MEDICATION LAW
AND BEHAVIOR

MEDICATION LAW AND BEHAVIOR

J. TYRONE GIBSON

Auburn University

A WILEY-INTERSCIENCE PUBLICATION

JOHN WILEY & SONS, New York · London · Sydney · Toronto

Library of Congress Cataloging in Publication Data

Gibson, J. Tyrone, 1943–
  Medication law and behavior.

  "A Wiley-Interscience publication."
  1. Drugs—Laws and legislation—United States.
2. Medical laws and legislation—United States.
3. Pharmacy—Laws and legislation—United States.
I. Title. [DNLM: 1. Drug therapy. 2. Legislation, Drug. 3. Behavior. WB330 G449m]

KF3885.G5   344'.73'042   75-36008
ISBN 0-471-29760-7

Printed in the United States of America

10 9 8 7 6 5 4 3 2 1

Preface

To anyone interested in health—and that includes all of us—it seems that most of the enormous outpouring of books today deal with health. Too many books have been written about one particular health problem: drug abuse. This is not a book about drug abuse or the drug abuse problem. It is a book about people and the medicine they consume. The book is designed to help the reader learn more about the influence of medication law on the behavior of health care personnel who assist in providing medication and medication services.

Most books represent a considerable input of resources. One part of a book is the preface, which in part explains why the book was written and also outlines for the reader the journey that lies ahead.

The title of this book was chosen to reflect the subject matter. *Medication,* the broad and important group of 1500 or so chemicals used to treat diseases, forms one of the three major referents for the content of the book. The words *law* and *behavior* were chosen because they indicate that law is created to command that those falling within its influence act in accordance with its provisions. The book deals primarily with the behavior of individuals as people who relate to medication. This approach to the subject is considerably different from most books on the subject because it is written from the viewpoint that control and regulation of physical products is accomplished only by directly regulating and controlling people.

Medication is unique in a number of respects, which accounts for some of the different ways it is controlled. Medication units are characterized by being individually small and at the same time numerous. No matter how potent a pill may be, most people do not view it as a potentially dangerous entity. Even though its particles may permeate every cell after entering the body, we tend to act somewhat nonchalantly about medication consumption. As consumers we are careful to differentiate between medication and "drugs." Paradoxically we value medication highly, as is suggested by the term *wonder drug*.

Chapter 1 sets the foundation for the book. The intent is to look upon the content as a set of concepts and principles which can be drawn from to decide the relative attractiveness of the behavior alternatives that exist and to provide a beginning for the reader to understand what behavior is prescribed for him by the law under diverse circumstances. Several systems of principles for decision-making are contrasted.

Chapter 2 describes in broad terms the medical and social purposes of drug therapy. The interrelationship of medication and other health system components is also reviewed briefly.

Some bedrock assumptions of medication consumption are discussed in Chapter 3. These are followed in Chapter 4 by a description of conceptual and actual effects on individual medication consumption, with emphasis on a description of variables that can be used to name or quantify drug effects. Alternative and nontherapeutic drug functions are also sketched.

A functional definition of medication is presented in Chapter 5. Disease and medication are matched conceptually in this chapter.

The most product-oriented chapter is Chapter 6, which contains a description of drug attributes that can be used as a basis for characterizing drugs in qualitative and quantitative terms. A major purpose of this section is to describe the purposes of drug attributes and to show how these characteristics influence human behavior—including their effects on the sick.

In Chapter 7 the major procedural end sought from the control and regulation of drugs is described in terms of a small set of principles which can be used to deduce the particulars of distribution control. The criteria for the major legal categories of drugs are presented here. Registration as a key control concept is also described and explained.

Chapter 8 introduces the concept of risk benefit as a paramount factor in medication use. The new drug investigational process is depicted as existing to generate information about the effects of a medication. The difficult task of weighing desired and undesired medication effects is described and several alternative methodologies are explored. Portions of this chapter are devoted to an explanation of the conceptual and legal means necessary and sufficient for estimating the relative benefit and risk of a chemical.

The purposes of drug information regulation are described in Chapter 9. The legal constraints and requirements pertaining to the description of risk and benefit from drugs are presented and explained. Officially approved labeling of drugs is described in terms of origin and content, and the point is made that only the medium may vary—the message must be relatively constant.

Chapter 10 is a description of the desired and actual ways of using drug information. An argument is presented for committing algorithms (or formulas) to memory for the application of drug information. The reader is urged to abandon the impossible task of storing in his head the enormous quantity of facts necessary for rational application of drug information.

The qualifications of providers licensed as agents to act on behalf of patients are described in detail in Chapter 11. The ethical, legal, and other norms used as referents for retrospective, concurrent, or prospective behavior evaluation are described and explained.

Chapter 12 considers the provider and the patient in their proper legal relationship. The conceptual model for the provision of medication to patients is broadly, but extensively discussed. The acts that must be performed by providers are identified, described, and explained.

The legal remedies for correcting deviance from the requirements of the spirit and letter of the law are contained in Chapter 13. The meaning of law from a broad societal view is expanded upon in this chapter. Malpractice as a control system is examined in detail and is evaluated in terms of effectiveness.

Chapter 14 is written especially for the scientifically oriented person who wishes to use certain legal references in the library. A means is described for efficiently and effectively communicating one's views about proposed or needed regulatory changes to those empowered to make these changes.

The limitations of this text should also be described. Since the book stresses concepts by throwing light on the particulars from which the concepts were derived, it will probably be necessary to consult specific regulations to ascertain the precise rule governing a given act. The intent here is not necessarily to provide all the particulars, but to assist the reader in framing a question properly. Only by understanding the concepts and principles of medication law and control can one hope to even begin to grasp the true meaning of what is going on. Indeed the particulars of individual laws and regulations are often short-lived. However, the basic model for the control and regulation of human behavior as it relates to medication has been relatively enduring; no basic changes loom on the horizon. Studying this book will aid in understanding existing and future laws and regulations. This book will not serve as a handbook in which one looks up a specific rule for a specific act. Yet, by referring to the references and guide for further study the reader will be able to progress from the conceptual model to the principle and ultimately to the specifics of the act of concern.

As even the casual observer realizes, the particular laws at a given moment in time pertaining to medication control and regulation enjoy only a short lifespan. Therefore it seems essential that the student establish as paramount the goal of becoming an intelligent consumer of information and knowledge pertinent to the subject. He must learn to examine carefully new laws, and the resulting behavior of participants within the system, in a critical and iconoclastic manner in order to understand the assumptions inherent in certain laws; and he must be prepared to challenge the inferences drawn from the evidence offered if they are at odds with his own answers obtained by this process. To paraphrase former Chief Justice Earl Warren: for most important questions—especially those that are of utmost importance or which must be answered within a matter of minutes—a person is his own judge, jury, prosecutor, defense lawyer, and ultimately Supreme Court.

During the course of this exposition, various examples will be used to describe certain points made; these may be of a current or present-bound nature. It is quite likely that the particular example used will become outdated. However, most of these examples are just that: examples. The underlying set from which these particular examples were obtained generally, and unfortunately, represents a set of problems that tend to be long-lived. While, for example, the medication chloramphenicol may fade from memory as a "medication problem," official and societal response to those vigorously advocating control changes for similar and related substances will insure the survival of similar drug problems as viable and inflammatory issues in the United States.

It is customary to thank various people for assistance in writing a book. First thanks go to my friend and assistant Samuel A. (Duke) Wilson who knows best how he has contributed to this book; without his assistance the book would not have been possible. I am grateful for the help of all my students who have contributed through their curiosity. Others who contributed in numerous and important ways are likewise thanked, even though their names do not appear here. Former professors and teachers who helped instill the curiosity necessary for producing a book serve as the bedrock foundation for the resulting structure; I am grateful. An author's family gives a considerable amount in order for a book to be written; one can only hope that the price paid is appropriate.

I take full responsibility for all errors. The subject matter is broad and deep; shortcomings and errors will be identified.

J. TYRONE GIBSON

Auburn, Alabama
November 1975

Contents

4 Expected or Hoped for Outcomes of Drug Therapy 24

5 Drugs and Medication Defined 29

6 Desirable Characteristics for Marketed Drugs 37

7 A Generalization of Various Major Drug Laws 59

8 Laws Governing the Derivation and Sources of Drug Labeling Information 82

Tables

Figures

MEDICATION LAW
AND BEHAVIOR

CHAPTER ONE

Introduction

Law neither regulates nor controls medication. What it does control and regulate is the behavior of people; and through people medication is controlled. Medication law is vital to many health care and other disciplines. It spells out in considerable detail many of the policies, procedures, duties, and task performance requirements of pharmacists, physicians, nurses, veterinarians, dentists, nurses' aides, and other health care providers in various environments that include the traditional pharmacy, physician's office, hospital, outreach clinic, and the institutional pharmacy. Punishment or other sanctioning measures are also within the province of this subject. Thus accountability is an important component of the model for medication regulation and control.

The primary thrust of this book is to describe, analyze, and conceptualize factors relevant to the behavior of participants in the use of medication in our society. The desired objective of drug therapy is simply stated but achieved (if at all) with considerable difficulty. Tentatively, the desired result of drug therapy is defined as the obtaining of the best match between a specific disease condition and a specific drug quantity. Both the disease and the drug must be sufficiently described for the drug to be utilized in the right place, by the right route, in the right amount, at the right time and under appropriate physical, social, and psychological conditions. The drug must be supplied according to legitimately mandated means. This book describes the claimed consequences of certain actions and the means prescribed in the relevant legislation for obtaining prescribed ends as these relate to medication use. Of necessity then, it also describes the social and other stimulants and constraints which impinge on the drug use process.

The information in this book consists of concepts, propositions, and laws. Concepts are class names applied to generalizations from particular stimuli having common characteristics. The class may correctly be viewed as a set consisting of elements. The elements which make up a set can be determined either by listing all elements making up a set or by formulating a rule for assignment to the set. The emphasis in this book is on the latter approach. Concepts may refer to objects, properties of objects, events and properties of events, and interrelationships among events and objects. Propositions refer to the "if event A, then event B" relationship between concepts A and B. A major purpose of this book is to describe the relationships of the various concepts and thus provide an enhanced understanding of medication use behavior.

Medication law and human behavior is a problem-oriented subject of study because the principles, laws, and procedures governing the subject affect providers and recipients of drugs and drug services and virtually all aspects of their drug manipulation behavior. In the past, unfortunately, this subject has been approached from a discipline-oriented perspective, which overemphasized law as an end in itself. A subject-dominated approach suggests that the student is being trained to be a practitioner and producer of law rather than a consumer of legal concepts and principles. Here, however, we take a problem-oriented approach and focus on the questions at hand, drawing knowledge or substance from any appropriate source that seems consistent with the overall purposes of the discussion.

In an age of increasingly sophisticated drug technology, pharmacists, physicians, nurses, and other affected health care practitioners are claiming increased expertise in medication use. It seems imperative that they not be limited to a working knowledge of the law as it exists, but that they understand *why* the law exists as well as what it may become to better achieve control and regulation of medication usage. Today when drugs can enhance the chances of conception, prevent blindness, cause the lame to walk, and prevent mental retardation, it is essential that providers of medication and their patients acquire a thorough knowledge of both legal principles and ethical principles.

Many students of medication law and behavior apparently fail to achieve a coherent understanding of the numerous federal and state laws that regulate the various health care providers. This book is designed to help students gain that understanding more readily. The major contribution of this book to the field of medication regulation and control is the creation of additional knowledge solely through coherent organization and classification of existing knowledge. These principles are worth absorbing since, by definition, a given principle can be applied to predict the behavior of people in various circumstances. Moreover extensive psychological research has conclusively shown that such information is retained for years, whereas the particular stimuli that spawned the principles are retained only briefly. Indeed, concepts and principles are frequently retained for the learner's lifetime. The description of the concepts and subconcepts contained within the various classifications should contribute to a further understanding of the important growing body of information used to guide, direct, prohibit, and mandate human behavior.

Traditionally, books about medication law and behavior have dealt with the adjudication of an alleged criminal encounter after the criminal event has occurred, and with the administration of criminal justice. Although these purposes are noble and worthwhile, they are inappropriate for most nonlawyer providers because in virtually all encounters between a provider and another person the provider and the patient much choose a course of action from the available alternatives. The provider, the patient, and society are best served when the course chosen is consistent with the statutory and common law principles regulating the behavior of both provider and patient.

While some laws on how to perform particular tasks will be considered here in great detail, emphasis will be given to the process of learning what tasks to perform and why they should be performed. Two authors writing in related fields have differentiated between training and education as follows: "Training is a process whereby one learns how to perform a task; education is the process whereby one learns what tasks to perform and why to perform them (1)." Education is the emphasis of this book.

1.1 RATIONALE FOR THE STUDY OF MEDICATION LAW AND BEHAVIOR

This subject matter has developed because of a congruence of interests and needs in our society, educational curriculum components, and practice needs and/or desires. Knowledge of this subject should enhance performance of the activities involved in the drug use process.

The major objectives of this study of medication law and behavior are: (1) to learn selected principles of jurisprudence, and (2) to discover how to apply these principles so that consumer, patient, and health care provider are all benefitted. Included as a major goal is the learning of rules and generalizations which must be followed by providers in practice, of rules and generalizations to which other practitioners must adhere and of how well these rules have achieved the purposes for which they were designed.

We will carefully consider medication law as it pertains to selected kinds of providers predominantly involved in patient and consumer needs. Emphasis will be placed on how this body of law works in relation to its real or claimed goals and purposes. Implicitly, it will address the effect of this body of law on the community. It will also address the issues raised by the question, "What should medication law and behavior be?" This book is based on the principle that law in general and medication law in particular represent a system of rules for directing human action. Its thesis rests on the assumption that drug laws are designed to protect and maintain public health, safety, and welfare by serving as rules, regulations, generalizations, guidelines, and directives for providers, patients, and consumers. These factors are useful in deciding which behavior characteristics to exhibit given a potential interaction between a provider or recipient and some other person, object, or idea.

Most law is written by lawyers for lawyers. The law is designed to help a third party resolve conflicts between two or more persons acting or wanting to act at cross purposes with one another. The rules are applied to ascertain right or wrong on a retrospective or "Monday morning quarterback" basis. Our primary assumption in this book, however, is that most two-party encounters whether resolved through actual courtroom battle or through speculation, are resolved without a third party. This process occurs for a number of reasons, not the least of which is the necessity for immediate action in the drug usage domain. Patients, pharmacists, physicians, nurses, and others must apply the rules of law on a prospective basis. Although trust is a major ingredient in most human interaction, it is even more evident in the realm of provider-patient medication use. Therefore it seems wise for provider and patient to understand the nature and scope of their relationship of mutual trust.

1.2 LAW CONTRASTED WITH OTHER AREAS OF KNOWLEDGE

Many systems, rules, and generalizations for directing human action have been promulgated by scholars in several fields. Sociologists describe and categorize normative behavioral expectations into four major types:

1. *Folkways*. Customary ways of doing things that involve no punitive measures for deviating from the customary modes of behavior.
2. *Laws*. An orderly and dependable sequence of events that generally take the form "If *A*, then *B*" where *A* and *B* each represent one or more conceptual acts (2). For example, if an individual is convicted of illegal possession of marijuana, he or she will be imprisoned for two years. Few drug laws are, however, so specific because of the relative inexactness of most legal concepts. Thus most drug laws might best be viewed as generalizations, so that "if A, then B" statement would be interpreted as "if A, then maybe B."
3. *Mores*. Behavior that is generally regarded as mandatory for a group's welfare and survival; sometimes termed "the must behaviors," for which there may or may not be official sanction and accompanying rewards and punishments.
4. *Technicways*. Behavior closely associated with a particular kind of technology, whose origin can be traced to or associated more or less with that technology. Important examples include the particular rules which must be followed rigorously when programming a computer or adding a drug to a large-volume parental solution in a laminar flow hood. These normative types constitute behavior that ought to exist, and contrast with actual behavior.

Some major normative systems of rules for directing human action that fall into one or more of these four categories are economic, legal, political, ethical, social-cultural, religious, psychological, biological, physical, and climatic/geographic. Most health care curricula require or recommend that the student study one or more courses on most of the topics mentioned.

A key concept pertains to the role of these content areas in defining means and ends. Some of these areas are primarily concerned with the selection of means for achieving ends, e.g., economics, whereas others are more concerned with selecting which ends to pursue, e.g., ethics.

The economic system is concerned with mankind's search for an optimum means of allocating scarce resources to unlimited wants and/or desires. The economic system is per se amoral and devoid of ethics. It is primarily concerned with what to produce, how to produce, and who will get what is produced. It does not exist in a vacuum and is affected by other systems. Thus economics, in essence, also provides an answer to the question "What can be produced?"

The ethical system of rules directing human action is not mandatory for individuals or society because of the difficulties of enforcement and for other reasons. There is no publicly sanctioned mechanism for this system of decision-making because it appeals to the moral and religious basis on which our culture is founded. Essentially it addresses the question of what ought to be done. Ethics is concerned with what is right, what is good, and how the pursuit of life, liberty, and happiness (whatever these may mean) might best be pursued. As a discipline it is concerned with explaining why some things are viewed as good. For example, we rely upon ethics as our system of rules for directing human action when questions arise about the societal objective of maximizing group pleasure versus individual pleasure. That is, should action be directed toward maximizing the collective utility and/or benefit flowing from the use of a set of drugs or should societal action strive toward optimizing the individual benefit?

The political system of rules directing human action primarily involves public debate on issues of interest in a social system in which various parties have conflicting and incompatible goals. This system consists largely of selecting rules for negotiation among more or less equally powerful parties. Basically it is concerned with who gets what and how much.

The psychological system of rules directing human action is the system whereby individual motives, drives, needs, aspirations, attitudes, interests, beliefs, and values culminate in particular action by the individual. Its unit of study is the individual. It approaches the basic question of how one might best secure fulfillment of his needs given the variety of alternatives available to any particular individual.

Other systems of rules for directing human action, e.g., religious, biological, physical, and climatic are as familiar to health care students as to health care educators, especially the religious and climatic systems. The physical system of rules is the best understood, most studied, and probably the most within our control. For example, it is a thoroughly accepted physical principle that gases expand when heat is applied, given constant pressure and other assumptions. The major thrust of most pharmaceutical curricula is toward mastering some of the fundamental physical principles for directing human action (although this situation is changing today). An example of such important knowledge is the fact that oxygen concentration must be controlled within a given range in the incubators of premature babies to prevent blindness from exposure to too great an oxygen concentration. Often, physical principles have become such a part of ourselves that they operate at a subconscious level, so that the individual is unaware of the real principles directing his actions. For example, the simple act of taping Christmas cards to the wall in a decorative fashion requires that one locate and place the tape in the top, center portion of the card and that the tape be attached to the wall. Although we may not pause to think about the principles giving rise to the location of the tape on the card, the principles of gravity direct our actions in this particular example because we know, for example, that if the tape is placed on the top right end of the card the card will not be horizontal to the floor (at an equilibrium state with the force of gravity) and will hang crooked. Physical principles will not be considered in this book except to the extent that the understanding of these principles is essential for mastering the other types of principles explained.

Probably the most fundamental premise of law is that within the context of a society, the ends achieved by obeying laws will result in justice for the citizens of that society. Stated as a principle, we can say: if laws are adhered to by the persons they affect, then justice will be the outcome for all concerned.

It is easy to forget, however, that whether learning is cognitive (thinking), affective (feeling), or psychomotor (doing), it is determined by a person's psychological attributes. The law, for example, depends largely upon the hypothesis that undesired behavior will, through punishment, be stopped and that such punishment will serve as a negative reinforcer to prevent other would-be wrongdoers from becoming actual wrongdoers. Whether this hypothesis should be rejected or accepted, we have mainly conjecture to go on rather than objective evidence due in part to the difficulty of conducting necessary experiments (3).

Likewise, laws can compel only behavior that is consistent with other facets of the world that direct behavior. A law that a nation's infant mortality rate will be halved within the next 12 months is doomed to failure. A law designed to compel parents to love their children is likewise doomed. A law that henceforth the sun will rise in the west will have no effect, and a law that "Wondermycin" will cure cancer will not yield the desired outcome. The point is that to be successful laws must be enacted in such a way that desired actions are not irreconcilable with other known behavior determinants. Many have argued that the laws banning certain drugs (e.g., marijuana, heroin, and LSD) are certain to fail because these drugs are simply supplied in response to the law of demand: as demand increases the price increases, and the quantity demanded at the "market" price will be supplied. Thus it follows that understanding areas of study other than law will yield considerable understanding of the law itself.

The reader should be careful to avoid a frequent logical error in making an analogy between the behavioral and the physical sciences: the former are concerned predominantly with predicting individual behavior, whereas the latter are mostly concerned with group behavior. Where would the physicist be if he were required to predict the behavior of single particles individually? The behavioral scientist cannot accurately predict which particular mothers will give birth to physically deformed infants. The assumptions are fewer for the physical sciences, and the premises of a law are likely to remain unchanged for a relatively longer time for the physical sciences. For example, the gas laws express a relationship among only three variables: temperature, pressure, and volume, and the application of the laws requires the meeting or presence of relatively few conditions. Thus in order to apply the gas laws successfully one needs only to assume a certain atmospheric pressure and a few other such items. The behavioral sciences, on the other hand, usually involve a large number of variables requiring an extremely large number of assumptions. For example, the number of cases of gonorrhea may depend in part on sexual mores, attitudes toward contraceptive use, the price of penicillin, subject age, the availability of alcohol, and the supply of gasoline.

1.3 PROCESS FOR APPLICATION OF LAW

The method used to teach the application of legal rules for directing human action will consist of the construction of an algorithm, whereby one first perceives that a decision must be made when a set of alternative courses of action exist. Given these circumstances, the reader will be expected to ascertain if the question is within the domain of, and therefore answerable by, the legal system. This analysis will require a process approach i.e., the student systematically asks: Does this decision belong in W, X, Y, . . . system for selecting a decision rule? Once the legal system is selected, the student will be directed toward determining the particular subsystem and, ultimately, the particular rule or generalization to be applied to select the correct course of action.

1.4 BRIEF SCOPE OF MEDICATION LAW

Later, in outlining a general set of concepts and principles pertaining to medication law and behavior, a categorization of the various general kinds of laws will be developed. At present, however, it is sufficient to explain that the various and diverse drug laws are enacted to protect American consumers from harmful and potentially harmful commerical products and to provide as many safe and effective products as technologically possible. They are generally intended to protect the consumer from the consumption of products which are:

1. *Adulterated*. They are defective, either in their ingredients or as a result of processing, packaging, or storage.
2. *Misbranded*. They have false or misleading packaging or labeling.
3. *Illegally marketed*. Lack of sufficient proof is provided to a sovereign that safety and efficacy have been established.
4. *Prohibited for consumption*. This involves protection of the consumer from his own ignorance, by preventing him from possessing and using certain named substances unless prescribed and demanding criteria are rigidly adhered to by the consumer and those supplying his needs.

Many of these criteria culminate in circumstances which function primarily as safeguards in directing the local, state, or federal government to protect the consumer from his own ignorance. Although this statement suggests the consumer cannot protect himself or herself, it will be shown that society is so structured that people are interdependent and act on the basis of mutual trust. We are all ignorant, but fortunately in different areas. The other side of the coin, when the statement is made positively, suggests that we are all knowledgeable, but knowledgeable in different areas. The consumer who relies on an expert, e.g., a pharmacist, for drug advice, may in turn furnish "advice" when he pilots the jetliner on which the pharmacist is a passenger. Mutual trust and interdependence go hand in hand, especially in a technologically sophisticated society.

Some questions that may be answered or made more understandable in this book are:

1. Does medication law retard and/or induce new drug development?
2. Should oral contraceptives be banned or made available with or without a prescription?

3. Is the diabetic patient best served by or without oral hypoglycemics?
4. Can advertisements for prescription drugs be believed?
5. Should prices for prescription drugs be advertised?
6. Why is alcohol legally available, and why is marijuana banned?
7. Are drugs which have different trade names but are chemically
   identical, equal in effectiveness?
8. What is meant by a safe and effective drug?
9. Who can prescribe, dispense, and administer particular classes of
   medication?
10. What is meant by control when a phrase such as "controlled
    substances" is used?
11. Can physicians do what pharmacists can do and vice versa?
12. Is it rational for physicians' assistants to prescribe drugs?
13. Why are some "effective" drugs available in Europe but not in
    the United States?
14. How does one discover the "good" effects of a potentially new
    medication?
15. Is there a general principle that can be relied upon to induce
    needed specifics of medication control?
16. Why does labeling accompany medication?
17. Should the patient be informed about his medication?
18. Is the current number of malpractice suits justified or too fre-
    quent compared to suits for drug-induced injury?
19. Does the "punishment" for failure to abide by medication law fit
    the "crime"?
20. If a patient is injured from consuming medication, under what
    conditions can he collect damages for malpractice?
21. Why are prescription drugs, aspirin, and other substances pack-
    aged in containers that are difficult for children to open?
22. Can aspirin be classified legally as a new drug?
23. What can a detail man legitimately tell a health care provider
    about a drug during a personal interview?
24. What is the risk of approving an unsafe drug relative to the risk
    of not approving an effective drug?
25. If the U.S. Food and Drug Administration (FDA) determines that
    an investigational new drug study should be stopped, can the
    decision be appealed?
26. Are the beliefs generally held about medication by the public
    consistent with the facts?

A foundation for an understanding of these complex issues is a necessary prerequisite for a complete understanding. Only by careful consideration of the underlying assumptions and theory of the drug use process can one fully appreciate the complexities of medication use.

REFERENCES AND GUIDE TO FURTHER STUDY

1. Chamelin, N. C. and Evans, K. R.: *Criminal Law for Policemen*, Prentice-Hall, Englewood Cliffs, N.J., 1971, p. xvi.
2. Zelermeyer, W.: *Introduction to Business Law: A Conceptual Approach*, Macmillan, New York, 1964.
3. Tittle, L. R. and Rowe, A. R.: Certainty of Arrest and Crime Rates: A Further Test of the Deterrence Hypothesis, *Social Forces* **52**:455 (June) 1974.
4. U.S. Food, Drug and Cosmetic Act and its Amendments, 21 *U.S. Code*, 301–392.
5. Title 21, *Code of Federal Regulations*.
6. U.S. Comprehensive Drug Abuse Prevention and Control Act of 1970, Public Law 91–513.

CHAPTER TWO

Personal and Societal Purposes of Drug Therapy

2.1 BRIEF HISTORY OF DRUG CONTROL AND LAW

Many social sciences characterize and classify human deviance. One of the simplest classifications consists of only two components. Whether the individual is responsible for his deviance determines which classification is appropriate for a given act. Instances in which the individual is held responsible are ordinarily construed as within the domain of the law and the law enforcers such as policemen, judges, lawyers, and other "insiders" within the judicial process. The other major kind of deviance is that for which the individual is not held responsible, i.e., medical deviance. Classification in this category is misleading because it suggests that the deviance is perceived mainly by the individual. Yet, it is possible and even probable for an individual to be afflicted with a disease and not be ill. This occurs because illness is defined as a state of affairs which exists when the patient decides he is "sick." On the other hand, disease is construed as a physiological, functional, or structural defect (deviance) that exists with or without the knowledge and awareness of the host organism. Ultimately in our society medical deviance is defined by physicians.

Traditionally drug control and drug legislation have been concerned with the control of the medical uses of drugs, i.e., deviant conditions for which the patient is not responsible. Generally, nonmedical uses are prohibited. Alcohol, tobacco, and caffeine are special cases and will not be treated specifically here. A brief digression is in order, however, to consider tobacco as a representative of the drug group. An interesting opinion of tobacco smoking was put forth by King James I in 1604, just seven years before his version of the Bible came out (1):

> A custom loathsome to the eye, hateful to the nose, harmful to the braine, dangerous to the lungs, and in the blacke stinking fume thereof; nearest resembling the horrible Stygian smoake of the pit that is bottomless.

Needless to say this was before the age of the "Marlboro Man" and his advertising colleagues. Nevertheless, tobacco is legally available today because of societal response to deviance.

2.2   RAPID EVOLUTION OF DRUG CONTROL AND REGULATION

Surprisingly, mankind managed to survive (many would say thrive) until the early 1900s without any significant amount of drug legislation (2). As recently as 1913 any drug could be readily purchased at one's neighborhood pharmacy or physician's office. A person was free to purchase such drugs as heroin, opium, and others generally regarded as dangerous and addicting today. Heroin, introduced at the turn of the century, was named "hero-in" because it was supposed to be an effective "hero" for curing morphine addiction. During prohibition alcohol was prescribed as a drug; today, caffeine seems to be moving toward classification as a drug. However, the late 1800s and early 1900s represented a period of unprecedented technological and social change. This change was accompanied by the risk associated with the technology of that and later periods. Although early attempts were made in this country to enact some very modest legislation, the Pure Food and Drug Act was not enacted until 1906. This act was devoted exclusively to considerations of adulteration and misbranding. Later, because of the increasing abuse of narcotic drugs and its accompanying perceived causal role in the social and moral degradation of American society, the Harrison Narcotic Drug Act of 1914 was enacted. Although this act was passed ostensibly as a revenue generating measure, it was actually aimed at prohibiting the consumption of certain named narcotic drugs and restricting the use of many other narcotic substances. Many persons have argued and continue to argue about the effectiveness of this and more recent legislation in relation to the claimed goals of the legislation. This issue will be discussed later.

2.3   RECENT RESTRICTIONS ON INDIVIDUAL
DRUG CONSUMPTION

The 1930s gave rise to legislation controlling the availability of marijuana and essentially prohibited the use of marijuana in all but very restricted situations. However, it continued to be listed in the U.S. Pharmacopeia (USP) until 1936 (USP XI). Also, during this period the sulfanilamide incident (in which 103 people lost their lives) gave great impetus to the passage of the 1938 U.S. Food, Drug and Cosmetic Act. The major thrust of this act was its requirement that drugs be proven safe prior to marketing, and this represented a significant departure from the earlier act, which placed the burden of proving a drug unsafe upon the government. However, the most significant conceptual deficiency of the 1938 act was its failure to require proof of effectiveness for marketed drugs. It did, however, serve as a significant milestone for further legitimizing the control and restriction of individual freedom within the broad domain of drug usage. In 1952 this act was amended by the Durham-Humphrey Amendments, which classified drugs into two major legal categories, one of which was called "legend" or prescription drugs (3). The term "legend" arises from the phrase in the act, viz., "Caution: Federal law prohibits dispensing without a prescription." (3) The term "legend" is used synonymously with the term "prescription drug." Under the law drugs cannot be purchased (and therefore cannot be consumed) by citizens without the permission of a duly licensed prescriber and dispenser (who may legally be one and the same person).

These amendments were followed by others in 1962, 1965, and 1972. The 1962 amendments (whose passage was facilitated by the thalidomide disaster of that period) represented an attempt to rectify apparent deficiencies of the FD&C Act of 1938, and were basically designed to supplement the Harrison Act by controlling the use of two major categories of drugs deemed especially hazardous, namely, barbiturates and amphetamines. The controls implemented by the 1965 amendments and earlier acts were mostly unsuccessful and were completely repealed by the 1970 Comprehensive Drug Abuse Prevention and Control Act and its substituent part, the Controlled Substances Act (CSA).

A short but significant amendment was enacted in 1972. For the first time the U.S. Food and Drug Administration (FDA) was given authority to inventory, and thus to require the reporting of the names of all drugs legally marketed in the United States. This procedure provided the FDA with a quantitative listing of the ingredients of these drugs.

The CSA of 1970 represented an attempt to control drugs based on their perceived hazard to society. These and later legal changes will be considered in detail in subsequent chapters.

2.4   MEDICAL AND SOCIAL ROLES OF DRUG THERAPY

The medical role of drug therapy is to treat some kind of functional deviance with which the patient is dissatisfied. This definition must be construed in its broadest meaning to include such drugs as oral contraceptives and fertility drugs (administered to healthy females), and sodium fluoride (administered to entire populations as well as individuals—both adult and infant). A simpler explanation may be that the individual is not satisfied with his current state of health or some other component of his life when medication is sought. This dissatisfaction results in much medical involvement on the part of persons acting as providers in the drug use process. Recall the point made earlier: when a person is ill he is not deemed personally responsible for this deviance. Yet, while not held accountable for his deviant condition, he is expected to do everything reasonably possible to recover and to seek technically competent help appropriate to his illness and his means. Seeking or accepting aid allows him freedom from blame for his illness and exempts him, in most cases, from normal roles and tasks.

Although only one serves to correct medical deviance, drugs may play any of the following functional roles: aesthetic, aphrodisiac, ego-disrupting, ideological, political, psychological support, religious, research, social control, war and conflict, and therapeutic.

The therapeutic category is commonly thought of as serving solely to define the role of drug therapy; exclusive emphasis on "therapeutics" stems from our failure to recognize and account for the social role of drugs. Therapeutic functions are those directed toward correcting or preventing medically deviant conditions. The expected or hoped for outcomes of drug therapy are discussed in Chapter 3. The social roles that drugs play, which include all but the therapeutic functions, will not be considered further here. An excellent description of drug roles can be found in Barber's work (4).

2.5   DRUG THERAPY AS A DETERMINANT OF HEALTH STATUS

Although we are only beginning to be aware of the numerous dynamic forces that act to define an individual's health status, this status is only

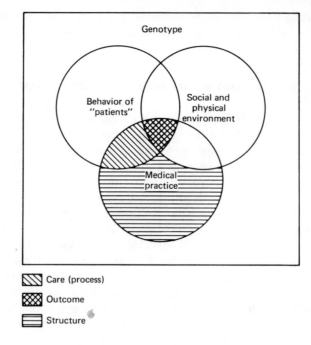

Figure 2.1.   Determinants of health status. *Source:* B. Starfield,: Health Services Research: A Working Model, *New England Journal of Medicine,* 289:132–136 (July 19) 1973.

partially affected by medical factors and, consequently, by drug consumption. Health status is best defined as a result of interaction among at least four major factors: genetics, environment, patient behavior, and provider practice (5).

Drug therapy as a determinant of health status must function primarily within the overlapping area depicted in Figure 2.1. The components of this area are provider practice, behavior of patients, and the social and physical environment within which the patient and provider exist. For example, patient behavior (eating habits) which results in obesity may produce an illness or disease for which medical and drug treatment are sought. In turn, the use of drugs produces serious illness and disease (e.g., the use of antiobesity drugs such as diethylpropion).

Of course, Figure 2.1 exists within a milieu largely determined by our particular culture and Judeo-Christian heritage, probably most important in determining an individual's health status. The structure of health care includes personnel, facilities, equipment, organization, information systems and records, and financing (5), i.e., people, things, ideas, and patterns of thinking. Since all of these structural elements involve the expenditure of various resources, the goal of optimum health status involves a good interaction and integration of these structural resources. Medication in itself does not form a significant component of this structure when all systems components are viewed in their entirety (6). Ultimately social, economic, or psychological factors may have a greater influence.

REFERENCES AND GUIDE TO FURTHER STUDY

1. Quoted in the *Houston Chronicle,* Jan. 12, 1964, Section A, p. 18, col. 3.
2. Quinn, T. M. and McLaughlin, G. T.: The Evolution of Federal Drug Control Legislation, *Catholic University Law Review* **22**(3):586–627 (Spring) 1973.
3. 21 *U.S. Code* 303.
4. Barber, B.: *Drugs and Society,* Russell Sage Foundation, New York, 1967, p. 165–186.
5. Starfield, B.: Health Services Research: A Working Model, *New England Journal of Medicine* **289**:132–136 (July 19) 1973.
6. Kaitaranta, H. and Purola, T.: A Systems-Oriented Approach to the Consumption Of Medical Commodities, *Social Science and Medicine* **7**:531–540, 1973. (This article depicts medication usage as a small subsystem of a much larger health care subsystem.)

CHAPTER THREE

Basic Assumptions of How Marketed Drugs Are Consumed

A critical assumption about the rational use of drugs is that understanding some basic principles of drug use will favorably affect one's health status. Inherent in the use of relevant drug information is the assumption that knowing only the disease/illness condition and a drug's uses is not enough to reasonably produce an improved health status from the use of these drugs. These principles are implicit in the remainder of this book. Examples include those listed in Section 3.1.1.

3.1 MOTIVE FOR CONSUMPTION OF DRUGS BY INDIVIDUALS

According to James Harvey Young the whole idea behind drug labeling rests on a favorite progressive era assumption ". . . that the average man was intelligent enough to plot his own course and would avoid risks if he was aware of them." (1) In other words, if given full information and the opportunity to choose among alternative courses, a person will opt for that course of action which is in his best interest. Young, however, fails to consider the basic concept of risk or benefit as an important element in the rational use of drugs. All drugs have a certain element of risk or possible undesirable effects that go hand in hand with the desired effect. Although the undesired effects usually cannot be eliminated, through careful planning they often can be reduced or minimized. Choosing medication on the basis of safety will be described in detail in Section 8.1.

3.1.1   Prescription Drugs

Basic assumptions for labeling drugs in a prescribed manner include the following:

1. Labeling will include only previously produced or discovered information derived from the experiences of person previously exposed to a drug, for the purpose of predicting the effects that will occur in future drug recipients.
2. Labeling is based on prediction from the general to the particular. Information derived from groups of similar people receiving a drug is assumed to be predictive of information about similar proposed uses.
3. Information acquired from a sample of individuals can be grouped to predict the effects of drugs on other individuals.
4. When a drug's effects have not been proved on groups of people, it will not be used except under controlled, planned circumstances.
5. Some drugs can be used properly only on the advice of experts.
6. Some drugs can be used properly without the advice of experts.
7. Some drugs can be used properly with only the information provided on the package label.
8. Drugs produce inseparable desired and undesired effects.
9. Observing relevant precautions will decrease the likelihood of experiencing adverse effects from a drug.
10. The true effects of a drug, described in its labeling, cannot be determined by testimonial evidence.

The foregoing points serve as a basis for deriving, selecting, and arranging information to best serve the patient. Some of the most important and most frequently overlooked assumptions about the manner in which drug information will be used by patients (and providers, to a lesser extent) include (1) the user can read, (2) the user will read what appears on the label, (3) the user will heed what he reads on the label, and (4) reading and heeding drug labeling information increase the chance that the drug will produce a favorable change in the user's health status.

The assumption that the buyer can read means that all words and all concepts used to describe drugs must be understandable when read and that the reader is made aware of what action to take by these words. The second assumption is that the buyer will read the directions on the label. The cliché "If all else fails, read the directions" shows that this assumption is not always sound. In an FDA-sponsored opinion survey, less than half the respondents answered that they thought other people read labels for nonprescription drugs, although about three-fourths thought label directions were adequate (2). The evidence that prescription label directions are not followed is overwhelming (see 10.4). Everyday experience with persons who fail to read directions before assembling toys and other devices, the failure of people to read road signs correctly, the failure of college students to read registration procedures, are examples which suggest that many people are not sufficiently motivated to read labels. Nevertheless, drug legislation and regulation are based on the assumption that whatever words appear on labels describing the effects of drugs and the ways these drugs are to be used will be read and understood. Also implicit in the third assumption is the belief that the buyer will act in accordance with the behavior suggested by his reading of the label. The many studies on drug usage, however, clearly show that patients fail to heed the label directions for consuming drugs (3). Many claim that much drug misuse by laymen and professionals alike can be traced to the failure to read and comprehend completely the relevant labeling and to act in accordance with the behavior suggested by it. Less conspicuous, perhaps, but implicit in these three assumptions is the ever-present idea that the drugs will be appropriately labeled for producing optimum action on the part of the consumer. The very existence of such instructions as "use as directed," and similar phrases appearing on prescription drug labels, suggests that often the implicit assumption that adequate information will be conveyed to the reader is not tenable.

For prescription drugs, it is assumed that labels for the patient will contain the name of the person who will consume that drug. This leads to the assumption that only the person whose name appears on the label will consume the drug. The many stories about individuals who exchange drugs (prescriptions) suggest that this assumption may also not be tenable.

Nonprescription Drugs

Many assumptions that apply to prescription drugs also apply to nonprescription products. The primary difference involves the need or lack of need for an intermediary (a pharmacist, physician, nurse, or other health care professional) to intervene between the patient's need for a drug and the information available describing that drug, the assumption being that the health professional who intervenes is capable (and the layman incapable) of translating the generalized information describing the effects of the drug to make it relevant for the needs of a particular patient. The need for an intermediary is assumed to be unnecessary for a nonprescription drug. A study on insulin (a nonprescription drug) utilization has shown that many diabetics consume either half as much or twice as much insulin as appropriate for their condition (4). This pattern of use strongly suggests that, at least in the case of this one nonprescription drug, individuals do not appear to utilize medication properly without intervention by a third party. It does not necessarily follow, however, that having someone serve as an intermediary to translate the information will necessarily result in patient behavior congruent with the directions appearing or suggested on a drug label.

A principle common to the use of both legend and nonlegend drugs is that a drug user cannot rely on information sources not directly associated with the drug to be consumed. There is also a strong suggestion of the necessity for drug labeling information being in writing on the dispensed container label. Available research allows the conclusion that the patient's (drug user's) memory is unreliable for storage and retrieval of information for directing the patient's drug consumption behavior.

The assumption for nonprescription drugs is that the user can arrive at, or somehow obtain, his own diagnosis and can then correctly prescribe an appropriate drug for his own needs. This is in opposition to the reason for creating prescription drugs, namely that the layman is assumed to be incapable of arriving at a suitable diagnosis for those medically deviant conditions amenable to treatment by prescription drugs. Regardless of the source of the diagnosis and the legal classification of a drug to be consumed, a diagnosis is always assumed. While the necessity for a correct diagnosis is obvious, experience suggests that treatment is often attempted with little or no attention to this critical need.

A common assumption about the use of both classes of drugs is that people are aware of the magnitude of usefulness of drugs in general, which also implies that people are aware of the limitations of drug therapy. The thriving existence of drug quackery in the midst of a therapeutic revolution suggests that this assumption is invalid.

Perhaps the most important of all the foregoing assumptions is that the label information describing the effects of a drug represents the best available information (the truth) about the effects (desirable and undesirable) of that particular drug. It supposes that the patient is aware of the benefits to be gained from a specific drug as well as the risks inherent in its use. It assumes that the author of the information on the drug label has written a truthful and correct message that communicates to the reader not only the positive benefits but the negative risks as well. The fact that less than 20% of legally marketed drugs reviewed by the FDA under its legally mandated Drug Efficacy Study Implementation program were shown categorically to be effective suggests that much remains to be accomplished before this assumption of full and correct disclosure is met (5). The *truth* about a specified drug may be a point of disagreement or controversy even among the most informed experts. Witness for example the ongoing controversy about the claimed effectiveness of Vitamin C for prevention of the common cold. Also, in our society it is in the short-run economic best interest of the retailer to sell the drug to the consumer whether or not it benefits that consumer. This practice also results in the inappropriate use of drugs. Compromising the buyer's best interest, however, may only be beneficial in the short run. Likewise, it may not be in the seller's best interest to communicate fully and truthfully the risk associated with the use of a drug. He may obfuscate his message by using more words than are necessary, by using a vocabulary incomprehensible to the buyer or by manipulating concepts of drug buyers in such a way that they are erroneously led to believe that drugs are effective for a broader range of conditions than is true.

The laws regulating drug usage assume that humans are rational beings free, for the most part, of behavior motivated by emotions and of other psychological and social characteristics. However, an individual may be fulfilling some nonrational need by the use of drugs. The person may be using drugs to secure affection, security, pride, freedom from fear, guilt, or shame, or for other emotional needs. To the extent that these nonrational factors operate, the foregoing assumptions are undermined. Some researchers claim that consumption or prescription of a drug by a physician serves to legitimize the illness of the patient. Prescription of a drug may also serve the prescriber's needs by legitimizing his position as a physician and by allowing him to exhibit evidence of having done something tangible for his patient. Thus the phsycian's intervention between the patient and the patient's disease is also legitimized: client approval is enhanced by prescribing a drug (6, 7).

REFERENCES AND GUIDE TO FURTHER STUDY

1.   Young, James Harvey: *The Medical Messiahs*, Princeton University Press, Princeton, N.J., 1967, p. 37.

2. Simon, M. E. and Kuehl, D. G.: FDA Listens: A Survey of Consumer Opinion on the Safety of Medicines, *FDA Consumer* **7**(4):8 (May) 1973.

3. Becker, M. H. and Naiman, L. A.: Sociobehavioral Determinants of Compliance with Health and Medical Care Recommendations, *Medical Care* **13**(1):10–24 (January) 1975.

4. Watkins, J. D. et al.: Observation of Medication Errors Made by Diabetic Patients in the Home, *Diabetes* **16**:882–885 (December) 1967.

5. National Academy of Sciences: *Drug Efficacy Study, A Report to the Commissioner of Food and Drugs,* U.S. Government Printing Office, Washington, D.C., 1969.

6. Freidson, E.: *The Profession of Medicine,* Dodd, Mead, New York, 1970, especially p. 158–184.

7. Smith, M. C.: Social Barriers to Rational Drug Therapy, *American Journal of Hospital Pharmacy* **29**(2): 120–127 (February) 1972.

8. Quinn, T. M.: The Evolution of Federal Drug Control Legislation, *Catholic University Law Review* **22**(3):586–627 (Spring) 1973.

CHAPTER FOUR

Expected or Hoped for Outcomes of Drug Therapy

Chapter 2 briefly discussed the medical and social roles of drug consumption. It was suggested that most legitimized functions of drugs fall within the therapeutic function. In this context the word *function* is used to describe phenomena that contribute positively (are rewarding) to the stability or survival of some part of society. Functional phenomena do not necessarily include all consequences. *Dysfunction* has the opposite meaning. In other words, drugs are only used to correct instances of medical deviance; this use is a functional role for this component of the health care sector. It has been shown that medical deviance may originate in patient behavior, from influences exerted on the patient by his social and physical environment and also from the medical practice component. Nevertheless, drug control and regulation seem to allow only correction of medical deviance. If the medical deviance to be treated arises from behavior of patients or from the social and physical environment or from medical practice, the correction of this deviance is permitted. However, when the person (would-be patient) desires to use a drug to correct what he perceives as an undesirable state, of a social, psychological, or other nature, he is usually prohibited from consuming drugs for this purpose. (Certain exceptions, e.g., alcohol, tobacco, and caffeine have been cited previously.) The functions of drugs contribute positively to the resolution of medically deviant conditions, and can be included in one or more of the following seven subcategories of expected or hoped for outcomes of drug therapy: longevity, activity, comfort, satisfaction, ease in relationship to dis-ease (disease), achievement, and resilience.

None of the foregoing categories allows for the use of a drug to produce (correct) behavior which is not medically deviant. It is, however, difficult to categorize the use of such drugs as oral contraceptives as being useful to correct instances of medical deviance, since this necessitates classifying normal, healthy women as diseased. This classification is most easily accepted by considering oral contraceptives as preventive drugs.

There is no provision within the categories mentioned earlier for the private, recreational use of drugs. Such uses are seen as being dysfunctional for the health care sector. The "passivity, pleasure, and escape from discursive thought provided by drugs seem wrong and this moral value is incorporated into drug control and regulatory laws . . . it seems destructive, or at best unfair, to find happiness, pleasure, and insight artificially, without the industry that usually precedes and lends such states value." (1) The use of drugs to produce a feeling of euphoria that may result in abnormal subjective concentration on trivia, loss of perspective, and focusing of attention on one object to the exclusion of all others is not provided for in drug control and regulatory law. To place this prohibition or omitted provision in another perspective it seems that drug law precludes the legalization of achieving certain desired psychic states by medication users. For example, the kind of pleasure derived from viewing television, majorettes, flowers, and mountain views is denied. This prohibition seems inconsistent and incongruent with the occasional article one sees on the forthcoming "learning pill" and similar drugs sought by many. Although a distinction between aspiration and duty seems appropriate for defining a minimum level of acceptable behavior, it seems questionable to place a limit on the kinds of feelings and psychic states a person may experience from drug use. The US Constitution clearly advocates the right to life, liberty, and the pursuit of happiness as basic to our society's well being.

4.1 ACTUAL EFFECT ON INDIVIDUAL BEHAVIOR FROM RESTRICTION OF DRUG USE

To view the spectrum of conditions for potential drug use as limited by the qualification that drugs be used only to alter conditions of medical deviance may be misleading. Consider the following in terms of the number of nontherapeutic functions not included within the many undesirable conditions suggested.

> We are buffeted by a seemingly endless stream of bad news, crises, and confrontations . . . with all forms of communications emphasizing social unrest, riots, crime, and breakdowns in traditional thinking." [We are] "helpless in the face of situations [we] can't control". [We are] "bogged down in traffic jams with honking horns, exhaust fumes . . . air-conditioners are turned down, or off. Lights dimmed . . . comfort, conveniences, and productivity suffer.

Under this overwhelming sensual assault, we have all experienced "that 'I give up' feeling of resignation . . . . For most people, it is an accepted part of everyday living." The foregoing quote was taken from three advertisements for a prescription drug called Ritalin (methylphenidate) (2–4). Apparently, from the projection of this advertisement, the limitation imposed upon drug use by the requirement that only medical deviance is treatable is minimal. Lennard et al. (5) conclude that our model of drug usage, which provides for treatment of conditions described in the foregoing quote, produces such undesirable occurrences as ". . . [an] anti-humanistic model of behavior, more than anything else, [which] makes possible actions such as high altitude bombing or the dumping of poisonous waste into rivers and lakes. It also facilitates the new psychoactive drug technology." If such claims of expanded use are true, we are justified in examining in depth the intended functional, therapeutic effects of drugs.

> If the present trend continues, within the next decade almost every person in the technologically developed countries will—according to the pharmaceutical industry—be on some type of daily drug regimen for the improvement or maintenance of his positive health. This habit is becoming modern man's response to his over-anxiety, overweight, overindulgence, and over-population. (6)

With few exceptions, e.g., euphoria from marijuana, we seem to accept chemical manipulation of mood as desired.

4.2 THE THERAPEUTIC FUNCTIONS OF DRUGS

The therapeutic functions of drugs are designed to prevent, alter or influence significantly the outcome of efforts to reduce the risks and dysfunctional effects of disease. Outcome is defined in terms of the seven categories mentioned earlier; this holds true for all treatments including the drug modality. Each of the categories is viewed as lying ". . . on a continuum between polar extremes: alive to dead, functional to disabled, comfortable to uncomfortable, satisfied to dissatisfied, without detectable disease to symptomatic disease, achieving to not achieving, resistant to vulnerable." (7) The effect exerted on a patient's health status by one or more drugs or combinations of drugs can be seen when these categories of outcomes are arrayed "in parallel and the position of an individual or population is located appropriately on each," the resulting pattern of effect from the joining of the points of two or more of the seven continua can be shown.

4.3   DRUG EFFECTIVENESS MEASURES

The effects of drugs on the health status of an individual may be most readily observed during dramatic encounters such as administration of insulin for diabetic coma, hypnosis adjuncts, drug-induced anesthesia, and epinephrine in treating shock. The interaction of two or more of the determinants of health status previously described in Figure 2.1 may affect the health status of the patient in a variety of ways that can manifest themselves in obvious or obscure signs and symptoms.

For example, longevity may be influenced by the use of an antibiotic to cure an infection and thus prolong life. The use of rabies serum to treat a person bitten by a rabid animal may avoid what would otherwise be certain death; this use obviously serves to prolong the recipient's life. Similarly, the activity of a patient may change from a disabled state to a functional state after using indomethacin and phenylbutazone to relieve the pain and swelling of arthritis-like disease and the accompanying immobilization of the patient. A patient may be made comfortable through the use of an analgesic drug to reduce his pain experience. On the other hand, a patient may be made uncomfortable by experiencing an adverse drug reaction such as nausea. A person may be satisfied through the use of mood-affecting drugs, other stimulants, barbiturates, and psychic energizers. Where failure to conceive leads to consumption of fertility drugs, detectable disease is made symptomatic through the adjunctive inducement of pregnancy. An unfavorable alteration of normal intestinal flow may change one's health status from resistant to vulnerable. The use of allergy desensitization drugs may cause a person to achieve due to removal of the respiratory and other symptoms accompanying the otherwise untreated allergic disease for which this substance is indicated. When two or more therapeutic functions are achieved by one or more drugs, it becomes clear that drugs can have a significant impact on human behavior and feelings. Nevertheless, it remains true that drug usage is not permitted to operate outside of the medical-deviance model (police-medical model) previously described. It is necessary, but not sufficient for legitimate drug use, that all deviant conditions treated with drugs be categorized as medically deviant conditions. The importance of this point will be made obvious when the pervasive effects of restricted access to medication are reviewed in Chapter 7. This factor serves to distinguish drug abuse (as the term is commonly used) from medication use.

REFERENCES AND GUIDE TO FURTHER STUDY

1. Zinberg, N. E. and Robertson, J. A.: *Drugs and the Public,* Simon and Schuster, New York 1972, p. 191.

2. *Journal of the American Medical Association* **215**:1583 (March)1971. (drug advertisement.)

3. *Journal of the American Medical Association* **215**:1021 (February 8) 1971. (drug advertisement.)

4. *Journal of the American Medical Association* **216**:58 (April 5) 1971. (drug advertisement.)

5. Lennard, H. et al.: *Mystification and Drug Misuse,* Jossey-Bass, Inc., San Francisco, 1971.

6. Stolley, P.: Assuring the Safety and Efficacy of Therapies, *International Journal of Health Services* **4**(1):143, 1974.

7. Starfield, B.: Health Services Research: A Working Model, *New England Journal of Medicine* **289**:134 (July 19) 1973.

CHAPTER FIVE

Drugs and Medication Defined

Drug is a four-letter word; it has assumed an undesirable connotation akin to some "locker room" four-letter words to such an extent that the word *medication* frequently replaces it when a medical setting is implied. Are alcohol, caffeine, cola beverages, or marijuana properly called drugs? During prohibition alcohol was frequently prescribed as a drug to treat medically deviant conditions. Indeed, alcohol as a principal ingredient of Hadacol was largely responsible for the phenomenal success of this preparation during the early 1950s. (The same item as sold today contains only about 11% alcohol.) Just what then is the meaning of this word which has undergone such a recent and rapid metamorphosis?

The statutory definition of drug seems to define the concept precisely. The statute lists five criteria for a substance to be considered a drug (1):

(A) articles recognized in the official United States Pharmacopeia, official Homeopathic Pharmacopeia of the United States, or official National Formulary, or any supplement to any of them; and (B) articles intended for use in the diagnosis, cure, mitigation, treatment, or prevention of disease in man or other animals; and (C) articles (other than food) intended to affect the structure or any function of the body of man or other animals; and (D) articles intended for use as a component of any articles specified in clause (A), (B), or (C); but does not include devices or their components, parts, or accessories.

The first criterion merely refers one to certain authoritative sources. Criterion B is the most useful. The key problem here is to ascertain what is meant by disease. Medical deviance is its construed meaning in practice. The phrase "intended for use" is the most useful concept contained here. It directs that the object being considered for classification as a drug be viewed in terms of the actions desired from its application to viable cells. It is difficult to cope with marijuana, caffeine, oral contraceptives, and sleeping pills within this definition. The third criterion is also difficult to apply because of the complexities involved in ascertaining when structure or function are affected. Do foods and soap and automobile injuries not affect structure or function? Only by declaration is food excluded as a drug. But the question of differentiation is fruitless. One is following a circular kind of reasoning, so that only after the declaration that a substance is a food can we determine whether it is a drug. The last element is important in that, if a substance is determined to be a drug, then any components used in the process of making the drug are likewise categorized as drugs. It is also important in placing limits on classification of devices or drugs. When all these criteria are considered singularly and as a whole, a coherent definition of drug is still lacking. The following discussion will further develop the concept of drug and will yield a coherent set of criteria for classification. This refined meaning of drug is essential for development of the legal classification of medication contained in Chapter 7.

Drug is a word that expresses an abstraction formed by generalizing from particulars; it describes the common characteristics of a group of objects. But what are the particulars or characteristics of the objects from which the generalization is formed? How are drugs like or unlike foods, trees, insects, professors, knowledge, kissing, thinking, running, and other concepts? Drug is a concept that has been deliberately invented or adopted for communicating a given image of a set of objects or object attributes from the sender to the receiver. Comparing a drug and a tree, for example, does not yield much information or knowledge although both trees and drugs have weight, beauty, density, etc. The same holds true for food, a concept that is difficult, perhaps impossible, to differentiate from the concept of drugs.

The meaning of the word *drug* can be defined in at least two ways. First, it can be defined simply by using other words: e.g., a substance utilized in the treatment of disease. Second, the actions or behaviors expressed or implied in the word can be described. This method requires that one specify what stimuli, actions, or behavior are associated with the meaning of the word. We will define drug here partially as phenomena that make a positive or negative contribution to the stability or survival of a person or a group of persons. When the contribution is rewarding, it will be termed functional, and when it is unrewarding or punitive, the contribution will be described as dysfunctional. The following approach was used by Barber in his functional definition of a drug (2): When the word is used to mean a legally available drug the only function of concern is the therapeutic one. (As stated previously, nontherapeutic functions are not permissible from the use of medication).

A way of describing the foregoing is shown in Figure 5.1. The shaded area represents a unique chemical entity, identified by chemical name and described by a certain set of words explaining the

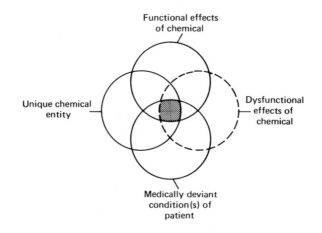

Figure 5.1. Conceptual definition of the term drug and its indications.

functional effects of the chemical to be used for treating a medically deviant condition. A description of dysfunctional effects is also necessary. Generally, a major change in any of the words used to describe a drug necessitates reclassification of the drug. When the connotation of the term "drug" as described in this section is essential for understanding, the capitalized term *Functional Drug* will be used unless the contextual use of the more familiar term drug suggests the meaning of Functional Drug. The nouns *Medication* and *Functional Drug* will hereafter be used interchangeably. The dashed circle in Figure 5.1 represents the dysfunctional effects of a drug. Labeling law requires that these effects be described in detail whenever and wherever functional effects are described. Thus, the intersection of the three circles plus all of the dysfunctional effects circle in this figure define the required "full-disclosure" information; the meaning of full-disclosure, further described in section 9.2.1, is easily understandable in terms of the four components of the figure. It will be shown in section 7.2.3, for example, that merely adding another part of the medically deviant circle of Figure 5.1 may necessitate reclassification as a "new drug."

One reason for the understanding that stems from the ordinary use of drugs is the relative dominance of the functional effects of a given substance (Functional Drug). Unusual foods or unusual quantities of food may yield an effect similar to that of a drug. The arguments among pharmacists, physicians, manufacturers, and more recently, patients seem to add yet another attribute to the definition of drug: the name of the manufacturer of the drug (or the drug's trade name).

The above definition yields a new entity each time any aspect of any of the informational units of the three nondashed circles (sets) change. In many, but not all, cases changes in the dysfunctional circle also result in definition of a new entity. As shown in Chapters 9, 10, 13, the battles (courtroom, scientific and lay press, educational institutions) fought, especially those fought by the drug labeler, clearly lead to the conclusion that the definition of drug presented here has de facto been "operationalized." Indeed, changing the inactive ion of a fairly inconsequential drug, as happened with synthesizing propoxyphene napsylate to replace propoxyphene hydrochloride in the drug armamentarium of a major drug company, was a sufficient change to secure another 17-year patent for the active moiety propoxyphene. Basically then, a drug is regulated by controlling the words that can be used to describe the overlapping area of Figure 5.1 plus the dysfunctional effects information set. It is easy to miss the significance of this de facto definition. It is the implicit definition used by drug manufacturers and the FDA. A Functional Drug is unique among commercial commodities because of the degree to which dysfunctional as well as functional effects must be described.

5.1   FUNCTIONAL USE OF DRUGS

Bernard Barber, in his significant book *Drugs and Society* (2) provides a comprehensive definition of drugs and their functions that clearly assumes that drug use is goal directed. The assumption also holds for medical deviance and also the prohibited social deviance corrective uses for drugs. By *function* we mean the natural or proper action for which a drug is suited or employed, excluding consequences of no interest or concern to the user, e.g., change in total number of molecules contained in the bloodstream. The functions of a drug may be viewed as a set of vectors where one vector consists of a list of elements reflecting the outcomes (indications for drug use) that can be achieved from use of the drug; the second vector consists of an array of conditions of medical deviance for which an altered state is desired. This process for functional use of drugs consists of conceptualizing the elements within the first array in such a fashion that the concepts form sets. A requisite of this conceptualization is that it be derived in such a manner that a relationship can be established between any of the elements existing within the second vector described. Any instance of drug usage assumes that the desired element is located within the second vector described; a diagnosis is, of course, always assumed. However, the probability of a given diagnosis may be anywhere from near one to near zero. Although problems of ties among diagnoses for a higher probability ranking complicate the situation, a diagnosis is considered a necessity.

The two arrays previously described define two distinct data sets. The indication elements described in the indications vector of the drug information consists of a data set derived from appropriate research that resulted in this information. The elements in the array making up the second vector described are derived from information describing the patient's medically deviant condition to be altered.

Feinstein (3) has described the data relevant to sick persons as consisting of three types; these are illustrated in Figure 5.2. His first

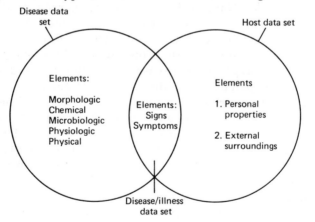

Figure 5.2.   Description of data sets and their resulting indications subset defining actions desired from medication use.

data set shown at the left in the figure, ". . . describes a disease in morphologic, chemical, microbiologic, physiologic or other impersonal terms." The second data set, shown at the right in the figure, ". . . describes the host in whom the disease occurs." This description of the host's environmental background includes the personal properties of the host before the disease began (e.g., age, race, sex, education) and also the properties of the host's external surroundings (e.g., geographic location, occupation, financial and social status). Illness is the third data set, shown as the overlapping portion of the host and disease data sets in Figure 5.2. Note that illness is defined by the interaction between the disease and its environmental host. The illness data set in turn consists of two subsets of clinical phenomena. These are signs and symptoms. Symptoms define the data subset consisting of sensations reported by the host and are relatively subjective. The data subset, signs, consists of relatively objective data determined during examination and interviewing of the host. These are the perceived conditions that are to be altered; they define the indications for which drugs are administered. The meaning of indications is "actions desired"; this is the access concept used to identify and select a drug. Actions desired represent the entry into the drug information process we shall describe in Chapter 10 (see especially Figure 10.2).

The patient, viewed from the perspective of the physician, exists as a medical deviant (or possible medical deviant) or as a nonmedical deviant. The deviance is described in temporal terms corresponding to the condition of the patient at examination (the present diagnosis), the past etiology and pathogenesis, and the future prognosis and treatment (therapy). The indications for the drug are such that administration of the drug will correct the deviant condition. The present diagnosis includes a description of the identified medical deviance as well as the name given to the disease. The pathogenesis describes the origin and development of the disease (3). Prognosis includes a description of the expected development of the disease with and without treatment. The treatment (therapy) is a description of what can be done about the present diagnosis and its future development and state. A drug's indications describe aspects of the treatment that will correct the medically deviant condition as expressed in terms of signs and symptoms.

Included in the desired actions (functional effects) of a drug is treatment or prevention. "In prevention, the purpose is to avoid the occurrence of a condition that does not yet exist, or to keep one already present from becoming worse. (3)"

The other action desired from the use of drugs is the altering of the patient's condition (medical or social); thus the purpose or goal of therapy is to remove or modify an existing condition. The FD & C Act defines a drug in a variety of ways, including its presence in named compendia, and in terms of the intended uses of articles deemed drugs. As has been shown, the definition is not adequately structured to differentiate functionally among various drugs, or among foods or devices and the component parts or accessories of devices, although it does exclude the last three categories of articles. Since drug use is goal directed, drug use is aimed at widely differing targets which are nevertheless consistent with the functional use of drugs. All of these targets (medically deviant conditions) obviously assume that the previously described data sets have been obtained. Feinstein (3) has classified the targets of treatment into three broad conceptual entities as follows:

1. The anatomic lesion, chemical dysfunction, or other basic abnormality of the disease itself.
2. Associated derangements manifested as abnormalities seen in the clinical tests performed on the patient or his specimens.
3. Clinical symptoms and signs, attributable either to that disease or to coexisting disorders.

Drugs exist for conditions in any of these three categories. These expected and desired effects (i.e., functional effects) are described in terms of indications for use in drug labeling. It is probably correct that the vast majority of drug therapy is targeted toward (indicated for) the third category, and that the first category is the most frequently sought target (indications class). Drug treatment may be indicated (1) for preventing a condition not yet existing or for preventing an existing condition from worsening, or (2) for removing or modifying an existing condition. Drug therapy is undertaken only when it falls into either or both categories; the condition toward which the drug is directed must be recognized for success to be determined. If the desired outcome is unknown, then its possible achievement cannot be known.

Any action of a drug that would be described by the seven categories listed in Chapter 4 could also be categorized within Feinstein's three comprehensive (more pluralistic) categories. The weakness exhibited by both systems of categorization is that they fail to fully distinguish between foods, drugs, devices, and related items on a functional basis. By consideration of the seven categories as units of measure of functional effect, however, the categorization described here can be used to classify medication effects.

The problems relevant to evaluating the actual effects achieved from a drug will not be considered in this section.

	Indications Vector	Illness Vector
Example A	1. Angioedema	
	2. Urticaria ——————————►	Urticaria Example A
	3. Preliminary emphysema	
	4. Regional ——————————►	Regional enteritis
	enteritis, etc.	
Example B	1. Oral contraception	Oral contraception Example B
Example C	1. (Relief from) ——————	Severe pain Example C
	severe pain	
	2. ———————— ————————►	Terminal cancer

Figure 5.3   Process of applying the functional effects of drugs in clinical treatment. The terms *illness* and *disease* are equally appropriate.

In summary, the functional use of drugs is illustrated in Figure 5.3. The first example is a simplified depiction of predisone therapy. Previous research has shown that predisone is indicated for treating the items listed in the indications vector (synonymous in meaning with "actions desired") of this figure, example A (other indications exist but are not shown). The illness data set derived from the interaction of the data sets previously described and illustrated in Figure 5.3, example A, has yielded the elements listed in the medical deviance (disease) vector termed illness vector in this figure. The targets of treatment consist of the elements in the medical deviance vector. These targets can be hit or matched only with like elements appearing in the drug indications data set. Figure 5.3, example B, depicts the process of applying the functional effects of a drug in the prevention of a condition that does not yet exist, namely, pregnancy. Here, the indications and medical deviance vectors contain identical elements. Since these match, the effects of the drug are functional for the prevention of pregnancy. Example C depicts actions desired (listed in the indications vector) for which no drug is indicated for this condition. The ideal indication would be for prevention of terminal cancer.

REFERENCES AND GUIDE TO FURTHER STUDY

1.   21 U.S. Code, 321(g)(1).
2.   Barber, B.: *Drugs and Society,* Russell Sage Foundation, New York, 1967, p. 165–186.
3.   Feinstein, A. R.: *Clinical Judgment,* Williams & Wilkins, Baltimore, 1967, see especially p. 165–186.
4.   Rapoport, A.: What Is Information? *Etc.* **10**:247–260 (Summer) 1953.

CHAPTER SIX

Desirable Characteristics
for Marketed Drugs

Even the occasional television viewer will recognize the advertising phrase "all aspirin is alike," intended to convey, because of its context, a meaning opposite to the literal meaning of the phrase. Obviously, the importance lies in how aspirin differs or is alike. Alike tends to suggest similarity in all important respects, although not necessarily in every respect, e.g., identical number of molecules. Differences tend to be important when major consequences result from the variation. Ultimately, the acid test of a drug's quality is the effect produced on the intended recipient. A great deal can be done to increase the chance of causing the desired effects.

One problem in showing drugs to be equal or unequal (in some variable) is that usually the very testing of the product destroys its integrity and thus renders it useless as a dosage form. The economics of testing drugs is obviously an important additional factor.

The focus of this chapter is on the physical, chemical, and other characteristics relevant to ascertaining the identity, purity, quality, and strength of a dosage form of a drug. The emphasis is not on the safety or effectiveness of a drug; these important concepts will be described in Chapter 8 and elsewhere. The emphasis is on insuring that a given substance, accompanied by a constant body of information, is just like the original substance used to prove the drug's effectiveness and safety.

The subject of this chapter does not seem as difficult on first encounter as its proponents and opponents treat it before both the lay and professional public. Before Senator Kennedy succeeded in 1974 in focusing the spotlight on his efforts to change certain behavioral attributes of people (via law), Senator Nelson, as chairman of the Subcommittee on Competitive Problems in the Drug Industry, succeeded in generating more than 10,000 pages of hearing transcripts encompassing more than 26 volumes. Roughly 30% of these pages were devoted to the subject matter of this chapter. A considerable proportion of comment on this subject is subsumed under the heading of generic equivalency/inequivalency. In 1974 the Office of Technology Assessment (OTA) produced a report on the subject (1). The OTA was commissioned to ". . . determine whether or not the technological capability is now available to assure that drug products with the same physical and chemical composition will produce comparable therapeutic effects." Implicit in their overall question was the question raised in the first sentence of this chapter. Their answers were equivocal because of an incomplete understanding of the meaning of quality and related concepts.

Understanding of this subject involves an understanding of several important and fundamental concepts (2, 3), such as adulteration, current good manufacturing practice regulations, identity, purity, quality, strength, statistical sampling theory, bioequivalence, compendial standards, process, and outcome.

The key variables are adulteration and sampling theory. This is true because an explanation of many of the other variables depends on an understanding of these two terms. The meaning of adulteration is best determined by reference to the FD & C Act (4).

A drug or device shall be deemed to be adulterated

(a) (1) If it consists in whole or in part of any filthy, putrid, or decomposed substance; or (2) (A) if it has been prepared, packed, or held under insanitary conditions whereby it may have been contaminated with filth, or whereby it may have been rendered injurious to health; or (B) if it is a drug and the methods used in, or the facilities or controls used for, its manufacture, processing, packing, or holding do not conform to or are not operated or administered in conformity with current good manufacturing practice to assure that such drug meets the requirements of this Act as to safety and has the identity and strength, and meets the quality and purity characteristics, which it purports or is represented to possess; or (3) if it is a drug and its container is composed, in whole or in part, of any poisonous or deleterious substance which may render the contents injurious to health; or . . . [if certain other criteria are met] . . . .

(b) If it purports to be or is represented as a drug the name of which is recognized in an official compendium, and its strength differs from, or its quality or purity falls below, the standards set forth in such compendium. Such determination as to strength, quality, or purity shall be made in accordance with the tests or methods of assay set forth in such compendium, except that whenever tests or methods of assay have not been prescribed in such compendium, or such tests or methods of assay as are prescribed are, in the judgement of the Secretary [of Health, Education and Welfare], insufficient for the making of such determination, the Secretary shall bring such fact to the attention of the appropriate body charged with the revision of such compendium, and if such body fails within a reasonable time to prescribe tests or methods of assay which, in the judgement of the Secretary, are sufficient for purposes of this paragraph, then the Secretary shall promulgate regulations prescribing appropriate tests or methods of assay in accordance with which such determination as to strength, quality, or purity shall be made . . . .

(c) If it is not subject to the provisions of paragraph (b) of this section and its strength differs from, or its purity or quality falls below, that which it purports or is represented to possess.

(d) If it is a drug and any substance has been (1) mixed or packed therewith so as to reduce its quality or strength or (2) substituted wholly or in part therefor.

A substance may be adulterated in the straightforward, common sense meaning of consisting of something other than what it is supposed to. The second criterion describes a substance as adulterated if certain conditions are met which may have contaminated it or where it may . . . have been injurious to health, even if it is not shown to consist of something other than what it should be made of. The third criterion is even more removed from the traditional meaning of adulteration. This declares that a drug is adulterated merely if it is not made according to certain statutory and regulatory requirements, with or without demonstration of the presence of something other than what should be present or the absence of what should be present. These requirements are termed Current Good Manufacturing Practice Regulations (CGMPs). The last major criterion declares that a drug is adulterated if it differs from the standards for identity, strength, quality, and purity set forth in listed compendia (mainly the USP). The stage is now set for careful examination of the remaining concepts.

Identity tends to be the most straightforward concept. Its meaning is implicit in the question "Is the drug actually what it is claimed to be?" If the drug is purported to be aspirin, is it actually aspirin or is it something else, e.g., penicillin? Note that identity suggests only some of the drug, presumably just enough to find out what it is by performing applicable tests. Identity suggests little about ingredient quantity, the presence of undesired substances, or the quality of the contents.

Strength is straightforward, too. Or is it? Strength relates to the question "Is just enough of the drug present per dosage unit, but not too much?" If an aspirin tablet is supposed to contain 300 mg, is it subpotent or superpotent if it has 1 mg too little or too much? What if it contains 60 mg over or under the required 300 mg; is this important? The USP and other compendia set the standards for the strength of a drug. For example, 300 mg aspirin tablets, USP, must contain between 285 and 315 mg. Any amount above or below this range represents unacceptable variance. Note that regardless of whether all aspirin is or is not alike, it is obvious that all aspirin tablets are not required to be alike since the upper limit represents 110% of the lower tolerance for aspirin. The difference might be significant for some patients, e.g., arthritics who may consume as many as twelve 5-grain tablets per day.

Quality is an elusive concept that is measured in terms of product attributes. All of the elements discussed so far pertain to quality. A "quality" drug product meets applicable standards of identity, purity, and strength. It is also reasonable that a product manufactured by a well-trained staff, in well-designed facilities, and according to well-written policies and procedures, has a legitimate claim to being a higher quality product when judged in relation to a product made under lesser circumstances. Basically, a high quality product is one which possesses the characteristics claimed for it; this is augmented when the product's attributes are precisely stated. In summary, a high quality product is one with characteristics necessary for its proper performance when used in accordance with its labeling.

A major and extremely difficult problem is how to discover the characteristics of a product in order to make a judgment as to its quality. Precise identification of the relevant characteristics to be measured can prove equally difficult. There are three basic approaches to measuring quality: structure, process, and outcome. The law utilizes all three meanings to ensure quality in marketed drugs. For ease in presentation the requirements pertaining to process and structure will be treated as one unit. The CGMPs as an entity encompass elements of structure and process. The official compendia [U.S. Pharmacopeia (USP) and National Formulary (NF)] relate to outcome requirements. Needless to say, the USP requirements and those of CGMP are related. The relationship can be simply stated: if CGMP requirements are adhered to, then USP outcome standards will be met.

The context in which outcome is used needs further explanation. Outcome refers to a product possessing a particular set of characteristics. Outcome in the restricted sense employed here does not connote a therapeutic result. However, the product characteristics and therapeutic effects are obviously closely related. The therapeutic effects (or therapeutic outcome) are assumed to have been demonstrated through appropriate means (see Chapter 8) and to be dependent on a product having agreed-upon characteristics. The outcome sought here is a product that is a duplicate in all relevant respects to a product that has previously been shown to yield the therapeutic outcome sought. The point is given additional emphasis because of the apparent confusion that seems to victimize interested persons. Frequently, debate rather than dialogue results from this confusion.

The reader is encouraged to maintain the distinction made here; it is easy to go astray. The bioequivalency report of the prestigious OTA (1) appears to have made a number of erroneous statements because it did not maintain the necessary distinctions (5). For example, consider the OTA and USP statements about the same subject. OTA statement:

> The disintegration tests currently called for in the compendia are relatively crude and require that an observer record the time necessary for the disintegration of six tablets. Since the average time for disintegration is about 30 mintues, a period long enough for the manufacture of hundreds of thousands of tablets, disintegration tests are clearly unsuitable for use in the monitoring and control of the manufacturing process.

USP critique of statement:

> The statement that disintegration tests are clearly unsuitable for use in the monitoring and control of the manufacturing process is not directly relevant to what is suitable for compendial monographs, but it is of peculiar interest since it demonstrates that the provider of this information appears to have no concept of the difference between the manufacturer's in-process quality control procedures and end-product batch release testing vis-a-vis the regulatory tests of the official compendia.
>
> By the absurd line of reasoning in the last sentence quoted, no test of any kind can be suitable for control of the manufacturing process of punched tablets, because all of them require a finite time interval, and in that time interval, modern high speed equipment might punch out . . . hundreds of thousands of tablets!

Many factors may act to influence a product's identity, purity, quality, and strength. This is especially true of quality. Examples pertaining to tablets include humidity, atmospheric pressure, wearing of dies, punches, and other equipment, slight changes in particle size of excipient or active ingredients, volume of granulation in feeder supplying its tablet puncher, water temperature, and so on. Variations, although numerous, tend to manifest themselves (for tablets) in changes in the following variables: hardness, weight, disintegration, dissolution, content uniformity, color, friability, size, geometric shape of dosage form, and so forth.

The main role of the USP is to issue standards for end products (finished dosage forms) and raw materials. These standards usually relate to one of the variables listed above that are needed to insure the presence of appropriate characteristics to meet quality requirements. Aspirin tablets, USP, serves as an interesting example. The relevant quality attributes of this item can be classified within the following categories: identification, strength, purity, disintegration, weight variation, and packaging and storage.

The attribute of purity for aspirin pertains mostly to one factor, namely, that significant amounts of nonaspirin not be present. The nonaspirin substance described in the monograph for this item is nonaspirin salicylates; no more than 150 μg/ml of a test liquid prepared from the tablets may be present. The tablets must pass the required specifications for nonaspirin salicylates contained in the monograph.

For a 5-grain (300 mg) aspirin tablet the strength is prescribed in the monograph. The actual amount of aspirin present may vary from 95% (285 mg) to 105% (315 mg). A determination of the actual number of milligrams present must be made only in accordance with an assay for aspirin described in the monograph.

Disintegration of the aspirin tablets must occur within 5 minutes. In other words, any given tablet that falls apart within 5 minutes meets the official disintegration standard. The USP contains a description of the disintegration test for these tablets. The procedure requires that at least 6 tablets be used for the determination. It is a straightforward and reliable procedure.

Aspirin tablets, USP, may contain several inactive substances. These serve to bind the tablet together, enhance disintegration, and reduce tablet breakage. The USP restricts the weight variation of these tablets. In some instances tablets which differ by as much as 10% in weight can successfully meet USP standards. For this attribute the procedure requires that 20 tablets be selected (method of selection is not given) and that their average weight be calculated. Variation from this mean is restricted. The weights of not more than two tablets must differ by no more than 5% ; no single tablet can differ by more than 10% from the mean tablet weight.

The qualitative identity tests required for a given "unknown" substance are described. These tests are designed to obtain a clear yes or no answer as to whether a substance alleged to be aspirin is actually aspirin.

The monograph specifies that this item must be packaged and stored in a certain way: "preserved in tight containers." Little explanation is given about the precise meaning of this phrase.

Quality as a concept allows for ignoring the factors about a product that do not alter its desired performance. For example, coloring aspirin green would not affect its strictly physiologic performance (although psychologically this may not be true). The shape of the tablet—within wide limits—would not affect the product's performance. Conducting tests to insure that all such tablets produced vary little or none in shape or color characteristics would be functionally meaningless. In the case of aspirin existing tests apparently do not result in bioequivalence of different aspirin tablets (1). The point is that once relevant product attributes are precisely described, the end product can usually be reliably tested to determine if a product being questioned meets these attributes. The product's quality is described in terms of how well it meets the standards defined for the product. Whether it meets other standards is irrelevant for determining product quality; one may measure its diameter, but the results do not pertain to measuring the product's quality unless this variable has been agreed upon as a relevant quality attribute for this particular product.

The notion of quality assurance is summarized in Figure 6.1. Note that the model depends on identification of relevant quality attributes and a feedback mechanism for correcting measured deviation from an established standard. Selection of a sample measurement unit is explained in the next section.

6.1   CURRENT GOOD MANUFACTURING PRACTICES

Testing of intermediate or finished products is accomplished by relying on information derived from a sample. By definition, a sample is some but not all units taken from a population. Thus, due to sampling variation, there will always remain some chance that defective units present in the population were somehow undetected in the sample taken. Increasing the sample size tends to decrease the chance of a defective unit falling outside the sample. But until all members of a population are sampled there is some (though perhaps small or inconsequential to most patients and providers) chance for a defective unit to escape detection. Table 6.1 summarizes the data describing the

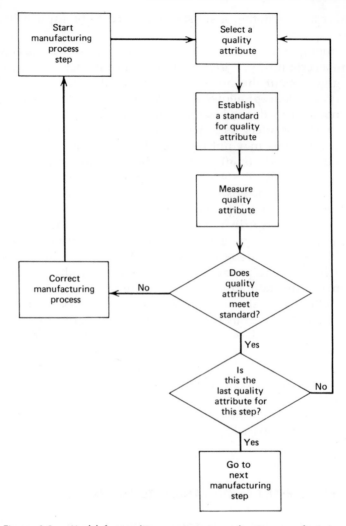

Figure 6.1. Model for quality assurance in medication manufacturing.

likelihood of accepting a batch of tablets as being within the disintegration test requirements when the listed percentages of the tablets do not meet the disintegration standard (1). For instance, batches of tablets with only 1% that do not meet the disintegration time requirement will almost always be accepted. A batch in which 10% do not meet this requirement would still pass 79 times out of 100. If only one tablet was not defective, the chance of acceptance would still be greater than zero. The CGMPs are designed to insure that every unit meets applicable standards.

TABLE 6.1   CHANCE OF ACCEPTANCE OF A SAMPLE OF TABLETS
AS A FUNCTION OF PERCENTAGE OF DEFECTIVE TABLETS

Percent Not Meeting Disintegration Standard	Chance of Acceptance
0%	1.0
1%	.995
5%	.96
10%	.79
20%	.39
30%	.15
40%	.004
Almost 100%	Almost .00
100%	.00

The Drug Control Amendments of 1962 contained a provision for FDA prescribing of current good manufacturing practices (6). The definition of current good manufacturing practices does not appear in the law; it is defined only indirectly by regulation. CGMPs specify criteria (7) for, buildings, equipment, personnel, components, master formula and batch production records, production and control procedures, product containers, packaging and labeling operations, laboratory controls, distribution records, stability, and complaint files. Elaboration of the meaning of each of these criteria follows.

1. *Buildings.*   Buildings are to be maintained in a clean and orderly manner and should be of suitable size, construction, and location to facilitate adequate cleaning, maintenance, and proper operations in the manufacturing, processing, packing, labeling or holding of a drug. Such items include provision for adequate space for placement of equipment and materials; provision for locker facilities, hot and cold water washing facilities for personnel; and provision for suitable housing and space for the care of all laboratory animals.

2. *Equipment.*   Equipment used for the manufacture, processing, packing, labeling, holding, testing or control of drugs should be maintained in a clean and orderly manner and should be of suitable design, size, construction, and location to facilitate cleaning, maintenance, and operation for its intended purpose. The equipment requirements pertain to such items as construction of surfaces that are not interactive with drug components. Lubricants or coolants should not in any way interact with drug substances. Construction and installation of equipment and its

cleaning, disassembly, and related procedures, should not interfere in any way with the manufacturing of a drug, and a provision must be made for excluding contaminants from the drug
product. Equipment should be of a suitable type, size, and accuracy for any testing, measuring, mixing, weighing, or other processing or storage operations required.

3. *Personnel.*   Specific requirements for education or experience of
persons manufacturing drugs are not specified in the regulations.
In one statement to a congressional committee, an FDA representative suggested that a person who drops out of pharmacy school
without completing his course of study or who fails his pharmacy
board examination and is legally barred from filling a patient's
prescription may nevertheless set up a drug manufacturing establishment and produce potent drugs to be dispensed by pharmacists all over the country. Whether this is the case or not, the
point is that the law applies to the performance of these manufacturing personnel rather than to their qualifications. A performance requirement is a rather marked departure from today's
societal norm of licensing persons ranging from automobile
mechanics to airplane pilots. Basically, the requirement for personnel is that responsible personnel directing the manufacture
and control of a drug shall be adequate in number and
background of education, training, and experience so that the
drug is assured of having the identity, quality, purity, and
strength that it purports to possess. All personnel are supposed
to possess capabilities commensurate with their assigned functions, a thorough understanding of the manufacturing or control
operations they perform, the necessary training or experience,
and adequate information concerning the reason for application
of pertinent provisions of the law to their respective functions.

4. *Components.*   All components and other materials used in the
manufacture, processing, and packaging of drug products, and
materials necessary for building and equipment maintenance, are
to be stored and handled in a safe, sanitary and orderly manner
upon receipt. Adequate measures are to be taken to prevent
mix-ups and cross-contamination of drug components and
finished drugs. Components are to be withheld from use until
they have been identified, sampled, tested for conformance with
established specifications, and released by a materials approval
unit.

5. *Master Production and Control Records; Batch Production and Control Methods.*   In order to assure uniformity in each drug batch, a

master production and control record for each drug product and each batch size of each drug product should be prepared, dated, and signed or initialed by a competent and responsible individual and should be independently checked, reconciled, dated, and signed by a second competent and responsible individual. The regulations describe the contents of the master production and control records. Basically, the requirements relate to a master "recipe" that specifies each ingredient and the quantities of each ingredient. When differing quantities are to be made the recipe must be individually written in proportion to the master recipe, so that the particular quantities desired can be manufactured according to a constant set of specifications each time a new batch is made. Explicit instructions specifying the steps in preparing a particular drug must be provided. Batch records must show each phase of production, including check weighing and other control checks necessary to prevent mistakes. A key requirement is that batch records be identified with a suitable number by which it should be possible to trace details of manufacture and control (the concept of tracing is treated in greater detail in Section 7.1).

6. *Production and Control Procedures.* These procedures are supposed to include all reasonable precautions necessary to assure that drugs produced have the identity, strength, quality, purity, and safety that they purport to possess. Such precautions include a double check in which all significant steps in the manufacturing process, e.g., selection, weighing, measuring, or adding components together are performed by a competent and responsible person and then independently rechecked by an individual of equal competence and responsibility. In the event that machines are used to check significant steps in the manufacturing process, these devices should be checked and monitored by a responsible person. The written record of the significant steps in each portion of the process should be identified by the name of the person performing the test and by the person charged with checking these significant steps. The names should be recorded immediately following the completion of each step.

All containers, liners, and equipment used during the production of a batch of the drug should be properly identified at all times to accurately and completely indicate their contents and, when necessary, the stage of processing of the batch.

Other procedures relate to cleanliness requirements and to minimizing microbiological contamination. Likewise, procedures designed to prevent cross-contamination of any drugs being made or stored are required.

In order to insure the uniformity and integrity of products there should be a set of adequate in-process controls. Examples include checking of weights and disintegration times of tablets, the adequacy of mixing, the homogeneity of suspensions, and the clarity of solutions. In-process sampling should be done at appropriate intervals using suitable equipment, personnel, processes, etc.

Samples of all dosage form drugs are supposed to be tested to determine their conformance with the specifications of the product; this must be done before release for distribution. Although particular requirements for sampling and procedures for random sampling have not been specified in the applicable regulations, they will be so specified in the near future.

Procedures for reviewing and approval of all production and control records, including packaging and labeling, are supposed to be done prior to the release or distribution of a batch of drug. Departures of a batch from any of its specifications should be thoroughly investigated and any discrepancies described and explained in detail.

7. *Product Containers and their Components.*   Suitable specifications, test methods, cleaning procedures and, when indicated, sterilization procedures are supposed to be used to assure that containers, closures, and other component parts of drug packages are suitable for their intended use. Product containers and their components should not be reactive or absorptive. Procedures should be implemented to provide adequate protection against external factors that can cause deterioration or contamination of the drug being made.

8. *Packaging and Labeling.*   The basic goal of this requirement is to insure that there is proper matching among proper containers, proper labeling, and proper packaging materials. It is quite possible for a drug to be manufactured in accordance with the most exacting requirements and yet for a mismatch of label and product to occur. For example, the best of aspirin when identified with labeling intended for phenobarbital will obviously be worse than a poorly made aspirin tablet. The packaging and labeling operations should be designed so that only those products that have met the standards and specifications established in their master production and control records are distributed. Proce-

dures should include measures to prevent mix-ups among drugs during filling, packaging, and labeling operations, to assure that correct labels and labeling are employed for the drug, and to identify the finished product with a lot or control number that permits determination of the history of the manufacturer and control of the batch (see section 7.1 for more on the last point). Numerous other controls are necessary on packaging and labeling operations. These include the separation of operations of different drugs being made, to avoid mix-ups between drugs or between batches of the same drug in order to minimize cross-contamination. In-house inspection of the facilities should be made prior to use to assure that all previously used drugs, packaging, and labeling materials have been removed. Basically, these labeling controls relate to restricting movement of persons, labels, packaging materials, and drugs once a given packaging and labeling operation has begun. Control is also achieved by inspecting, examining, or laboratory testing of packaging and labeling materials after the final labeled and packaged product is ready for shipment.

9. *Laboratory Control.* Basically, laboratory control requires that scientifically sound and appropriate specifications, standards, and test procedures be established in order to assure that components, in-process drugs, and finished products conform to prescribed chemical and physical standards. The master record for a given product should contain appropriate specifications for the acceptance of each lot of drug components, product containers, and their components used in drug production and packaging, and a description of the sampling and testing procedures used for them. The regulations provide that samples be representative and adequately identified, although no requirements for random sampling are specified. However, the master record is supposed to contain a description of the sampling procedures for finished drug products. Special requirements should be adhered to for drugs purported to be sterile and for those with critical physical properties, e.g., ophthalmic ointments (which should be free from foreign particles or abrasive substances). Sustained-release products should be adequately tested to insure that they conform to the release specifications in their master production record.

10. *Distribution Records.* Basically, distribution records are required to facilitate tracing the movement of the various ingredients of the drug through the manufacturing process, so that the finished

product with its lot number identification can be traced to or from its destination. This subject is discussed in detail in Section 7.1.

11. *Stability and Expiration Dating.* The manufacturing process should insure that a drug will remain basically as it was when manufactured for a reasonable amount of time. The manufacturing process should provide for stability testing by spelling out specific testing methods. It is important that products be stability tested in the same container-closure system in which they will be marketed. Special requirements should be followed for dry drug products that are to be reconstituted at the time of dispensing; stability testing should be performed on the dry product itself as well as on the reconstituted product. Note that these requirements for stability testing furnish a good argument for dispensing drugs in their original containers rather than transferring them to some other container. Regulations have recently been written which require, for example, that nitroglycerin be dispensed only in its manufacturer-tested container.

Expiration dating is intended to assure that drug products that are liable to deteriorate meet appropriate standards at the time of use. An expiration date should be justified by readily available data derived from stability studies. Stability testing and expiration dating must be appropriate for the storage conditions that the drug may encounter.

12. *Complaint Files.* A drug manufacturer must maintain records of all written and oral complaints received regarding each of his products. The manufacturer must investigate each complaint to find out if it is legitimate and if changes in the manufacturing process should be instituted.

6.2   USE OF SAMPLING THEORY IN QUALITY ASSURANCE

Randomness is a means of knowing the chances of a drug possessing a given attribute. It is also a means of maximizing the chance that the sample will yield the best estimate of the properties of its universe. Sampling is the taking of a portion of a universe to stand for the universe as a whole. Random sampling is a method of sampling in which each entity in the universe has the same or equal chance of being selected. Sampling is based on the assumption that one can make fairly accurate statements about the attributes of a large group by examining only a small portion of the members (units, items, entities) of that group. A population or universe represents some whole or "complete" set of items about which one is seeking information. A sample represents some function of the universe taken according to some method; when the method is random sampling, the fraction obtained is a random sample. Technically, facts about a population are called parameters. Facts about a sample are known as statistics. The difference that exists between a statistic (a sample fact) and a parameter (a population fact) is called sampling error. If a population fact is known, there is no good reason to concern oneself with a sample fact because a sample fact is only an estimate of the population fact. Sample facts contain sampling error, and they will differ in value from a population fact. The main point of sampling is to infer something about the population fact.

If a sample is drawn and a statistic calculated, that statistic ideally is equal to the parameter. However, if several different samples from a population are drawn, each statistic will differ from the others a little. The differences in the statistic from sample to sample yield an estimate of the sampling error of the statistic. Such variation leads to the concept of sampling distribution (8):

> A sampling distribution is a theoretical probability distribution of the possible values of a sample fact which would occur if one were to draw all possible samples of the same size from a given population.

If the sampling distribution is bell-shaped (normal), the mean of the distribution is termed the expected value of the statistic. The standard deviation of the sampling distribution is the standard error of the statistic. Generally, the smaller the standard error the greater the confidence that can be placed in inferences made.

> The standard deviation of a sample of size 'n' is given by the square root of the sum of the squared deviations from the mean divided by $n-1$ (9).

The standard error of a statistic is influenced considerably by the sample size. In general large samples are better than small ones because the sample standard deviation is more likely to be equal to the population standard deviation as the sample size increasingly approximates the population size. Carried to its extreme, the best estimate of a parameter is based on a sample that consumes the entire population. Figure 6.2 roughly expresses the relationship between sample size and error (10).

The obvious problem of large sampling previously alluded to is that most drug testing is destructive. The absurd outcome is that when one

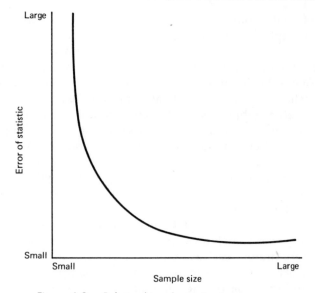

Figure 6.2.   Relationship of sample size to error.

is most assured of the values of variables describing drugs (e.g., dissolution, bioavailability, disintegration, tablet compressibility), no drug remains for patient treatment.

Irrespective of the wide applicability of such statistical concepts in industry (e.g., canned beverage manufacturing), drug manufacturers have been slow to apply this information. As recently as 1975, the CGMPs were virtually silent on such considerations as (1) the method of sampling, (2) the rationale for specifying the number of units (sample size) to be tested, and (3) the statistical criteria for permitting a batch or lot of a finished product to pass. The more pressing need for application of these concepts is with products that have a narrow margin of safety, e.g., large-volume parenterals, digitalis preparations, and sodium warfarin.

Due to great variability and considerations relevant to producing a given drug with a given set of characteristics (e.g., safety, efficacy, identity, purity, quality, strength), it is preferable that the CGMPs require that each manufacturer maintain in writing sampling and testing plans adequate to meet the three points raised in the preceding paragraph. Detection of batches containing, say, more than 5% defective units, whatever the measure may be on the unit, can be accomplished by following the principles described in this section. This procedure requires,

1. Choosing sample sizes in accordance with the average quality deemed necessary;
2. adoption of sequential sampling and testing procedures;
3. recognition that the acceptance or rejection of a batch should be determined not on the basis of the individual tests alone, but on the totality of the tests on all important characteristics.

Basically, a firm decides that it will test the following hypothesis:

$$H_0 : U_1 = V_i$$
$$H_1 : U_1 \neq V_i$$
$$\alpha = 0.05$$

For this hypothesis U may represent any one of a number of things or statistics. Included are such indicators of identity, purity, quality, and strength as tablet disintegration, dissolution, content uniformity, bioavailability, particulate matter in the air, granule size, or other variables described in this chapter. H_0 in this hypothesis represents the null hypothesis or what is thought or plannned to be the value (V_i) of the item (dissolution rate, for example) being measured. H_1 depicts the alternative hypothesis. Patient's risks, signified by α, represents the chance of accepting a defective batch. (The producer's risk, signified by β, is the chance of rejecting a good batch. While not described here, β is important to both the producer and consumer because of the increased production cost of rejecting acceptable batches.)*

Application of this generalized hypothesis to the USP dissolution tests will make the meaning clearer. For example, if the USP dissolution test reads that (1) tablets are acceptable if 6 tablets initially tested for dissolution properties properly meet the specifications or (2) if 1 or 2 units fail to meet the requirements, the test should be repeated on six additional units, and at least 10 of the 12 units tested must meet the specifications, then the chances of acceptance can be summarized in a table. Assuming some specific batch size and producer's risk, Table 6.2 lists the chance of acceptance as a function of percentage of defective tablets. Note that when 5% or less of the tablets are defective the batch will be accepted 98% of the time.

---

* If the same terminology is applied to criminal law, α represents the chance of convicting an innocent person and β represents the probability of acquitting a guilty person. Thus the criteria for conviction of "beyond a reasonable doubt" would fall in the neighborhood of 5% error.

TABLE 6.2 CHANCE OF BATCH MEETING DISSOLUTION TEST SPECIFICATIONS AS A FUNCTION OF PERCENTAGE OF DEFECTIVE TABLETS

Percent Defective Tablets	Chance of Acceptance
1%	.9998
5%	.98
10%	.90
20%	.58
30%	.28
40%	.10
50%	.03
60%	.006

Hypothesis testing must be repeated for each variable (statistic) deemed relevant to a drug's identity, purity, quality, and strength. Each time a sample is drawn, it must be drawn randomly according to the sampling plan designed specifically for that product. (Rejection of any one hypothesis disqualifies a drug from meeting its standards.)

Industrial application of the statistical concepts discussed here are described in quality control textbooks in the language of operating characteristic curves. Basically an operating characteristic curve contains the type of data listed in Table 6.2 plus specification of a value for producer's error and sample size. Detailed descriptions of sampling theory applications can usually be found in a textbook on quality control (11).

A review of the quality of FDA enforcement of CGMPs is outside the scope of this book. A General Accounting Office (GAO) report revealed that 48% of producers studied critically deviated from CGMPs (12). The same report showed that 16% of drug producers were not inspected at all within the required two years. Nonenforcement of the best of regulations is unlikely to result in drugs possessing the attributes necessary for safe and effective drug use. Critics of generic equivalency among drugs seem to have a persuasive argument. How can a legitimate defense of the equality of drugs be made on the basis of equality of manufacturing requirements when considerable discretion can be exercised in manufacturing operations? Equality of manufacturing operations must be made a reality.

6.3 POISON PREVENTION PACKAGING REQUIREMENTS

The Poison Prevention Packaging Act of 1970 (PPPA) prescribes certain packaging standards for all prescription drugs, nonprescription aspirin, and a few other nonprescription drugs (13,14). These requirements do not constitute antiadulteration standards. Apart from certain legal, technical reasons, these requirements are termed misbranding because they relate to the container and not to the contents of the container. Although adulteration standards also relate to the container, the PPPA standards do not in and of themselves affect the product; the regulations require that the intended use of the drug not be adversely affected. The PPPA standards are aimed at preventing the product from being inadvertently used for an unintended purpose. Because of their (product container standards) similarity to adulteration considerations, the requirements of the PPPA are described here rather than in the chapter on labeling.

Unquestionably, the PPPA has affected the behavior of providers, adult consumers and, to some extent, children. The basic aim is to control the behavior of children, i.e., to reduce the 300 or so deaths and roughly 100,000 injuries due to accidental ingestion, from the perspective of the adult responsible for the child, and purposeful ingestion by the child himself.

The basis for the PPPA provisions is the assumption that a package be used that can be opened by adults, but not by children less than 5 years of age. A number of other events may intervene, however. For example, adults may leave the top of the medication off to avoid the effort of reopening the container, or may place the drug where it is accessible to children.

The philosophy behind the act is well stated by a consumer representative (13):

> . . . our investment in our human resources—children—is too great to permit continued inaction. The curiosity which killed the cat should not be allowed to continue to kill children. Children must be protected from themselves; the cost of doing nothing is too high.

About half the deaths and injuries from poisons occur from ingestion of medicines. Aspirin, alone or in combination with other drugs, is the product most frequently involved.

The PPPA governs four classes of substances including drugs. It provides for the establishment of standards for special packaging if a household substance is determined to present a hazard to children. Factors to be considered in making this determination are reasonableness of the standard, nature and use of the drug, feasibility of special packaging, industry manufacturing practices, and data describing injuries occurring from such substances.

To ensure that a container is in fact a poison prevention container, a test protocol has been established. A sample of 200 normal, healthy children between 42 and 51 months old, evenly distributed by sex and age should be selected. According to proper principles of research design, the children are allowed up to 5 minutes to open the drug container. Those unable to open it are given instructions, (e.g., "you can use your teeth,") on how to open it. At least 85% of children not receiving instruction and 80% of those receiving instruction must be unsuccessful. An adult use effectiveness test of at least 90% is required; testing must be done on adults ages 18 to 45 (15).

Special drug containers are required for (1) all oral dosage form prescription drugs (see Section 7.2 for a definition of drug categories), and (2) aspirin-containing nonprescription over-the-counter (OTC) drugs. Certain exceptions have been made to the OTC aspirin category, e.g., the exemption of Alka-Seltzer®. Certain exemptions for prescription drugs are allowed, e.g., nitroglycerin sublingual tablets, and most drugs in aerosol dosage form. In addition one noncomplying package (of OTC drugs) can be packaged provided that it carries the statement "this package for households without young children."

A prescriber (physician) can stipulate, if in his opinion the patient's state of health merits it, that standard (nonspecial) packaging is desirable. A patient may also request of a dispenser (e.g., pharmacist, or physician) that standard packaging be used. If the dispenser's opinion is that the patient's condition or reasons warrant use of a standard package, he may acquiesce.

This act raises a number of questions. For instance, would the cost of changeover and the additional expense of special packaging (an estimated $75 million) be more effective if spent for other purposes, e.g., research on the causes, prevention, and treatment of so-called crib death which kills about 10,000 infants annually? The ethical issues raised by this question are considered in more detail in Section 11.1.

Is it fair to demand that the 75% of households not having children less than 5 years of age tolerate safety containers and pay for their additional cost? As one poster claims: Is there not an adult responsible for every child accidentally poisoned annually? Since children can't read labels, since they learn by exploring their environment, and since they can't appreciate the potential hazards from drug ingestion, shouldn't their responsible adult be held responsible? The dramatic testimony at Senate hearings, describing the pain and suffering that resulted when a curious 18-month-old boy underwent a tracheotomy to permit breathing and a tube was inserted in his stomach to receive nourishment, strongly suggests that society is willing to tolerate safety containers (16).

Another serious question in this regard involves the actual effectiveness of special packaging. There is no provision for premarketing approval of the effectiveness of special packaging containers. Manufacturers are supposed to report their data, derived from use of the required protocol, showing the effectiveness of a particular container. At least one study has resulted in the conclusion that the fear of leaving safety closure containers where children have access to them is not valid (17). This same study showed that adults who are intolerant of safety closures leave the top off, transfer the contents to another container, etc. The blister pack container was shown to be the most effective (child-proof) but also the most difficult for adults to open. One study has added an encouraging finding, from a broader perspective of poisoning from drugs and certain other substances, by showing that a poison prevention program is cost-effective (18). Another study (19) has shown that pharmacists are reluctant to use safety closure containers. There is also ample anecdotal evidence that dispensing physicians use less safe containers than do pharmacists. Generally, however, qualified studies have shown that safety closures are effective (20,21) for relatively large populations considered in the aggregate.

Ultimately responsible consumers and providers are responsible for their respective behavior. The pharmacist who features the one adult size of aspirin packaged in "regular" (nonpoison prevention) containers in a special sale is not acting responsibly. It is impossible to enact enough laws to deal with the irresponsible consumer or provider.

REFERENCES AND GUIDE TO FURTHER STUDY

1. Drug Bioequivalence Study Panel: *Drug Bioequivalence,* Superintendent of Documents, Washington, D.C., July 15, 1974, 78 p.
2. 21 *U.S. Code,* 351(a)(2)(B).
3. Title 21, *Code of Federal Regulations,* 133.0.
4. 21 *U.S. Code* 351.
5. Heller, W.: Letter to Senator Kennedy, July 18, 1974. In Werble, W. (Ed.) *The Gold. Sheet* **8** (7): 5–14 (July) 1974.
6. Drug Control Amendments of 1962, Public Law 87–781.
7. Title 21, *Code of Federal Regulations,* 133.
8. Kelly, F. J., et al.: *Multiple Repression Approach,* Southern Illinois University Press, Carbondale, Ill., 1969, p. 14.
9. Freund, J. E. and Williams, F. J.: *Dictionary/Outline of Basic Statistics,* McGraw-Hill, New York, 1966, p. 103.

10. Kerlinger, F. N.: *Foundations of Behavioral Research*, Holt, Rinehart & Winston, New York, 1964, p. 61.

11. Lachman, L. et al.: *The Theory and Practice of Industrial Pharmacy*, Lea & Febiger, Philadelphia, 1970, p. 719–736.

12. Comptroller General: Problems in Obtaining and Enforcing Compliance with Good Manufacturing Practices for Drugs, *In Competitive Problems in the Drug Industry*, Part 24, Feb. 20, 21; March 5, 6, Superintendent of Documents, Washington, D.C., 1974, p. 10519–10564.

13. President's Committee on Consumer Interests: Letter to H. O. Staggers, *U.S. Code Congressional, and Administrative News*, **3**:5332, 1970.

14. Poison Prevention Packaging Act of 1970, Public Law 91–601.

15. 38 *Federal Register* 1700, p. 21249.

16. Corrigan, J. J.: The Poison Prevention Packaging Act, *FDA Papers*: 14 (March) 1971.

17. Oberda, G. M. et al.: *Child Resistant Containers—Safe for Children and Usable by Adults?* Unpublished manuscript, 29 p.

18. Norwood, G. J. and Rotello, N. D. An Accidental Poisoning Prevention Program, *Journal of the American Pharmaceutical Association* NS 13 (3): 131 (March) 1973.

19. Chmielewski, D. H.: An Analysis of the Value of Poison Prevention Containers, *Journal of the American Pharmaceutical Association* NS 11 (1): 16 (January) 1971.

20. Stracener, C. E. et al.: Results of Testing a Child-Resistant Medicine Container, *Pediatrics* 40 (2): 159 (August) 1967.

21. Krain, L. S. et al.: Dramatic Trends in Childhood Poisonings in Los Angeles County, *Journal of the American Pharmaceutical Association* NS 11 (1): 13 (January) 1971.

CHAPTER SEVEN

A Generalization of Various Major Drug Laws

Drugs are among the most regulated of commodities in the United States and in most other countries. Drugs are regulated through various and diverse laws at the national, state, and local levels. Laws regulate the activities of manufacturers, growers, and consumers. They also control the intermediaries which exist at opposite ends of the drug use continuum between consumers and producers of drugs or drug components. Often these laws duplicate, overlap, and are in conflict with each other. They seem incomprehensible and lacking in general governing principles. Closer examination shows, however, that general principles regulating drug supply and demand do exist and that the system also tolerates many exceptions to the overall plan of regulation and control.

The laws regulating drugs in this country, regardless of their level (federal, state, or local), can be categorized under several general kinds specifically designed to relate to drugs and drug-related products:

1. Laws governing the record of movement of drugs and related items through various distribution channels.
2. Laws governing the information content of drug labeling.
3. Laws defining the qualifications of persons responsible for both the movement of drugs through the various distribution channels and for the labeling of drugs.
4. Laws defining the scope of the legal duty owed by the various practitioners involved in the provision of drugs and drug related services.

5. Laws regulating the quality and nature of a drug and its container.
6. Laws defining the punishment and/or civil penalty for non-compliance with medication law.
7. Laws affecting the supply and demand of drugs by direct and indirect controls on internal and external competitive practices.
8. Laws directing that certain categories of the public be provided with drugs dependent only on their categorical membership.

This discussion will only indirectly and peripherally consider the fundamental question of why drugs have been selected and isolated for their intensity of regulation. However, some brief comments about this fairly modern state of affairs have been and will be made.

Categories 7 and 8 are outside the scope of this text. The latter category is usually studied as an important component of the external factors is a course in drug marketing, and pertains to provisions of drugs and drug services to eligible recipients by various third-party programs. The Kerr-Mills program enacted in 1960, followed by the Medicaid program in 1965, provided the first major influence of this type. Regulations under these programs are likely to exert an increasingly important effect on future drug use. Ample evidence of the impact of such programs is available by examining the *Conditions of Participation* for Medicare and Medicaid. The revised condition for Medicare patients, finalized in 1974, requires that the pharmacist review each patient's chart monthly; this review is the first significant step outside the military for true clinical pharmacy involvement. The specific duties of the pharmacist under these programs are described in Section 12.6.6.

7.1   RECORD OF MOVEMENT OF DRUGS THROUGH DISTRIBUTION CHANNELS

Drugs in this country are regulated at the federal level primarily according to their legally defined category. Some of these legal categories have already been briefly described. Criteria for classification as legend drugs, nonlegend drugs (OTCs), investigational new drugs, new drugs, old drugs, veterinary legend drugs, veterinary nonlegend drugs, controlled substances, drugs intended for animal feed purposes, and drugs not intended for use in human or animals will be described in part in this chapter. Based on the category in which a particular drug appears, it is possible to describe the physical movement and the records of movement of the drug product through its distribution channels prescribed by applicable law or laws. Confounding the problem of describing the movement of drugs through their various channels of distribution is the fact that the legal categorization of drugs is such that a particular drug may, under a wide variety of circumstances (e.g., the drug's intended use, location of use, potential for abuse, previous knowledge or experience with the drug), be placed in any one or all of the foregoing legal categories. For example, a common drug such as aspirin may sometimes be classified not only as an old drug as it is usually classified, but also as a prescription drug if it is offered (that is, marketed) for a new and novel purpose. Aspirin may be considered a new drug if it is marketed as a timed release preparation; it may be considered a veterinary legend drug if it is offered for a new and novel veterinary purpose; and if it is shown to be addicting or subject to abuse under certain circumstances, then it could conceivably be marketed as a controlled substance. On the other hand, tetracycline (available only as a prescription drug when intended for use in humans) can be obtained as a veterinary nonprescription drug for treating diseases of tropical fish.

Nevertheless, drugs are usually distributed in such a way that the record of the movement and the persons causing and authorizing the movement of a drug through interstate commerce can be traced from the origin of the basic chemical constituents all the way to the ultimate consumer; it must also be possible to trace the drug from consumer back to basic chemical constituents (Figure 7.1). For example, in the case of a common drug such as aspirin, USP, the physical product must contain certain information according to federal law including a manufacturer's (or distributor's) name and address, so that a particular drug can at least be traced to that manufacturer. The manufacturer is also required to maintain records so that he can determine the lot of origin of the package, the ingredients in that particular lot of aspirin, and the origin of each ingredient.

It is not possible to trace the movement of the drug from the intermediary points in the distribution channels unless the manufacturer maintains records by lot numbers so that he can state to whom and when the particular lot was shipped. That shipper in turn should be able to indicate when and to whom portions of the particular lot of aspirin were assigned. However, for the most controlled legal category of drugs (controlled substances), e.g., codeine sulfate, the law requires that every ingredient comprising a lot that makes up a particular dosage form be traceable as it flows into the particular dosage form within a manufacturing plant, so that all significant steps and the

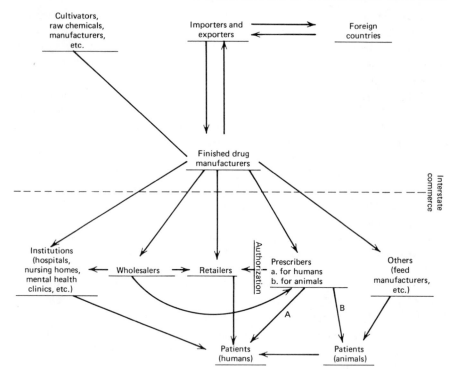

Figure 7.1. Major and traditional elements in the legitimate drug distribution channel in the US. Only selected elements and relationships are shown. *Note:* A single entity, i.e., a hospital, may contain a number of channel elements simultaneously, e.g., patients, pharmacists, physicians, and nurses. Multiple channel functions are sometimes performed by a single channel entity.

persons performing these steps and the time of performance can be ascertained. It is also necessary that its movement be traceable to the consumer whose name appears on the dispensed prescription label or who possesses a properly labeled nonprescription container. For example, if a dispensed prescription package contains codeine sulfate tablets (or some other controlled substance), the law requires that the container label identify the pharmacy which, in turn, must be able to ascertain from its records the supplier who made the drug available. This requirement applies to any particular lot number involved. Once the pharmacy identifies the supplier from which the codeine sulfate supply was obtained (generally a wholesaler), the supplier must be able to ascertain from his records the date and source which furnished the drug. Each of the critical steps involved in the movement of this drug and its records must also be accessible according to law. Once the wholesaler ascertains his source of supply (generally a basic pharmaceutical manufacturer), he must be capable of identifying the manufacturing batch records containing the drug and be able to identify all individuals, times, pieces of equipment, etc., relevant to the manufacture of the drug.

In the example of codeine sulfate, its individual ingredients in turn must be traceable to their suppliers. This applies to all inactive ingredients contained in the final dosage form. For example, if a basic supplier (e.g., Penick) of raw chemical ingredients supplied the codeine sulfate to the manufacturing firm, then the firm must be capable of identifying Penick and ascertaining the date and the persons authorizing the movement of the drug from Penick to the manufacturers; the same must be true for Penick. If Penick receives the drug from someone else, the chain of events must also be traceable as per the preceding description. If Penick grew the opium (the source of codeine) in its own field, then the records must be traceable to the very seeds.

In summary, the procedures for recording the physical movement and maintaining enabling documents for the movement of a drug through its distribution channels are demanding. The basic requirement is that (to varying degrees) the flow of the drug and the people authorizing the movement together with the times of authorization of the physical movement and the records of this flow be traceable from the origin of the basic ingredients to the ultimate consumer.

Of equal importance is the requirement that any registrant be able to reconcile his receipts and the drugs he has disbursed. (Briefly, a registrant is a person or firm who indicates to an agency such as a Board of Pharmacy that he intends to engage in some phase of drug distribution or production at a particular address. This concept is described in detail in Section 7.3.) The documentation of sources of supply and disbursement must be readily identifiable. A drug's legal category determines the scope, nature, and criteria of record keeping and authorization for movement and other aspects of its control under the law.

7.2 CRITERIA FOR DETERMINING THE LEGAL CATEGORY OF A DRUG

For each major drug category certain criteria must be used to determine on a drug-by-drug basis to which, if any, legal category(ies) the drug belongs. The classification categories range from illegal to legal.

Illegal _____ Legal
Category   Category

The intended use and the claimed effects of a drug are of paramount importance to category determination. Classification as legal or illegal is entirely unsatisfactory for predicting the degree of behavioral control of the people desiring to consume the drug. The following examples will illustrate this point. Drug X may be an illegal (banned) drug because its purported effects are not useful for correcting instances of medical deviance. Drug Y may be illegal because research results have failed to demonstrate a favorable risk/benefit relationship from use of the drug. Drug Z may be illegal because "substantial evidence of effectiveness" has not been demonstrated. This lack of substantial evidence may be due entirely to the unfavorable economic potential of the drug; i.e., it simply costs too much in relationship to anticipated sales to justify the necessary research expense to secure marketing approval by the FDA. (However, some drugs are made at a loss in order to serve the patient; some critics claim that this also serves to prevent government entry into manufacturing.) Consumer and provider behavior is thus curtailed because the drug is unavailable for consumption.

The legal category may consist of a drug, e.g., Drug A, available only from approved outpatient clinics where only designated prescribers may permit patients to consume the drug (only in the presence of other providers). Drug B, however, may be legally purchased or sold by anyone anywhere, without identification or other evidence of the purchaser or seller.

Nine major legal categories of drugs exist under federal law, and each contains additional subcategories. Figure 7.2 depicts the major categories and some of their interrelationships. Any one drug, depending on a number of factors that will be described later, may simultaneously be classified within one or more of the sets shown in Figure 7.2.

The wavy line in the central portion of Figure 7.2 is the dividing line between old and new drugs; old drugs are to the left of the line and new drugs to its right. Banned substances and non-approved new drugs are neither new nor old drugs. The universal set of all possible drug substances is described by the outermost rectangle. One can only hope that drugs potentially available are underrepresented in the universal drug set. The topmost inner rectangle represents the prescription drug set. Note that prescription drugs may also be classified as new or old and as controlled or noncontrolled. The second, third, and fourth rectangles depict the nonprescription, veterinary prescription, and veterinary nonprescription drug sets, respectively. Any of these legal categories can be further subclassified as controlled or noncontrolled and/or new or old drugs.

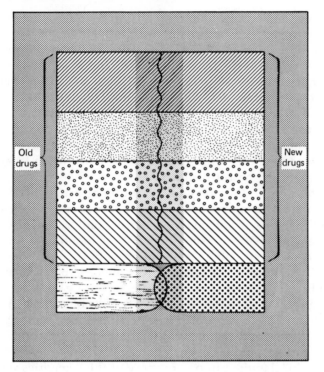

	Approximate percentage of total in category
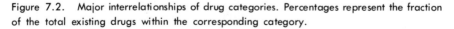 Prescription	85%
Nonprescription	15%
Veterinary prescription	50%
Veterinary nonprescription	50%
Nonapproved new drugs undergoing clinical trial	1%
Banned substances	1%
Universal set of drug substances	?
Controlled substances	15%
Old drugs	50%
New drugs	50%

Figure 7.2. Major interrelationships of drug categories. Percentages represent the fraction of the total existing drugs within the corresponding category.

The controlled substances category overlaps all other legal categories. It is important to note that future drugs may also be classified as controlled substances.

The solid dots on the bottom of the inner rectangle depict the set of nonapproved new drugs undergoing clinical trials. This set may overlap the controlled substances set and the banned substances set (depicted by horizontal markings). Examples of banned substances are heroin, lysergic acid diethylamide (LSD), and marijuana. An example of a controlled substance undergoing clinical trials (the overlap of the controlled substances set with the "undergoing clinical trials") is methadone. Recall that classification is determined on the basis of intended use as labeled. Methadone is classified as an old drug and a controlled substance when labeled for use as an analgesic, but as a nonapproved new drug and a banned substance when labeled for use as a treatment for narcotic addiction.

Close attention to the previous definition of drug will show that an object becomes a drug only when some functional outcome or good, described in terms of longevity, activity, comfort, satisfaction, ease, achievement, or resilience (see Chapter 4), is identified for the particular object considered only in association with its one or more desired effects. In determining the category to which a substance belongs, one can simplify the process by thinking of a drug in terms of words describing its functional effects (indications) rather than in terms of a unique chemical substance. As will be shown in Section 9.2 a drug* can exist legally only when it is accompanied by certain kinds of descriptive information. Given a constant chemical entity, any substance may be classified in one or more of the categories described in Figure 7.2 simultaneously. For example, aspirin is usually regulated as an old drug and as an OTC drug. However, if it is to be marketed as a time-release product (reflected in the labeling by, as a minimum, differing intervals for consumption), it will be classified as an unapproved new drug until required data from clinical trials and other sources are obtained.

The criteria and ways of establishing conformance vary widely from one category to another. The burden of proof for admission to a category may rest upon the marketer or would-be marketer; and proof is necessary for categorization as an approved new drug. On the other hand, the burden of proof may rest with the marketer to prove that a given product does not belong in a particular category; this is true for categorization as an old drug. Efficiency in study is, nevertheless, accomplished by studying categories of drugs and criteria for classification. When a category is determined for a labeled drug, all the laws, regulations, procedures, cautions, etc., controlling the behavior of people who desire to use a drug in that category apply to the uniquely labeled drug.

* A few exceptions exist; e.g., drugs termed "chemical orphans" because no therapeutic claims are made (see especially reference 1 and Section 9.2.5.).

Figure 7.2 is designed so that any Functional Drug can be appropriately placed within its proper cell or cells. For example, since Aspirin Tablets, USP, is properly classified as an OTC old drug, it is excluded from the controlled substances cell and the new drugs cell. Timed-release aspirin is classified identically except that it lies within the new drug cell and is still excluded from all other cells except the OTC and universal cells. Morphine sulfate lies within the old drug, prescription, and controlled substances cells. When used to treat addiction, methadone is classified as a controlled substance, and as an unapproved new drug undergoing clinical trials. Since it is not labeled as a prescription drug for this indication, it lies outside the prescription cell. To classify a drug in the controlled substances cell precisely requires subdividing the controlled substances cell into its five divisions (schedules); the resulting parts, not shown in Figure 7.2, are described in the next section.

7.2.1   Controlled Substances

Drugs classified as controlled substances are those that the FDA and the Attorney General have determined to be potentially abusive (2). In deciding whether a drug has a potential for abuse, the following factors must be considered (3):

1.   Actual or relative potential for abuse
2.   Pharmacologic effect if known
3.   Current scientific knowledge regarding the substance
4.   History and current pattern of abuse
5.   Scope, duration, and significance of abuse
6.   Risk, if any, to the public health
7.   Dependence liability (physiologic or psychologic)
8.   Whether the substance is an immediate precursor of a controlled substance.

When a substance is determined to be in the category of controlled substances it must be placed in one of five schedules according to the criteria listed in Table 7.1. (See Section 14.2 for description of an instance in which a citizens group attempted to force the Drug Enforcement Administration to abide by its own criteria.)

No drug or other substance may be placed in any schedule unless the criteria described in Table 7.1 are met (4). In short, the law determines which category a drug will fit into when the particular therapeutic criteria are defined.

When a controlled substance's proper schedule is determined, each

TABLE 7.1   CRITERIA   FOR   CLASSIFICATION   OF   CONTROLLED   SUBSTANCES   BY SCHEDULE

	Schedule				
Criteria	I	II	III	IV	V
1. High Potential for Abuse	Yes	Yes	<II	<III	<IV
2. Accepted medical use	No	Yes	Yes	Yes	Yes
3. Accepted safety	No	Yes	Yes	Yes	Yes
4. Psychological dependence	Not applicable	Severe	High	<III	<IV
5. Physical dependence	Not applicable	Severe	Moderate or low	<III	<IV

Source: Public Law 91-513, Controlled Substances Act, Section 202.

container of that substance must show an emblem clearly designating its schedule on the drug label (5). The symbols must be at least twice as large as other letters on the label and must be located in the upper right-hand corner of the label's principal panel on the commercial container. Symbols may also be overprinted on the label, but they must be at least one-half the label size and in a contrasting color to all other printing on the label.

Legally, controlled substances must be identified as such. This is accomplished by display of the appropriate symbol on the retail package supplied to the dispenser. Symbols must be as follows (5):

Schedule	Symbol
Schedule I	I or C-I
Schedule II	II or C-II
Schedule III	III or C-III
Schedule IV	IV or C-IV
Schedule V	V or C-V

7.2.2   Criteria for Classification as Prescription Drugs

The approach to category definition is first to list relevant criteria. The basic FD&C Act lists these criteria for classification as a prescription drug (6):

1. Any drug in a list of 17 named habit-forming drugs listed in another section of the Act (e.g., morphine, peyote).

2. Any drug which because of its toxicity or other potential for harmful effects, or the method of its use, or the adjunctive measures necessary to its use, is not safe for use except under the supervision of a practitioner licensed by law to administer such a drug.
3. Any substance so named as a prescription drug under the new drug provisions of the Act as being a component of an approved new drug application.

Several interesting and instructive points can be made about these criteria. The first criterion is of little consequence, since it is mainly concerned with a relatively small number of drugs listed in the Act itself. Likewise, the third criterion is an intermediate way of getting to the second most basic criterion. Thus if criterion three is applied to a drug during the course of its development as an "approved new drug" then it is to be so labeled. Criterion two is clearly the most important. A careful look at this yardstick reveals that ". . . not safe for use except under the supervision of a practitioner licensed by law to administer such drugs . . ." is a key phrase. The phrase modifying this quoted portion is an explanation and listing of some of the reasons why a drug cannot be labeled so that it can safely be used by laymen, i.e., intervention by another person is essential to insure safe use of the drug.

The layman is deemed to be incapable of rationally following instructions and other advice contained in the drug labeling as approved either implicitly or explicitly by the FDA. Several other points must be made regarding the overall classification of substances as legend drugs. Significantly, legend drugs shall be dispensed only "upon a written prescription written by a practitioner licensed by law to administer such drugs . . . ." In practice administer is construed to mean prescribe (7).

Procedurally, classification as a legend drug is accomplished by declaring a drug misbranded if it is not legally labeled as a legend drug after it has met the classification criteria. Conversely, the Act provides that a drug is misbranded if it is labeled as a legend drug when in fact it does not meet the classification criteria. The law achieves identification of prescription drugs by requiring that the statement "Caution: Federal law prohibits dispensing without prescription" appear on all drugs classified as legend drugs and by prohibiting this phrase on labels of drugs which do not meet the statutory and regulatory criteria for legend classification (8). If examination of a drug's label reveals this phrase, then it is a legend drug. Likewise, if the statement "Caution: Federal law restricts this drug to use by or on the order of a licensed veterinarian, or on his prescription order," then the drug is a veterinary prescription drug.

Although one might at first be led to believe that these are fairly objective criteria, close examination indicates that considerable difficulty occurs when classification of a given substance as prescription or nonprescription is attempted. For example, how is it that insulin, contraceptive foam, oral contraceptives, ophthalmic glucocorticosteroids, antihistamines (e.g., 8 mg chlorpheniramine maleate), pyrvinium pamoate, digitalis, and other substances have been differentially classed as prescription or nonprescription drugs? The meaning for a given substance of "toxic or harmful" and "whether its method of use or the adjunctive measures necessary in order to ensure safe use" are not clear; whether the drug can be used by the patient also becomes unclear. Is it not possible to label oral contraceptives safe for use by the layman? Consider pyrvinium pamoate, which is administered for a very specific indication (pinworms), when only one dose is necessary and when a noted pharmacology textbook implies that it is virtually harmless. Can it not be labeled to be used safely by the layman (9, 10)?

The following section will examine some of the effects on patient behavior brought about by restricted access to prescription drugs. The requirement for third-party intervention between the practitioner and the seller will be explored in brief, since this subject seems to have escaped the attention and interest of most persons writing on the broad subject of drug use.

Effects of Limited Access to Prescription Drugs on Patient Behavior

The exclusive right to control access to drugs makes it impossible or at best extremely difficult for the average layman to manage his problems independent of expert (prescriber) advice. By being the legally appointed gatekeeper for a large and significant class of essential products, the prescriber gains considerable power—sanctioned by society—to at least require the patient (sometimes reluctant) to take, or appear to take, his advice as a necessary condition for purchasing a given drug. Although the layman may feel that he knows precisely the drug product he needs for his ailment, and may even be correct in his selection, he must acquire a prescription to purchase the drug legally. Thus, the prescriber must duplicate the layman's selection or make an independent selection in order for the layman to gain access to the desired drug.

This procedure is in direct contrast to the only prerequisite for purchasing other commodities, namely, that one possess the required amount of money to pay for the commodity.* To purchase a replacement exhaust muffler in an automobile parts store, one need not seek permission from a mechanic to make the desired purchase. Society allows the purchase despite a known hazard to the automobile user from poisonous carbon monoxide fumes emanating from improperly installed exhaust mufflers. But the automobile mechanic is not a professional; he does not have exclusive control over the *social object*, in this example, the mufflers (11).

Establishing a class of drugs which can be obtained only by the permission of a consenting third party assumes the existence of only two classes of people. In brief these two classes are (1) the "ignorant class," or those so uneducated about the use of members of this class of drugs that the advice of an intervener must be obtained, and (2) the "educated class," or those informed enough to give advice to the ignorant class. This two-category classification has the disadvantages of most gross classification systems. The ignorant label places university presidents and college students, generals and privates, teachers and students, children and their parents, the sane and the insane, the imprisoned and the free, all into the same general class. Such heterogeneity among class members is certain to create some misgivings on the part of at least some class members. The basis for classification as a prescription drug is frequently misunderstood by both professionals and laymen. Some infer that the basis for classification is whether or not the patient can reasonably be expected to arrive at his own correct diagnosis. For example, insulin is used to treat diabetes mellitus when the body produces the hormone in inadequate amounts because of a malfunction of the adrenal cortex. Diabetes mellitus is a difficult disease to diagnose, its prognosis is variable and unpredictable, and it may be confused with a number of other diseases. Nevertheless, insulin is legally categorized as a nonprescription drug. Others see the prescription classification as a basis for broad protection of the uninformed and relatively ignorant consumer. Two authors, writing in a pediatric medical journal, expressed such an opinion (12). They treated a patient who mistakenly ingested camphorated

---

* Certain exceptions to this exist, e.g., the age requirement for purchasing alcohol and, in some states, tobacco products; the requirement in some states that a person be of some minimum age in order to purchase certain poisons; and the requirement that one be of legal age to purchase certain firearms, get married, incur financial obligations, drive a car, etc. Note that these requirements are class-based rather than individually based.

oil thinking it was castor oil, and who shortly thereafter gave birth to an apparently normal baby who had a distinct odor of camphor from the mouth, skin, and amniotic fluid. Their remedy for preventing such future occurrences was ". . . as camphorated oil has no therapeutic value, it has been requested that the drug be available only by prescription." The foregoing examples illustrate the confusion that can result when one strays too far from the basic criterion for labeling a drug so that the reasonable man can discern desired behavior from a reading of the label.

Regulations and controls have not always been the same. For example, we seem to have completely reversed the direction of control existing in England during the reign of Henry VIII (13).

Be it ordained, established, and enacted by the authority of this present parliament, that at all time from henceforth, it shall be lawful to every person, being the king's subject, having knowledge and experience of the nature of herbs, roots, and waters, or of the operation of the same, by speculation or practice, within any part of the realm of England, or within any other the king's dominions, to practice, use, and minister in and to any outward sore . . . of the kind listed in the preamble any herb or herbs, ointments, baths, pultess, and emplasters, according to their cunning experience, and knowledge in any of the diseases, sores and maladies aforesaid, and all other like to the same, or drinks for the stone, strangury, or agues, without suit, vexation, trouble, penalty, or loss of their goods. . . .

The reader should not conclude from the foregoing argument that we should undertake a vast reclassification of many legend drugs from prescription to nonprescription. The previous discussion was designed to raise the question of how much control of individual behavior should be allowed to a person in order for him to achieve the optimum health standard possible with current medical and health care technology. Section 10.4, which examines layman capability in drug information processing, is rather discouraging about the layman's ability to act rationally in processing drug information so that the therapeutic outcome he desires is likely to be achieved. Perhaps a solution would be to enlarge the number of persons allowed to prescribe. Creation of a third class of drugs intermediate between the present prescription and nonprescription class has long been advocated by the American Pharmaceutical Association. (A third class already exists for Schedule V and certain other controlled substances which can only be sold by a pharmacist; see Section 12.6-8.7.) While this proposal has considerable merit, there is a question of possible conflict of interest if the prescriber and dispenser are one and the same. Although so-called dispensing physicians presently account for almost one prescription in ten, this practice has received considerable criticism, including that of organized pharmacists. More than two drug classes may be needed. These should probably be categorized as follows:

1. Drugs that can be sold by any vendor without a prescription.
2. Drugs that can be dispensed without a prescription, but only by a pharmacist.
3. Drugs that can be dispensed by prescription only, any physician could authorize dispensing.
4. Drugs that can be dispensed by prescription only, only select physicians possessing special qualifications could authorize dispensing.

Recent research based on the Delphi technique (a technique for scientific prediction based on expert opinion) has suggested that such a reclassification may occur within the next 20 years. An interdisciplinary California legislative commission has already made such a recommendation (14, 15). The development of clinical pharmacy (clinical pharmacology applied by pharmacists rather than physicians) will be a major factor in determining future classification.

Nevertheless, the point here is not whether a vast reclassification of legend drugs should be undertaken, but what degree of individual control is to be exchanged for some increased measure of health. Ultimately, the ends which can be achieved through current technological means may not be those which a society should strive toward (16). Friedson has succinctly and lucidly summarized this point (17).

> A profession and a society which are so concerned with physical and functional well-being as to sacrifice civil liberty and moral integrity must inevitably press for a scientific environment similar to that provided laying hens on chicken farms—hens who produce eggs industrially and have no disease or other cares.

As further evidence of the questionable desirability of the ultimate technological answer a quote from a noted educator and physician is in order (18). The author created a composite picture of a person who had taken maximum advantage of existing technology to minimize his risk of developing atherosclerosis. His description follows:

. . . an effeminate municipal worker or embalmer completely lacking in physical or mental alertness and without drive, ambition, or competitive spirit; who has never attempted to meet a deadline of any kind; a man with poor appetite, subsisting on fruits and vegetables laced with corn and whale oil, detesting tobacco, spurning ownership of radio, television or motorcar; with full head of hair but scrawny and unathletic appearance, yet constantly straining his puny muscles by exercise. Low in income, blood pressure, blood sugar, uric acid and cholesterol, he has been taking nicotinic acid, pyridoxine, and long term anti-coagulant therapy ever since his prophylactic castration.

7.2.3   New Drugs

Any drug or substance purported to be a drug, but not proven to be safe and effective for its intended uses, is deemed an unapproved new drug; in Figure 7.2 unapproved new drugs are termed "drugs undergoing clinical trials." An approved new drug must meet the requirements of Section 505 of the FD&C Act. These requirements will be comprehensively described in a later section. The FD&C Act (19) defines a new drug as:

> (1) Any drug . . . the composition of which is such that such drug is not generally recognized, among experts qualified by scientific training and experience to evaluate the safety and effectiveness of drugs, as safe and effective for use under the conditions prescribed, recommended, or suggested in the labeling thereof, except that such a drug not so recognized shall not be deemed to be a "new drug" if at any time prior to the enactment of this Act it was subject to the Food and Drugs Act of June 30, 1906, as amended, and if at such time its labeling contained the same representations concerning the conditions of its use; or
> (2) Any drug . . . the composition of which is such that . . . as a result of investigations to determine its safety and effectiveness for use under such conditions, has become so recognized, but which has not otherwise than in such investigations, been used to a material extent or for a material time under such conditions.

This definition uses "new" to mean used for the first time. A drug may become new when it is used for an additional use for the first time. If the conditions under which the drug is prescribed, recommended or suggested change, then because of these changes the drug may become a *new* drug. Likewise, a drug may remain classified as a new drug because it has not been used extensively for a long enough time under the labeled conditions. Any chemical or other substance not previously used in man for the treatment of medical deviance is a new drug. Combinations of new approved drugs or of old drugs may be classified as new drugs even though the entities comprising the combination may be classified otherwise. A new indication for a drug, new or not new, may require that it be considered a new drug. That is, "The use of a drug *in vitro* as a diagnostic agent when this use will influence the diagnosis or treatment of disease in a human patient may cause the product to be regarded as a new drug." (20)

To exhaustively define *new drug* would be difficult and lengthy, and any newly discovered instance would not be included in this definition. Considerable understanding and parsimony is achieved by recalling the definition of Functional Drug (medication), which includes a constant meaning of information that must exist with the unique chemical itself. Changes in any of the contributing concepts to the definition of Functional Drug require treatment of each Functional Drug thus created (or defined) as unique. In other words, changes of any sort in the unique chemical entity, the medically deviant condition information set, or the information set used to describe the subset formed by the overlap of the chemical information, medically deviant information, and functional effects sets may render the resulting Functional Drug a new drug. Thus it may be concluded that any given Functional Drug is either an approved new or old drug, and that once it is classified as an old drug it will remain in that category until the legal definition of new drug changes.

Generally, a new drug cannot be identified by reference to its label. For a nonprescription new drug, the presence of a quantitative list of ingredients is suggestive, but not conclusive. A check of a comprehensive index to drugs will lead one to a description of old and new drugs. (see Section 14.1).

7.2.4 Other Categories

Veterinary legend drugs and veterinary nonprescription drugs will not be described here. A separate but similar section of the basic FD&C Act describes the criteria for their classification. These important drugs will probably be even more important in the future. These drugs must carry on the dispenser's package the veterinary legend listed in Section 7.2.2.

No treatment other than that in the introductory chapters of this book will be devoted to banned substances. Part of Chapter 8 explains the criteria for reclassifying an unapproved new drug to an approved new drug. Technically, antibiotics and insulin are not classified as new drugs. The distinction in the criteria applied to insulin and antibiotics is relevant only in a technical, legal sense. The insulin and antibiotic certification requirements are discussed briefly in Section 7.3.2 and in Chapter 6.

Although there are other classification schemes which affect the behavior of persons dealing in drugs within the class, e.g., caustic poisons, they are beyond the scope of this book.

7.3   REGISTRATION AS A MEANS OF CONTROL

Control of drug movement through distribution channels rests upon a comprehensive system of registration. This system requires that certain people (mainly physicians) and other entities (mainly hospitals, community pharmacies, drug wholesalers, and educational institutions dealing in certain classes of drugs) engaged in the distribution of drugs must register periodically with designated agencies. (Common carriers are exempted by law from registration, provided certain documents and information possessed by them is made available upon request; when this information is provided by the common carrier, the common carrier is exempt from prosecution based upon this information.)

Registration is required by a number of different acts including the FD&C Act and the Controlled Substances Act (CSA) at the federal level (21, 22). In addition, registration is usually required at the state level by the State Uniform Controlled Substances Act or its equivalent, the State Pharmacy Practice Act, and/or the State Food, Drug, and Cosmetic Act. Generally, the registrant must provide his name and the address of his place of business. Usually, he will also be asked to provide a description of his type of operation, the size of his establishment, and the classes of drugs handled by his firm. Under the US FD&C Act each registrant is supposed to be inspected every 2 years by the FDA. This inspection is performed as a control measure to ascertain if the registrant is complying with the conditions he agreed to.

Registration requirements depend on the category of the drug being handled by the registrant. Generally, under the US FD&C Act, only firms or individuals relabeling drugs or labeling drugs for the first time are required to register (23). Ordinarily, this category includes cultivators, raw chemical manufacturers, and importers and exporters who handle drugs in drug packages. The major registration category under the US FD&C Act requirements relates to the finished drug manufacturer. Generally, retailers such as general purpose sundry shops, gasoline service stations, department stores, animal feed retailers, etc., are exempt from registration under this portion of the law if they do not engage in labeling or relabeling of drug products. (These types of businesses are forbidden to deal in controlled substances or human prescription drugs.) Likewise, pharmacies do not ordinarily have to register under this portion of the Act because they do not generally engage in labeling or relabeling finished drug products within the meaning of these words as defined in the Act. * A similar exemption applies to prescribers for drugs they make for their patients. However, the CSA requires registration of virtually all entities in the distribution chain engaged in the manipulation of controlled substances regardless of whether labeling or relabeling is accomplished by the channel member, with the sole exception of the consumer (22). Generally, the registration requirement for controlled substances dealers or others involved in authorizing controlled substances movement extends to all channel members with the exception of the patient, who is not restricted as long as he does not transfer the drug to someone else. The registration requirements under the US CSA are ordinarily duplicated for those channel members existing within the confines of a particular state. (More than 60% of the states in the US have enacted a State Uniform Controlled Substances Act.)

By law, the FDA must inspect all manufacturers of prescription and nonprescription drugs at least once every two years for compliance with the FD&C Act and especially the Good Manufacturing Practice Regulations of the same Act. (As discussed in chapter 6, this is not always done by the FDA). Nonprescription drugs may be sold by any person who receives a properly labeled drug in inter- or intrastate commerce. The movement of prescription drugs, however, can be accomplished only upon permission of a practitioner authorized by law to initiate or continue movement of a drug in interstate commerce. This is made possible by state licensing laws of physicians (prescribers), pharmacists (dispensers), and other practitioners engaged in prescribing, dispensing, and administering drugs. The patient does not

---

* Pharmacies are exempt in part because of the requirement of the various states that each pharmacy secure a permit to operate and that each pharmacist register (secure a license) from the State Board of Pharmacy. Each pharmacy permit and pharmacist registration must be renewed at required intervals.

have to meet any licensing requirement, just as he is exempted from any registration requirement.* Many states have also seen fit to register all retailers of legend drugs; many states have imposed a similar registration system upon wholesalers of prescription and nonprescription drugs. Analogous registration requirements have generally been required for retailers and wholesalers, prescribers, dispensers, and administers of veterinary prescription and veterinary nonprescription drugs. Veterinary nonprescription drugs can be bought, sold, and otherwise handled in a fashion similar to human nonprescription drugs.

7.3.1   Registration of Products

The Drug Listing Act of 1972 (technically an amendment to the FD&C Act) coupled with the desired symbols which must appear on controlled substances labels for commercial products (see Section 7.2.1) effectively requires registration of products themselves. Firms and persons dealing in any legitimately available drug class must register annually with the FDA the names of these drugs, their strengths, ingredients, and certain other relevant information. Pharmacies and certain other organizations are exempt from registration of products under this act if there is no labeling or relabeling of products offered for sale outside the normal course of pharmacy business. A similar exemption for prescribers also applies to physicians and certain others designated by regulation.

7.3.2   Special Registration Requirements

Many states have enacted a Uniform Controlled Substances Act (UCSA), which duplicated the federal regulation of persons handling controlled substances with the exception of patients. This involves another duplicate system of registration of prescribers, dispensers, retailers, and wholesalers including those dealing in veterinary drugs, regardless of whether they are legend or nonlegend drugs.

* As previously noted, for some few especially selected drugs he is warned via the labeling that certain acts on the part of the patient are illegal.

An almost completely closed system is insured by the provision for setting quotas for substances listed in Schedule II under the requirements of the CSA (24). The traceability of these substances is greatly aided by the requirement that Schedule II substances be ordered only by the use of a specially designed order form. With the exception of prescribers, movement of a Schedule II controlled substance cannot occur without appropriate use and record keeping via this special order form, issued in triplicate by the DEA to registrants only. One copy is retained by the dispenser, one copy is sent to the vendor (usually a wholesaler), and one copy is sent to the DEA. Since the DEA maintains records of quantities manufactured and quantities ordered by dispensers, and since written prescriptions are the sole basis for an authorized prescription, the system is almost a closed one. If a supply of special forms were issued to prescribers and added to the reconciliation, the system would probably be nearer a completely closed network. Obviously a major drawback is the enormous effort necessary for complete record keeping and reconciliation. As computer use is adopted by members of the distribution channel, especially prescribers and dispensers, the record keeping problem will diminish.

Similarly, the FDA maintains a record of the quantities of certain antibiotics and insulin certified during the course of a year. This is roughly equivalent to registration of the quantities of these products. An estimate of the number of dosage units actually used compared with the number that should have been used can be derived by comparing the total quantities of antibiotics and insulin certified with the disease incidence for which these drugs are indicated. Thus a crude estimate of the quality of the control system can be produced. Considerable refinement of this description is necessary for implementation of the reconciliation suggested here. (The FDA has paid for a contract based on this methodology (25).)

Recently the FDA took a significant step in the stringent control of a noncontrolled substance drug with the announcement of the distribution requirements for medroxyprogesterone acetate (MPA) (26). The drug is a long-acting injectable contraceptive marketed as Depo-Provera. Prescribers ordering the drug from the manufacturer must do so on a special order blank signed by the prescriber. Pharmacies that order the drug will receive in each carton a postage-paid card which must be returned to the manufacturer with the name of the prescriber. The manufacturer in turn must maintain a registry of prescribing physicians. Thus by comparing the medication ordered and dispensed, a complete tracing of the movement of this drug can be achieved. (The requirement that the physicians obtain the patient's informed consent before administration of MPA is discussed in Chapter 11.) The exact date of implementation of these requirements is to be determined, because the initial regulation was delayed by a subsequent one (27, 28). A certain brand of intrauterine device (IUD) must be distributed and controlled in a similar fashion.

Some specific labeling and record-keeping requirements used to achieve the statutory degree of control are described in Section 12.6.8.

REFERENCES AND GUIDE TO FURTHER STUDY

1. Reilly, M. J.: ASHP Survey of Use of Nonapproved "Drugs," Third Annual Midyear Clinical Meeting, American Society of Hospital Pharmacists, December 9, 1968, Washington, D.C., 10.

2. Public Law 91-513, Section 201(b).

3. Public Law 91-513, Section 201(c).

4. Public Law 91-513, Section 202(b).

5. Title 21, *Code of Federal Regulations,* 1302.03.

6. 21 *U.S. Code,* 353(b).

7. DeMarco, C. T.: The Legal Basis for Clinical Pharmacy Practice, *American Journal of Hospital Pharmacy* 30(11):1070 (November) 1973.

8. 21 *U.S. Code,* 353(b)(4).

9. Goodman, L. S. and Gilman, A.: *The Pharmacological Basis of Therapeutics,* 4th ed., Macmillan, New York, p. 1079.

10. Aviado, D. M.: *Pharmacologic Principles of Medical Practice,* 8th ed., Williams and Wilkins, Baltimore, 1972, p. 1098.

11. Freidson, E.: *Professional Dominance,* Atherton Press, New York, 1970, p. 117.

12. Quoted from *Clin-alert,* Dec. 22, 1973, No. 233.

13. Stevenson, L. G.: Official Control of the Administration of Drugs, *Experimental Medicine and Surgery* 22:148 (January), 1964.

14. Goyan, J. E. (Chairman): Report to the Speaker of the Assembly by The Advisory Commission on Pharmacy pursuant to H.R.-21, 1973–74, San Francisco, Nov. 5, 1974, 63 p.

15. Report to the Speaker of the Assembly, *ibid.,* Part 2, Appendices, 281 p.

16. Zola, I. K.: Medicine As an Institution of Social Control, Sociology Conference of the British Sociological Association, Western-Super-Mare, U.K., November 5–7, 1971, 22 p.

17. Freidson, E.: *Profession of Medicine,* Dodd, Mead, New York, 1970, p. 354.

18. Lasagna, L.: *Life, Death, and the Doctor,* Alfred Knopf, New York, 1968, p. 215–216.

19. 21 *U.S. Code,* 321 (p).

20. Gyarfas, W. J. and Welch, A.: The IND Procedure: Assuring Safe and Effective Drugs, *FDA Papers,* 3:27 (September)1969.

21. 21 *U.S. Code,* 360(L).

24. Public Law 91-513, Section 306.

25. Food and Drug Administration: Request for Proposal Number 641-4-118, Proposal for Analysis, Pilot Operation and Evaluation of a Drug Use Trends Analysis Information System, U.S. Food and Drug Administration, Rockville, Md., 1973.

26. Food and Drug Administration: Postcoital Diethylstilbestrol, *FDA Drug Bulletin*:2(May) 1973 (issued irregularly).

27. *Federal Register*, Oct. 30, 1974 p. 38226.

28. Food and Drug Administration: Depo-Provera for Contraception: Approval Stayed, *FDA Drug Bulletin:* 2 (January-March) 1975 (issued irregularly).

CHAPTER EIGHT

Laws Governing the Derivation and Sources of Drug Labeling Information

This is the first of three chapters devoted primarily to a description of drug information. Figure 8.1 depicts a model for starting with a hypothesis about the relationship between a chemical and its effects. This is used to generate information about a drug useful for disease treatment. This chapter includes a description of all the components of the model through approval of the drug for disease treatment; this is indicated in Figure 8.1 by the first dashed line between approval and output. Chapter 9 is a description of information about medication; this appears as the output component of Figure 8.1. How this drug information is used for input in disease treatment is the subject of Chapter 10. The aspects of disease treatment that produce certain actions desired were discussed in Chapter 5. The interface of disease effects that need to be modified and medication actions were illustrated in Chapter 5.

Figure 8.1 depicts an information system. The activating element of the system is an idea; someone must derive a hypothesis about the effects of a chemical. The disease treatment component in Figure 8.1 is only briefly considered here because the most relevant aspect of diagnosis and prognosis to medication usage is the information produced from the process. The "actions desired" is the key and vital output of diagnosis and prognosis; medication usage cannot proceed without it.

It should be recognized at the outset of this chapter and throughout this book that labeling per se is a means rather than an end. It is a

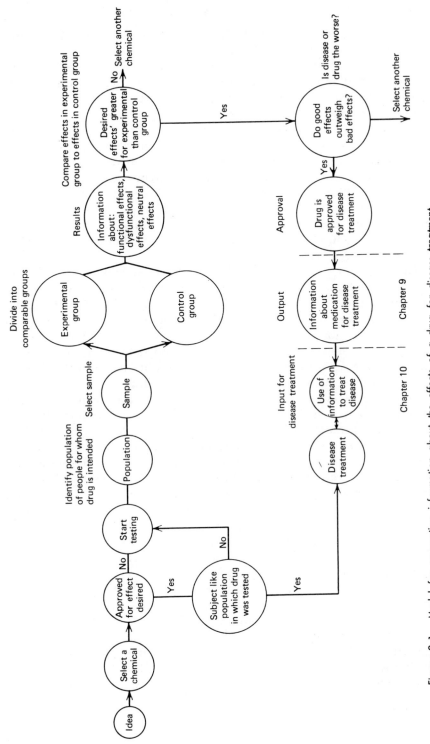

Figure 8.1. Model for generating information about the effects of a drug for disease treatment.

principal mechanism by which all drugs are regulated in this country. Basically, some action can be taken against the possessor of a drug (except for most cases of consumer possession) who is holding it for distribution if the drug's labeling deviates from legal requirements. Illegal acts are almost always of the illegal possession, misbranding, or adulteration type.

The process of generating drug information can be assimilated and understood by recalling the earlier statement that a drug is best viewed as (1) a unique chemical entity, (2) words describing its functional effects, and (3) the use of which is directed toward a medically deviant condition. If one or more of these three items are changed in any manner, the "unit," i.e., the Functional Drug, generally takes on a meaning different (although usually quite similar) from the original unit. Changes in information about dysfunctional effects can likewise create a different meaning.

The basic controlling federal law is the U.S. FD&C Act. The Act provides that no drug can be marketed in this country unless approved by the FDA as safe and effective for the conditions indicated on the label. Its claimed usefulness must be established according to acceptable standards and only these uses may appear on labels and supporting materials. If a drug is a new substance that has not been shown to be safe and effective for the conditions indicated on the label, it will be classified as a new drug. If a drug is a new substance that has not been proven or is not generally recognized as safe and effective, then it is the responsibility of the would-be marketer to prove it. He must carry out sufficient animal testing followed by human clinical testing to substantiate the safety and effectiveness of the drug. (This is a dramatic departure from the ways of determining drug effects throughout man's history, up to 1938. Until 1938 drugs were used mainly because of their placebo effect. It was thought that administering a drug to a patient and relying on intermittent observation or on the patient's own reporting of the drug's purported effects was all that was required to ascertain a drug's effects.) In order to market the drug, it is necessary to label the usage for which it is planned only with those uses approved by the FDA. Unless it can be proven according to established rules and laws that the candidate for marketing is both safe and effective, it is not possible to market the drug legally in interstate commerce in the United States.

The law provides that certain items of information must appear on all drug labels. Drugs without labels or labeling are almost always misbranded, i.e., in violation of the law. A description of a drug's desirable effects must be accompanied by a description of possible undesirable effects. The nature of the information appearing on a particular drug label again depends on the drug's particular legal category. The matter is complicated by the previously described possibility that a particular chemical entity will be classified in one or more legal categories, depending on the drug's intended uses. Labeling requirements pivot on whether it is a nonlegend drug or a legend drug.

For nonlegend drugs, certain information must be provided on the drug container introduced in interstate commerce. These items must include sufficient information to achieve traceability of the drug through interstate commerce in the manner previously described (Chapter 7), and also to allow the patient to use the drug safely and effectively without provider intervention.

For legend drugs, certain items of information not required for nonlegend labeling must be provided in the drug labeling. The basic FD&C Act requires that a legend drug introduced into interstate commerce be "fully disclosed." It should contain the following basic information on the label and/or labeling accompanying the drug—name, description, clinical pharmacology, indications and uses, contraindications, warnings, precautions, adverse reactions, dosage and administration, other relevant information including references. This chapter describes how this information must be generated.

Although this information must be present on the label or labeling of the drug, a drug made available to patients can be exempted from these requirements under certain circumstances. If a drug is provided to a patient by a licensed prescriber who has established a contractual practitioner/patient relationship, or if the medication has been dispensed by a licensed dispenser (via prescriber authorization) who has in turn established a contractual practitioner/patient relationship, then such a dispensed drug is exempt from the full disclosure labeling requirements if certain information appears on the prescription label.

This information consists of seven principal parts (1) which will be discussed later. This exemption applies to all drugs made available to a patient via the route described above, and also to any category of professional who makes the drug available, i.e., physicians, pharmacists, and others must comply with these labeling requirements if they dispense a drug to a patient in order to qualify for an exemption under this portion of the Act.

The required categories of drug information necessary for a drug moving in interstate commerce are exacting. The nature of the information to be included under each heading is described explicitly in the appropriate section of the *Code of Federal Regulations*.

The discussion above represents a brief overview of labeling requirements. These requirements are discussed more fully in Chapters
9 and 10. Emphasis will be devoted to the principles of labeling,
although considerable detail is necessary to develop and fully explain
these principles.

8.1 CONCEPT OF RISK/BENEFIT

The saying "every rose has a thorn" applies to drug usage because
along with the desired effects of a drug are some undesirable ones
which occur. Conversely, the desired effects of the drug may not
occur. Taking an aspirin tablet, for example, may not relieve one's
headache, but may yield an unpleasant, burning sensation in the
stomach. (The reader should distinguish between the requirement that
the benefit merely outweigh or exceed in some way the expected risk
from use of a drug and the requirement for the marketing of certain
other items, e.g., food additives, which are approved on the basis that
there be some benefit and that risk be zero (or virtually zero). Thus,
for example, although cyclamates as a low-calorie sweetener yield
obvious benefits, their use is restricted because they apparently induce cancer in animals. The use of cyclamates is unlikely unless
favorable data are generated by a current study scheduled for completion in 1978. The criterion for legal use of drugs is relative safety
whereas for food additives, color additives, and certain other items the
criterion is "absolute" safety.)

8.1.1 Conceptual Overview

The different effects produced by a given drug or class of drugs may
be desirable, undesirable or both (2). Almost without exception, drugs
do not have a specific effect which can be selected for a given drug-
organism encounter. A general set of functional and dysfunctional
physiologic effects occur in an organism, and they are classified according to whether they represent a desired change in the organism's
deviant condition. This is probably due to the nonspecific interaction
between drug elements and receptor sites. All receptor sites of a given
nature may react with a drug, even though only a subset of these
receptor/drug moiety elements are desirable. "Even a highly selective

drug is . . . likely to react with some structure other than the one for which it has been designed. In other words, absolute selectivity is a chemical impossibility (3)."

Problems in Functionally Evaluating Drug Effects

The eminent sociologist, Bernard Barber, has listed several general functional problems pertaining to the evaluation of the effects, benefits, and risks of using drugs. These include the following (4):

A.   The same general set of phenomena, things seen by the same, single, loose term, may have multiple functions.
B.   Even the same drug substance may have different functions in different dosages and in different social and psychological circumstances.
C.   The different functions which the same drug or class of drugs has may be partly positive, or eufunctional, and partly negative, or dysfunctional.
D.   One of the reasons for the various functional effects of a given drug agent is that there are always indirect as well as direct effects of this action.
E.   There may be important differences in the short-run and long-run functional consequences from the activity of a drug.
F.   The functional consequences of a drug may be unintended as well as intended, and unintended as well as intended consequences may be either good or bad.
G.   As in social and psychological systems, the general problem of a functional calculus, or the weighing up of good and bad effects, arise in connection with drugs and their effects on physiological systems.

There are three major categories of information describing the effects of drugs:

A.   Information describing the effects of a drug; these effects may be either functional or dysfunctional.
B.   Taxonomic/nomenclature information and;
C.   procedural information describing how a drug is to be administered and manipulated.

The first category describes the kinds of information useful for estimating the effects of a drug in a person. The second category describes data useful for indexing, locating, and otherwise referring abstractly to a given chemical entity and its effects. This type of information serves a function analogous to that of the alphabetized list of names in a phone book. Category three describes the type of information that provides instruction for the use of a drug to achieve optimum effects. Only the information describing the functional and dysfunctional aspects of drugs will be considered in this section.

Irwin distinguished among drug use, misuse, and abuse. He states (5):

> Drug use results when the sought for effects of a drug are realized with minimal hazards, whether or not used therapeutically, legally or prescribed by a physician. Drug misuse occurs when a drug is taken or administered under circumstances and at doses that significantly increase the hazard to the individual or to others. Drug abuse follows when a drug is taken (sporadically, repeatedly, or compulsively) to such degree as to greatly increase the hazard or to impair the ability of the individual to adequately function or cope with his circumstances.

Essentially, Irwin's definition defines drug use as functional usage and divides nonfunctional usage into drug misuse and drug abuse. Implicit within each of these three categories, however, is the concept that undesirable effects occur.

Problems Arising from Ignorance of the Concept

Public and professional discussion of drug consumption generally fail to consider adequately the concept of risk versus benefit. A study conducted for and funded by the FDA seems to confirm this assertion (6). A national probability sample of 2005 people stratified by geographic area, type of community, age of respondent, income, and educational level was interviewed. Respondents were asked to rate five classes of products by means of a safety "thermometer." "They were asked to place the products on the temperature scale, in terms of their own opinion of safety, with 100 degrees designating the most safe and 0 degrees the most dangerous." The ranking of safety was (6):

Most safe
| Foods
| Prescription medicines
| Cosmetics
| Toys
↓ Nonprescription medicines
Most dangerous

More than half the respondents rated prescription drugs as "most safe," whereas less than one-fifth rated nonprescription drugs in this category.

When the reasons why people answered as they did were probed, it appears that the public's notion of risk/benefit appears to be mainly a notion of benefit with risk—maybe. Table 8.1 is a summary of the reasons given by respondents for viewing prescription or nonprescription drugs as safe or unsafe.

TABLE 8.1 REASONS WHY MEDICINES ARE SAFE OR UNSAFE AS REPORTED BY RANDOM RESPONDENTS

Reasons	Percent of Public Who Would Give Indicated Reasons	
	For Prescription Medication	For Nonprescription Medication
Safe		
Confidence in doctor	63.8	—
When used properly	10.5	13.4
Confidence in druggist	6.2	1.1
Government regulation	2.4	7.1
Personal experience has been good	1.4	4.1
Confidence in manufacturer	0.8	3.3
"Blind faith"	—	8.1
Careful buying	—	8.1
	85.1	45.2
Unsafe		
Side effects, allergies	9.4	11.1
Doctor error	6.5	—
Patient error	3.0	12.2
Drugs of unknown safety are sold	1.6	1.6
Druggist error	1.4	—
Bad personal experience	1.2	0.9
Can't rely on manufacturer	0.2	0.6
	23.3	26.4
Other		
People should not use OTC medicines	—	15.1
Vague or don't know	6.1	21.9
	114.5[a]	108.6[a]

[a] Totals more than 100% due to multiple answers.
Source: M. E. Simon and P. G. Kuehl: FDA Listens: A Survey of Consumer Opinion on the Safety of Medicines, *FDA Consumer* 7(4):7 (May) 1973.

TABLE 8.2   OPINIONS ABOUT NONPRESCRIPTION MEDICINE LABELS OF RANDOM RESPONDENTS

Question:	Percent of Public Who Would Say			
	Agree	Disagree	No Opinion	Total
1. Do OTC labels provide enough information to tell consumers how to *use* the drug safely?	72.2% Many or most people	23.8% Hardly any people	4.0% No opinion	100.0% Total
2. How many people read OTC labels for safety information?	47.7% All of the time	37.0% Most or some of the time	11.7% Hardly ever or never	3.6% No opinion	100.0% Total
3. How often do OTC labels correctly state *all* the ingredients of the medicine?	17.7%	68.6%	6.1%	7.6%	100.0%

Source: M. E. Simon and P. G. Kuehl: FDA Listens: A Survey of Consumer Opinion on the Safety of Medicines, *FDA Consumer* 7(4):8 (May) 1973.

Note that almost three-fourths of the reasons for considering prescription drugs safe is due to confidence in the prescribing physician and dispensing pharmacist. The appropriateness of this confidence will be examined later. The lack of a fully developed concept of risk was suggested by the 9.4% and 11.1% of those questioned who viewed prescription drugs and nonprescription drugs, respectively, as unsafe because of side effects or allergies. Perhaps the 15% who responded that people should not use nonprescription (OTC) medicines at all have a more developed risk/benefit concept, but one wonders why a significant fraction did not respond similarly in regard to prescription drugs. This suggests that probing respondents more deeply might have produced evidence of an understanding of risk/benefit. Table 8.2 summarizes responses pertaining to safety aspects of nonprescription labels. Unfortunately no such data were presented for prescription drug labels. Note that 24% of those questioned felt that not enough information was provided on labels to enable safe use, and that almost half of the respondents reported that they believe many or most people read such labels for safety information. Another puzzling finding was the one-third to one-fourth of consumers who believe unsafe medicines reach the market "a lot." Perhaps they feel they can avoid buying such products.

It seems clear from a careful study of the pharmacology of drugs that the risk of drug usage varies along a continuum from almost no risk to a high risk, including risk of death. Clearly, a risk may also be incurred from not using an indicated drug, and those concerned with safety too frequently fail to consider this point adequately. The question of functional value for a drug always depends upon the particular circumstances and uses for which it is intended. For example, prescribing or consuming morphine for or by a terminally ill cancer patient negates the need to consider the problem of addiction or the related problem of physical and psychologic dependence. The hazard from using morphine in this example is relatively minor when only the psychologic and physical dependence aspects are considered. Irwin has provided a list of important criteria in judging drugs ordinarily considered to be drugs of abuse. His criteria also seem appropriate for judging the risk associated with almost any drug entity to be consumed by people. These criteria include (7):

. . . The possibilities for death from an overdosage or during withdrawal;
irreversible tissue damage;
physical deterioration;
mental deterioration (as with an organic brain syndrome or psychosis);
social deterioration;

reduction of violence or passivity (amotivation);
rapid loss of control;
psychomotor impairment (coordination, memory, judgment, vigilance
and perception);
psychotic reaction;
easy overdose at use levels;
and special hazards when taken intravenously or in combination with
other drugs. It is only when these factors indicate major hazards that the
presence of psychological and physical dependence (which reinforce drug
taking) take on significance. For example, the high psychological dependence liability of tobacco would be of no concern, to the individual or to
society, if it were not for the tissue damage produced by long exposure.

An example of the foregoing hazard potential of drugs has been
provided by Irwin. Using the criteria quoted above for evaluating the
diminishing hazard of certain substances, Irwin has produced an
interesting table in terms of (1) hazards to the individual, and (2)
hazards to society.

Table 8.3 was derived by Irwin by evaluating the relative hazard
from each substance listed on the basis of the criteria listed in the
preceding paragraph. "For hazard to the individual, death was given a
score of 100 points and seven physicians or scientists were asked to
assign point scores to each of the other items to reflect their judgment
on the hazard of each in relation to sudden acute death. The same was
done for the items representing hazard to society. In this case violence
was given 100 points and the other items were assigned points relative
to it (7)."

The rating was scored on a 6 point scale. The median scores for each
item rated were computed in terms of relative adjusted values for a
maximum total score of 122 points for individual and 116 points for
social hazard (8). For example, coffee received its 10/9 value (see Table
8.3) as follows:

Criterion	Points
Psychomoter impairment (judgment)	1
Health (physical deterioration)	1
Health (mental deterioration)	2
Social deterioration, violence	2
Drug dependence	1
Psychologic	3
Rapid loss control	1
Physical—severity	1
	12

TABLE 8.3 DRUGS AND RELATED SUBSTANCES IN ORDER OF DIMINISHING HAZARD WITH MAXIMUM CHRONIC ABUSE

Drug	I/S[a]	Hazard
Alcohol[b]		
Distilled spirits (45%)	81/79	Very high
Wines (12%)	77/79	
Secobarbital	65/83	
Methamphetamine	63/69	
Cocaine	61/69	
Food[b]	53/16[d]	High
Diazepam (Valium)	42/69	
Δ^9-THC	40/55	
Hashish	39/50	
Heroin	48/47[c]	Intermediate
Methylphenidate (Ritalin)	37/48	
Methadone	40/44[c]	
Cigarettes[b]	37/0[d]	
LSD-25	31/41[c]	
Codeine	29/41[c]	
Opium	28/40[c]	
Beer (6%)	27/42	
Chlordiazepoxide (Librium)	21/37	Low
Marijuana (1.2%)	25/29	
Caffeine	23/22	
Cigars[b]	13/0[d]	Very low
Coffee	10/9	

[a] % of maximum possible score (100%).
[b] Significant tissue damage.
[c] Much lower hazard with continuous use because of tolerance development (6/6).
[d] High individual hazard scores only with prolonged abuse.
Reprinted from Contemporary Drug Problems, Volume II, No. 1, page 21. © 1973 by Federal Legal Publications, Inc. 95 Morton Street, New York, N.Y. 10014

The total score, 12, was used as the numerator to compute the maximum individual hazard due to coffee. The ratios 12/122 and 13/116 yield the scores of 10/9 or 10% maximum individual hazard and 9% maximum social hazard, respectively, as shown in Table 8.3. Note that food is rated more hazardous to the individual than cigarettes, cigars, and heroin.

While Irwin's depiction is certainly not that of society, based on the relative degree of control of these items, the future may hold such a view. This possibility is suggested by a full-page advertisement in a national magazine, pointing out the dysfunctional effects of sugar. A portion of this ad is reproduced as Figure 8.2. This ad, paid for by a Ralph Nader-affiliated organization, makes the important point that sugar is not a necessary part of a balanced diet. Will sugar be limited to prescription in the future?

An Example of Dysfunctional Effects

A sample problem encountered in coping with dysfunctional effects of drugs is the use of allergy desensitization to treat people allergic to pollens, household dust, and other common substances. A person receives an allergy desensitization injection after a series of diagnostic tests have served to identify the allergens causing the symptoms, and to determine the proper amount of the substance needed to make the patient's body resistant to these aggravating agents. As long as he continues to receive these injections, the patient will experience few or no effects from his allergic condition. When the injections are withheld, however, he will experience systemic symptoms of allergen exposure with discharges from the nose and eyes, reddening and inflammation of the eyes, itching in various body areas such as the eyes, nose, and hairy areas of the body. This systemic effect, however, will be a direct function of the dosage being withheld; i.e., if only half the needed dosage is withheld, only a part of the full range of intensity of symptoms will be experienced ordinarily. This example is analogous to physical addiction and the ensuing withdrawal symptoms that occur when the addicting agent is withheld from the afflicted individual. The analogy continues in that as long as the narcotic recipient or the allergic desensitization injection recipient continues to receive his "drug," he will experience no or a minimum amount of adverse effects.

The effect of the 1974 gasoline shortage is another example that sheds further light on this concept. Some immediate effects of the gas shortage included a marked reduction in automobile induced deaths and injuries. Thus, viewed from the perspective of those whose lives were saved, the changes brought about by the shortage were functional. Society also viewed these effects as functional. Other effects included marked reduction in the need for emergency medical technicians, emergency wrecker service, a need for funerals and flowers,

America has turned into a nation of sugar addicts. In 1972 we consumed an average *126 pounds* of caloried sweeteners per person. More than two pounds a week for each and every one of us. Enough sugar to cause serious danger to your teeth, general health and possibly even your heart.

If you think you're not eating as much sugar as the average American, you're probably mistaken. Much of our sugar intake is *hidden* in sweetened foods like snacks and soda pop, cakes and candy, desserts and cereals, and even in sauces and frozen vegetables.

It's high time we stopped the sweet talk about that sweet stuff. Here are some bitter facts from doctors, nutritionists and the U.S. government:

Sugar contains *no* vitamins, *no* minerals, *no* protein.

Sugar contains *only calories*—as many as 30 per rounded teaspoon.

Sugar is *not* a necessary part of a balanced diet—you do *not* need to eat sugar at all since a healthy body converts all the energy it needs from other foods.

Sugar rots your teeth. Tooth decay afflicts 98% of Americans. And a dental bill can hurt even more than a toothache. Evidence indicates that sugar is the primary villain in causing tooth decay. The sour candy you suck on or the soda pop you suck up drenches your teeth in sugar.

Sugar can make you fat. When you eat sugar it's easy to take in more calories than you need because sugar is *nothing but calories*. And you only need a little sugar to get a lot of calories.

Sugar may affect your heart. Recent studies suggest a relationship between high sugar intake and heart disease. Some doctors believe that eating too much sugar could be as harmful to your heart as excess fat consumption.

Sugar interferes with good nutrition. If you substitute sugar for good nutritive foods, you dilute your nutrient intake. If you add sugar on top of a balanced diet, you'll probably get fat.

What should you do about this sour view of sweet stuff? Now that you know that sugar is not all sweetness and light, here are a few suggestions. Skip presweetened cereals, try a little fresh fruit on regular cereal instead. Put less sugar—or none at all—in your coffee or tea. Stop using sweets as a reward to children for good behavior (or you run the risk of giving them a sweet tooth for life.) Switch to snacks and drinks like nuts, raw fruits, whole and skimmed milk and unsweetened fruit juices.

Actually, the best thing you could do is to completely stop adding sugar to your food. But that's a pretty tall order. What you and your family should do is *cut down on sugar*. You'll be amazed at all the fun things to eat that aren't sweet!

Figure 8.2   Advertisement depicting sugar as a dysfunctional substance. *Source:* Advertisement, *The Progressive*, April, 1974, p. 67.

automobile and human body repair, and related products. From the viewpoint of the affected emergency medical technicians, wrecker owners and drivers, morticians and florists, mechanics and surgeons, and providers of related products and services, these effects were economically dysfunctional. Clearly, the criterion for functional determination rests with the achievement of objectives from somebody's (or group of somebodys) perspective.

Minimization of Risks Accompanying Drug Usage as a Goal of Drug Control

The previous argument suggests that the goal of modern drug use is not realistic when it suggests eliminating drug hazard by eliminating medication use. On the contrary, the aim of modern drug usage is (or should be) to minimize the risk of drug use while maximizing its benefits; this is an optimizing goal between the deleterious risk effects and the desirable benefit effects. A vast number of persons in our society use drugs; within any given 24-hour period, approximately one-half of the adult population experiences the effect of one or more medications (9,10). Clearly, a goal directed toward elimination of drug use will not be successful, since societal mores have already been established on the basis that drug use is desirable. Whether a person experiences undesirable effects from a drug may not be a direct function of the drug's pharmacologic effect in and of itself. Destructive drug use may depend more on failure to adhere to established principles of consumption behavior, failure of the social system to provide information to a drug user, or some other nonpharmacologic (nondrug) attribute.

A synopsis of this argument is that given a desired drug action, the goal of drug therapy is to choose the safest drug available from a given set of drugs producing the desired effect. The key question remains: Which is worse, the drug or the disease?

Irwin has described a safe drug as (11):

> . . . one (1) with only moderate psychologic dependence liability; (2) for which tolerance and physical dependence is minimal or absent; (3) where large increases in dosage are required to obtain substantial increases in biological effect; (4) which does not produce tissue damage or significant mental or social deterioration; (5) which is unlikely to produce death from overdosage; (6) and which does not significantly impair judgment, coordination or increase aggressiveness in the doses commonly taken.

An Analogy to Further Explain the Concept

The concept of risk/benefit may be viewed in physical terms analogous to the ubiquitous scale of justice. This model provides that on the one hand the benefit (whatever it may be) must outweigh the risk on the other end of the scale. The idea is that whenever the benefit end of the scale is higher than the risk end, use of the drug is favored. Alternately, when the risk end outweighs the benefit end, drug use is not indicated for the individual. It is imperative that the risk/benefit determination be made from the perspective of the potential individual drug consumer.

This is an analogy that appears repeatedly in the drug literature and appears to be implicit within the basic FD&C Act. What is lacking in this seemingly simple analogy is a description of what is placed onto the respective ends of the scale. What are the units used to measure risk and benefit? One such approach in describing the risk associated with drug usage and the accompanying undesirable or dysfunctional drug effects that may occur is to express the units of benefit and risk in terms of time lost from maximum potential functioning (probably best expressed in hours). This concept would place lost time in juxtaposition to a drug producing the functional and dysfunctional effects described.

For example, the symptoms of the common cold might deprive the person of 10 hours per day of optimum functioning and a reduction of 10% of his function to yield about 1.0 hours of potential benefit time associated with this disease entity. The same reasoning might also be applied to each undesirable effect associated with drugs used to treat the common cold. If these risk/benefit time combinations could be calculated, and if a joint probability of happening could be associated with each of them, then a risk/benefit calculation could be performed for each common cold drug treatment. The methodology might be extended to the top 200 drugs, or all drugs, or merely be limited to an individual's medication determination.

Alternate Candidates for Quantifying the Concept

Slovic (12) has suggested that the measuring of risk and benefit be done in terms of the percentage of functional reduction for various ailments and drug-induced problems. He suggests that one might use direct judgments of a large number of experts and laymen. He raises the question that "hours lost" may be too simple and incomplete a criterion. He cites as an example that drug-induced loss of hair may lead to less loss of efficiency than the effects of some other drug, but it might well be the more severe complication. He suggests that some general criterion such as disutility might be a better measure for comparing drug effects with ailments.

Slovic suggests as an alternative scaling possibility that it be performed for social disutilities. This process would entail treating the effects of illness or drug-induced complications as multidimensional entities. He suggests as examples the dimensions of risk as entailing pain, time loss, probability of permanent damage, probability of death, etc. He rates each consequence on each dimension, and dimensions are given relative weights as well. These could all be amalgamated into an overall disutility for the illness or drug by a formula such as this additive equation:

$$D = A_1U_1 + A_2U_2 + \ldots A_nU_n$$

where A represents the relative importances of the dimension, the U values are the scale values for the individual consequences, and n represents the number of dimensions evaluated.

Model for Quantification of Risk/Benefit

Zeidner has described a model for decision making based on expected utility and risk theory (13). His model is designed to synthesize or integrate joint probabilities for specific therapeutic effects desired. It is constructed to yield a single numerical index of utility, and is probably of most value in that it requires each component of drug effects to be considered in relation to its risk/benefit potential.

When both the risk and the benefit that may occur from exposure to a drug are determined, there remains the difficult task of deciding how much risk one is willing to tolerate given a certain quantity of benefit. If there is a 1:20,000 chance of death, should the risk be taken?

The Zeidner model is best understood from the following example. Propoxyphene (Darvon-N) as the napsylate salt is used as an example because its effects are, relative to many drugs, not pervasive or numerous and because it is a well-known, popular drug. Figure 8.3 shows a utility matrix, joint probability matrix, and resulting expected utility matrix for this drug. The package insert indications characterize the nature of the drug's benefit or therapeutic effect as "relief of mild to moderate pain." The package insert adverse reactions also characterize the negative effects of this drug. The therapeutic effect in this example is rated rather simply in terms of complete, partial, or no relief of mild to moderate pain. For the purpose of illustration and for simplification, adverse reactions are not treated individually but are grouped in three categories plus a "no adverse effect" category.

Matrix A contains a subjective estimate of the value of each combination of therapeutic effect and adverse effect. For example, the combination of no adverse effect and complete relief is valued highest at 35; the 35 represents utility units. The lowest value is given to the combination of central nervous system (CNS) effects and no relief, and

Indication: Relief of mild to moderate pain

	Adverse Effect			
	None	CNS[a]	GI[b]	Skin[c]
No relief	−5	−15	−15	−7
Partial relief	20	−5	−5	15
Complete relief	35	20	20	25

Matrix A: Utility matrix

	Adverse Effect			
	None	CNS	GI	Skin
No relief	0.15	0.10	0.10	0.05
Partial relief	0.65	0.15	0.25	0.10
Complete relief	0.75	0.25	0.35	0.15

Matrix B: Joint probability matrix

	Adverse Effect				
	None	CNS	GI	Skin	
No relief	−.75	−1.5	−1.5	0.35	
Partial relief	13.0	−0.75	−1.25	1.5	= 51.10
Complete relief	26.25	5.0	7.0	3.75	

Matrix C: Expected utility matrix (A × B)

[a] = Central nervous system effects: dizziness, headache, sedation, somnolence, paradoxical excitement, insomnia.
[b] = Gastrointestinal effects: nausea, vomiting, abdominal pain, constipation.
[c] = Skin rashes.

Figure 8.3 Utility/disutility assessment of propoxyphene napsylate.

also to gastrointestinal (GI) effects. In application by a clinician, trial values would optimally be assigned by a large number of experts. The clinician might choose to modify the values for his patient because of some attribute of his patient that justifies a different value.

Matrix B is a joint probability matrix which expresses the likelihood or chance of the therapeutic effect and adverse effect occurring together. For example, the likelihood of partial relief and no adverse effect is assigned a probability of 0.65; this may be interpreted as a

65% chance of this combination occurring simultaneously. In practice, however, the probability estimates would be obtained by simply dividing the number of people with each combination of effects by the total sample size (number of people receiving the drug). In this example the probabilities represent merely educated guesses rather than real data. Also, the possibility of a patient developing more than one adverse effect is not discussed, although such a consideration is desirable for the most effective use of this model.

Matrix C is the expected utility matrix obtained by multiplying the utility values of matrix A by the corresponding cell expected utility of matrix B. For example, the value of 3.75 in matrix C was obtained by multiplying 25 in matrix A by 0.15 in the lower right-hand cell of matrix B to yield $(25) (0.15) = 3.75$. The value of 51.10 in matrix C was obtained by totaling the numbers within the cells of matrix C.

The scale of the numbers (ordinal, interval, ratio) entered into the first matrix (matrix A) is important. Usually, ordinal numbers will be used, meaning that a value of 35 cannot be interpreted as 1.75 more than a value of 20, but can be interpreted only as of a magnitude > 20 or any other number < 35.

The major value of this model is that it makes explicit what is usually treated only implicitly. Currently the FDA, prescribers, and most importantly, patients are looking qualitatively and usually univariately at the kinds of data shown in Figure 8.3 and trying to make a decision about benefit and risk. To varying degrees they are considering data describing adverse reactions, therapeutic reactions, reading case studies, looking at experimental designs, and then, trying to weigh all this information and make a decision. When a decision is made, it is unclear precisely what reasoning has been used or how to communicate the basis for the decision to other persons or groups. Although this particular method needs further refinement (as do the other methods described), it does have the worthwhile attribute of forcing the people involved in making any risk/benefit decisions to list more precisely relevant gains and losses, singularly and jointly, so that a given decision is less "seat-of-the-pants" than is currently the practice. Participants in the decision-making process can have a much clearer idea of the quality of a decision if they have been forced to list the positive and negative contributions of a drug to a given patient or to society. People often fail to maximize payoffs and probabilities because of their ignorance, inability, or unwillingness to make the optimizing choice. Psychological experiments (14, 15) have documented this behavior; people tend to attend to either risk or benefit but not both. The Knapps (15) have shown that physicians prescribing drugs for simulated patients tend singularly to consider risk *or* benefit. If there is to be a meaningful best answer when benefit/risk decisions are made, both must be dealt with simultaneously and systematically.

The reader of this may have decided by now—especially if his background is in the biological sciences—that he should simply abandon understanding the model's application instead of recognizing that it or other models offer useful possibilities for practice. What do such terms as joint probability matrices have to do with drug use? The reader is reminded that (16)

> . . . this jargon is no more imprecise or irrelevant than cyclic AMP (adenosine monophosphate) and enzyme turnover rates in pharmacology. In fact, [one] might argue that this is more pertinent to the type of decision-making the practicing clinician actually does than the nature of cyclic AMP at the receptor of an alpha blocking agent.

Magnitude of Risk Toleration

Some perspective needs to be given to the concept of risk. Consider these relative benefits and risks:

Benefit	Chance of Dying
Halt aging process	1/100
Aphrodisia	1/1000
Contraception	1/10,000
Relief of mild pain	1/1,000,000
Dying during first year of life	1/50
3-year "arrest" of a cancer	1/10
Relief of anxiety	1/100,000
"Cure" of infection	1/25,000
Make pregnancy possible	1/60,000

Which of these risks if any would people or patients be willing to take if the benefit (also described as a probability estimate) were available in the form of medication? Starr has arrived at the following generalizations about the magnitude of risks acceptable, given specified quantities of benefit (17):
1. The public is willing to accept voluntary risks roughly 1000 times greater than involuntary risks.
2. The acceptability of risk is roughly proportional to the third power of the benefits (real or imagined).

3. The statistical (average across the population) death rate appears to be a psychological gauge for judging the tolerability of other risks.
4. "The social acceptability of risks is directly influenced by public awareness of the benefits of an activity, as determined by advertising, usefulness, and the number of people participating."
5. The acceptability of risks is inversely proportional to the number of people engaging in an activity.

Some figures on risk-taking for activities of a diverse nature are (17):

1. 1 accident/100,000 automobile miles.
2. 1 death/1,000,000 automobile miles driven.
3. 1 chance/100 of any one person (on the average) dying each year.
4. 1 death/50,000 miles flown in "general aviation" aircraft.
5. 1 death/1,100,000 "airliner" miles flown.
6. 4 deaths/1,000,000 persons in fossil fuel electric plants.
7. 1 chance/10,000,000 of dying in a natural disaster.
8. 1 chance/2,000 of a mother dying during childbirth.
9. 1 chance/86 of a pregnancy resulting in the birth of fraternal twins.

Table 8.4 shows the risk of dying for selected age periods. In Table 8.4 and in each of the items listed above it is predictable that during the course of a year the listed fraction (percentage) of persons will experience the listed event. Treating all people equally in a statistical sense means that any person engaging in any listed activity has the listed chance of experiencing that event, e.g., dying. Flying in general aviation aircraft is the most dangerous of the activities listed.

Table 8.5 lists the number of deaths (approximately equal to the chances of dying) per operation performed. Note that these are average figures, and although they are true in general vary widely with the nature of the procedure and patient attributes.

One important generalization based on the mortality statistics above is that many drugs are as likely to cause death as are a number of other events. Especially noteworthy is the similarity between surgical death rates and the death rate for several drugs. Indeed, methotrexate use reportedly results in 33 deaths per 10,000 drug issuances (18). The overall mortality due to drugs, as estimated by the Boston Collaborative Drug Surveillance Program, is in the range of 29 deaths per 10,000 hospitalized patients (19).

The set of five generalizations listed at the beginning of this section offers stimulating thought about drug use. The first generalization,

TABLE 8.4   CHANCE OF DYING FOR SPECIFIED AGES GIVEN KNOWLEDGE OF AGE
ONLY

Age Period (Years)	Chance of Dying[a]
0 to 1	0.0190
1 to 5	.0033
5 to 10	.0021
10 to 15	.0020
15 to 20	.0055
20 to 25	.0072
25 to 30	.0072
30 to 35	.0084
35 to 40	.0121
40 to 45	.0182
45 to 50	.0280
50 to 55	.0423
55 to 60	.0643
60 to 65	.0937
65 to 70	.1339
70 to 75	.1946
75 to 80	.2852
80 to 85	.3953
85 and over	1.0000

[a] To be read as: (1) 1.9 chances in 100 of a person dying during the first year of life; (2) a person age 20 to 25 has 0.72 chances in 100 of dying during that 5-year period or roughly 1.44 chances in 1000 of dying during any one year in the 5-year interval.
Source: Public Health Service: Vital Statistics of the U.S. for the Year 1971, Vol. II, Section 5, Life Tables: 1972, DHEW Publication No. (HRA) 75-1147, U.S. Government Printing Office, 1974, p. 5–18.

would suggest that the more informed and in control of their own drug use patients are, the more inclined they will be to consume potentially risky drugs. The practice of some pharmacists, physicians, and nurses to withhold drug information from patients remains a puzzle when this generalization is considered. Why is it that one often hears statements from health care providers maintaining that if the patient were told of all the adverse effects, he wouldn't take the drug. This behavior is even more puzzling when we consider results of a study which showed that individuals will select a higher amount of risk for themselves than they will for others (20). This study suggests that the more involved patients are in selecting their drug therapy, the higher the risk-taking will be.

TABLE 8.5   CHANCE OF DEATH PER OPERATIVE PROCEDURE[a]

Operation	Deaths Per 10,000 Operations[b]
Tonsillectomy without adenoidectomy	.3
Ligation and division of fallopian tubes	.5
Partial mastectomy	7.4
Extraction of tooth	17.4
Abdominal hysterectomy	20.4
Appendectomy	35.2
Radical mastectomy	40.3
Prostatectomy, transurethral	164.1
Open reduction of fracture	474.2
Partial gastrectomy	579.2
Resection of colon	846.9
Exploratory laparotomy or celiotomy	1,328.2
"Average operation"	150.0

[a] Deaths following the listed operation.
[b] Based on data from 1,281 hospitals, 4,332,814 operated patients, and 65,985 deaths.
Source: Commission on Professional and Hospital Activities: PAS Reporter 9(12):1–3 (Oct. 25) 1971.

The generalization pertaining to the direct relationship between public awareness of benefits and the propensity for risk-taking suggests that drug advertising would encourage otherwise reluctant people to consume drugs. This generalization may help to explain the rather large per capita consumption of nonprescription drugs. The public tends to learn almost exclusively about the beneficial aspects of prescription drugs while learning very little about the concomitant risks from these drugs; this was suggested in the items in Table 8.1. In light of the more than $1 billion currently expended on various forms of drug promotion, this relationship deserves further study (21). Perhaps as consumers attend more to drug abuse as a concept, they also acquire a tendency to undertake greater risks (e.g., physiologic, or psychologic damage, or arrest by police). The recently mounted campaign to increase patient compliance with their hypertensive drug regimen may ultimately meet a similar fate. Patients learn more about the risks from uncontrolled hypertension but concomitantly become willing to tolerate a higher risk level.

8.1.2 Requirements for Assurance of Safety

As already described, any given chemical substance may produce diverse and unpredictable effects on human beings. A slight change in the nature of the drug or the attributes of the recipient may yield a significant or even drastic change in the effects experienced by the organism. The only way to be certain of the effects of a drug on a particular person is to administer it and observe its effects over a very long period. Even then the actual effects may escape the observer, as occurred for example with the delayed effects of diethylstilbestrol (DES) in producing vaginal and uterine cancer in the female offspring of pregnant females receiving DES during gestation (22). Because of the difficulty of predicting the effects of drugs in humans (based on knowledge of the physical and chemical aspects of a drug), the principal basis for the assurance of safety from drug use rests on a cautious system of careful and deliberate exposure of animals and humans to a particular drug.

Before a drug can be administered to determine its effects in humans, it should be studied thoroughly to get an idea or understanding of its possible effects through a study of its chemical and pharmacological properties, if they are known. Usually, chemical properties such as water solubility, protein binding, and dissolution in body fluids, can be determined through *in vitro* studies. When suitable *in vitro* studies have been completed, animal studies must be performed. These studies generally consist of administering the substance, which has yet to be termed a drug, to two or three animal species. Generally, some idea of the functional effects thought to occur in humans will be determined in animals.

Animal studies, however, are usually directed toward ascertaining the pharmacologic and toxicologic effects of the drug in living beings rather than to determining its clinical effects. This phase of research usually involves determining metabolism, elimination route, absorption, minimum effective dose needed to produce a particular effect, the amount of the drug required to produce death in 50% of the subject animals (LD_{50}), and other related variables. Only after these tests have been completed can the drug reasonably and legitimately be administered to human beings. The basic conceptual model for discovering the true dysfunctional effects of a drug will be shown in the next section. This model is identical to the one used for discovering the functional effects of a given substance except for one fundamental difference. Whereas the model for discovering the functional effects assumes that a dependent variable, Y, is known and defined prior to beginning the experiment, the dependent variable is generally unknown when dysfunctional or undesired aspects are involved because the dysfunctional effects which occur from exposure of the organism to the drug may not be known. In addition, although some effects may be known from previous research, the goal of assuring safety includes establishing all the undesired effects that occur from the use of the drug. Nevertheless, the chance that previously unexpected effects will occur is always present. When an effect is identified or suspected, however, then planned *a priori* research can be carried out to ascertain whether these suspected or expected effects actually occur in persons receiving the drugs.

Phase one of the investigational new drug procedure (IND) is almost exclusively devoted to determining the pharmacologic and toxicologic properties of the drug. This phase is primarily related to the safety aspects of the drug. Phase two, which involves limited use of the drug in people afflicted with the disease for which the drug is indicated, also involves ascertaining the dysfunctional, undesired, or safety aspects of the drug's affects on living tissue. The relatively widespread use for treating patients having the disease for which the drug is thought to be indicated is termed phase three, and includes use of the drug by office-based physicians. There is relatively little observation and supervision of patients in this phase. Phase four, which follows the approved new drug application, will be used to ascertain the dysfunctional or safety aspects of the drug's use in humans. This phase relies on the epidemiologic method (described in section 8.1.3 on efficacy) for ascertaining the unknown dysfunctional variables.

Before considering in greater detail the requirements of the law and the regulations themselves, one can profit by considering the complexity of the task confronting those who desire to determine the dysfunctional effects of drugs. The difficulty of ascertaining the dysfunctional effects of diethylstilbestrol has already been suggested. This example involved the administration of diethylstilbestrol for the functional effect of preventing the premature termination of pregnancy. However, it took some 20 years to determine that the female offspring of the pregnant women who received DES would develop vaginal or uterine cancer in a significant number of instances (22). Likewise, over 100 people died from the toxic effects of elixir of sulfanilamide before it was conclusively determined that ethylene glycol is toxic to humans.

A more recent episode resulting in the deaths of more than 5000 people in several countries is another unfortunate example of the difficulty of determining the undesired effects of drugs (23). In this instance a common drug, isoproterenol, had been administered in many countries in a lower strength (0.08 mg/spray). When administered in a greater strength (0.40 mg/spray), by the inhalation route, marked increases in toxicity occurred as compared to earlier methods of use. Again, this dysfunctional effect was conclusively demonstrated only after more than 5000 people died from the use of this drug. Phocomelia, or seal-like babies, were born to a large number of women in Germany and other European countries and also in some Latin American Countries before it was shown conclusively that thalidomide produced this particular undesired effects in the offspring of certain pregnant recipients who were given the drug as a sedative. An example (Table 8.6) which compares the mortality rate of newborn infants receiving any one of four treatment groups is perhaps the extreme of a study designed in part to ascertain or confirm the dysfunctional effects of a drug. Since the undesired effect, death, was thought to be likely, it could be planned for and anticipated. As will be shown, this study used the classic, comparative randomized trial to ascertain the safety or dysfunctional effects of various selected treatments when administered to children. Ordinarily such experiments are not executed because of the obvious disadvantage of destroying the life of a significant number of subjects. However, the method of this particular experiment produces needed answers to complex questions of drug safety. (Ethical aspects of this study are described and evaluated in Chapter 11). It demonstrates clearly the need for adequate requirements to ensure subject safety. Safety is too important to be left solely to researchers—supervision is essential.

8.1.3   Methods of Determining Efficacy and Safety

Some chemicals act to relieve pain, prevent seizures, relieve anxiety, induce anesthesia, assist conception, etc. Others cause pain, induce seizures, produce anxiety feelings, prevent induction of anesthesia, prevent conception, etc. A key question which has persisted from biblical times (see the first chapter of Daniel in the Old Testament for a description of a nutritional experiment) is: How can one know, prior to consumption of or contact with a given chemical, just what the effects experienced will be? Will the chemical cause more harm than good? Will only desirable effects be experienced, or will only undesirable effects be experienced? Will a mixture of desirable and undesirable effects be experienced?

TABLE 8.6 APPLICATION OF CONCEPTUAL MODEL TO DETERMINE THE EFFECTIVENESS OF SELECTED DRUGS IN INFANTS

Birth Weight (grams)	Group I[a]		Group II[b]		Group III[c]		Group IV[a]	
	Total Infants	% Who Died	Total Infants	% Who Died	Total Infants	% Who Died	Total Infants	% Who Died
1000	1	100.0	0	0	3	100.0	1	100.0
1001–1500	5	40.0	5	100.0	2	0	4	100.0
1501–2000	9	22.0	9	67.0	4	75.0	11	90.0
2001–2500	17	5.9	16	50.0	24	0	15	40.0
Total	32		30		33		31	
Average		19.0		60.0		18.0		63.0

[a] No treatment.
[b] Chloramphenicol.
[c] Penicillin and streptomycin.
[d] Penicillin, streptomycin, and chloramphenicol.

Source: L. E. Burns: Fatal Circulatory Collapse in Premature Infants Receiving Chloramphenicol; *New England Journal of Medicine* **261**(26):1318 (Dec. 24) 1959.

Examination of a listing of drugs regarded as lacking substantial evidence of effectiveness and/or safety suggests that not only is this question difficult, but that one is likely to arrive at the wrong conclusion. This outcome is suggested because the list of drugs referred to consists of more than 200 pages of drug names and companies marketing the disapproved drugs. Only some 19% of already marketed drugs were unqualifiedly evaluated as effective in the FDA's initial round of Drug Efficacy Study Implementation Action (26).

The long and successful history of quackery involving drugs amply indicates that the actual effects of drugs and the alleged or perceived effects of drugs may be literally at opposite poles to one another. The failure of legitimate practitioners to properly separate the actual versus the claimed effects of drugs further suggests that what at first appears relatively easy, i.e., to ascertain the effects of a drug, may be a more difficult undertaking than one would imagine. Indeed, one eminent physician has stated (24): "Random experiments by thousands of doctors on millions of patients produced practically no positive results." He might have gone on to say that overreliance on practical experience exists today, albeit less than in the recent past. Contemporary debates pertaining to the safety and effectiveness of oral hypoglycemics and contraceptives provide considerable evidence that not everyone is in agreement about the methods and/or procedures most appropriate for discovering the true effects of drugs (25). One major factor that helped to speed up and secure enactment of the 1938 FD&C Act was the death of 107 people caused by ethylene glycol, a substance not previously tested in humans (27).

Even today there is a widespread latent belief among physicians, patients, and others that the mere administration of a drug will produce readily discernible effects. There is, of course, a certain element of truth in this statement. Can a person not tell from his own sense of pain if relief from a headache is obtained following ingestion of a particular drug? Using this statement as a prototype, it will be shown to contain the proposition "If A . . . , then B . . . ," where A represents the ingestion, administration, or other contact with a drug by an organism afflicted with condition C and where B is the effect, described in terms of condition C, experienced or reported by the patient or provider (pharmacist, physician, nurse, veterinarian, etc.) A principal problem in ascertaining the true effects of a drug will be shown to be the logical basis for concluding that B, the effect, is caused by A, the action. Many instances of drug consumption will be shown, especially in those illnesses controlled by the central nervous system, that actually result in the claimed effect experienced or observed.

To return to the original headache example, it seems reasonable that a person can tell whether or not the headache is present, has been altered, eliminated, or otherwise perceptually changed. The answers to questions of true safety and effectiveness are best explained by relying on basic logical premises, principles of experimental design, and the general principals inherent in the scientific method. For it may well be that a person with a headache may experience its attenuation or elimination when no drug is consumed. For example, the complexity of ascertaining that ingestion of a drug causes relief of pain is suggested by a study which showed that tolerance to pain is affected by age, sex, and race (28). Could not variables of this nature account for the claimed drug effects rather than the drug itself? Although the answer is an unequivocal yes, it is not always yes or always no. The fact that these variables could account for the effects sought doesn't prove that the drug is also responsible for the desired effects.

A careful and detailed conceptual model for discovering the true functional and dysfunctional effects of a drug will be described. The use of a conceptual model as a referent for realized models provides a means of organizing data and information, so that a better grasp of the overall problem can often be achieved. The conceptual model described will incorporate the least assumptions and still provide an answer to the basic question: What are the functional and dysfunctional effects of this drug? It is presented as an aid to differentiating appropriately conducted research from unacceptable research. Its main purpose is not to show how research is done because the reader plans to do it; the view is that the reader needs to know if proper reasoning has been followed when drug claims are made.

The basic conceptual model requires a minimum of two groups: one group receives the drug and the other something else. All other factors must be equal, or those elements that might affect perception of the drug effects must be measurable in order for a cause-and-effect relationship to be inferred. The factors necessary and their essential inter-relationships and comparisons are depicted in Figure 8.4. Ideally all patients who are potential recipients of the experimental drug (termed Drug X here) should be identified. An appropriate number (this is based on statistical theory, and for normally distributed samples 30 or more subjects are usually judged as a minimum) of subjects are randomly selected and randomly assigned to receive Drug X. R represents random assignment of subjects to treatments (experimental and control). The symbol X_e in Figure 8.4 represents Drug X and the symbol X_c represents Not Drug X. It makes no difference if Not Drug X consists of a placebo or some alternative drug, as long as a comparison is

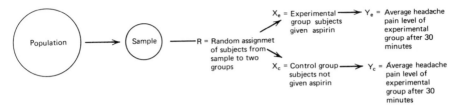

Figure 8.4.   Conceptual model for discovering true functional effects of a drug.

possible. The variable, Y, consists of a measure of the effects of Y sought for and defined before the experiment is performed. That is, Y simply stands for the desired (specifically and precisely defined) effect. Ordinarily the functional effect, Y, will be expected, or hoped for. Many fine drugs have, nevertheless, been produced or discovered by serendipity or by a heuristic process. Even in these instances where some unplanned but functional effect is identified and described, it is usually desirable or necessary to plan an experiment whereby the heuristically derived effects can be tested in the same fashion as other anticipated Y effects and thus unequivocally confirmed. (Propranolol is such an example. It was originally approved and marketed for treating heart arrhythmias and, while being used for this purpose, was identified and later shown to be effective in treating angina pectoris.)

The testing of the effect of aspirin to determine if it is effective in relieving headache pain can be used profitably as an example, as illustrated in Figure 8.4. In this example Drug X would be aspirin and Y would be a measure of headache pain. Nondrug X could be a placebo or any other drug with known effects; the control is listed as simply nonaspirin in the figure. Subjects randomly chosen from the potential aspirin recipient population should be randomly assigned to receive either aspirin or placebo (experimental or control, respectively). After a predefined lapse of time, e.g., 30 minutes, a measure of headache pain should be obtained and the headache pain level of the aspirin-receiving subjects and nonaspirin-receiving subjects compared; these measures would be represented by the numbers (or values) assigned the Y_e experimental and Y_c control group members. Although it is unlikely that subjects would be randomly selected from the potential population, random assignment could be accomplished when a suitable subpopulation (or new universe) has been defined. (A slight improvement in design could be achieved by securing a preexperimental measure of relevant variables: in this example, relief of headache pain.) However, complications are also introduced, and for this reason

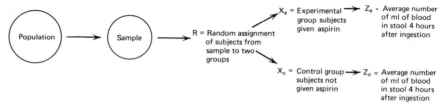

Figure 8.5.   Conceptual model for discovering true dysfunctional effects of a drug.

and others the potential refinements in the design will not be considered further.

Figure 8.5 depicts the conceptual model for discovering the dysfunctional effects of a drug. This model is identical to that used for discovering the functional effects (Figure 8.4) except for one fundamental difference. In Figure 8.4 the dependent variable, Y, was known and defined prior to beginning the experiment; in Figure 8.5, however, the dependent variable, Z (undesired effects; dysfunctional effects), may or may not be known. The dysfunctional effect, "ml of blood in stool," is illustrated in Figure 8.5 and is identical in all relevant aspects to the functional model. Since all dysfunctional effects are seldom, if ever, known, the identity of all Z components is virtually always unknown. Note that variable Z should be conceptualized as an array of effects consisting of the elements $Z_1, Z_2, Z_3 \ldots Z_i$ where the vector Z_i formed by the array Z consists of identified elements, but the total number of universe elements in Z_i are never known. This is a key concept because one must forever watch for other unknown Z_i elements. Absolute knowledge of toxicity is impossible. Obviously, if the identity of Z is unknown, then developing a measure of Z will be impossible. Moreover, experiments are predominately designed to ascertain functional effects, although it will be shown later that the required Phase I and to some extent Phase II of clinical research required by law are fundamentally concerned with ascertaining dysfunctional drug effects.

The major advantages to the conceptual design of Figure 8.4 (the classical design of scientific research) are:

1. It has a built-in control system, i.e., a comparison between equal groups receiving and not receiving the drug is provided for.
2. In theory it can be extended to any number of different drugs or drug strengths.
3. Several hypotheses can be tested at once if multiple variables are examined at the same time.
4. The design rests on fundamentally sound statistical and probability theory principles.

5. Different experimenters in various places can get the same resluts using the model.

Although this design encompasses a minimum set of assumptions, it is not the ultimate design. Its practical application may also be limited because of the requirements of probability or statistical theory. It is an effective design, however, for two major reasons: (1) A provision is made for comparing the experimental drug recipient group to the group receiving a placebo or other nonexperimental drug. Thus the fundamental requirement for comparability is achieved. (2) The randomization requirement provides that the groups being compared are statistically equal in all relevant variables. Such equality derives from the statistical principles of randomization, if a sufficiently large sample is obtained.

The experiment suggested by the design of Figure 8.4 assumes that there is probable cause to suspect that the drug under study will produce the effect sought. Many diverse sources may be called upon to generate this hypothesis. The chemical properties may suggest the action of the drug, and animal data may also support or give rise to the hypothesis. Similarity to an existing proven drug, effects reported by the patient or suspected by the experimenter, physician, nurse or pharmacist, and a variety of other reasons may all produce a hypothesis about the effects of the drug to be studied further. More attention will be given to this point later in this section.

Some Alternative Compromised Models in Man

Several models representing a compromise between the conceptual model and the demands of patient treatment are examined here. The examination of alternative models will be dispassionate and thus may escape the pejorative terminology one frequently encounters relative to this subject. Regardless of the model, the basic question of discovering the functional (and later, dysfunctional) effects of Drug X remains. Included as a corollary of the basic purpose is a subordinate but essential question of controlling the variance of the effects actually produced by Drug X.

Anecdotal or Uncontrolled Observations. The type of design lacking formal controls can be depicted as shown in Figure 8.6. Some effect, Y (depicted as C_e, the number of colds in Figure 8.6), is observed and it is known that the patient has been exposed to the drug, thus giving rise to the hypothesis that Drug X caused effect Y. A person experiences fewer colds this year than last year and recalls that he has

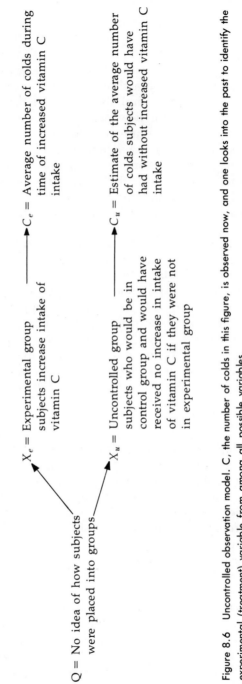

Figure 8.6 Uncontrolled observation model. C, the number of colds in this figure, is observed now, and one looks into the past to identify the experimental (treatment) variable from among all possible variables.

increased his vitamin C intake. Is there a cause-and-effect relationship here? Although the term uncontrolled is in a strict sense correct, a control of sorts is nevertheless implied. The control consists of what the observer believes would have occurred had no drug been administered. The patient or his physician thinks he would have had more colds in the absence of increased Vitamin C. The utility of this design depends upon the success of convincing oneself and others that what one thought would occur in the absence of the drug is a realistic assumption. Note that this design provides no placebo or other drug for comparison; there in only one group (the experimental).

However, one may again have a "mental control" in that the control may be the effect the observer would have expected had a comparative drug been included; this is illustrated as group C_u in Figure 8.6. For disease treatment it is difficult to meet the assumption that the disease condition would not have spontaneously and independently changed for the better. How does a person know how many colds would have occurred in the absence of Vitamin C? Moreover many diseases, particularly those that are degenerative diseases such as the arthritic diseases exhibit spontaneous remission and regression. Many sure cures of the past (and probably of the present) owe their existence to the difficulty of ascertaining what the characteristics of the disease would have been if the drug had not been administered. The use of chaulmoogra oil for the treatment of leprosy is an example of this type of drug. Early clinical trials with penicillin and cortisone therapy show that for some drugs with pronounced and dramatic or life-preserving effects, where there is no drug having a similar action, it is sometimes possible for the assumptions of the model to be met. In these instances the course of the disease was virtually certain, i.e., 100% mortality was the normal course. No probability statement can be made, however, about a cause-and-effect relationship between Drug X (illustrated as Vitamin C) in Figure 8.6 and its effect, Y (illustrated as C, the number of colds), in Figure 8.6.

Challenge-Rechallenge. The challenge-rechallenge type of trial is actually a special type of uncontrolled trial as shown in Figure 8.6. This trial method involves administering a drug to a patient, then withdrawing the drug and observing the effect. It merely demonstrates that the drug administered has an effect. However, the assumptions for the model depicted in Figure 8.6 must also be met. It may represent a slight improvement if one can realistically assume that the patient reverts to his former status without the drug. The disadvantages described for its parent uncontrolled model also apply here.

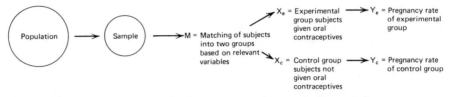

Figure 8.7.   Case-matching model for discovering functional effects of drugs.

Case Control or Case-Matching.   The case-matching type of trial is depicted in Figure 8.7. A given patient who receives Drug X, the treatment (oral contraceptives, in Figure 8.7), is matched, depicted by the symbol M, and is thought to be identical with or at least very similar to all relevant variables. The second patient receives a placebo or some other drug. The control group X in Figure 8.7 is illustrated as noncontraceptive receiving subjects. The principal departure from the conceptual model of Figure 8.4 is that, albeit with difficulty, random selection of patients is still possible, but no random assignment can be accomplished. However, to the extent that matching requirements are achieved, the results obtained by comparing the Y values will be persuasive. Studies of drugs such as oral contraceptives have shown the difficulty of achieving an acceptable match because of important differences that affect assessment of the treatment outcome. These include previous diseases, especially thromboembolic disorders, socioeconomic class, age, etc. If nothing else differs on matching, there may be relevant genetic variations manifested by differing blood types, etc. Many experiments that would otherwise be impossible can sometimes be fitted to this model. Thus the model is important and valuable as long as it is not used when a more reliable model can be employed.

Epidemiologic.   Vital statistics, such as birth rate, death rate, conceptions, abortions, etc., can be used to discover the functional and dysfunctional effects of drugs. Figure 8.8 depicts the vital statistics model, where X represents the administration of some Drug X to a population and Y represents a measure of some vital statistic, e.g., the death rate. The hypothesis that Drug X affects the death rate arises from the observation that the overall death rate due to some specific disease is lower for the experimental group (diethylstilbestrol receivers in Figure 8.8) than for the control group (no diethylstilbestrol receivers).

Of course, this hypothesis has the major shortcoming of most *ex post facto* research in that it is necessary to look back into time and

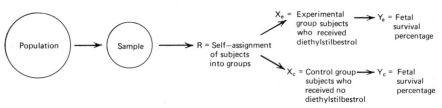

Figure 8.8. Vital statistics model for discovering the true effects of drugs.

select the variables causing the change measured in the vital statistic variable. Although it can be established that the vital statistic index has changed, the doubt rests with the causative relationship between the administration of some Drug, X, and the observed difference in the two measures of the vital statistic being studied.

Figure 8.8 illustrates an example of an approach initially used to determine the efficacy of DES in preventing premature births and thus helping to preserve the lives of newborns. The experimental variable, Y_e, is expressed in terms of the fetal survival percentage of mothers who received DES during their pregnancy. The control variable, Y_c, represents the fetal survival percentage of babies whose mothers did not receive DES. If Y_e exceeded Y_c, then it would follow that DES was effective in increasing fetal survival. Basically this reasoning was employed to justify the widespread use of DES. Later, a well-controlled study failed to support the efficacy of DES. The earlier reasoning was defective in a number of ways. Poor record keeping, lack of knowledge about the similarity of the groups being compared, etc., could have been responsible for the erroneous conclusion. If, for example, the Y_e group had been of a higher economic class than the lower group, this may have been sufficient to account for any observed difference between Y_e and Y_c.

This same model was used to discover the causative relationship between vaginal adenocarcinoma and DES use (22). Moreover, it was successfully used to identify the apparently causative relationship between a certain strength and inhalation route of isoproterenol and asthma mortality (23).

This type of design differs from the uncontrolled design of Figure 8.6 mainly in its superior data quality. The uncontrolled design suggests observation with very limited recording or with records being kept in the head of the researcher. Both suffer from being retrospective, i.e., one looks back into the past to identify variables thought to be causative of the observed difference in Y_e and Y_c.

Before the vaccine for the prevention of poliomyelitis was discovered, it was observed that people contracting this disease had a higher exercise rate, such as increased swimming, prior to contracting the disease. In this example, Y was represented by measures of exercise. Y_e - experimental represents the exercise measure for polio victims and Y_c - control represents the exercise measure for control (nonpolio) people. Drug X is represented by the extent of exercise. The error occurred in identifying exercise rather than the poliomyelitis virus as the etiologic or causative agent, i.e., C, the poliomyelitis virus, was incorrectly identified as exercising.

Other examples abound. At one time grape juice was heralded as a cure for cancer by many laymen. It was claimed that cancer victims who recovered or experienced a remission had a greater intake of grape juice than did noncancer victims. In this instance grape juice played the role of Drug X. The error was merely the fact that Drug X consumption happened to be correlated with the incidence of cancer. The results of such reasoning can be tabulated using contrived figures as follows:

	Cancer Remission (%)		
	Yes	No	
Grape juice	25	25	50
No grape juice	0	50	50
Total	25	75	100

Clearly, these highly exaggerated figures show an association between cancer remission and grape juice consumption. The only error lies in the unfortunate lack of a causal relationship. For unknown reasons the two kinds of phenomena were associated. It is also unlikely that a careful tabulation would be kept.

Professional and Lay Judgment and Sales Volume. "Judgment" means "the mental ability to perceive and distinguish relationships or alternatives . . ." (29). This definition implies that some analytical model is to be used rationally by the judge. Although judgment as a process could be used with any of the foregoing models, it is usually thought of in the context of the case-matching model depicted in Figure 8.7. Essentially it involves the same principles, advantages, and disadvantages of the case-matching model and has the added disadvantage that the usual application of the model to ascertain the true functional effects of drugs relies almost exclusively on one person's ability to store and recall information. Once the information is recalled the problem of handling and analyzing the data is similar to that required for the model depicted in Figure 8.7. The major disadvantage lies in the poor ability of people to selectively perceive or retain information. Selective perception is a psychological concept which describes the tendency of people to perceive information based on preexisting data, values, attitudes, education level, etc. Selective retention is a similar concept describing the tendency of people to store or "input" only selected information; it is also affected by one's values, attitudes, etc.

Comparative Randomized Trial. The use of the highly lauded, comparative randomized trial (CRT) as an approach for discovering the true functional effects of a drug is essentially that described previously in Figure 8.4. Surprisingly, this model is primarily a product of this century. Although there are historical instances of this nature, in a strict sense they were not well controlled. The famous trial by Lind on *H.M.S. Salisbury* using citrus fruits to treat scurvy represents a compromise in comparability of cases since random assignment was not achieved (30).

The CRT is a trial in which patients are randomly assigned to treatment. The minimum treatment consists, as described earlier, of one group which receives the experimental drug of interest and another group which does not. This nonexperimental drug group may receive an alternative drug or a placebo. The dependent variable measures for Y are compared to ascertain if the Y measures for the experimental and control groups are equal. In the earlier headache pain example, Y_a represented some index of headache pain. The requirements of the CRT specify that the subject and the experimenter not know which drug the subject receives. Since the subject and the experimenter are "blind," (unaware of the drug's true identity), the experiment (trial) has been given the name "double-blind." It is important to remember that even this method establishes the probability only within a quantifiable limit of the hypothesis that a cause-and-effect relationship exists between the administration of a drug and the measured effect. From the *New England Journal of Medicine* we have an example of an experiment that appears to incorporate the principle of random assignment of subjects to treatment. The study was undertaken (31)

... of premature infants born twenty-four hours or longer after spontaneous rupture of the fetal membranes, because of a higher mortality in this group than in the premature infants whose membranes had ruptured at birth. Routinely, these infants had been placed on antibiotics shortly after birth because of assumed exposure to infection. The role of antibiotics in this higher mortality was questioned. A comparative study of these infants on different treatment schedules was conducted from March, 1958, to February, 1959. . . .

The portion of the study describing the methodology used implies that subjects were randomly assigned to one of four treatment groups. Since the subjects were newborn babies they obviously were "blind" to the identity of the treatment received. The persons administering the various treatments apparently did not know the identity of the treatments. Since the dependent variable was whether the subjects lived or died, the importance of this knowledge to the subjects was minimal, since death is very objective. The results of the study were as follows:

Table [8.6] lists the results of the study. The mortality rates in the nontreated group and the group treated with penicillin and streptomycin are similar. The mortality in both groups given chloramphenicol is strikingly higher than that in the groups not receiving it. The higher mortality is most obvious in the infants weighing 2001 to 2500 gm., that of the babies given chloramphenicol being 45 per cent and that in those not given it 2.5 per cent.

Although neither the results nor discussion clearly state that statistical tests were performed, such tests would be necessary to establish that the results were not obtained by chance. The design of this study is placed into the context of the model earlier depicted in Figure 8.4 using Figure 8.9.

As described earlier, R represents random assignment of newborn babies to one of the four treatment groups. Group 1 received no drug, Group 2 received chloramphenicol alone, Group 3 received penicillin and streptomycin, and Group 4 received penicillin, streptomycin, and

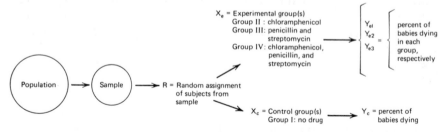

Figure 8.9. Application of the conceptual design for discovering true effects for a reported drug therapy trial.

chloramphenicol. The dependent variable, Y_i, represents the percentage of newborn babies who died after receiving the corresponding i^{th} numbered treatment. In order to infer a cause-and-effect relationship between no drug and some drug, the control (no drug or Group 1) group was essential. The randomization assured the experimenters (with a calculable probability of being wrong) that each of the four treatment groups of babies was equal in a statistical sense.

The method and example used have shortcomings. The most obvious are ethical in nature, and these will be described and discussed in Section 11.1. The experimenters could have concluded that no difference existed because of small sample size, errors in determining if the babies were dead, errors in administering the drugs (treatments), observations attributable to chance, etc. Falsely concluding that mortality was caused by the differential treatments can be erroneous. For example, if no control group (nondrug group) had been included, the researchers might have failed to consider the high mortality rate of babies arriving under the conditions described. Most of the possibilities for erroneously concluding that no effects were achieved apply here.

There always remains the statistical error of falsely concluding that treatment effects were achieved. Improper doses, improper frequencies of administration, etc., of any drug could have influenced the results obtained. For example, since the mortality rate of the Group 4 babies was almost four times that of the Group 1 babies, and since the symptoms of the babies who died followed a clearly distinguishable pattern, the nurses and others administering the Group 4 treatment might have guessed a cause-and-effect relationship and refrained from giving treatment four (i.e., give treatment one), or might have substituted treatment two or three. To the extent that this was done (if it had been done), the results from the experiment would have been less clear. The advantage of "blinding" (not informing persons involved of the specific identity of the substance being administered) is that there would be no way of ascertaining that some of the four treatments were obviously more toxic than others and thus of substituting a less toxic drug. The integrity of the experiment is maintained through blinding.

A Caveat to Those Searching for the True Effects of Drugs

Although we may carry on current arguments about the effectiveness or lack of effectiveness of a particular chemical, let us not forget the advice of the French physician, Pierre Louis, who dealt bloodletting its death blow. In concluding his not very famous but invaluable treatise on bloodletting, Louis said:

> Let those, who engage hereafter in the study of therapeutics, pursue an opposite course to their predecessors. Let them not think that they have done anything effectual, when they have only displayed their own theories, or stated what is done by the most celebrated physicians in search of such a case. But let them labor to demonstrate, rigorously, the influence and the degree of influence of any therapeutic agent, on the duration, progress, and termination of a particular disease (32).

Louis' advice was not well received by his contemporaries. His treatise was first published in 1836; the practice of bloodletting lingered on long enough to help usher Abraham Lincoln into an early grave. Oversimplification of the task of discovering the true effects of chemical agents has significantly retarded the identification of effective therapeutic agents. While experience may be the best teacher, as the cliche goes, it is too expensive. Too expensive in modern usage includes the expense of ascertaining that thalidomide produces deformed phocomelia babies, that vaginal and uterine cancer is produced in the female offspring of women receiving diethylstilbestrol, that isoproterenol in large doses introduced by inhalation causes the death of persons in all age ranges, that clindamycin and lincomycin apparently cause severe colitis, and that ethylene glycol is especially toxic to children.

People should attempt to search dispassionately for the truth wherever it may lead. Moreover, selection of a noneffective treatment leads to the expenditure of resources toward encouraging moderation in exercising on hot days rather than investing resources in identifying the poliomyelitis virus as pathognomic of the disease. The person who faithfully drinks large quantities of grape juice in the hope of curing uterine cancer instead of seeking a surgical remedy diminishes the chances of successful surgery if it is finally resorted to. True education frees us from the tyranny of demons, mystery, ignorance, provincialism, bias, and prejudice. This applies not only to patients who may be educationally deficient pertaining to medication use (in the broadest sense of the term), but is especially important for the many practitioners who, when confronted with many of the truly heart rending tragedies of disease, must remember that their principal role is to act rationally under circumstances which are adverse in a direct manner only to the patient. There is, however, no harm in the use of grape juice when clearly no known treatment is of any value. Such instances justify discarding the garb of the healer and scientist in white and donning the garb of a human being who has done his best, when best is not good enough. Sympathy, not abandonment or false treatment, would then seem to be the medication of choice.

8.1.4   Requirements for Efficacy Determination

New Drugs

Imagine a medicinal chemist who believes that the powder he has just synthesized is an effective and safe drug. Moreover, he explains that this powder is the result of long years of research devoted to a drug that insures perpetual youth, prevents and cures heart disease, cancer, and the common cold. But the chemist also explains that he has just this instant completed his synthesis; his powder has yet to cool. He adds the explanation that this substance has not been synthesized before, and therefore there have been no chemical or other tests performed on the new substance except to identify it as a new substance. No animal toxicity tests or exposures to humans have been done. Would someone take the drug? Would someone take the drug if he or she were certain that it would be another 10 years before a dose could be synthesized? Would someone with heart disease take the dose? Someone with cancer? Someone with a common cold? Would someone who thought he might get old or contract these diseases take it? Would the answer change with pregnancy, or if the person was six months old, or if the person was of retirement age? If the person had other diseases, e.g., hypertension, would his or her answer change? If a large sum of money was offered to take the dose would the answer change? If the person was an orphan, mentally retarded or ill, or a prisoner, would the answer change? What would the answer be if other effective drugs were already available for the indications described?

Such questions as these suggest the need to know what the effects from a chemical coming into contact with living human tissue *in vivo** will be. Federal law requires that a person (such as our chemist) who wants to use a drug for treating humans must prove the effects of the drug in humans. Moreover these effects, which include known functional and dysfunctional effects, must be clearly and unambiguously communicated to those using the drug. The information must be

---

* *In vivo* means literally in a living organism; it is contrasted with *in vitro*, which means in a test tube or in an inanimate object.

sufficient so that persons using the drug can make the most reasonable estimate possible based on known effects of the drug's anticipated benefit and risk. This requirement is predicated on the paramount assumption of medication use that only when expected benefit exceeds expected risk will a drug be consumed by a person. The FD&C Act sets forth a mechanism for providing this need via the new drug section of the Act, Section 505 (33).

Technically, antibiotics and insulin have different requirements for marketing as new drugs (34). However, these ostensible differences fade when it is noted that these requirements are essentially identical to those of the new drug section of the Act. Therefore, separate treatment of insulin and antibiotics will not be included. (It is important to note that the Act does require that insulin and selected antibiotics be certified on a batch-by-batch basis to have met applicable standards of identity, purity, quality, and strength (35) described in Chapter 6.

Any Functional Drug not generally recognized as safe and effective by those persons qualified to determine its safety and effectiveness is deemed to be a new drug. The only new drugs that can legally be marketed in the United States are those for which an approved new drug application (NDA) exists. ("Legally marketed" is a term construing commercialization of the drug and excludes drugs intended for investigational purposes.) It will be shown that the requirements for securing approval of an NDA are demanding.

An approved NDA includes adequate provision for the following major elements.*

1. Decide if a drug† can be tested.
2. Approve who shall test it.
3. Approve on what and on whom it can be tested.
4. Approve where it will be tested.
5. Approve how it will be tested.
6. Determine when the testing may start and stop.
7. Determine when enough testing has been done.
8. Decide whether the product can be marketed.
9. Decide to whom the drug can be marketed.
10. Decide whether the drug is safe and effective.
11. Decide what the labeling may contain.
12. Decide what advertising may contain.*

* Providing interstate commerce is involved.
† Technically, a substance that is only potentially medication.
* Technically, advertising is not approved in advance of publishing, but can be removed from communication channels if it departs from legal requirements.

13. Decide what its salesman may say about it.
14. Decide how it can be distributed.
15. Decide who can distribute it.
16. Decide whether a patient must secure the assistance of a pre-
     scriber in order to benefit from the use of a drug.
17. Determine the abuse potential of a drug.

Items 11 through 17 are only indirectly a product of an approved NDA.
The first 10 elements describe the core of the impact of an approved
NDA on the marketing of a new drug.

Although the preceding list seems all encompassing, it is not. No
requirement for proof of relative efficacy is included. It is not necessary that a drug be proven to be more effective than existing drugs
with the same indications, or as effective with greater safety. It will be
shown that proof of effectiveness requires only comparison with no
drug (in effect, a placebo). It is not necessary that a more favorable
risk/benefit comparison be shown for a drug than exists for drugs
already marketed with the same indications. One major reason for
such a lack appears to be the difficulty of such an undertaking. Also,
drugs usually have multiple indications.

Note also that a drug must only be proven safe and effective. There
is no need to prove, show, or explain why it is effective. Such a
requirement would drastically inhibit the introduction of new substances into the market. May such a requirement be anticipated for the
future?

8.1.5 Major Steps for Introducing a Drug in Interstate Commerce

The legal steps necessary to achieve introduction of a drug in interstate commerce represent the procedures adopted for implementing
the model to generate information about the effects of a drug for
disease treatment (Figure 8.1). The major requisites for securing approval of a new chemical to become a Functional Drug are:

1. The Investigational New Drug Application.
2. The New Drug Application.

The investigational new drug application is a legal provision for shipping a nonapproved new drug in interstate commerce. When approved by the FDA, this application provides an exemption for the
shipping of a nonapproved new drug. A person or drug company
(termed a sponsor) who wishes to initiate studies of the drug in

Sponsor activities   FDA activities

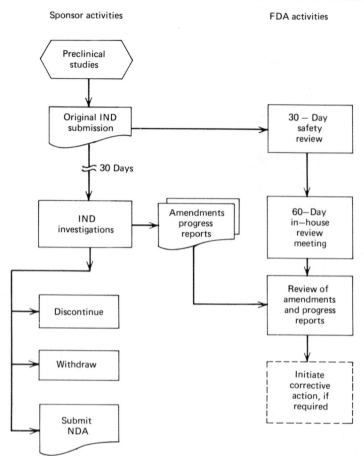

Figure 8.10.   Major elements of the IND process. IND = Investigational New Drug; NDA = New Drug Application. *Source:* H. B. Landau: Comprehensive Designs for Improved Paper Work and Information Systems Associated With the Review of Investigational New Drug Applications, National Technical Information Service, PB No. 220324, Springfield, Va., 1973, p. 1–7.

people must submit a Notice of Clinical Investigational Exemption for a New Drug (IND). After a 30-day waiting period the sponsor may begin the clinical study of the drug if the FDA does not require a delay. These points are summarized in Figure 8.10.

Once the research described in the IND and certain other work is completed, an NDA must be submitted. This includes the data derived from the IND and other essential information primarily directed toward assurance that the drug can and will be properly manufactured and promoted. A complete and detailed description of all the phar-

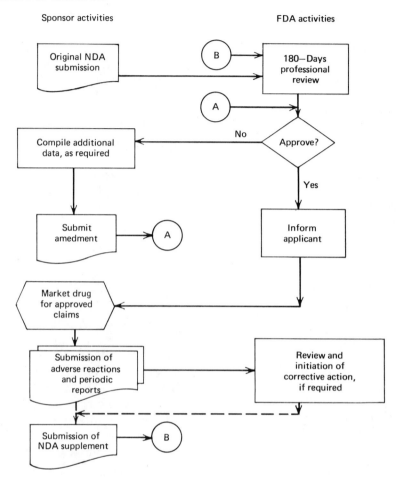

Figure 8.11. Major elements of the NDA process. NDA = New Drug Application. *Source:* H. B. Landau: Comprehensive Designs for Improved Paper Work and Information Systems Associated With the Review of Investigational New Drug Applications, National Technical Information Service, PB No. 220324, Springfield, Va., 1973, p. 1–9.

macologic, biopharmaceutic, chemical, manufacturing, and clinical information must be included. Proposed labeling, which summarizes the clinical pharmacology of the drug and contains the necessary information for administration of the drug, and sufficient information to classify and uniquely name the drug must be included. After the NDA is filed, the FDA has 180 days to approve or disapprove it; the sponsor must be notified in writing of the action taken (36,37). It may be that the 180-day figure is in practice circumvented by the FDA. These points in the NDA process are illustrated in Figure 8.11.

8.1.6   IND Content

An IND is filed by completing a special form (Form FD-1571). The IND actually constitutes a plan for research in humans to determine the effects of a drug and a promise by the sponsor to follow the plan. Form FD-1571 appears in the regulations to the FD&C Act (38). The information composition of the IND is shown in Table 8.7. Tables 8.8 and 8.9 outline the information content of Forms FD-1572 and FD-1573. These statements must be signed by the clinical pharmacologist and investigator named therein.

The heart of the method of conducting clinical research described in the IND resides in what is termed Phases I, II; III. The most salient aspects of these are summarized in Figure 8.12. Phase IV, not formally described in the regulations, is also sketched.

Description of Phases I, II, and III

The basic purpose of all three phases of the investigational new drug procedure (see Figure 8.12) is to produce new information about the drug under study. The type and nature of information sought from the various phases differ. Phase I is mainly concerned with determining whether the substance under study has an effect on man, and if it does, what kind of effect. This phase is primarily short-run in orientation. To avoid acquiring a distorted notion of the effects of the substance it is usually best to use healthy volunteers, because diseased persons may yield spurious results. Frequently the substance will be given to just one healthy volunteer, and other volunteers will receive the drug only after a suitable observation period has elapsed.

This phase seeks data on various toxicologic parameters of the universe of patients who may later receive the drug. Data is also sought on toxicity, metabolism, absorption, elimination, distribution, and other pharmacologic actions of the substance. The first dose administered to the first person or first few people will usually be 5 to 10 times smaller than the amount expected to show clinical activity. The dose will also be many times smaller than that associated with adverse effects in animals; these are usually estimated on a proportionate-weight basis. As more is learned about the drug, the dose is increased or decreased until desired or untoward effects are encountered. If reasonably satisfactory results are obtained, the number of new subjects will be increased gradually to about 20.

During and after the period of drug administration, the subjects are [usually] interviewed and examined regularly and the laboratory tests

TABLE 8.7   OUTLINE OF INFORMATION COMPOSITION OF IND[a]

Item 1:   Name and description of drug including its chemical structure, and route of administration.

Item 2:   List of all components of the drug, including any reasonable alternates for inactive components.

Item 3:   Quantitative composition of drug, including reasonable variations expected during the investigational stage.

Item 4:   Description of source and preparation of any new-drug substances used as components.

Item 5:   Methods, facilities, and controls used for manufacturing, processing, and packing.

Item 6:   Results of all preclinical investigations, including animal pharmacology, toxicology, and metabolism data. Any available clinical data, e.g., from other countries, or from a combination of data from previously investigated or marketed drugs.

Item 7:   Informational materials to be supplied to each investigator, including labeling. "Full disclosure" in the sense of what is known must be provided.

Item 8:   A statement of the training and experience requirements required of investigators by the sponsor.

Item 9:   Names and credentials of investigators and monitors. Record keeping, informed consent, and supervision of subjects' requirements are included.[b]

Item 10:   Outline of the clinical investigation, including a description of Phase 1 and Phase 2 (clinical pharmacology) and Phase 3 (clinical trial).

Item 11:   Agreement to notify FDA if the investigation is discontinued and why.

Item 12:   Agreement to notify investigators if NDA for drug is approved or if IND is discontinued.

Item 13:   If the drug is to be sold, an explanation as to why this is noneconomically necessary.

Item 14:   Agreement to wait 30 days after FDA receives IND to begin implementing plan.

[a] Designated as Form F-D-1571.
[b] This is accomplished via Form F-D-1572 or F-D-1573, statement of Clinical Pharmacologist and Investigator, respectively.
Source: 21 Code of Federal Regulations 130.3(a)(2).

repeated once or twice weekly. The clinical and laboratory data are carefully recorded on special forms, usually provided by the sponsor. If an assay [for the drug] is available, blood and urine specimens are obtained at appropriate intervals and analyzed for the test drug and its metabolites. Thus absorption, distribution, and elimination data are developed and

TABLE 8.8   OUTLINE OF INFORMATION COMPOSITION OF FORM F-D-1572: STATE-
MENT OF CLINICAL PHARMACOLOGIST

Item 1.   Statement of education and training of qualifications as a clinical
          pharmacologist.
Item 2.   Name and address of research facility where clinical pharmacology
          will be conducted.
Item 3.   The expert committees or panels responsible for approving the ex-
          perimental project.
Item 4.   Estimated duration of the project, and the maximum number of
          subjects that will be involved.
Item 5.   The general outline of the project to be undertaken (modifications
          allowed).
Item 6.   A statement that the investigator understands the following condi-
          tions governing his receipt and use of the investigational drugs.

      a.   Sponsor must supply full preclinical information.
      b.   Maintenance of adequate records of the dispositions of all re-
           ceipts of drug, including dates, quantity, and use by subject and
           disposition of unused amounts must be done.
      c.   Case histories designed to record all observations and other data
           that is relevant must be prepared and adequate case histories
           maintained.
      d.   Investigator must furnish reports to the sponsor and must report
           certain adverse reactions and adverse effects that are alarming
           immediately.
      e.   Records shall be maintained for two years after approval of the
           NDA or two years after discontinuation of the IND. The inves-
           tigator also agrees to make certain records of subjects and other
           records available to authorized FDA employees.
      f.   Certification that the drug will be administered to subjects only
           under the personal supervision of the investigator or under addi-
           tional named investigators (whose names must be listed under
           Item f) and a statement that the drug will not be supplied to any
           other investigator for administration to subjects.
      g.   Certification that informed consent will be obtained from sub-
           jects except under unusual circumstances.

Source: 21 *Code of Federal Regulations* 312.1(a)(12).

the drug blood levels can be correlated with any pharmacodynamic action
which may have occurred. The relationship, or its lack, between drug
blood levels and a pharmacodynamic effect such as lowering of blood
pressure or sedation may suggest whether the drug or a metabolite is

TABLE 8.9 OUTLINE OF INFORMATION COMPOSITION OF FORM F-D-1573: STATE-MENT OF INVESTIGATOR

Item 1.   Statement of education and experience in detail including a list of selected publications.

Item 2.   A list of sites where investigations will be conducted.

Item 3.   A statement that the drug will be used in accordance with a plan of instruction to be submitted to include the following components:

   a.   An outline of the plan of investigation including approximation of the number of subjects to be treated and the number of controls, if any.
   b.   Clinical usage to be investigated.
   c.   Characteristics of subjects by age, sex, and conditions.
   d.   The kind of clinical observations and lab tests to be undertaken.
   e.   Estimated duration of investigation.
   f.   A description or copies of report forms to be used to maintain an adequate record of observations and test results obtained.

Item 4.   A statement attesting to an understanding of the conditions governing receipt and use of the drug including the following:

   a.   The sponsor must supply the investigator with full preclinical information.
   b.   Adequate records must be maintained of the disposition of all receipts of the drug, etc.
   c.   Adequate and accurate case histories designed to record all pertinent data must be prepared and maintained for each individual receiving the test drug or acting as a control.
   d.   Statement acknowledging that a report must be provided to the sponsor, and that adverse effects must be reported to the sponsor, and that alarming adverse effects be reported immediately.
   e.   Agreement to maintain records of disposition of the drug for required time periods, and an agreement to allow authorized FDA employees to inspect relevant patient records.
   f.   A certification that the drug will be administered only to subjects under his personal supervision or other subjects to be named within this Item, and a statement that the drug will not be supplied to any other investigator or to any clinic for administration to subjects.
   g.   A statement that informed consent will be obtained from subjects except under unusual circumstances.

Source: 21 *Code of Federal Regulations* 312.1(a)(13).

Time	Preparation for Clinical Testing	
6 to 12 months		Prepare chemical supplies and dosage forms
	Phase I.	First human administration. Who? Normal volunteers—small number.
12 to 21 months		Why? Determine biologic activity and metabolism in man. By whom? Clinical pharmacolgists.
	Phase II.	Early portion. Who? Selected patients—small number.
21 to 33 months		Why? Determine potential usefulness and dosage range. By whom? Clinical pharmacologists.
		Interim review of data by intra- and extramural experts. Initiate chronic toxicity studies in animals. Special animal studies for effects on reproduction and fertility.
	Phase II.	Later portion. Who? Selected patients—larger number for longer duration. Why? Determine final dosage form. More data on metabolic activity. By whom? Clinical pharmacologists.
39 to 57 months	Phase III.	Broad clinical trial. Who? Large sample of specified patients. Why? Determine safety and efficacy. By whom? Clinical investigators.
42 to 69 months		Prepare and submit New Drug Application (NDA). Obtain FDA approval.
continues for life of drug	Phase IV.	Post-NDA approval stage: revision of estimate of drug's functional and dysfunctional effects.

Source: Adapted from K. L. Melmon and H. F. Morrelli: *Clinical Pharmacology*, Macmillan Company, New York, 1972, p. 11; and H. A. Clymer: The Changing Costs and Risks of Pharmaceutical Innovation. In J. D. Cooper (Ed.): *The Economics of Drug Innovation*, Center for Study of Private Enterprise, American University, Washington, D.C., 1969, p. 117.

Figure 8.12 Outline and description of major phases of drug trials required for an investigational new drug.

responsible for the action. Time-course studies may also provide information about the accessibility of the drug in the blood to the target tissue or receptor. Furthermore, the metabolic data can be compared with that previously obtained in animals to provide guidelines for further animal studies, and to suggest the degree of relevance the earlier animal pharmacologic studies may have for man (39).

Many more or less routine measurements are usually obtained, including blood pressure, pulse, and electrocardiogram, and simple physical observations about drug effects.

For example, the size of the pupil of the eye is sensitive to many types of drugs. Other variables studied depend on the anticipated actions of the drug. For instance, many substances enter the brain and affect the electroencephalograph. Several specific patterns have now been described. If the test drug affects sympathetic nerve tissue or receptors, pressor sensitivity tests with pyramine and norepinephrine may delineate the exact mechanism of action (39).

Another way of viewing the basic purpose of Phase I studies is to look upon Phase I as identification of possible Y effects previously described in the discussion of the model for discovering true dysfunctional effects. The goal in Phase I might be viewed as an attempt to identify and quantify all relevant Y variables of a functional and dysfunctional nature.

Phase II studies involve administration of the drug to a limited number of patients for specific disease treatment; i.e., to patients having medically deviant conditions which the drug seems to be effective in treating. Phase II is also concerned with eliciting additional pharmacologic data concerning safety and efficacy. Thus Phase II studies represent in part an expansion of Phase I activities.

The prime purpose, however, is to establish the clinical activity of the new agent. In consultation with medical statiticians and investigators expert both in the disease or condition for which the drug is intended and in the conduct of clinical trials, protocols are devised which describe in detail the questions being asked, the controls and treatments to be used, and the measurements to be made (40).

Studies in all phases must adhere to the requirements of the FD&C Act.

The exact protocol for a Phase I or II study depends on the nature of the test drug. The completion of Phase II studies marks another major decision point in the life of a new drug. The sponsor must consider whether the evidences [sic] of efficacy and safety now available warrant the broad clinical trials, chronic animal toxicity studies, manufacturing commitment and the many other activities which must be done to make the drug a candidate for marketing. An affirmative decision launches Phase III (40).

Phase III is extremely important because it represents a significant investment in time, money, and other resources by the sponsor, investigators, and subjects. Of equal or greater importance is the risk subjects in Phase III studies must take in order for relevant, necessary data to be produced. Phase III studies involve well-controlled studies not only by clinical pharmacologists, but qualified investigators. These researchers include practicing physicians whose training and experience in drug evaluation is less than that of clinical pharmacologists but is, nevertheless, adequate for Phase III studies. About 20,000 physicians have qualified for this role.

Phase III trials are a massive effort to provide the 'substantial proof of efficacy' based on 'adequate and well controlled clinical investigations' required by the FDA before marketing can be considered (40).

A few hundred patients are usually adequate for this phase. However, sometimes hundreds or even thousands of patients may become involved in Phase III studies, e.g., the testing of polio vaccine. During this phase the sponsor prepares preliminary labeling describing the drug's functional and dysfunctional effects as well as procedural and nomenclature information necessary for administering the drug. This information is, of course, incomplete at this stage. A brochure is usually provided that describes not only the dysfunctional effects, but also the specific clinical indications for which the drug is thought to be effective. This information is supplied to the investigators.

The expanded clinical trial tends to elicit additional dysfunctional effects. Likewise, efforts will be made to further identify dysfunctional variables previously described under the conceptual model for determining the true effects of drugs. Diverse data are correlated with the effects discovered and identified. This may include determination that the drug has a peculiar effect in the presence of renal disease, particular genetic makeup, or other effects specific to the drug. For example, certain enzymes may yield pronounced effects when present in certain concentrations. As the sample size and the number of persons exposed to the drug increase, allergic and idiosyncratic reactions begin to appear. The investigator reports these adverse reactions (as per his agreement) on a special form. In summary, Phase III studies can be characterized by protocol planning, solicitation of investigators, multi-purpose and combined clinical trials, data collection and evaluation, chronic animal toxicity studies, and solidification of formulation, quality-control, and manufacturing procedures. When all of this is done, an encyclopedic document known as a new drug application is prepared and sent to the FDA to seek approval for marketing (40).

Although reports of the length of NDAs submitted are frequently exaggerated, some of them are quite lengthy. Lasagna (41) has listed the page content of several NDAs submitted to the FDA: the NDA for ketamine contained 72,200 pages, for Norlestrin 12,370 pages, and 439 pages for pyrvinium pamoate. The date of approval may account for the page count variation, since the shortest NDA was approved in 1949 whereas the others were more recent. Regardless of the volume or number of pages, it is safe to conclude that an NDA contains an enormous amount of information, including raw data.

If all goes according to plan (the exception rather than the rule) an NDA will be filed with the FDA. As was previously suggested, an NDA consists of a large amount of information to be read and studied by the FDA staffers in order to make an informed decision for or against approval of a new drug. The NDA regulations allow some of the major items to be sutstituted; Table 8.10 contains what is termed an "optional expanded summary and evaluation" of the major items of information included in an NDA. In order to better communicate the nature, quantity, detail, and complexity of the information in the NDA, the table shows a reproduction of a slightly edited version of this "Optional Expanded Summary and Evaluation."

One important item remains to fully document the major pathways traveled by an approved new drug: the regulations defining principles for the conduct of clinical investigations. These regulations will be listed, the reactions to their promulgation described, their relationship to the conceptual models for determining the true functional and dysfunctional effects discussed, and some observations of grass roots practitioners and others summarized.

The regulations describing principles for conducting clinical investigations are relatively brief. They serve to interpret the meaning of the phrase ". . . adequate and well-controlled clinical investigations . . ."; i.e., these principles serve as a definition of the term appearing in the Act. Note that the full statutory definition of substantial evidence is

evidence consisting of adequate and well-controlled investigations, including clinical investigations, by experts qualified by scientific training and experience to evaluate the effectiveness of the drug involved, on the basis of which it could fairly and responsibly be concluded by such experts that the drug will have the effect it purports or is represented to have under the conditions of use prescribed, recommended, or suggested in the labeling thereof (42).

Dissection of this item yields the following major conceptual components: (1) adequate and well-controlled investigations, and (2) experts qualified by scientific training and experience, on the basis of which it can fairly and responsibly be concluded that the drug will have its claimed effect.

Probably the most important component is the first item. Note that the noun investigations is plural. The meaning of investigations is interpreted by the FDA to mean that at least two well-controlled investigations constitute the necessary minimum. Under this criterion, the testimony of 50,000 physicians about their experience with 500,000 patients does not constitute the statutorily required kind of evidence.

TABLE 8.10 OPTIONAL AND EXPANDED SUMMARY EVALUATION CRITERIA FOR A NEW DRUG APPLICATION

A. Chemistry:

1. Chemical structural formula or description for any new-drug substance.
2. Relationship to other chemically or pharmacologically related drugs.
3. Description of dosage form and quantitative composition.

B. Scientific rationale and purpose the drug is to serve.

1. Clinical purpose.
2. Highlights of preclinical studies. The reasons why certain types of studies were done or omitted as related to the proposed conditions of human use and to information already known about this class of compounds. Emphasize any unusual or particularly significant pharmacological effects or toxicological findings.
3. Highlights of clinical studies. The rationale of the clinical study plan showing what types of studies were done, amended, or omitted as related to preclinical studies and prior clinical experience.
4. Conclusions. A short statement of conclusions combining the major points of effectiveness and safety as they relate to the use of the drug.

C. Reference number of the investigational drug notice(s) under which this drug was investigated and of any notice, new-drug application, or master file, any contents of which are being incorporated by reference to support the application.

D.   Preclinical studies: All findings should be presented including all adverse reactions which are interpreted as being incidental if not drug-related. The summaries of the individual tests described hereinafter should include a brief statement of methodology with results and interpretation of the test. Each test should be referenced to the proper page number(s) and volume number of the detailed report or to the table of contents preceding the basic scientific data. Include a table of contents referring by volume and page number(s) to the summary and to the location of the complete data and reports in the application and any documents incorporated by reference.

1.   Pharmacology. Studies on pharmacodynamics, endocrinology, etc., as appropriate.

a.   Studies of activities related to primary therapeutic activity.

b.   Studies of activities related to secondary therapeutic activity.

c.   Studies of miscellaneous pharmacologic activities of the compound that may be considered pertinent to the efficacy or safety of the drug.

d.   Metabolism.

i.   Absorption.

ii.   Tissue distribution.

iii.   Detoxification.

iv.   Excretion.

2.   Toxicology and pathology.

a.   Acute toxicity. Summarize by species and route of administration. Give levels and number of animals per dose level with weights, sex, and maturity. In some unusual circumstances, a brief description of the method may be needed. Give LD_{50} values with standard deviation, signs of toxicity, times of deaths, and other pertinent information. It is desirable that species and/or sex differences be pointed out and that the ratio of the oral to parenteral $LD_{50's}$ be indicated.

b.   Subacute and chronic toxicity studies (present by species).

i.   Method. Give duration of study, route of administration, dose levels, and method of giving drug (diet, gavage). Include number of animals per dose level and range of weights at initiation. Indicate parameters studied, including pathology.

ii.   Results. List pertinent observations, including pathology, with statement that other parameters were not affected. If necessary, indicate which alterations were related to pharmacodynamic activity and which were related to toxicity.

c.   Reproduction and teratology studies (present by species).

i.   Method. Give dose levels employed and time of drug administration relative to stage of pregnancy. List parameters examined. State method of examination of young.

ii.   Results. Describe effect on mother and on the various parameters of pregnancy and the fetus. Discuss relationship of drug doses to the therapeutic and toxic doses.

d.   Miscellaneous studies. Include studies designed to explore drug toxicity beyond the more routine acute, subacute, and chronic studies. Studies on tissue irritancy, ciliary motility, etc., and special tests of pharmaceutical formulations should be included.

e.   Evaluation of effectiveness and safety. This section should be the final evaluation of effectiveness and safety based upon the known attributes of the new drug in animals.

E.   Clinical studies. All material should be referenced to the investigator and to the volume and page number of the raw data. Include a table of contents referring by volume and page number(s) to the summary and to the location of the complete data and reports in the application and in any document incorporated by reference.

1.   Special studies. Include all studies that do not clearly have applicability elsewhere. If anything is known about absorption, distribution, excretion, and fate of the drug, it should be included here. Correlations with similar animal data should be drawn. Drug studies on circulation, respiration, volunteer extraordinary safety studies, and overdosage effects are examples. Studies of dose findings are not to be included.

2.   Dose-range studies (individual and collective analysis). Include for each study:

a.   Investigator.

b.   Plan.

c.   Materials used.

d.   Diagnosis.

e.   Age and sex of patients and, if applicable:

i.   Drug codes.

ii.   Control agents.

iii.   Statistical methods.

iv.   Results, adverse reactions and experience, and other side effects.

3.   Controlled clinical studies. A brief description of each giving:

a.   Investigator.

b.   Detailed design of study: crossover, double crossover, stratified sample or matched groups, double-blind, single-blind, randomized, etc.

c.   Control agents (placebo, reference compounds).

d.   Drug codes.

e.   Design for selection of control and drug groups.

f.   Primary and secondary diagnoses, including severity and stage of disease, of patients in drug and control groups with numbers, sex, and age distribution.

g.   Detailed criteria of effectiveness, objective and subjective.

h.   A brief description of adverse experiences looked for by the subject or patient and by the investigator. Include laboratory tests and time of observation.

 i. Control and drug periods and kind and number of observations made in each.

 j. Adverse reactions and all adverse experience by system and organ, general and local.

 k. All results, positive, negative, or inconclusive.

 l. Statistical analysis where possible, kind and applicability.

 m. Conclusions. Overall conclusions of controlled clinical studies.

 4. Other clinical reports. Depending on the nature of the investigation, this could be divided between incompletely controlled studies and reports of uncontrolled use. The presentation of the plan and method of analysis could be governed by the criteria in "3. Controlled clinical studies" and by the situation.

 5. Clinical laboratory studies related to effectiveness. A description and summary of results. If applicable, use pre- and posttreatment tables and graphs.

 6. Clinical laboratory studies related to safety.

 a. The general plan giving the number of studies, duration of therapy, controls, number of control determinations, etc.

 b. A description and summary of the results for each study, including all variations irrespective of the significance, the investigator's name (with reference to volume and page number of the raw data), the results of laboratory determinations, the number of patients, the range of normal values for each laboratory, and what standardization procedures each laboratory employs. Discuss variations fully and make a judgment of the significance of variations with supporting reasons. Submit explanatory tables and graphs wherever useful.

 7. Summary of clinical literature reviewed by applicant. All studies, including controlled studies, that yield data pertinent to safety and effectiveness of the drug and all reports of adverse experience should be abstracted, utilizing the criteria in "3. Controlled clinical studies" under "E. Clinical studies."

 8. Overall results and conclusions. This category should combine findings from all categories in this item E (clinical studies) and present composite, balanced conclusions.

 a. Table of all investigators, academic affiliation, number of cases reported and nature of the study (special, controlled, double-blind, single-blind, randomized or not, etc.). A statement should be made as to why the study was discontinued, if it was, or a statement that it is continuing, if such is the case. (If this information has been submitted elsewhere, it may be incorporated by reference.)

 b. Table of age range for all studies giving totals in each age group and number of males and females in each age group.

 c. Table of various dosage schedules by duration and number of patients.

 d. Effectiveness.

 i. Summarize evidence separately for each claim cited in the package circular. Give results by claim either by blending the results of equivalent types of studies done or by citing the results of the other well-done studies separately and then drawing a conclusion.

  ii. Include summary tables containing the primary and secondary diagnoses, the number of patients and controls, the dosage schedule, duration, and responses.

  e. Safety.

  i. Includes tabulations listing all side effects or adverse experience, by age and sex, whether or not the applicant considers them to be significant, showing whether therapy was stopped and showing the investigator's name, with a reference to the volume and page number in the application and any documents incorporated by reference where the complete data and reports may be found. Indicate which side effects and adverse experiences are regarded by the applicant as possibly drug-related.

  ii. Append the investigator's and the applicant's discussion of the basis for deciding whether or not the adverse experience is drug-related and the significance of possible drug-related experiences.

  f. Overall conclusions about safety and effectiveness.

  i. Concisely compare kind and incidence of beneficial experience with kind and incidence of adverse experience found in clinical studies. Tabulate adverse reactions and experiences with percentage of incidence that were derived from studies designed to seek such data, if possible. Concisely state effective and recommended clinical dosage range on a mg/kg basis and state mg/kg dosage levels which showed adverse effects in animals and adverse experience in clinical studies.

  ii. To the extent known, or from studies by the applicant, concisely compare therapeutic index (effective vs. toxic dosage) and incidence of beneficial and significant adverse effects with related drugs.

  iii. Summarize findings with regard to habit-forming or addiction potential, when applicable.

  9. Annotated package circular.

  a. For each claim or indication, give references supporting it in the summary, or give statements that are in turn referenced to the summary.

  b. For each side effect and adverse experience contained in the submitted summaries and raw data, and for each contraindication, warning, and precaution suggested by such data, give references to it in the summary and cite the disclosure contained in the package circular, or explain its omission. Similarly, cite or explain the omission of such additional disclosures based on experience with related drugs.

Source: 21 *Code of Federal Regulation* 130.4(d)(2).

TABLE 8.11   REQUIREMENTS FOR EFFICACY DETERMINATION—NEW DRUGS

Assumption	Substantial evidence is determined on an individual drug basis.
Goal	Substantial evidence must be shown that the drug will, when exposed to humans, have the effect it purports or is represented to have under the intended conditions described or suggested in the proposed labeling.
subgoal	Based on a fair evaluation of all material facts, the proposed labeling summarizing the substantial evidence must not be false or misleading in any way.

Table 8.11 summarizes briefly the major assumptions and goals pertaining to the requirements for efficacy determination. The principles themselves appear in Table 8.12. They are certainly brief, especially in relationship to the NDA generated from following these principles. Although grumbling about the workload and complaining in general is observed in the literature and heard at professional meetings and in individual conversations about the overall enormity of the task of securing approval of an NDA, most comments regarding these principles are not meant to be taken too seriously. It appears that many of the problems suggested by the term "future shock," coined by Toffler (43)—a term used to characterize the problems of people overwhelmed by rapid change and an expanding information base— surface because of the reaction generated by these principles. The most difficult problem identified by application of these principles is that of communicating the enormity of the information involved when the NDA procedure is under consideration. Four of the most difficult and important problems arise in relationship to physicians. These are the physician's inclinations to (1) seek action rather than knowledge, (2) rely on "results" rather than theory; that is, to act as a pragmatist, (3) trust firsthand experience rather than book learning, and (4) overemphasize the individuality of a person as a genetically unique entity (44).

The third item may have the most significant effect on drug use. This relates to the physician's tendency to ignore, or place in a less than primary perspective, information not generated from personal experience, e.g., data yielded by an NDA. No less a person than the (then) executive director of the Academy of Internal Medicine told a Senate hearing:

TABLE 8.12 PRINCIPLES FOR CONDUCTING CLINICAL INVESTIGATIONS FOR THE SHOWING OF "SUBSTANTIAL EVIDENCE" OF SAFETY AND EFFECTIVENESS

(a) The plan or protocol for the study and the report of the results of the effectiveness study must include the following:

(1) A clear statement of the objectives of the study.

(2) A method of selection of the subjects that

(i) Provides adequate assurance that they are suitable for the purposes of the study, diagnostic criteria of the condition to be treated or diagnosed, confirmatory laboratory tests where appropriate, and, in the case of prophylactic agents, evidence of susceptibility and exposure to the condition against which prophylaxis is desired.

(ii) Assigns the subjects to test groups in such a way as to minimize bias.

(iii) Assures comparability in test and control groups of pertinent variables, such as age, sex, severity, or duration of disease, and use of drugs other than the test drug.

(3) Explains the methods of observation and recording of results, including the variables measured, quantitation, assessment of any subject's response, and steps taken to minimize bias on the part of the subject and observer.

(4) Provides a comparison of the results of treatment or diagnosis with a control in such a fashion as to permit quantitative evaluation. The precise nature of the control must be stated and an explanation given of the methods used to minimize bias on the part of the observers and the analysts of the data. Level and methods of "blinding," if used, are to be documented. Generally, four types of comparison are recognized:

(i) No treatment: Where objective measurements of effectiveness are available and placebo effect is negligible, comparison of the objective results in comparable groups of treated and untreated patients.

(ii) Placebo control: Comparison of the results of use of the new drug entity with an inactive preparation designed to resemble the test drug as far as possible.

(iii) Active treatment control: An effective regimen of therapy may be used for comparison, e.g., where the condition treated is such that no treatment or administration of a placebo would be contrary to the interest of the patient.

(iv) Historical control: In certain circumstances, such as those involving diseases with high and predictable mortality (acute leukemia of childhood), with signs and symptoms of predictable duration or severity (fever in certain infections), or in case of prophylaxis, where morbidity is predictable, the results of use of a new drug entity may be compared quantitatively with prior experience historically derived from the adequately documented natural history of the disease or condition in comparable patients or populations with no treatment or with a regimen (therapeutic, diagnostic, prophylactic) the effectiveness of which is established.

(5) A summary of the methods of analysis and an evaluation of data derived from the study, including any appropriate statistical methods.

Source: 21 *Code of Federal Regulations* 130.12(a)(5)(ii)(a).

I do not pay much heed to all this scientific testing, this measurement of blood levels, this testing in animals. I am accustomed to certain brands and I have good luck with them. The final test is the patient himself. If I want to know if a drug is any good or not, I ask may patients (45).

This statement contrasts meaningfully with a statement appearing in the consumer magazine, *Family Weekly*, provided as a supplement to Sunday newspapers. In an article entitled "Medicine Chest: At-A-Glance Bulletins from the Changing World of Medical Science," the author argued that Gerovital H$_3$ should be available in this country for its alleged rejuvenation effect. The author said:

It (Gerovital H$_3$) is used throughout the world for rejuvenation . . . people have flocked to Europe for the treatment and returned with glowing reports of its effectiveness . . . . The subjects do look (and apparently feel) indefinably younger (46).

Apparently the physician's and the layman's views on this subject have something in common. In Chapter 10 a review of how drugs are actually used in relation to how they are supposed to be used, as defined by FDA-approved labeling shows that the available evidence strongly suggests it is not at all unusual to deviate from approved uses. (Such deviation is sometimes desirable and in the patient's best interest; cf. duty owed in Section 12.7.)

Again, the layman and the physician seem to share a common view of the genetic uniqueness of the individual. A nationwide study commissioned by the FDA to ascertain health beliefs of laymen yielded the interesting findings that the layman views himself as unique, i.e., when he was made, they threw away the mold (47). This seems merely to be an extension of the medical maxim that there is no such thing as the average patient—they're all unique. A logical conclusion which can be drawn by both layman and physician, given the foregoing premise, is that since the person to receive a drug is unique, then the only way to find out if a drug will work is to try it. This conclusion, at least for the layman, is documented in the Health Practices Study (47). A journal article directed to members of hospital pharmacy and therapeutics committees suggests that physicians may share this view (48). The theme of the article was largely the same as that in the Health Practices Study.

Although there is a grain of truth in almost any statement, the fact remains that no two people (with the possible exception of identical twins) are genetically equal. This does not, however, preclude two or more people from being the same height or from having the same number of teeth, the same visual acuity, shoe size, blood pressure, or prothrombin time. One can be confident, for example, that the "average" 70 kg man will be encountered frequently. By studying people having a body weight of 70 kg one is best able to predict the effects on a person weighing exactly 70 kg, other things being constant. The effects of a drug if ascertained from a sample of men exactly 5 ft. 10 in., are likely to be different than the effects derived from its administration to a person two feet or ten feet tall. Likewise, a drug tested in a sampling of persons having a given prothrombin time will produce different effects in a person with prothrombin time differing markedly from that of the people in the sample. It remains true, however, that for the average patient (assuming a normal or known distribution) the drug's effects can be predicted with considerable accuracy. As already argued, the very essence of life, law, and medication use is prediction. Each new drug recipient, unique or not, is compared to the people before him who have received the drug, to anticipate the effect that new recipient will experience. To the extent that those being compared are equal (disregarding research design factors for the moment), the effects experienced by the new person will be identical to those experienced by the prior drug recipient.

Recall that a generalization is an abstraction formed by generalizing from particulars; that a certain drug will exert certain effects under certain circumstances is an example of such a statement. However, the particulars from which the generalization was formed are never more than a sample from the universe of particulars relevant to the principle. As more particulars (for drugs, more and more patients) are encountered, the generalization either gradually erodes and is cast aside in deference to some new generalization, or it is enlarged upon and refined. Initially it is possible to say, for example, that a certain drug is safe and effective within the meaning of the law for children 6 years of age or older. Later, as more children less than 6 years old receive the drug, we are able to modify this principle and say that it is or is not safe and effective in younger children. Figure 8.1, described at the beginning of this chapter, illustrates this point. If the subject is unlike the population from which a sample was drawn and tested, then an experiment is necessary to accurately predict the drug's effects on this "new" subject.

A number of forces cause practitioners, especially physicians, to seek action rather than knowledge. Some of these forces are the lack of a time frame for in-depth study, the expectations of a society which may have a distorted and unrealistic set of expectations from drugs, and the lack of a social reward for seeking knowledge (49). Some sage has observed that there are too many people writing and too few reading. Modern technology is not applied to the processing of drug information. The old methods of using the mind for inputting, storing, controlling, processing, and outputting data and information do not seem to work anymore. Those most involved in drug information application should start making greater use of their minds for the processing of algorithms for data and information manipulation. (Chapter 10 on labeling will address these processes in greater depth.) There also seems to be little effort directed toward simplification of drug information itself, e.g., elimination of trade names, and the stuffing of package inserts with words to discourage rather than encourage reading.

The most pervasive problem in medication use is the failure to allow personal experience deference to the method of the controlled study. Too many people in the health care field are eager to veto volumes of data and information by virtue of the slightest amount of evidence from personal experience (see Section 12.7 for examples of this type of reasoning). The criterion established in the FD&C Act is most amazing for its very presence. While wading through hundreds of pages of testimony by well-educated physicians and scientists one encounters the sometimes obvious and sometimes subtle overreliance on individual experience. This results in bewilderment: Who then was responsible for the effectiveness requirement in the Act? At the same time, one acquires an in-depth appreciation of the eagerness of people of all ages to blandly accept a drug on face value. (This issue is discussed further in Chapter 10.)

SUMMARY

The foregoing discussion of the requirements for efficacy determination forms the skeleton upon which further knowledge can be built. The key requirements include:

1. Placing the burden of proof of safety and effectiveness on the sponsor of a drug.
2. The requirement that a drug be proven safe and effective by providing substantial evidence of safety and effectiveness from well-controlled clinical trials.
3. The provision for an IND and an NDA which serve as research plans and include the requirements

a) that sufficient preclinical testing be done to justify clinical testing as seen through the eyes of the FDA;

b) that (usually) normal volunteers receive the drug first under
carefully controlled conditions;

c) that clinical studies begin only after a 30-day waiting period
subsequent to FDA receipt of the IND;

d) that the FDA continuously review the IND as the IND develops;

e) that reports and summaries of all studies must be submitted
with the NDA; and

f) that raw data be submitted as part of the NDA along with
reports and summaries of data.

4. The provisions that for approval an NDA must contain substantial
evidence of safety and effectiveness.

5. The provision that appropriate ethical standards be followed, including securing the informed consent of subjects.

6. The provision that a mechanism (although in need of improvement) be established to upgrade information as additional experience with the drug is obtained.

A general summary developed to encourage simplification of Cana-
dian drug laws is given in Table 8.13 and provides a concise checklist
for assessing a therapeutic trial report. The list can be used to check
therapeutic reports issued subsequent to the writing of approved
labeling, i.e., the package insert. Understanding of the foregoing
bases and procedures for experimentation on humans is assumed.
The major categories in Table 8.13 pertain to the objectives of the
study: an adequate description of the study, how it was conducted,
and the information derived from it. The checklist represents a broad
statement of major requirements. It should be used somewhat like a
road map showing only interstate highways; one must remember that
many other roads exist and influence traffic on the highway.

Abbreviated New Drug Applications

A basic change in the requirements for approval of a new drug was
announced in 1968. Little publicity or attention was devoted to the
provision for approval of Abbreviated New Drug Applications
(ANDA), perhaps because it was viewed as an interim measure to
assist the FDA in its Drug Efficacy Study Implementation (DESI). The
ANDA was designed to provide a means for drug manufacturers to
show effectiveness for certain drugs that had been reevaluated, after

TABLE 8.13 CHECKLIST FOR ASSESSING A THERAPEUTIC TRIAL REPORT

1. Aim: specific ☐, or not clear ☐; single ☐, or multiple ☐.

2. Description of subjects, drug administration, etc. *Are the following specified?*

Healthy subjects or patients?	Y N	
Volunteers or not?	Y N	
Age	Y N	
Sex	Y N	
Race	Y N	
Criteria of selection	Y N	
Contraindications	Y N	
Presence of disease other than that treated	Y N	
Whether additional treatments were given	Y N	
If they were, are they described?	Y N	
Daily dose	Y N	n/a
Frequency of administration	Y N	n/a
Hour(s) o'clock when given	Y N	n/a
Route of administration	Y N	n/a
Source of drug (e.g., name of manufacturer)	Y N	n/a
Dosage form (e.g., tablet, syrup, etc.)	Y N	n/a
Timing of drug administration in relation to factors affecting absorption (e.g., meals)	Y N	n/a
Checks that drug was taken	Y N	n/a
Other therapeutic measures (if a drug was not used)	Y N	n/a
If yes, are they described?	Y N	
Total duration of treatment	Y N	n/a
Persons who made the observations	Y N	n/a
Inpatient/outpatient	Y N	
Setting (e.g., one or several hospitals/clinics/wards)	Y N	
Dates when trial began and was completed	Y N	

3. Methods and Design

Are the methods of assessing therapeutic effects clearly described?	Y N
Were these standardized methods?	Y N
Were control measures used to reduce variation that might influence the results?	Y N

If *yes*, specify:

Concurrent controls	☐	Patient his own control	☐
Stratification or matched subgroups	☐	Identical ancillary treatment	☐
Run-in period	☐	Other	☐

Were controls used to reduce bias?	Y N

If *yes*, specify:

"Blind" observers	☐	"Blind" patients	☐

Matching dummies   ☐   Random allocation   ☐

4. Assessment of the trial

Were the subjects suitably selected in relation to aims?	Y	N
Were the methods of measurement valid in relation to the aim?	Y	N
Were they adequately standardized?	Y	N
Were they sufficiently sensitive?	Y	N
Was the design appropriate?	Y	N
Were enough subjects used?	Y	N
Was the dosage appropriate?	Y	N
Was the duration of treatment adequate?	Y	N
Were carry-over effects avoided or allowed for?	Y	N n/a
If no controls were used, were they unnecessary?	Y	N
If controls were used, were they adequate?	Y	N
Was comparability of treatment groups examined?	Y	N n/a
Are the data adequate for assessment?	Y	N
If statistical tests were not done, were they unnecessary?	Y	N
If statistical tests are reported		
(a) Is it clear how they were done?	Y	N
(b) Were they appropriately used?	Y	N D

5. Are the conclusions justified?

   Completely ☐   Partially ☐   No ☐

6. Is the trial acceptable?

   Definitely yes ☐   Probably yes ☐   No ☐

7. Are unwanted effects, or their absence, mentioned?   Y   N

8. Is the summary completely accurate?   Y   N   n/a

Y = yes   N = no, or not clear
D = doubtful   n/a = not applicable
Source: J. C. Ryan and J. Leger: Accelerating the Review/Approval Process, *Med. Mkt. Media* **8**(2):32 (Feb.) (1973).

the 1962 amendments required that all drugs marketed between 1938 and 1962 be reassessed. For such drugs, evaluated by the FDA as effective, the notice of effectiveness published in the *Federal Register* includes a finding on other conditions that must be met if the drug is to continue as an item in interstate commerce. In effect the drug is exempt from the requirement that it be proven effective. The ANDA requires only the following (50, 51):

1. Description of components and composition of dosage form.
2. Place of manufacture.

3. Name of suppliers of active ingredients.
4. Assurance that the drug will comply with appropriate specifications.
5. Outline of methods to be used in manufacture.
6. Description of manufacturing and packaging facilities to be used.
7. Certification that the drug will be made in accordance with current good manufacturing practices.
8. Evidence of bioavailability, if deemed necessary.
9. Other necessary information as required by the FDA.

The assumption implicit in the ANDA requirements is that if a drug can be made chemically and physically identical to a drug already proven safe and effective, then the new product will also be safe and effective. Bioavailability may or may not have to be proven, depending on the drug and the circumstances. Chemical equivalence is deemed equal to bioequivalence, and is assumed unless evidence to the contrary is presented. Although there is a great amount of rhetoric to the effect that safety and effectiveness cannot be assumed under the circumstances described, there have been only a few (at least one, and possibly as many as fourteen) cases in which chemical equivalence has not produced therapeutically equivalent blood levels. However, even in these few instances it was not shown that different blood levels affect the disease process (although such an argument can be made quite easily).

The U.S. Department of Health, Education, and Welfare (DHEW) policy on reimbursement, debated during 1974 and 1975, stimulated considerable resolution of much of the controversy surrounding this issue. Clearly, chemically equivalent drugs are therapeutically equal or else the law is being circumvented by those empowered to enforce it. (See Chapter 6). However the overall issue of antisubstitution, the substitution of a chemically equivalent drug for a given trade-name drug, has been viable since 1888 and will probably linger on for years.

The ANDA procedure creates some labeling practices that are difficult to understand. Some of the notices published in the Federal Register include the entire labeling, whereas others include only the indications part of the labeling. The result can be labels suggesting different effects for supposedly identical drugs (52–54). This point will be elaborated on in the section on labeling.

Since considerable interest is shown by the lay and professional press, the news media, economists, and congressional committees on the subject of the effect of the US drug development laws, it is instructive to mention such laws in other countries (55,56,57).* Few countries in the world have investigational and development drug laws as demanding as those of the United States. Of the Western countries only Sweden, Switzerland, Canada, and the United Kingdom have laws that are as stringent as ours. Table 8.14 shows the differences between these countries and the United States in relation to new drug studies, approval, and clinical investigation procedures. Some countries may await approval in the United States before allowing distribution of a drug in their own country.

The question of the effect of US new drug laws on the rate of production of new, significant chemical entities for disease treatment is a broad topic for discussion. Only two points will be considered here, however. One is the likelihood, suggested by Visconti and Smith (56), that a suitable answer is best withheld pending more data. The other is a basic difference in the ethical philosophy of the two disagreeing sides, which seems to have escaped the attention of both sides. The issue seems to be: Should drugs be marketed to produce the greatest good (benefit) for the greatest number or the greatest benefit for each individual? At first glance the two seem identical. Consider an example. By taking a cohort sample of 1,000,000 people it might be possible to select 1,000 of them and use them for experimental purposes to discover new and effective drugs. Assume for the sake of simplicity that the members of the cohort were all 20 years old with equal life expectancies of 50 remaining years. The net benefit measure would be represented solely as years lived. The total years lived would be 50 (1,000,000) or 50,000,000 net years, in the absence of experimentation. If 1,000 people were used for experimental purposes and a drug that would increase life expectancy 5 years were made marketable, the net benefit would be (55 (999,000) − 50 (1,000)) − 50,000,000 = 4,895,000 net years saved. This is equal to 69,928 extra 70-year lives or a return on investment (the investment of 1,000 lives for 50 years) of 4, 895,000/50,000 = 9800%. Clearly, this is a superb investment. The only difficulty would seem to arise in selecting the 1000-person cohort as a sample. Who would want to be selected or to volunteer? As previously argued, many areas of knowledge are investigated in the search for answers to behavioral questions. In this instance law, ethics, religion, and economics are clearly looked to for an answer. Cost/benefit analysis alone may yield an undesirable answer.

---

* The best single source of a review of both sides to the question of the effect of our drug laws on the rate of new drug laws on the rate or new drug development is included in reference 55.

TABLE 8.14 COMPARISON OF THE SYSTEMS OF VARIOUS COUNTRIES FOR CLINICAL INVESTIGATION AND NEW DRUG STUDIES AND APPROVAL PROCEDURES

	Sweden	Switzerland	United Kingdom	Canada	United States
Clinical investigation.	Normal volunteers: no IND[a] required, but are considering it. Patients: IND required, trials begin immediately.	No IND required either for patients or normal volunteers.	Normal volunteers: no IND required. Patients: IND required. Trials delayed until approval granted by extramural committee.	Normal volunteers: IND required. Patients: IND required, trials begin only after agency approval (up to 120 days, but this will be shortened).	Normal volunteers: IND required. Patients: IND required, trials begin ater 30 days.
	Continuous review of IND as it develops.		No review of IND after initial submission until application for renewal every 2 years. Serious adverse reactions in humans and animals must be reported immediately.	Continuous review of IND as it develops.	Continuous review of IND as it develops.
	Preclinical toxicology requirements flexible depending upon drug.		Preclinical toxicology requirements defined.	Preclinical toxicology requirements defined.	Preclinical toxicology requirements defined.

(Continued on next page)

TABLE 8.14 (continued)

	Sweden	Switzerland	United Kingdom	Canada	United States
Year of introduction of IND requirements.	1964		Voluntary 1964, mandatory 1971.	1963	1963.
New drug application date requirements.	Summaries of studies; published literature. Firms not required to submit all known studies.	Summaries of studies; published literature. Firm not required to submit all known studies.	Summaries of studies; published literature. Firms not required to submit all known studies.	Summaries and raw data; published literature. Firms not required to submit all known studies.	Summaries and raw data; published literature. Firms required to submit all known studies.
Final approval or nonapproval responsibilities.	Extramural committee	Extramural committee	Extramural committee	Agency	Agency.
Year of introduction of new drug application.	1934	1942	Voluntary 1964, mandatory 1971.	1961	1938

a Investigational new drug application.

Source: Competitive Problems in the Drug Industry, Hearings Before the Senate Subcommittee on Competitive Problems in the Drug Industry, Part 23, Feb. 5, 6, 7, 8, and March 14, 1973, U.S. Government Printing Office, Washington, D.C., 1973, p. 9360.

REFERENCES AND GUIDE TO FUTHER STUDY

1. 21 *U.S. Code*, 353(b)(2).

2. Barber, B.: *Drugs and Society*, Russell Sage Foundation, New York, 1967, p. 180.

3. Talaalay, Paul (Ed.): *Drugs In Our Society*, Johns Hopkins Press, Baltimore, 1964 p. 41.

4. Barber, B.: *Drugs and Society*, Russell Sage Foundation, New York, 1967, p. 178–183.

5. Irwin, S.: A Rational Approach to Drug Abuse Prevention, *Contemporary Drug Problems* 2(1):11 (Spring) 1973.

6. Simon, M. E. and Kuehl, D. G.: FDA Listens: A Survey of Consumer Opinion on the Safety of Medicines, *FDA Consumer* 7(4):6 (May) 1973.

7. Irwin, *ibid.*, p. 16.

8. Irwin, *ibid.*, p. 17–19.

9. Andjelkovic, A. et al.: International Comparisons of Medical Care Utilization, *New England Journal of Medicine* 277:516–522 (September 7) 1967.

10. Rabin, D. L.: Use of Medicines: A Review of Prescribed and Nonprescribed Medicine Use, *Medical Care Review* 29(6):668–699 (June) 1972.

11. Irwin, *ibid.*, p. 23.

12. Slovic, P.: Personal Communication, Oregon Research Institute, Corvallis, Oregon, 1973.

13. Zeidner, J.: The Philosophy of Evidence, In Cooper, J. D. (Ed.): *The Philosophy and Technology of Drug Assessment*, Volume 3, Interdisciplinary Communication Associates, Washington, D.C., 1971, p. 193–218.

14. Slovic, P.: From Shakespeare to Simon: Speculation—And Some Evidence—About Man's Ability to Process Information, *Research Monograph*, 12(12) Oregon Research Institute, Covallis, Oregon 1972.

15. Knapp, D. E., Knapp, D. A., and Oeltjen, P. D.: *The Benefits-to-Risks Ratio as a Factor in Drug Choice by Physicians* (unpublished manuscript), 1971, 87 p.

16. Cooper, *ibid.*, p. 222.

17. Starr, C.: Social Benefit Versus Technological Risk, *Science*, 165:1232–1238 (September) 1969.

18. New Drugs Used for Nonapproved Purposes (methotrexate for psoriasis), Hearings before the House Intergovernmental Relations Subcommittee, July 29, and 30, 1971, U.S. Government Printing Office, Washington, D.C., 1971, p. 122.

19. Miller, R. R.: Drug Surveillance Utilizing Epidemiologic Methods, *American Journal of Hospital Pharmacy* 30(7):588 (July) 1973.

20. Kogan, N. and Zalesha, M.: Level of Risk Selected by Individuals and Groups When Deciding for Self and for Others; *Proceedings*, 77th Annual Convention, American Psychological Association, 1969, p. 423–424.

21. Rucker, T. D.: Economic Problems in Drug Distribution, *Inquiry* 9(3):44 (September) 1972.

22. Herbst, A. L., et al.: Adenocarcinoma of the Vagina: Association of Maternal Stilbestrol Therapy with Tumor Appearances in Young Women, *New England Journal of Medicine* 284(16):878–881 (April 22) 1971.

23. Stolley, P. D.: Asthma Mortality: Why the United States Was Spared an Epidemic of Deaths Due to Asthma, *American Review of Respiratory Diseases* **105**(6):883–90 (June) 1972.

24. Dunlop, D.: The Assessment of the Safety of Drugs and the Role of Government in Their Control, *Journal of Clinical Pharmacology*, **7**(4):184–192 (July–August) 1967.

25. Cooper, J. D. (Ed.): The Quality of Advice, In *The Philosophy and Technology of Drug Assessment*, Volume 2, Interdisciplinary Communications Associates, Washington, D.C., 1971, p. 227–324.

26. Drug Efficacy Study, A Report to the Commissioner of Food and Drugs from the National Academy of Sciences, U.S. Government Printing Office, Washington, D.C., 1969.

27. Young, J. H.: *The Medical Messiahs*, Princeton University Press, Princeton, N. J., 1967, p. 185.

28. Woodrow, Kenneth M. et al.: Pain Tolerance: Differences According to Age, Sex and Race, *Psychosomatic Medicine*, **34**(6):548 (November–December) 1972.

29. Morris, W. (Ed.): *American Heritage Dictionary*, Houghton Mifflin Company Boston, 1969, p. 709.

30. Lind, J. A.: *A Treatise of the Scurvy*, Sands, Murray and Cochran, Edinburgh, 1753.

31. Burns, L. E.: Fatal Circulatory Collapse in Premature Infants Receiving Chloramphenicol, *New England Journal of Medicine* **26**(26):1318–1321 (December 24) 1959.

32. C. G. Putnam: (English translation) *Researches on the Effects of Bloodletting in Some Inflammatory Diseases and on the Influence of Tartarized Antimony and Vesication in Pneumonitis*, Hillar, Gray and Company, Boston, 1836, p. 96–97.

33. 21 *U.S. Code*, 355.

34. 21 *U.S. Code*, 356 and 357.

35. 21 *U.S. Code*, 356(a) and 357(a).

36. Title 21, *Code of Federal Regulations*, 130.10.

37. Title 21, *Code of Federal Regulations*, 130.12(a)(6).

38. Title 21, *Code of Federal Regulations*, 130.3(a)(2).

39. Abrams, W. B.: Introducing a New Drug into Clinical Practice, *Anesthesiology* **35**(2):186–187 (August) 1971.

40. Abrams, *ibid.*, p. 188.

41. Lasagna, L.: Research, Regulation and Development of New Pharmaceuticals: Past, Present, Future, Part I, *American Journal of Medical Sciences*, **263**(1):15 (January) 1972.

42. 21 *U.S. Code*, 355(d).

43. Toffler, A.: *Future Shock*, Bantam Books, New York, 1970, p. 2–5.

44. Smith, M. C.: Social Barriers to Rational Drug Use, *American Journal of Hospital Pharmacy* **29**(2):125 (February) 1972.

45. Competitive Problems in the Drug Industry, Hearings Before the Senate Subcommittee on Competitive Problems In the Drug Industry, July 16, 29, 30 and Oct. 27, 1969, Part 13, U.S. Government Printing Office, Washington, D.C., 1969, p. 5017.

46. Cyan, E. D.: Medicine Chest: At-A-Glance, *Family Weekly*, p. 14, April 28, 1974.

47. National Analysts, Inc.: *Health Practices and Opinions*, National Technical Information Service, Springfield, Va., PB-210 978, June, 1972, p. 57–61.

48. Cosmides, G. J.: Human Variablity and the Safer, More Effective Use of Drugs, *Hospital Formulary Management* **8**(1):7–15 (January) 1973.

49. Smith, M. C., *ibid.*, p. 128.

50. Geismar, L.: Abbreviated New Drug Applications, *FDA Papers* **4**:9–116 (December–January) 1971.

51. 39 *Federal Register*, March 29, 1974, p. 11723.

52. Gibson, J. T. and Sterling, S.: Generic Equivalency and the Use of Drugs According to Approved Usage: Antibiotics, *Hospital Formulary Management* **9**:6–14 (January) 1974.

53. Gibson, J. T.: Generic Equivalency and FDA Approved Usage, *Hospital Formulary Management* **9**:39 (November) 1974.

54. Gibson, J. T.: Estimation of Risk-Benefit Expected From Hypotensives/Cardiovasculars, *Hospital Formulary Management* **10**(2):69 (February) 1975.

55. Competitive Problems in the Drug Industry, Part 23, Hearings before the Senate Subcommittee on Competitive Problems in the Drug Industry, Feb. 5, 6, 7, 8 and March 14, 1973, U. S. Government Printing Office, Washington, D.C., 1973.

56. Smith, M. C. and Visconti, J. A.: On the "Costs" of the 1962 Drug Amendments, *Inquiry* **11**(1):65–68 (March) 1974.

57. Defelice, Stephen L.: *Drug Discovery: The Pending Crisis*, Medcom Press, New York, 1972.

58. Friedman, A. P. (Chairman): Drug Trials for Headache, Principles and Methods, Public Health Service Publication #1741, NINDB Monograph No. 6, U.S. Dept. of Health, Education and Welfare, National Institute of Neurological Diseases and Blindness, Washington, D.C., 1968, 60 p. (Describes protocols and procedures for clinical testing of potential headache remedies.)

59. Poprick, M.: Consumer Perception of Safety: A Survey. ACPE Report 1, U.S. Food and Drug Administration, Washington, D.C., about 1972, 231 pages, see especially p. 97–156.

CHAPTER NINE

Laws Governing the Information Content of Drug Labeling

Virtually everyone knows that a person deprived of air will die. It may be less obvious, but a person deprived of information may also die. To anyone who has reflected on the problem variously known as "information explosion" and the more dramatic "future shock," there seems to be too much to know. The problem is confounded by the difficulty of selecting information from among many related sources which often overlap or even duplicate one another. Paradoxically, there also seems to be a dearth of relevant, useful information.

Consider briefly the role of information in a typical person's life. Upon awakening he needs information before a decision can be made to go back to sleep or to get up. He looks at his watch and observes that it is 7 o'clock. He must remember that it is 7:00 A.M., or ascertain this information by observing the amount of natural light outside. Our sleeper must know the day of the week. Is it a workday or a leisure day? Is today an exception, e.g., a holiday or vacation day? Our typical sleeper will have processed a surprising amount of information by the time he arrives at work.

Many areas of activity have a rapidly increasing and changing information base. This is clearly true for medication; it is in the forefront of this evolution. The reader has already been exposed to the notion that such and such a fraction of the drugs of today were not available 5 years ago. Indeed, comparison of the today's drug base with that at the turn of the century shows very little overlap.

Today there are only a little more than 1000 distinct chemical entities that are Functional Drugs; a recent *National Drug Code Directory* lists 1273 (1). Several hundred medications are added when combinations are considered in the total. The complexity and actual number of drugs are increased by the information used to describe each drug. Although the actual number of functional drugs is unknown, it probably exceeds 25,000. The expanded number is the result of adding information elements in various combinations; e.g., new route of administration or use.

Frequently students express surprise and even amazement when they learn that obtaining an optimum match between a drug and a disease (indications and actions desired, respectively) is a complex undertaking. This is due in part to the nature of the information that accompanies all drugs and diseases.

A careful look at the nature of information and language is necessary to fully understand the enormity of the tasks confronting the marketers and controllers of prescription and, to a lesser extent, nonprescription drugs. It will be shown that the structure of language itself largely accounts for much of the problem of information overload regarding drugs and drug therapy.

Information in general, and drug information in particular, is transmitted in the form of symbols. These symbols are usually words (composed of the 26 letters of the alphabet plus 1 space), numbers, or chemical symbols. When properly used these symbols convey the same meaning to various perceivers. Basically the problem of communication arises from the arbitrary assignment of symbols and especially words to convey certain meanings. The term "anaphylactic shock" has a different meaning for someone who has witnessed it than it does for a person who has only read about it. Words are used to represent objects, events, and interrelationships between objects and events. Perhaps the most frequent use of words is to represent objects. Drugs are objects and are thus represented by words. It is easy to miss the significance of language to mankind's survival. Imagine the impossibility of communicating the meaning of virtually anything without words. The sentence "I ran" would necessitate demonstrating physically the art of running to communicate the message desired. Symbols must be used precisely and rigidly in order for transmission of information to occur. A given symbol must always refer to the same entity and only that entity. The frequent appearance of the word "semantics," which refers to the problems arising from inconsistent relations between a word and its referent is evidence of failure to conform to this rule. Thus two basic principles of communication are (1) establish clearly the purpose of the communication in the mind of the receiver before transmitting the information, and (2) use symbols having a meaning common to both the sender and the receiver.

The second principle can be stated in an alternate way by saying that the sender and receiver must establish exactly and unambiguously what the referent is for a particular word in a given context and maintain a constant understanding of the referent-word relationship. Defining the referents for words can be extremely difficult. Two basic methods can be used: one presents an actual example and the other uses other words to define the word at issue. "Look, that is a go-go dancer," or "look, that is a mouse" establishes an unambiguous relationship between the word and the object.

Nouns, as in the foregoing example, generally have demonstrable referents. Verbs require action that must be either demonstrated or described in terms of other words. Crying is an act that requires certain kinds of expressions, sounds, and attitudes; a demonstration of crying, however, may not be easy. Drugs are largely concerned with altering of body processes. The usual instance is for something or someone to do whatever the verb specifies, since a verb (according to grammar) must have a subject. Consider the verb "absorbs" in the sentence "It absorbs negative ions." Interest is focused on the process of absorption, therefore showing absorption probably transmits its meaning better than describing it in other words.

The problem described above will be made clearer by the use of an example. When one locates the word "infant" in a standard dictionary, it is described as meaning "1. a child during the earliest period of its life, especially before being able to walk, baby. 2. Law. a person who is not of full age, especially one who has not attained the age of 21 years; a minor. 3. a beginner; . . . novice" (2). However, the regulations in the FD&C Act require a more precise and special meaning. Therein "infant" is defined only in relation to dietary foods as "a child not more than 12 months old" (3). FDA policy suggests that "Until the term is more precisely defined by legislation or formal regulation, where the exact meaning of the term is significant, manufacturer should qualify any reference to 'infant' to indicate whether it refers to a child who is not more than one year of age, or a child not more than two years of age" (4).

In order for the reader of the term "infant" to receive the same information (meaning) sent by the writer of the information a common agreement must be reached about the referent of a word. Specification of the purpose of the communication helps establish the context of the meaning. If confusion or ambiguity can easily arise regarding as common a word as infant, imagine the ambiguity of the term "mild pain." (This example also serves to explain a major purpose of this book, namely, to generalize. By constructing a generalization one loses some of the preciseness gained through dwelling on the particulars, but gains in that it becomes possible to see the whole. One is thus able to grasp the existence of the forest and select his particular trees for scrutiny as the need arises.)

Physicians, pharmacists, nurses, and other health providers are fond of noting that only a particular role occupant (usually the physician) is competent to prescribe drugs, diagnose disease, or recognize adverse drug reactions because of the other members lack of "clinical experience". Clinical experience takes on a special, almost religious connotation. The amount of rhetoric surrounding the use of the term is so great and voiced so emotionally that the original meaning of the term is lost. The term "paroxysmal tachycardia" means an intermittently, rapidly beating heart. However, only a physician or other person who has experienced the sometimes audible beat and has observed the motion of the patient and his surroundings created by this type of heart condition as well as the victim's emotional reaction to this condition can fully appreaciate the meaning that this term should convey. Actually, although only the patient can fully know many of the sensations experienced in this condition, he is unaware of possible subconcious effects of the condition or of his own facial expression, attitude, etc. The indefiniteness or ambiguity or (as many critics would say) nonmeaning conveyed by a term such as "behavioral drift" immensely complicates the problem of describing the effects of drugs. (The advertisement featuring behavioral drift as an indication for the use of nortriptyline hydrochloride was a major focus of several days of congressional hearings and was ultimately the subject of informal FDA action) (5).

If the words and terms describing the functional and dysfunctional effects of drugs are viewed as concepts, the difficulty of communicating the desired drug information becomes clearer. Consider the concept "mild pain," which is assimilated from personal sensations and the sensations of others. One observes or listens to reports from persons said to be exhibiting pain. A constellation of stimuli are observed, and the similarity of common characteristics which clearly seem to be associated with mild pain forms the concept in part. To fully develop the concept, however, one must observe or listen to reports from people with slight to excruciating pain. Since provider and patient alike have probably experienced mild pain and to the extent that symbols with equal meaning for both parities are used, communication occurs as intended. The meaning in the mind of the sender is thus interpreted identically by the receiver.

9.1   PURPOSE AND ENDS SOUGHT FROM THE REGULATION OF THE INFORMATION CONTENT OF DRUG LABELING

The broad purpose of drug labeling is to promote the rational use of drugs. The goals of drug information use are (1) communication of the expected benefit and risk from the use of a drug in a patient, and (2) transmission of information from the labeler using symbols having identical meaning for seller and provider or patient. The content of the message that can be transmitted is limited to the information derived from IND and NDA activities. Only information produced according to statutory requirements can be communicated to potential providers or patients. The problems of drug information stem mainly from the different attitudes of the writer of the labeling (usually, but not always, the manufacturer) and the labeling approver (always the FDA), who have different purposes in selecting the symbols to convey the meaning intended for the affected parties.

It seems fair to say that the marketer of the drug would tend to favor a more positive approach to describing his drug. The FDA, on the other hand, prefer to adopt a conservative approach to labeling. Yet neither position may be the most desirable for best communicating the known benefit and risk information about the pharmaceutical product involved.

Before delving into the regulations specific to drug labeling, a definition of drug information will be presented. The major elements of drug information sought by prescribers and others will be described for a hospital environment and for information sought by a nationwide sample of primarily non-hospital-based physicians.

A comprehensive, nonlegal definition of drug information follows:

> . . . any objective, scientifically derived and documented, data or knowledge involving the pharmacological, toxicological, and therapeutic use of drugs. It includes, but is not necessarily limited to, such particular items of knowledge as chemical names, structures and properties, identification, diagnostic or therapeutic indications, mechanisms of action, time of onset and duration of action, recommended doses and dosage schedules, administration, absorption, metabolism, detoxification, excretion, side effects, adverse reactions, contraindications, interactions, chemical and therapeutic incompatibilities, costs, advantages, signs, symptoms and treatments of toxicities, clinical efficacy, comparative data, clinical data, drug use data, and any other information useful in the diagnosis and treatment of patients with drugs (6).

In general drug information describes the effects of medication on living organisms and, conversely, the effects of living organisms on drugs. Its function is to reduce the uncertainty generated by identification of a medically deviant condition and thus to improve the chances that a drug will be effective.

Table 9.1 lists the strictly therapeutic elements of drug information from an established, ongoing drug information service provided by a hospital. Note that almost half the elements fall into four categories: indications, toxicity, dosage, and availability. Table 9.2 lists information elements of a strictly pharmaceutical nature obtained from the same source.

TABLE 9.1   THERAPEUTIC INFORMATION ELEMENTS RECEIVED BY A DRUG INFORMATION SERVICE INVOLVED IN 491 INQUIRIES RECEIVED DURING A YEAR

	Number of Elements	% of Total
Indication for use	29	14.15
Toxicity	25	12.20
Dosage	23	11.22
Availability	21	10.24
Bibliography/references	19	9.27
Route of administration	11	5.37
Milliequivalents	9	4.39
Pharmacology	7	3.41
Equivalent dose	7	3.41
Skin tests	7	3.41
Adverse or side effects	7	3.41
Therapeutic incompatibilities	6	2.92
US equivalent product	6	2.92
Drug of choice	5	2.44
Site or mechanism of action	4	1.95
Sodium content	3	1.46
Overdose	3	1.46
Absorption	2	0.98
Metabolism	2	0.98
Rate of administration	2	0.98
Laboratory tests interference	1	0.49
Contraindications	1	0.49
Antidote	1	0.49
Duration of action	1	0.49
Teratogenicity	1	0.49
Safety	1	0.49
Total	205	100.00

Source: Drug Information Services: Two Operational Models, U.S. Government Printing Office, Washington, D.C., about 1972, p. 35.

TABLE 9.2   PHARMACEUTICAL INFORMATION ELEMENTS RECEIVED BY A DRUG IN-
FORMATION SERVICE IN A YEAR

	Number of Elements	% of Total
General information[a]	56	16.87
Composition	44	13.25
Identify	38	11.45
Manufacturer or source	35	10.54
Physical or chemical incompatibilities	30	9.04
Cost	13	3.92
FDA approval	12	33.61
Product identification	10	3.01
Investigational drugs	8	2.41
Stability	7	2.11
Strengths available	7	2.11
Formulary status	5	1.51
Dosage forms	5	1.51
Definition or terminology	4	1.21
Spelling	3	0.90
Trade name	3	0.90
Drug abuse pamphlets	3	0.90
Investigational drug consent forms	3	0.90
Sterility	2	0.60
Formulas for calculations	2	0.60
Other	42	12.65
Total	332	100.00

[a] Usually desired physiologic or pharmacologic action, side effects, use, contraindications, dosage, administration.
Source: Drug Information Services: Two Operational Models, U.S. Government Printing Office, Washington, D.C., about 1972, p. 36.

Again, only four information categories, i.e., general information,
composition, identity, and source account for about half the information requests. The information is specific for one highly sophisticated,
university-based hospital and may or may not be generally applicable.

A nationwide probability sample of physicians showed somewhat
similar results (Table 9.3). The information elements obtained from the
most frequently used source of drug information are listed in Table 9.3
(the sources of drug information are described in Section 10.4). Note
that here also only a small number of elements satisfy most searches
for information and that the cost of drugs seem unimportant. There is
usually considerable reliance on memory for much drug information.

TABLE 9.3 INFORMATION ELEMENTS SOUGHT FROM THE MOST FREQUENTLY USED SOURCE OF DRUG INFORMATION[a]

	What Are the Main Things You Use PDR For? (N = 501)	What Prescribing Information, If Any, That You Need Is Not Available in PDR? (N = 501)
Principal elements mentioned	100%[b]	100%[b]
Dosage	71	4
Contraindications/side effects	58	5
Indications	37	7
Dosage forms/packaging	20	1
General information/refreshing memory	17	4
Identification of specific drugs	16	3
Some drugs omitted	0	16
None, nothing, nothing special	1	48
Don't know, no answer	1	3

[a] The Physicians Desk Reference, Medical Economics Co., Oradell, N.J. was the most frequently used drug information source.
[b] Percentages represent the fraction of total respondents answering yes to the corresponding item.
Source: Adopted from Opinion Research Corporation: *Physicians Attitudes toward Drug Companies*, Opinion Research Corporation, Princeton, N.J.) June, 1968, p. 12.

Indeed, it seems likely that the prescriber has already selected an indicated drug before he begins his search for the information sought from the elements described in Table 9.3. Information elements appeared to be relatively complete if the drug was listed in the source. (*What* was sought from sources of drug information actually used, was reviewed under "Assumptions of How Drugs are Used" in Chapter 3, and a description of the frequency and nature of use of sources appears in Section 10.4).

Perceived information needs of nurses differ markedly from those of physicians; the best available study on the nurse's need for drug information did not, unfortunately, use categories directly comparable to those of Table 9.3 (7). However, doasage and side effects were also listed as the most important drug information elements needed by nurses.

It is important to underscore the profound effect of the application

of drug information to patient treatment. To prescribe or not to prescribe may be just as important as it was with Hamlet because selection of either alternative may result in life or death. Thus a principal
goal of drug labeling is to increase the chances of a favorable
therapeutic outcome.

To say that drug labeling is the continuing subject of intense controversy is to understate reality considerably. Drug labeling will become even more controversial as drugs become potentially more beneficial and probably more risky as new developments occur. (For
example, a "tamper-proof" pack capable of releasing an individual
dose at a designated time by means of its own automatic control
mechanism or upon receipt of an electronic signal from the prescriber
is already technologically possible) (8). Descriptions of drug labeling
(termed "package insert") vary from "a distillation of the results of a
long and laborious process of research to provide reliable information
for the prescribing physician" (9) to opinions that a package insert
derives from a process in which "the physical characteristcs are determined by the amount of empty space in the package which the
stuffer has to fill in order to prevent rattling" (10). The following
sections will assist the reader in formulating his own opinion of the
package insert.

9.2 LABEL AND LABELING DEFINED

The statutory definitions of the terms label and labeling state:

> The term 'label' means a display of written, printed, or graphic matter
> upon the immediate container or any article; and a requirement made by
> or under authority of this Act that any word, statement or other informa-
> tion appear on the label shall not be considered to be complied with
> unless such word, statement, or other information also appears on the
> outside container or wrapper, if any there be, of the retail package of such
> article, or is easily legible through the outside container or wrapper. The
> term 'labeling' means all labels and other written, printed, or graphic
> matter (1) upon any article or any of its containers or wrappers, or (2)
> accompanying such article (11).

These definitions contribute little toward a description or understanding of the information content in labels or labeling; the words
"all" and "accompanying" are construed to have the broadest possible
meaning. The law also requires that the labeling of drugs (all drugs)

contain "adequate directions for use" (12). The FDA, by exercising its rule-making authority, has seen fit to define "adequate directions for use" to mean

> . . . directions under which the layman can use a drug or device safely and for the purpose for which it is intended. Directions for use may be inadequate because [among other reasons] of omission, in whole or in part, or incorrect specification of:
>
> (1) Statements of all conditions, purposes, or uses for which such drug or device is intended, including conditions, purposes, or uses for which it is prescribed, recommended or suggested in its oral, written, printed or graphic advertising and conditions, purposes or uses for which the drug or device is commonly used; except that such statements shall not refer to conditions, uses or purposes for which the drug or device can be safely used only under the supervision of a practitioner licensed by law and for which it is advertised to such practitioner.
>
> (2) Quantity of dose [including usual quantities for each of the uses for which it is intended and usual quantities for persons of different ages and different physical conditions],
>
> (3) Frequency of administration or application,
>
> (4) Duration of administration or application,
>
> (5) Time of administration or application [in relation to time of meals, time of onset of symptoms, or other time factors],
>
> (6) Route or method of administration or application,
>
> (7) Preparation for use (shaking, dilution, adjustment, or temperature, or other manipulation or process) (13).

The reader will recall that the principal distinction between prescription and nonprescription drugs is that the former cannot be labeled safe for use by the layman without prescriber intervention. Although recent emphasis on communication to the patient suggests that drugs prescribed by a clinician, e.g., oral contraceptives, can be labeled in such a way that the patient can use her informed judgment to decide whether to take them, the very definition of prescription drugs stands in opposition to this suggestion.

However the FDA, in what appears to be a roundabout way, has ruled that under certain circumstances a prescription drug can be exempt from the requirement for "adequate directions for use" (14). The "certain circumstances" require that the labeling of a drug bear adequate information to enable prescribers to administer the drug safely and for correctly intended purposes (note the statutory appearance of the word "administer" where one would expect the word "prescribe") (15). Thus meeting the requirements for 'full disclosure' via the package insert makes the PI the answer to drug labeling information requirements in terms of content and, to some extent, of form. For new drugs and for antibiotics the labeling information can contain only that information approved as part of an NDA or for a certified antibiotic. (Essentially, the requirements for marketing of an antibiotic are identical to those for marketing other drugs except for the batch certification requirement, and will not be treated separately in this text.) The package insert thus meets the legal requirement for labeling and in the process provides full disclosure of the functional and dysfunctional effects of the drug. Therefore, full disclosure is equivalent to providing adequate directions for use. Full disclosure is directed to professionals.

The regulatory definition of full disclosure evolved as an answer to the need of the patient or his proxy for data and information on a drug describing its functional and dysfunctional effects. (This need did not include the promotional and advertising information about a drug although these are highly related). The 1906 Pure Food and Drug Act made no attempt to control the content of drug information except to loosely require that such information not be both false and fradulent. The 1938 Act added the requirement for adequate directions for drug use. It was not until 1951, however, that a statutory classification of drugs as prescription or nonprescription was enacted with the passage of the Durham-Humphrey amendment to the FD&C Act. Prescription drugs enjoyed a *de facto* exemption from meaningful or communicative labeling until, stimulated by the thalidomide birth defect disaster and the Kefauver Senate hearings, a regulation requiring full disclosure was added by the FDA in 1961. The drug amendments of 1962 added strength to the 1961 regulation. Not the least of these additions was the requirement that a drug be proven to be effective for each indication appearing on its label.

9.2.1.   Information Content of the Package Insert

The package insert (PI) must carry the message approved by the FDA and the identical message should be conveyed to the recipient. The regulations developed pertain not only to the content but also to the type, order of information, arrangement of information, and context in which the information occurs. These regulations are all supported by the doubtful assumption that the labeling will be read completely and that only the intended message (as approved by the FDA) will be transmitted. The regulation specifically describing the information in the PI recommends that a certain "suggested format and order of the headings used in drug labeling" be followed in writing a PI (13). As first finalized by the FDA the regulation recommended the following section headings in the order listed:

1. Name of drug.
2. Description.
3. Clinical pharmacology.
4. Indications and usage.
5. Contraindications.
6. Warnings.
7. Precautions.
8. Adverse reactions.
9. Dosage and administration.
10. Overdosage (where applicable and available).
11. How supplied.

Optional sections included:

12. Animal pharmacology and toxicology.
13. Clinical studies.
14. References.

These headings, except for the optional ones, are recommendations only and can be modified in unusual circumstances. Since (for new drugs) the FDA must approve labeling as part of the NDA approval, it is in a position to encourage following its recommendations.

Even though these headings and listings are being modified, the changes will be more in form than in substance. Nevertheless the changes will be important and will take a more realistic approach to the questions of if and how package inserts are read and studied (16, 17). In Section 8.1 we encountered a better arrangement of drug information than that listed above. However, although the underlying assumptions of drug information use are unlikely to change much (17), the changes will reflect a better understanding of the importance of the underlying assumptions. For these reasons the package insert headings are listed and described and, in addition, a description is added of the assumptions underlying the reasoning that a given category of package insert information is desirable or needed.

1. *Name and description.* The established name (generic name is frequently used in trade and lay communication) of the active ingredients must be listed. The description includes such items as physical

and chemical characteristics, e.g., chemical formula and structure, melting point, solubility, color, taste, etc. For prescription drugs and certain nonprescription drugs, the quantity of each ingredient must be listed. Inactive ingredients, e.g., vehicles, preservatives, must be listed for parenteral dosage forms.

Assumptions pertaining to heading:

    a. Name: The name of a drug serves the primary function of uniquely identifying it and giving it a characteristic different from that of other drugs. The assumption is that having a name associated with a chemical entity allows the substance to be described symbolically without ambiguity. Naming serves as a means for abstractly referring to a particular chemical substance so that it is uniquely identified and described.

    b. Description: It is assumed that certain words and symbols can be used in such a way that by observing the chemical entity one can ascertain whether or not it meets the requirements of its verbal description. The description is thought to assist in some way in identifying uniquely the chemical entity as well as to assist the user in some fashion in manipulating the drug.

2. *Clinical pharmacology.* In what was termed the actions section, the basic pharmacological effects of the drug are explained. When available, information on peak time of action, site of action, onset, absorption, metabolism, and duration of action is given. The emphasis here is not on functional or dysfunctional effects, but on the physiologic changes in body elements.

Assumptions of heading: It is assumed that a unique chemical entity has pharmacologic actions that are describable and predictable in the human organism, and which operate according to known scientific principles. Knowing the action of a drug is assumed to assist in manipulating the drug so that its most favorable functions are achieved while minimizing dysfunctional effects.

3. *Indications.* This is probably the most important and controversial heading. The therapeutic claims and desirable therapeutic actions that may be produced by a drug are found here. The therapeutic claims must be as specific as possible, e.g., leukopenia, not blood dyscrasia (if leukopenia is the only known instance). If the drug is to be used in adjunctive or supportive therapy, this must be listed. If substantiated, relative efficacy may be included (18), although this is

not mandatory even if known. Limitations of the drug may be listed, e.g., a low pH is required for effective action of an antibiotic.

Assumption pertaining to heading: It is assumed that a given chemical entity is effective for treating a subset of all existing and/or known diseases. Moreover, it is assumed that each distinct chemical entity has limited usefulness and is useful only for the conditions in which it has been proven to be effective. Knowing the information about a drug other than its indications is not sufficient to predict the clinical usefulness in treating the known disease conditions or states for which the drug is useful so that a favorable benefit/risk solution is obtained. A fundamental assumption is that substantial evidence of effectiveness describing the effects of the drug has been presented according to publicly known scientific rules.

4. *Contraindications.* Reasons why a drug should not be given (absolute contraindications) and reasons why it should not be given if another treatment can be substituted (relative contraindications) appear here. Absolute contraindications may be listed for patients with certain attributes: e.g., preganancy, certain disease states, certain ages, concurrent use of other drugs (e.g., monoamine oxidase inhibitors). Relative contraindications may include, for example, use of sympathominetic animes (e.g., pseudoephedrine) when the patient has diabetes mellitus or hypertension, and use of cholinergic drugs (e.g., propantheline) when glaucoma is present.

Assumptions pertaining to heading: It is assumed that even though a drug entity is effective for treating a disease condition, conditions may exist which prohibit the consumption of the drug entity due to an anticipated unfavorable risk/benefit comparison influenced by the contraindicated factor. Relative contraindications exist on the assumption that even though undesirable effects are known to occur, sometimes the benefits from the use of the contraindicated drug outweigh the risks of using these drugs. A relative contraindication reduces the risk/benefit margin but the margin is still positive, whereas the margin of difference produces an excess of risk for an absolute contraindication.

5. *Precautions.* This heading pertains to actions to be taken in advance of drug administration to protect the patient against possible adverse effects from conditions that may arise or affect the body/drug interrelationship. These are to be observed for routine and special conditions. The idea is to plan ahead so that measures that could help

increase beneficial effects or minimize dysfunctional effects can be implemented. Relative contraindications, warnings, and possible drug/drug interactions may appear here and in other headings.

Assumptions of heading: It is assumed that taking certain precautionary or preventive measures reduces the probability of adverse effects and that beneficial effects are changed to the patient's detriment or benefit, as the case may be.

6. *Warnings.* Statements in the warnings make the reader aware of potential or actual damage that may occur from use of a drug, e.g., "safety in pregnancy is not known," "drug may mask signs of infection," "use with certain other drugs may induce glaucoma." Other salient warnings which must be considered in the benefit/risk decision include habituation potential, toxicity of some drugs, use by the suicide-prone patient, or duration of therapy.

Assumption of heading: It is assumed that by observing certain most important conditions the probability of some dysfunctional effects occurring is minimized while the probability of obtaining some functional effects is maximized.

7. *Adverse reactions.* This section lists effects contrary to the goals and well-being of the patient, i.e., dysfunctional effects, which may (or may not) occur. Adverse drug reactions thought to have a probable causal relationship to a drug are listed; the requirements for listing do not demand the rigorous proof required for listed indications. Initially, those adverse drug reactions in the labeling approved as part of the NDA must appear here. New adverse reactions can be added as new experience (not research) suggests. The "Dear Doctor" letter, sometimes required of drug manufacturers by the FDA, is usually concerned with rapidly informing providers of new adverse drug reactions. Also, adverse drug reactions common to the particular class of drug may be listed en masse in this section. Adverse reactions usually begin with "nausea" and end with "death has been known to occur from use of this drug," with almost any possible undesirable effect appearing somewhere in between depending on the drug under consideration. At present no indication of the frequency of occurrence of adverse drug reactions need be mentioned for the typical drug, although as labeling is revised such statements will be required (16). One has little information to predict the likelihood of, for example, diarrhea, if he does not know whether diarrhea occurs in about 25% of the patients (e.g., as with lincomycin) or in only about 10% of patients (e.g., as with tetracycline hydrochloride).

Assumptions of heading: It is assumed that certain dysfunctional effects will be experienced by the drug consumer. Some known probability of occurrence is thought to exist (which is not likely to be known or to be precisely known) for each distinct undesired or dysfunctional effect. These dysfunctional effects are thought to be comparable in a fashion that allows a computation of the risk of dysfunctional effects which may occur from the use of the drug and the benefits which may accrue from the functional effects hoped for from the use of the drug. The drug is expected to be used only after a calculation is made on an individual basis and a prediction of a favorable risk/benefit relationship is made. These adverse or dysfunctional effects are expected to occur in accordance with their expected probability only when the precautions and warnings described in the foregoing sections are rigorously adhered to. It also assumes that the other instructive portions of the drug labeling will be followed in a rational manner. Apparently, it is also assumed that drug effects are not selective but are diverse in that all receptors exist to receive the many elements of the drug.

8. *Dosage and administration.*   This heading contains a description of how much drug to administer and how to administer it. The amount of drug and the route of administration is specified as to indications, ages, presence or absence of other diseases, etc. The frequency with which a drug is to be administered and the duration of therapy are described here: e.g., children with upper respiratory tract infections should be given 125 mg every 4 hours by the oral route for 10 days.

Assumptions of heading: It is assumed that only certain routes are to be used for each drug entity. The stated probability of functional and dysfunctional effects holds true only when the described routes are followed. Desired effects are thought to be best produced from certain quantities of the drug being exposed to the organism in a prescribed fashion when relevant conditions are observed. It is assumed that a drug produces its functional effects in this predictable fashion when just enough drug is consumed to produce the functional effects desired, but not enough to produce more than the predicted quantity of dysfunctional or adverse effects. Again, it is assumed that directives for using the drug described in previous information categories will be adhered to rigorously. The person receiving a drug is assumed to be identical in all relevant attributes to the persons on whom the drug's dysfunctional and functional effects were determined; this is an especially difficult assumption to meet for reasons described previously.

9. *How supplied.*   This section contains merely a description of the dosage forms, strengths of these forms, package quantity, and product characteristics of the available product. For example, "aspirin tablets, USP, 5 grains, in bottles of 100, white, scored tablets."

10. *Overdosage.*   Data on overdosage, if available, can be included. If special instructions are required for treatment and recognition of toxicity symptoms, they will also appear here. For example, "oxygen should be administered concurrently with stomach gavage due to the inhibition of respiration."

11. *References.*   Included here is a listing of other sources of drug information for the drug. For a new drug only the articles cited in the approved or supplemental NDA can be listed here. These are limited to those references which have met the FDA's criteria for controlled studies.

Assumptions of heading: Other relevant information describing the effects of the distinct drug entity are assumed to exist. Moreover, it is assumed that one may rationally consume or direct the consumption of a distinct drug entity without the aid of initial information other than a basic education. Under certain circumstances one may seek information in references that might shed light on a person who did not meet the assumptions described in the foregoing information categories, e.g., a study done on the effects from concurrent administration of the drug with aspirin. The assumption is made that additional information pertaining to animal pharmacology, human pharmacology, toxicology, and other pharmacologic, biologic, physical and social information is relevant to increasing the probability of securing the designated functional effects while minimizing the dysfunctional effects.

12. *Animal pharmacology and toxicology; clinical studies.*   This category involves findings of the investigational studies in the various IND phases. Animal pharmacology and toxicology information may describe the toxicity reactions observed and the amount of drug per unit of animal weight, usually expressed in terms of LD_{50} or ED_{50}, that will produce the effects. The findings of studies done with humans will pertain to the same variables, but will be described under a clinical studies section. These findings are limited to those approved as part of the original or a supplemental NDA. It is assumed that knowing why a drug produces its effects will increase the rational use of the drug.

Each package insert must also be dated, and only the most recent can appear in drug packages. This date can profitably be used to save time in a literature search if one begins his search around the time of the package insert date and searches from that date to the present.

While these sections and headings are the most commonly encountered, other names are sometimes used to indicate these same segments of the package insert. "Composition" may be seen instead of "description," "side effects" instead of "adverse reactions"; a section of advantages may be added, actions and use (indication) may be combined, and warnings may be included with precautions; these are examples of just some of the variations that may be encountered. Especially lacking in clear-cut distinctions are the portions of the package insert on contraindications, warnings, and precautions. The package insert category in which a particular statement appears was once discretionary on the part of the drug company (or the FDA). The package insert as it exists today is only about 5 years old, and the concept itself was introduced only 14 years ago. Many criticisms of the current package insert could not be foreseen when it was first required. The changes in the package insert, which first received *Federal Register* attention in 1974, are due mainly to new knowledge gained from years of experience (40). We hope that as the labeling is revised, the changes will correct many of the deficiencies of the package insert and will avoid creating new problems.

Physical and Related Aspects of the Package Insert

The package insert* is a piece of paper with words and other symbols recorded on it. It accompanies drug containers and describes the contents and probable effects of the contents on users of the drugs. The PI may be glued to the outside of the container, placed in the cap as a sort of buffer, cellophane-taped to the container, placed in the container with the drug, or simply affixed to the container with a rubber band. A typical PI is hard to describe because they are printed in a variety of colors, shapes, sizes, and qualities of paper. One wonders if the charge that it exists merely to prevent rattling of the contents may be near the truth. The manufacturer does comply with the labeling requirement by providing a PI for each and every prescription drug container (except for the regulatory exemptions and the pre-1938 drugs "grandfathered" by the original 1938 FD&C act). After considerable indecision, single unit packages were exempted from a PI requirement for every container provided a PI appears in multiple containers of unit dose drugs.

---

* The term *package insert* is shorthand terminology for officially approved prescription drug labeling. Non-prescription drugs often contain labeling in the form of a package brochure; such labeling is excluded from the meaning of PI in this book by operational definition.

The estimated $10 million spent annually on the required PIs, encourages manufacturers to use thin paper and small print. Regulations do indirectly control print size and specifically require that established names be at least one-half the print size of trade names (19). In addition, an approval of an NDA includes approval of the proposed PI and vice versa. Unfortunately, most PIs are not utilized properly.

The physician does not get PIs, except from a sample drug given to him or from a detailman or "mailer." Several million dollars are thus spent to make PIs available, which are only seen by physicians in unusual circumstances. (The physician does however, have access to a large number of PIs through the Physicians' Desk Reference—the PDR). Even when a systematic filing system is attempted for PIs, their physical characteristics make it a rather formidable task.

Advertising and Promotion: Influence on Information Meaning

To better appreciate the role of advertising and promotion, attention to the basic goals of these activities is necessary. (Advertising and promotion will be used as equivalent terms here.) Advertising originally was designed to merely inform the potential buyer of the availability of a product; promotion was more concerned with persuading the buyer that he needed the product by showing him how it would or could contribute toward achievement of his objectives. Persuasion was accomplished by describing the various positive attributes of a product in terms the potential buyer could understand. The goal of promotion is an increase in sales.

Promotional practices of the drug industry have been the target of several influential groups for a number of years. The Kefauver Senate hearings of the late 1950s were mainly concerned with the high cost of drugs and the relationship between promotion and cost. Since 1967, Senator Nelson's Subcommittee on Competitive Problems In the Drug Industry has succeeded in keeping the promotional practices of the industry in the limelight. Representative Fountain has served the same purpose in his role as Chairman of the House Subcommittee on Intergovernmental Relations. More recently, Senator Edward Kennedy's Senate Subcommittee on Health, whose hearings have received widespread publicity, has focused more intensely on promotional practices at the retail, wholesale, and manufacturer levels. The pharmacist, who had usually escaped the severest criticism, received more adverse publicity from the Kennedy committee than from any previous investigative body. The pharmacist practice of allowing drug company salesmen to review pharmacy prescription files was the major focus of the criticism. Numerous other ctitics of promotional practices abound. However, this section is devoted to explaining the information content of promotional messages and is only peripherally concerned with its economic aspects; the two are related. All too often drug promotion has been the subject of debate rather than of dialogue and explanation.

The portion of the FD&C Act devoted exclusively to advertising consists of only 300 words. A key requirement is that advertisements contain "in brief summary" (19) information relating to side effects, contraindications, and effectiveness in a form prescribed by FDA regulations; these regulations appear in the *Code of Federal Regulations* (20). Here, a regulation was introduced by the requirement that promotional labeling be "the same in language and emphasis" as that in the package insert (18). Since a "brief summary" and "full disclosure" are required in order to comply with the requirements for advertising and labeling, an advertisement must contain information meeting both requirements (21). Only a careful reading of the regulations themselves will convey the regulatory detail inherent in this method of communication.

The PI has been sketched as the information base or universe from which advertisements may be constructed. The regulations provide that the information must be constant. The only variations allowed apply to the substitution of one set of symbols for another; the total meaning of the words and other symbols of the PI must remain constant. Different media may be used to convey the allowed meaning, and in some instances all indications or subset of indications (less than the total PI indication) may be featured in an advertisement (22).

The message—the symbols used and the meaning conveyed—is the focus of advertising regulations. The advertisement viewed as discrete bits of smaller information units and the ad as a whole, including its context, are major factors in regulatory considerations. Virtually all modern modes of communication are regulated as advertising. When describing a prescription drug, these include the following (23):

1. Ads in published magazines, journals, newspapers and other periodicals.
2. Ads using radio, television, and telephone communication systems.
3. Brochures.
4. Mailing pieces.
5. Booklets.
6. File cards.

7. Bulletins.
8. Calendars.
9. Price lists.
10. Catalogs.
11. House organs.
12. Filmstrips.
13. Letters.
14. Motion picture films.
15. Lantern slides.
16. Sound recordings.
17. Exhibits.
18. Literature, reprints.
19. Published references.

Often the feeling persists that those who advertise drugs are not to be trusted. Lest one get too comfortable while trusting the regulators (in this case, the FDA), it's worth remembering that Oliver Wendell Holmes was attacked professionally and even personally by the respectable medical establishment of his time when he advocated certain changes (mainly, handwashing) in obstetrical procedure to prevent deaths due to puerperal fever. No one, of course, has a monopoly on wisdom. With this concept in mind, a brief comparison of some US ads with advertisements from selected countries will be presented.

The next three figures (Figures 9.1, 9.2, 9.3) present ads intended to lead the reader to conclude that US advertising might tend to be grossly misleading in the absence of existing regulations.

LOOSEN UP . . . WITH RHEUMOPYRINE®

RHEUMOPYRINE®

For the treatment of rheumatic disorders and
relief of pain in other conditions.

INGREDIENTS:
Coated tablets
Phenylbutazone 0.125g.
Aminopyrine   0.125g.

POLFA (NIGERIA) LIMITED
12 Market Street, P. O. Box 1556, Lagos, Nigeria

Figure 9.1 Nigerian advertisement for a combination prescription drug. *Source: African Journal of Pharmacy and Pharmaceutical Sciences* **2**:58 (April) 1973.

DOPAMET   SWIFTLY, SMOOTHLY LOWERS
Brand of
Methyldopa BP   BLOOD PRESSURE

WITHOUT POSTURAL EFFECTS

Dopamet lowers blood pressure by competing for the enzyme responsible for converting dopa to dopamine, thus reducing the amount of noradrenaline formed from dopamine, with the resultant lowering of blood pressure. Dopamet tablets contain the equivalent of 250 mg anhydrous methyldopa BP in packs of 50 & 100.
Further information on request
Biode Pharmaceutical Industries Ltd.
P.O. Box 3022
Mile 10¼ Ikorodu Road
Lagos, Nigeria

Figure 9.2 Nigerian advertisement for a brand of methyldopa. *Source: African Journal of Pharmacy and Pharmaceutical Sciences* **3**:84 (April) 1973.

"WARNING—THIS DRUG MAY CAUSE FATAL AGRANULOCYTOSIS.

"CAUTION: This drug should be used only in those conditions in which it is specifically indicated and in which other less toxic drugs have proved ineffective or are not tolerated. The potential benefit accruing from the use of this drug must be weighed against the possibility of fatal agranulocytosis.

"Indications for use. Aminopyrine and aminopyrine derivatives (dipyrone preparations) should be restricted to use for their antipyretic effect in serious or life-threatening situations where salicylates or similar drugs are known to be ineffective or are contraindicated or not tolerated.

"Duration of administration. Fatal agranulocytosis has been reported after short term use, intermittent use, and after long-term administration. Therefore, the use of these agents should be as brief as possible.

"Precautions. Frequent white blood cell and differential counts should be carried out. However, it is emphasized that agranulocytosis may occur precipitously without prior warning. The drug should be discontinued at the first evidence of any alteration of the blood count or sign of agranulocytosis, and the patient should be instructed to discontinue use of the drug at the first indication of sore throat or sign of other infection in the mouth or throat (pain, swelling, tenderness, ulceration.)

"Dosage. Adults: The usual antipyretic dose should not exceed ½ to 1 gram per dose, nor should more than 3 grams total daily dosage be used. If the desired effect is not achieved within a very few days, use of the drug should be discontinued.

"Children: 250 to 500 milligrams per dose, repeated in 3 to 4 hours if necessary. Use of the drug should be as brief as possible."

A quantitative statement of aminopyrine content plus certain other required information must be included.

Figure 9.3 Information content for US aminopyrine advertisement. *Source:* 21 *Code of Federal Regulations* 3.44.

Figures 9.1 and 9.2 are examples of ads for drugs (categorized as prescription drugs in the United States) for sale in Nigeria; vignettes have been deleted and the type size emphasizing the drug's trade name and indications appears as all capitals, in smaller type than in the original full-page (about 9 in. × 6½ in.) ads in a pharmacy journal. The most interesting feature of both ads is the relatively small amount of information presented; one is reminded of ads for nonprescription drugs on U.S. television. Note that no information is given about the dysfunctional effects of these drugs. Aminopyrine (Figure 9.1) is virtually banned in the United States because of its tendency to induce fatal blood dyscrasias. A U.S. label or ad for aminopyrine must contain the information listed in Figure 9.3 (24). Note that in the United States the drug is to be used only for serious or life-threatening situations. Experience with aminopyrine and similar unnecessarily hazardous substances has led to the formation of the International Association for Medical Assistance to Travelers (IMAT) to prevent undue risks to travelers from drugs (cf. reference 25). Comparable U.S. advertisements for phenylbutazone (popular U.S. trade name is Butazolidin), the other ingredient in rheumopyrine, and for methyldopa (Dopament in Figure 9.2) are not presented here due to space limitations.

A quick consultation in the index of a current or recent issue of *Physicians' Desk Reference* (26) will yield a copy of the required package insert for phenylbutazone. The reader will note that 2082 words are used to describe phenylbutazone, as contrasted with a total of about 30 words for the two ingredients of rheumopyrine in Figure 9.1. In all fairness it should be pointed out that only 634 words were used to describe phenylbutazone in the pre full disclosure volume of the PDR published in 1960 (27).

A note of caution is in order about drawing conclusions from drug advertisements. The approximately one billion dollars spent on drug advertising (this amount is equal to the cost of financing all the teaching activities of all the US Medical Colleges annually) purchases the talents of some of the most creative people in the United States (28). These people are increasingly highly skilled in the behavioral sciences. They know what their goals and objectives are. Even though the information content is supposed to be the same as that contained within the PI, it is obvious that additional information can be found in an ad. The point can be argued that use of colors, catchy phrases, thinly clad beautiful women, large or variable type size, or other additions to PI information exist merely to get the attention of the reader. The best way to determine whether medication ads add to or detract from PI information is to compare a current PI (or PDR entry) and an advertisement in a medical journal. Virtually any medical journal will contain about as many pages of medication ads as it does of editorial matter. Specific points of comparison should, of course, begin with a comparison of the basic PI categories in the ad and in the PI itself. Estimate the probability that a reader will peruse all of either document. Estimate the chances of a reader going beyond the largest type and the best done, most colorful illustrations. Which elements have the highest probability of being retained—the pictures, graphs, illustrations, bold type, small type, the one complete page of type, etc.? What are the relative chances that the trade name will be remembered rather than the established name? (The reader's estimate of the number of appearances of the trade name and of the established name is relevant here).

A study was commissioned by a large pharmaceutical company to determine the factors influencing the prescribing of erythromycin (29). After reading the summary referenced here, the reader should reconsider his opinion of drug advertisers. Do they know what they're doing? Is their money likely to be spent effectively? What is the quality of their educational activities versus those undertaken by the typical student in the health professions?

9.2.2 Dispensed Prescription Labeling Requirements

The requirements for labeling a prescription dispensed for a particular patient by a duly authorized, licensed prescriber (presently including physicians, osteopaths, podiatrists, dentists, veterinarians, and psychiatrists but excluding clinical psychologists, optometrists, and chiropractors) arise from an exemption provision in the Durham-Humphrey amendment to the FD&C Act (30). A prescription drug is exempted from the full disclosure information requirement if the label contains certain alternative information, i.e., a PI need not be provided with a dispensed legend drug if the required alternative information is contained on the label. The required information is listed in Table 9.4 together with that prescribed by other laws; suggested or desirable information is also listed.

Surprisingly, the law requires only directions for use, the patient's name, and applicable cautionary statements (31), if these items are stated in the prescription used as authorization to dispense the drug to a patient. This labeling requirement pertains to new, refilled, writ-

TABLE 9.4 COMPARISONS OF THE TYPE OF INFORMATION REQUIRED ON OVER-THE-COUNTER DRUG LABELING WITH THAT REQUIRED ON THE CONSUMER'S PERSONAL PRESCRIPTION PACKAGE

Type of Information	Drug Label Information[a]		
	a. Required for over-the-counter drugs	b. (1) Required for prescription drugs (consumer's package)	b. (2) Optional information physician may choose for prescription drugs
Identity of product	Name and address of manufacturer or distributor	Name and address of pharmacy	
	Established name* with or without trade name	Name of doctor prescribing	Trade or established name
		Prescription number	
	Names of active ingredients		
	Strength of each dosage unit for specified drugs		Strength of each dosage unit
	Quantity, kind, and proportion of any alcohol, and other specific ingredients		

How, when, how much, how often to take	Route of administration if not for oral use	Date of writing or original filling of prescription	Route of administration
	Suggested number of units per dose		Number of units per dose
	Suggested frequency of dose		Frequency of dose
	Suggested time to take		Time to take
	Suggested duration of use		Special directions for irregular use or "as needed"
Preparation for use	Directions for shaking, diluting, measuring, etc., as necessary		Necessary directions
Warnings and cautions	Wide variety of warning statements required by law (See 21 C.F.R. 369; 21 C.F.R. 330.1(g))		
For whom	Suggested age limitations, particularly for young children		Name of patient
	Contraindications for persons with certain physical problems		

[a] Only as described by federal statutes and regulations.

[b] Established name—the law authorizes FDA to establish simple, useful common or generic names for drugs.

Source: Adapted from the Food and Drug Administration, The Use and Misuse of Drugs, Superintendent of Documents, Washington, D.C., FDA publication #46, pamphlet, about, 1968, p. 9; see also 39 *F.R.* June 4, 1974, p. 19881.

ten, and oral prescriptions (32). Dispensing a drug contrary to the requirements that the prescription be authorized by a person licensed by law to administer the drug regardless of how it is labeled constitutes misbranding. (Reference 33 discusses the peculiar choice of the word administer when the meaning appears to be prescribing (27).) Refilling prescriptions is permitted only if a duly authorized person authorizes the refill. The exemption provision is not available for the misbranding portion of the act which requires that necessary special packaging and instructions for storage be provided for drugs especially liable to deterioration, e.g., nitroglycerin tablets and reconstituted antibiotics (34).

The lack of a requirement that the dispensed drug's lot number be recorded on the prescription or dispensed prescription label impedes tracing distribution. Thus, a pharmacist may be unable to identify which patients received drugs of a given lot number. This deficiency was removed by Medicare regulations (35) for Medicare patients; however, at the time of this writing, Medicare still did not pay for outpatient drugs. Drug recalls at the patient level are, fortunately, relatively rare. The United Mine Workers Union currently requires that prescriptions paid for under its insurance plan contain the diagnosis for which the drug is indicated. This notation is essential for the pharmacist to review a patient's drug regimen effectively and comprehensively.

The Controlled Substances Act (CSA) resulted in a change in the regulations to the FD&C Act which requires that a transfer statement (Table 9.5) appear on the label of any dispensed, controlled substance prescription (36). The absence of this statement results in misbranding of the dispensed drug. The individual responsible for separation of the controlled substance from the transfer statement would appear to be responsible for the misbranding.

The other information listed in Table 9.5 would facilitate the identification of a drug, the tracing of a drug's movement through its distribution channel, or the rational use of a drug by a patient. In child poisoning cases, for example, it is frequently a problem to identify prescription drugs because no name is on the drug label and the pharmacist cannot be reached for some reason. About 25% of consumers participating in a recent FDA survey indicated that they would like to see adverse reactions and cautions on prescription labels. In the same study about 33% of the participants indicated that they would like the drug's name on the label, and about 30% wanted the label to list the drug usage clearly, e.g., diuretic.

It is legal to put more than the minimum information on prescrip-

TABLE 9.5 DISPENSED PRESCRIPTION LABELING INFORMATION REQUIRED OR
SUGGESTED

---

1. {Name and address of dispenser} and registration number
2. {Serial number of prescription}[a]
3. {Date of Rx (initial filling}
4. {Name of prescriber}, address and registration number
5. {Name of patient} and address
6. {Directions for use}
7. {Cautionary statements,} if any
8. Dispenser's phone number
9. Name of drug[b]
10. Strength of drug
11. Manufacturer's control (lot) number[b]
12. Expiration date, if any
13. Name of person dispensing
14. Statement of refill status
15. Transfer statement[c]
16. Diagnosis, diagnostic code, or use
17. Special instructions for storage
18. Specific indication(s)
19. Name of manufacturer or trademark[b]
20. National Drug Code number

---

[a] Braces indicates Rx labeling requirements of CSA and FD&C Act except #15
is required only by the CSA; underlined items are optional under FD&C Act if
not specified in the prescription.
[b] Required by Medicare (20 CFR 405.1027).
[c] Required of Controlled Substances in Schedules 2, 3, 4, but not 5. Statement
reads: CAUTION: Federal Law prohibits the transfer of this drug to any
person other than the patient for whom it was prescribed. (21 C.F.R. 1.109).
Notes: 1. CSA—U.S. Controlled Substances Act.
2. CSA labeling requirements are generally duplicated by states
which have enacted a uniform Controlled Substances Act.
3. FD&C—U.S. Food, Drug and Cosmetic Act as amended.

tion labels, although pharmacists seem reluctant to do so. Eckerd's
Drugs, a large drugstore chain, has for some time had a policy that the
drug name be listed unless the prescriber states (presumably without
explanation) that the drug name is not to be listed. Both the trade
name and the established name should be listed. The proposed increase in the number of drugs with package inserts which can be given
to the patient may be the ultimate solution for providing more information to consumers. However, the experience from the debate surrounding provision of a patient PI with oral contraceptives teaches us

that organized medicine will oppose patient PIs, although individual physicians may support them. For a variety of reasons patients may not read labels or other instructional materials provided.

The tendency of patients not to abide by directions on labels suggests that changes are needed to promote rational drug therapy. The information supplied to a patient with a prescription appears to be an excellent candidate, as discussed at the beginning of this chapter.

9.2.3 Over the Counter Labeling Requirements

Section 9.2 described the meaning of "adequate directions for use" in considerable detail. Table 9.4 lists these requirements in summary form and contrasts them with drug label information requirements for the consumer's personal prescription package. Some points of interest include the lack of a requirement that a disclosure be made of what firm manufactured the drug, and the failure to require that a quantitative listing of a drug's ingredients be provided (except for certain drugs listed in the statute). After considerable debate and opposition by organized pharmacists to an initial ruling that OTC labeling carry the phrase saying in effect: "for more information, see a physician," but not contain the added phrase "or pharmacist" a significant change in OTC labeling was ordered (37,38). OTC labels must now contain the statement: "Keep this and all drugs out of the reach of children. In case of accidental overdose, seek professional assistance or contact a poison control center immediately."

9.2.4 Criticism of the Content and Access to Package Insert Information

The criticism of package inserts ranges from the view that since it is approved by the government it is totally unreliable to the view that since it is produced by the manufacturer it is totally biased, and vice versa. Some of the more important points made about the PI are:

1. It is more seen than read.
2. It is poorly organized.
3. It is repetitive and redundant.
4. It is advertising oriented instead of therapeutically oriented.
5. It need not contain relative efficacy information.

6. The incidence of adverse reactions is usually absent.
7. It is not current.
8. It excludes large blocs of potential patients through its warnings and precautions, e.g., Darvon was listed as contraindicated for pregnant women as late as the 1975 Edition of the PDR (39).

Its major strong point is that its information content is approved by a government agency (FDA) not only on the basis of the scientific publications about the drug, but also on the basis of a review of the raw data.

The foregoing criticisms all contain considerable truth. Although the PI is seen, the extent to which the PI message as an entity is perceived, read or studied is not clear. (Section 10.4.2). It does seem clear that changes are needed and the changes suggested (by means of an "informal" *Federal Register* notice) and first made public in 1974 ought to be welcomed by a broad base of the population (40). The criticism pertaining to excluding large blocs of potential patients will be considered first in some detail.

The problem of excluding large blocs of potential patients by means of PI labeling (especially by warnings, precautions, and dosage and administration sections) has become known as "therapeutic orphaning." This term is meant to convey that the absence of full disclosure information for some groups of people, especially children, deprives these people of the therapy available from a given drug. Just a superficial overview of PIs yields a large and varied number of phrases which may serve to produce a therapeutic orphan. Some of these phrases are:

1. Usage in children under 5 years of age is not recommended.
2. Not recommended for children under 3 because of the absence of clinical data with respect to safety and efficacy.
3. Administration to infants under 1 year of age is not recommended until additional data is available.
4. Dosage for children 2 years and younger has not been established.
5. Since clinical experience in children under 12 years of age is limited, use in this age group is not recommended.
6. Safety for use in the aged and debilitated has not been established.
7. For administration by the oral route only.
8. Do not administer when patient has been shown to be allergic to drug.
9. Contraindicated in senile patients.

10. Safety for use during lactation has not been established.

11. Contraindicated in women who may become pregnant.

The term "therapeutic orphan" is usually applied to children, but correctly describes anyone falling into an orphaning category. A therapeutic orphan is a person who is excluded from drug therapy available to others because orphaning clauses in the PI precludes this. The orphan patient must either participate in an unplanned experiment or do without the drug. For example, the comatose patient needing a drug whose safety has been proved by mouth only is *de facto* deprived of the use of the drug.

For children at least Lockhart has described cyclical factors that give rise to therapeutic orphans (41). She sees the cycle (depicted in Figure 9.4) as starting with a basic ethical reluctance to test drugs in children. The necessary data for showing "substantial evidence" of effectiveness in children are prevented from being produced. Drugs must be labeled to reflect the population characteristics of the subjects participating in various research phases; children are thus excluded on the basis of the labeling. Since they are excluded there is reluctance to use or test such drugs in children.

This progression (Figure 9.4) also holds true if the word "children" is substituted with terms such as "pregnant women," the "aged," or "debilitated."

The reluctance to test drugs in children is understandable. Investigating the effects of drugs in children carries a stigma that inhibits the drug manufacturer and the clinical investigator from conducting needed research; public opinion can be persuasive. Parents are also understandably reluctant to give their consent for a drug evaluation study involving their sick child, even if the need is understood. One can imagine the public outcry if drug evaluation studies were conducted using healthy volunteers in the pediatric group as required in phase I of the IND process, i.e., experimental drug usage for nontherapeutic purposes. Also it is questionable whether parents can, in certain situations, grant permission for drug testing in their children since the common law rights of minors are involved. Breese, in a respected medical text, recommends that office or home practice is preferable for pediatric research involving drugs (42). Nevertheless, litigation-wary physicians may be hesitant to undertake experimental use of drugs on pediatric patients. As a result of the efforts of the FDA and several medical pediatric organizations, proposals have been made to establish programs for determining drug safety and efficacy in children (43). At present, however, a user of a drug that is a therapeutic orphan for that type person (e.g., a child, a pregnant woman, a

Reluctance to test

drugs in children

Absence of data on drug

effects in children

Drugs are labeled to

exclude use in children

Results: therapeutic orphans

Figure 9.4 Cyclical factors giving rise to therapeutic orphaning.

person also taking tricyclic antidepressants) must undertake drug use on the basis of his own guess as to what the results will be. In Section 8.1.3 we have already seen some of the ethical problems of determining the adverse effects of chloramphenicol on children, and now we know that the deaths occur mainly because newborn infants lack the necessary glucuronide conjugation mechanism for metabolizing the drug. To date there is no clear-cut answer to this problem.

Some encouraging findings have been reported by Alexander (44) in his study of patients in a pediatric hospital. Many of the fears expressed have been based more on speculation and personal experience than on hard data. Alexander correctly cautioned the extrapolation of his data to larger populations, but there seems to be no compelling reason for his findings to be different from those that could be found in similar hospitals. Bias in his data would tend toward overstating the amount of orphaning. His study was concerned with the agreement of actual therapy with that described in PIs. Specifically, he compared the agreement between contraindications in the patient's medical record with those in the PI; the agreement between the age of the patient and the age, if any, specified in the PI (the "orphaning" age); and the actual dose given compared with the PI recommended dose. In each of these categories considerable agreement was reported. The agreement between each of the three PI categories is summarized

TABLE 9.6   PEDIATRIC PATIENTS "ORPHANED" BY CONTRAINDICATIONS, AGE RE-
STRICTIONS, AND DOSAGE REQUIREMENTS EXPRESSED AS DEGREE OF AGREEMENT
WITH PACKAGE INSERT SPECIFICATIONS

	Frequency	%
Contraindicated	8	0.9
Possibly contraindicated	29	3.3
Not contraindicated	843	95.8
Age not recommended	44	5.0
Age possibly not recommended	20	2.3
Age recommended	816	92.7
Ratio of actual daily dosage to package insert suggested dosage	880	1.1[a]

[a] Computed by dividing each patient's actual daily dosage by the package
insert suggested dosage and then computing the average for all patients. For
statistical reasons, the direction of this number was adjusted by subtracting 1
and taking the absolute value prior to averaging.
Source: V. L. Alexander: Relationship Between Manufacturer's Recommendations and Actual Drug Usage in the Pediatric Patient. Unpublished M.S.
thesis, University of Houston, Texas, 1972, p. 73, 74, 78.

in Table 9.6. (Note that the maximum clear-cut deviation for the first
two categories was 5%). Since this study involved the drug therapy of
200 patients receiving 880 different drugs, it seems reasonable to
believe that most important drugs were represented.

A study to develop guidelines for conducting therapeutic research
offers promise toward resolving some of the problems identified here.
Some of the ethical problems are likely to remain with us in the
foreseeable future. The new guidelines for conducting pediatric research will serve as a partial remedy for this important problem (61).
These include the provision that adequate studies be done in pediatric
patients before marketing approval is given; that tests be done only in
children who require treatment; that the test drugs be shown to be
reasonably safe and effective in adults before testing is done in children; and that labeling include a strong proscription against use in
children and pregnant women for drugs not studied in children.

Age and Recentness of Package Insert Information

It is easy to think and act as if we have established the truth about a
given drug or other referent, but one must recognize that virtually the
only basic truth of science lies in its method of producing information.

Just as one theory of the infectious process supplements another, so does new information replace or supplement existing information—to do otherwise would be most unscientific. Even aspirin is suspected of having an action heretofore unknown which seems, fortunately, functional for treating heart disease in that it may be effective for retarding myocardial infarction.

Another way of expressing the evolutionary nature of scientific and drug information is to say simply that once it is in print, the information is probably outdated. Clearly, PIs should be revised or reviewed frequently. The so-called "phase-4" of the IND, or simply the use of drugs in an increasing, more diverse population, tend to identify effects previously not matched with the drug. More effective dosages, additional routes of administration, additional dosage forms, and new indications are frequently identified after approval of an NDA. Information in a PI that pertains to dysfunctional effects of a drug may be added by a manufacturer if he chooses, without FDA approval. If a firm fails to include "negative information" pertaining to precautions, warnings, adverse reactions, or other information of a dysfunctional nature, the FDA may require its addition. The FDA's ultimate weapon is to withdraw an NDA if its labeling becomes defective. If a manufacturer desires to add information pertaining to new or additional indications, the firm must submit a supplemental NDA containing "substantial evidence" of the effectiveness and safety for use as suggested under the changed indications. Since the tendency is to use drugs outside the PI indications, the company has little incentive for undertaking the needed research because sales are made anyway.

Whether the FDA can compel a firm to add an indication to an already approved drug is an important question. The conclusion reached in published results of a conference about the PI in 1969 was that the FDA could not require such an addition (45). In 1972 a statement of FDA policy seemed to contradict and nullify the previous conclusion (46). This policy was specifically concerned with the use of approved drugs for unapproved purposes. So the context of this paragraph requires that the question be phrased in terms of whether the label for a drug already being employed for a nonapproved use must be revised to incorporate the new use, and whether the FDA can compel this act. In this more restricted instance the FDA apparently can compel addition of an indication. The FDA has three alternatives (46) (1) require a change in the labeling to warn against or to approve the unapproved use (after receipt of substantial evidence), (2) restrict the channels of distribution. (A recent Supreme Court case involving the FDA versus the American Pharmaceutical Association forbids restriction of distribution to only one type of pharmacist (47), and (3) withdraw approval of an NDA (and thus remove it from the market).

The FDA maintains that the regulations require the labeling to contain adequate information for effective and safe use of a drug for each and all intended uses of that drug. The Supreme Court decisions of June, 1973, strongly support the view held by the FDA on this matter. A key point is "intended use." If use occurs but was not intended by the manufacturer, there is little the FDA can do.

The lack of a relative efficacy requirement for comparing a given drug with a standard or other available drug will probably not be remedied until pharmaceutical and other technologies are able to produce the data necessary to substantiate such a requirement. Former FDA Commissioner Goddard has argued for such a requirement (48), and at least one significant bill introduced in Congress by Senator Nelson contained a relative efficacy provision (49). Currently, however, such a requirement remains remote and improbable. Indeed, the American Medical Association's second edition of its drug evaluations book (50) did considerable backtracking on its relative efficacy statements on drugs; the furor created by this issue allegedly resulted in the abolishment of the AMA's Council on Drugs. A relative efficacy requirement would be a significant step forward and would probably stimulate research, discovery, and development of significant new medications. Assessment of effectiveness would have to be precise for relative efficacy to be a constructive requirement.

Restrictions on Detailing Content and Publishing

In 1967 the question of FDA censorship of textbooks reached its peak when an incident involving drug dosage in an authoritative medical textbook surfaced. A textbook dose of 2 to 4 times that of the FDA-approved PI dose, caused a "therapeutic mishap," the death of an 8-year-old child (10, 51). The FDA met with invited representatives of the publisher, and the cry of censorship was long and loud. The result was the not surprising conclusion that an author of a textbook is free to express his opinion concerning a drug and that the FDA has no jurisdiction over textbooks and related material, since textbooks and similar items fall outside the definition of labeling. A reasonable author might prefer to list his deviation from the approved labeling and to explain his reasons for such a deviation. A defendant physician, pharmacist, or other provider might have to justify his deviation in a court (see Section 12.7).

A bill introduced by Senator Kennedy in 1974 and reintroduced in

1975 seems to require explicit control of the professional service representative's (detailman's) detail of a drug to a physician. There was at that time some question as to whether the full PI would have to be recited as part or all of a detail (52). Although the weight of information suggests that the new legislation was technically unnecessary, it does not eliminate all doubt. The Legislative Reference Service of the Library of Congress, seemed to say that yes, maybe the FD&C Act does give authority to control the content of the detail to a prescriber. A memorandum on this subject reads (53):

To: Senate Subcommittee on Antitrust and Monopoly (attention Mr. Gordon).
From: American Law Division.
Subject: Does Food and Drug Administration have authority over oral statements of drug manufacturer's representatives who contact physicians directly.

No specific authority is conferred on the Food and Drug Administration to deal with the matter in question. The Food and Drug Act deals, in pertinent part, with labels and labeling. A drug shall be deemed to be misbranded in several situations set forth in the law. See 21 U.S.C. § 352. We have located three court decisions involving prosecutions under the Food and Drug Act for oral representatives which apparently were misstatements respecting the product to which they relate. None of these, however, were concerned with statements to physicians. In U.S. v. Hohensee, 243 F. 2d 367 (1957) the evidence was sufficient to sustain the conviction of the defendant who subsequent to shipment of harmlessly labeled food products in interstate commerce to pre-arranged towns, went to such towns to give lectures and distribute literature promoting the use of such products to promote health. The case of Nature Food Centres, Inc. v. U.S., 310 F. 2d 67 held that defendants selling drugs identified on attached labels as dietary supplements could not meet branding requirements of the Federal Food, Drug and Cosmetic Act through sale of 'lecture notes' concerning the drugs where some of the drugs were destined for sale at stores where notes were not available and, even at halls where lectures were delivered and drugs were available, notes were obtainable only upon payment of additional price. In U.S. v. Article of Drug, etc., 362 F. 2d 923 the court held that the evidence supported the finding that the drug company claimant adopted as its own representation a radio broadcaster's claim that vitamins were efficacious for prevention and treatment of human disease, and that claimant intended its products to be used for general purposes recommended by broadcaster, as asserted by the government which charged misbranding in that claimant's catalogs failed to contain adequate directions for use.

These three cases involving oral statements would appear to have but limited application, if any, to the question presented. It seems to us that there is no clearly defined authority for the exercise of control by the Food and Drug Administration over oral statements of manufacturer's representatives to physicians in all situations.

On the other hand, William Goodrich (then) General Counsel to the FDA, stated unequivocally that the FDA does possess such authority, (54, 55). Regardless of the law, the important question of enforcement remains to be resolved. If the FDA's position is correct, the detailman's visit to the physician creates the paradoxical situation of a busy physician with little time for careful study of drug information being read to or listening to a recitation of a PI by a relatively less educated person who is frequently virtually a layman. There is also the questionable value derived by society from the average $15 spent by the drug manufacturer for the detailman's visit to the physician (56). Since the typical PI takes more than 7 minutes to read, an estimate of a minimum of 10 minutes for a recitation of a typical PI seems reasonable. In a study reporting on the number of minutes per detail, the time spent varied from a low of 4.6 minutes to a high of 30.4, with a median around 20 minutes depending on the physician's age and specialty (57). It appears that some older detailman do spend enough time with the physician to enable them to recite the PI. However for most physicians, if one drug is discussed, and all the time is used to describe drugs, then full oral disclosure may not only be possible but may actually occur. The situation created results in a too constrained time-frame; it may be that the detailman is disinclined to spend precious minutes, frequently gained after hours of waiting, in describing a drug's dysfunctional effects. He would most likely prefer to concentrate on functional drug effects. Available evidence, although meager, suggests that physicians are not as concerned as is warranted with dysfunctional effects.

9.3   INFORMATION CONTENT OF PROMOTIONAL COMMUNICATIONS

The FDA regulates the promotion of prescription drugs by declaring in effect that advertising and promotional information are labeling. The FDA has ruled that

Information for use contained in any promotional labeling for a prescription drug must be the same in language and emphasis as that contained in the labeling approved in the new drug application or the same as that contained in the labeling required for its certification (18).

This in effect means that an advertisement must contain a copy of the package insert.*

Studies of drug information sources used by physicians consistently show that the PDR (58) ranks near the top among the most frequently used sources of written drug information. Interestingly, the PDR has been held to contain labeling rather than advertising by one court (59). The same case involved the legality of paraphrasing rather than quoting the PI in the PDR. Although the court's opinion was that the paraphrasing in the contested instance was as accurate medically as the language of the PI, the foreword to the current PDR contains a statement to the effect that products described within the PDR meet the "same in language and emphasis" requirement using the PI verbatim, since the FDA interprets this phrase to mean verbatim (60). The PDR is distributed free to all practicing physicians in the country, and is sold for about $12 to others. Its distribution is paid for by the pharmaceutical companies who pay for the space for listing their products in the PDR.

All large, brand name companies are represented. The current PDR, which lists about 2600 products, consists mainly of the more frequently prescribed products of brand name companies. The PDR is arranged so that it is easy to use if the user can remember both the brand name and its manufacturer. The bulk of the PDR consists of an alphabetical listing of products by manufacturer and alphabetically by brand name under each manufacturer's name. (Brand name and trade name are used as equal in meaning). If the user remembers the brand name and manufacturer, he can locate the manufacturer (listed alphabetically in the main body of the PDR), then alphabetically locate the brand name which will identify the PI information. The PDR is organized so that several other ways of locating a listed drug can be used all of which involve additional steps if the manufacturer and brand name cannot be recalled. These include a section with color pictures of popular drugs, their brand names, and dosages. These pictures serve to aid the user (mainly the physician) in identifying a product and probably in discussing a drug which he or she has not seen. (Drug sampling usually resolves this problem.) There is no index per se to specific actions desired, although there is a broad index of major therapeutic categories that can lead one to a specific trade name and specific page number for it. The AMA's *Drug Evaluations* (50) is apparently the only drug information publication to carry such an index; however, it is not classified as advertising but as a textbook/reference book.

* In this context PI is used to mean the minimum labeling necessary to meet FDA requirements.)

While the PDR is clearly a promotional device, and a collection of PIs, it may be regarded in surveys of drug information sources as a recognized drug compendium. Indeed, the PDR and the PI may be categorized separately. Physicians have been known to remark that PIs are not reliable sources of drug information since they represent "company propaganda," whereas the PDR serves as a reliable source of drug information. (The use of various drug information sources is treated in greater depth in section 10.4.2.)

Prescription drug advertising is big business, and expenditures for advertising exceed $1 billion annually (28). It seems reasonable to believe that advertising is done to match a company's drug with the conditions for which it is indicated. A less charitable view would be that the purpose is to secure sales and let the disease and indications watch out for themselves. Advertising may cause some of the problems attributed to it by its critics. However, to single out advertising as the sole reason for some of the problems of medication use is to use energy and resources improperly that could more profitably be devoted to other problem areas. To avoid this temptation, it is necessary to scrutinize the statutory and regulatory bases for control of drug promotion and advertising. Countries that allow little or no advertising seem to have problems similar to ours. Underusage of such an important drug as Rho-GAM (a preventer of erythroblastosis fetalis in infants) and most of the antihypertensive drugs, as well as a curtailed therapy period for antibiotics, serves to raise interesting questions. Although one may believe that more than $1 billion spent in advertising is enough, the facts do not all support either a pro or con position. More definitive information is needed.

ACKNOWLEDGMENT

I am indebted to Vance L. Alexander for his contribution to this chapter.

REFERENCES AND GUIDE TO FURTHER STUDY

1. Food and Drug Administration: National Drug Code Directory, June, 1974, U.S. Government Printing Office, Washington, D.C., 1974.
2. Stein, J. (Ed.): *Random House Dictionary of the English Language,* unabridged Ed., Random House, New York, 1971, p. 728.
3. Title 21, *Code of Federal Regulations,* 125.1(e).
4. 22 *Federal Register,* November 31, 1957, p. 9593.

5. Competitive Problems in the Drug Industry, Hearings before the Senate Committee on Competitive Problems in the Drug Industry, Part 13, July 16, 29, 30; Oct. 27, 1969, U.S. Government Printing Office, Washington, D.C., 1969, p. 5344–5354.

6. U.S. Department of Health, Education and Welfare, Drug Information Services: *Two Operational Models*, U.S. Government Printing Office, Washington, D.C., about 1972, p. 2.

7. American Journal of Nursing Company: The Nurse and Drugs Administered in Hospitals, *Medical Marketing and Media* **9**(6):13–23 (June) 1974.

8. Office of Health Economics, Medicines in the 1990's: A Technological Forecast. In Stimson, G. V.: *Obeying Doctor's Orders: A View from the Other Side*, Social Science and Medicine **8**:104, 1974.

9. Goddard, J.: FDA Papers, *Clinical Pharmacology and Therapeutics*, **8**:753 (July–August) 1967.

10. Modell, W., FDA Censorship, *Clinical Pharmacology and Therapeutics* **8**:361 (May–June) 1967.

11. 21 *U.S. Code*, 352(k, m).

12. 21 *U.S. Code*, 352(f).

13. Title 21, *Code of Federal Regulations*, 1.106(a).

14. Title 21, *Code of Federal Regulations*, 1.106.

15. 21 *U.S. Code*, 503(b)(1)(i).

16. Title 21, *Code of Federal Regulations*, Parts 1, 3.

17. *Federal Register*, April 7, 1975, Labeling for Prescription Drugs used in Man, p. 15392–15399.

18. 33 *Federal Register*, October 8, 1968 and Title 21, *Code of Federal Regulations*, 1.106(b)(4)(i).

19. 21 *U.S. Code* 352(n).

20. Title 21, *Code of Federal Regulations*, 1.105.

21. Title 21, *Code of Federal Regulations*, 1.106(b)(4).

22. Title 21, *Code of Federal Regulations*, 1.105(e)(3)(ii).

23. Title 21, *Code of Federal Regulations*, 1.105(k).

24. Title 21, *Code of Federal Regulations*, 3.44.

25. Rx for Travelers, *Newsweek* **84**(6):73 (August 5) 1974.

26. *Physicians' Desk Reference*, 29th ed., Medical Economics, Inc., Oradell, N.J., 1975, p. 797.

27. *Physicians' Desk Reference*, 14th ed., Medical Economics, Inc., Oradell, N.J., 1960, p. 677.

28. Rucker, T. D.: Economic Problems in Drug Distribution *Inquiry* **9**(3):44 (September) 1972.

29. Market Research Summary of Physicians' Attitudes Toward Antibiotics, Competitive Problems in the Drug Industry, Part 22, May 9, 10, June 21, July 19, 1972, U.S. Government Printing Office, Washington, D.C., 1972, p. 8727–8731.

30. 21 *U.S. Code*, 353.

31. 21 *U.S. Code*, 353(b)(2).

32. 21 *U.S. Code*, 353(b)(1).

33. De Marco, C. T.: The Legal Basis for Clinical Pharmacy Practice, *American Journal of Hospital Pharmacy* **30**(11):1070 (November) 1973.

34. 21 *U.S. Code*, 352(L).

35. Title 20, *Code of Federal Regulations*, 405.1027.

36. Title 21, *Code of Federal Regulations*, 1.109.

37. 39 *Federal Regulations*, June 4, 1974, p. 19881.

38. Title 21, *Code of Federal Regulations*, 330.1(g).

39. *Physicians' Desk Reference*, 29th ed., Medical Economics, Inc., Oradell, N.J., p. 875.

40. 39 *Federal Register*, March 7, 1974, p. 8946.

41. Lockhart, J. D.: The Information Gap in Pediatric Drug Therapy, *FDA Papers* **4**:6–9 (February) 1971.

42. Breese, B. B.: Experimentation in Clinical Pharmacology in Private Practice. In Shirkey, H. C. (Ed.): *Pediatric Therapy*, 3rd ed., C. V. Mosby, St. Louis, 1968, p. 52–80.

43. Proceedings, Conference on Pediatric Pharmacology, U.S. Department of Health, Education and Welfare, Washington, D.C., 1967, p. 4.

44. Alexander, V. L.: *Relationship Between Manufacturer's Recommendations and Actual Drug Usage in the Pediatric Patient*. Unpublished M.S. thesis, University of Houston, Houston, Texas, 1972.

45. Adriani, J. (Chairman), AMA Council on Drugs: Notes on the Package Insert, *Journal of the American Medical Association* **207**:1335–1338 (February 17) 1969.

46. 37 *Federal Register*, August 22, 1972, p. 16877.

47. United States District Court for the District of Columbia: *Journal of the American Pharmaceutical Association* NS **14**(8): 400–403 (August) 1974.

48. Stolley, P. D. and Goddard, J. L.: A "Relative Efficacy" System for New Drugs, *Annals of Internal Medicine* **73**(3):479–480 (September) 1970.

49. Omnibus Drug Act, Senate Bill 2812, 92nd Congress, 1st Session, November 4, 1971.

50. American Medical Association Council on Drugs: *AMA Drug Evaluations*, Volume 2, American Medical Association, Chicago, 1973.

51. Goddard, J. L.: FDA Papers, *Clinical Pharmacology and Therapeutics* **8**:753 (July–August) 1967.

52. Drug Utilization Improvement Act, Senate Bill 3441, 93rd Congress, 2nd Session, May 6, 1974.

53. Competitive Problems in the Drug Industry, Hearings before the Senate Subcommittee on Competitive Problems in the Drug Industry, Part 8, May 2, 3, Sept. 17, 1968, U.S. Government Printing Office, Washington, D.C., 1968, p. 3517.

54. Competitive Problems in the Drug Industry, Part 8, *ibid.*, p. 3481.

55. Competitive Problems in the Drug Industry, Hearings before the Senate Subcommittee on Competitive Problems in the Drug Industry, Part 9, Sept. 18, 19, 25, 1968, U.S. Government Printing Office, Washington, D.C., 1968, p. 3559.

56. Hess, S. W.: Communicating With Physicians, *Journal of Advertising Research* **14**(1):17 (February) 1974.

57. Hess, *ibid.*, p. 17.

58. Opinion Research Corporation, *Physicians' Attitudes toward Drug Compendia*, Opin-

ion Research Corporation, Princeton, N.J., July, 1968 (also see 10.4.2 and references).

59. Martin, E. W. (Ed.): *Hazards of Medication,* J. B. Lippincott Company, Philadelphia, Pa., 1972, p. 99.

60. Baker, C. E. (Ed.): *Physician's Desk Reference,* 29th ed., Medical Economics, Oradell, N.J., 1975, foreword.

61. Report to Food and Drug Administration, American Academy of Pediatrics, in Werble, W. (Ed.): *FDC Reports* 36(45): T and G 8 (November 11) 1974.

CHAPTER TEN

How Drug Information
Is Used

*It is not what you say to people that counts, it
is what you have them do (1).*

Earlier the point was made that drug information is a necessary means
to rational drug use.* Chapters 7 and 8 considered how drug information is produced, acquired, verified, recorded, and disseminated. Here
the ways in which drug information is used are described, with attention focused on both prescription and nonprescription drugs.

Drug information retrieval has been defined as the act of getting
answers to questions about a selected drug product, given a set of
actions desired from the drug. An average drug is described in approximately 1400 words, about the equivalent of five double-spaced,
typed pages. Thus, about 1000 such pages would be needed to describe the top 200 drugs. When we consider that many of these drugs
are available in several dosage forms, strengths, and dosage ranges, it
seems formidable just to remember these data. How is a drug information retriever able to define, analyze, develop, select, execute, and
evaluate the relevant drug information for a given medically deviant
condition? The answer is: with difficulty. To remember only the dosage requirement for each of the top 200 prescription drugs, with only
one fact to match to each name, some 200 discrete facts would have to
be memorized. Since enormous amounts of money have been spent to
produce information that will be seen and may be read, it seems
reasonable to use this information in a manner that best achieves the
objectives sought from the application of drug information. Since a

* Even for irrational uses a number of items of information must be known, e.g., that it
exists, a method of administration, rough dosage estimate, etc.

favorable risk/benefit relationship generally predicts a successful drug experience, it seems reasonable to focus on the how of communicating.

Optimally, all the full-disclosure information should be considered for each drug issuance. Available data suggest, however, that there is not enough time to consider adequately the relevant drug information. The average physician spends only about 4.5 minutes with each patient. A minimum of about 7 minutes is required simply to read the PI for diazepam (Valium), the most prescribed drug in the country (3). The average time for reading the average PI is probably longer than 7 minutes. Available information suggests that pharmacists and nurses also do not read the PI for each drug issuance they process. Clearly, an alternate, more rapid procedure is used by these providers. Possible procedures that are or can be used by providers will be explored here. Consideration will be given to eliciting questions necessary for acquisition and processing of optimum drug information.

10.1 GOALS SOUGHT FROM DRUG INFORMATION USE

The objective sought from the use of drug information can be described as minimization of patient morbidity or mortality. The best match between an indicated drug and a medically deviant condition is the immediate goal of therapy. The principal shortcoming of such statements, aside from the difficulty of their quantification, is that they yield little in directing the actual use and application of the relevant drug information. A more detailed analysis is essential of subgoals, and sub-subgoals, etc., until a goal is reached which leads to explicit direction on how to use relevant information. A suitable ending point must be identified because one arrives at the point of saying, for example, that the information to be read from a drug label must be turned right side up. The level where one should stop has been defined as "the smallest unit of performance which can be identified as having a distinct and independent purpose" (4).

Figure 10.1 depicts a dynamic model of how drug information is related to treatment outcome. The model assumes that drug information will be used to influence action, that since all information cannot be communicated selection must occur, and that one needs to know only selected information. A major influence on the way drug information is used is suggested by depicting information as being processed or ordered to fit the perspective of the receiver. The receiver is seen as

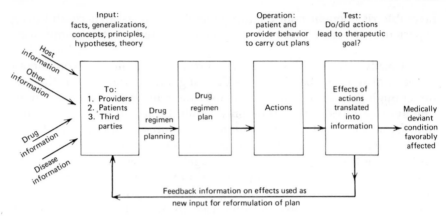

Figure 10.1.   A model of how drug information is related to treatment outcome. Patient and provider behavior incorporate some social components of behavior as listed in Section 10.2.

having stored certain facts, generalizations, concepts, principles, and theory, and as capable of employing these facts toward guiding his thinking to the point of formulating a drug regimen plan. This plan will consist of a set of instructions addressed to both patient and provider, premade decisions which order the behavior sequence in relation to the goal to be achieved. The decisions implicit in the plan are only tentative and are subject to modification by feedback information. Prescription drugs were defined earlier in terms of whether they could be properly labeled to be used safely by the layman. It appears that the layman's inadequacy lies mainly in deficiencies within the facts, generalizations, concepts, and principles components of Figure 10.1: he is not properly "programmed." To a lesser extent, he is also limited in his ability to select information for input and to translate actions into information congruent with that derived from other sources.

In one sense the most distinguishing aspect of the Input component of Figure 10.1 is the extent of programmed capability present in the decision-maker. This idea can be used to advantage to differentiate prescription drugs from nonprescription drugs more clearly. An analogy can be drawn between processing numbers in multiplication and processing drug information, where the knowledge of the multiplication tables corresponds to the facts, generalizations, concepts, principles, and theory of drug information use. The parallel conclusion to be drawn is that one who does not know the analogous drug information process cannot multiply numbers when they are provided, and thus cannot rationally use drug information when it is provided. The layman does not know enough to understand the PI. Complicating the analogy may be the knowledge that the answer obtained is or is not correct in multiplication, whereas the processor of drug information may erroneously arrive at an answer, i.e., a benefit/risk decision. He may believe false information to be true and, may not even suspect that his information is incorrect.

Science is concerned with prediction. Drug information use is also concerned with achieving a certain desired outcome. Plans and, when implemented, actions are goal directed. All these statements are similar in that prediction and production of certain effects rests upon an assumed set of conditions. A drug regimen plan states a relation between actions sought from a drug and a set of conditions. For example, controlling diabetes with insulin rests on the condition that the insulin be injected intramuscularly. Conditions are usually numerous, complex, and frequently overlooked.

Consider a person starting a car. The driver predicts that the turning of the ignition key will set up an electric circuit, which will cause the gas and air mixture in the cylinders to burn rapidly to produce energy that will result in the rotation of the wheels. The car will not start unless a set of conditions is met. These include adequate gasoline, adequate air, a functioning battery, a switch key, proper connection of mechanical parts, etc. Failure to meet these conditions will affect the car's performance. Recollection of the sum total of knowledge required to make a car (mechanical and electrical system, mostly) of today's quality will convince one that the example is not trivial. Cars are usually started on the basis of personal decisions rather than technical ones. A similar view can be taken for making the decision to use drugs; this is explored in Section 11.2.

Drug use plans are similar to the foregoing reasoning in principle. They are a mechanism to be used for the accomplishment of a therapeutic objective. Unfortunately such plans are not as reliable as the car starting plan for a number of reasons, the most fundamental being the level of medical and social complexity involved. Our knowledge of drugs is not as extensive or precise as our knowledge of the electrochemical and mechanical systems of cars. Unfortunately, we seem to be less aware of our ignorance about drugs than we are of our lack of knowledge about cars, although both are items with which most people have contact every day. A second problem is that drug use plans are comparably deficient. Action based on less than perfect knowledge is the only choice available; mankind would be immobilized otherwise. Performance should be based on the best available information at the time the decision is made rather than at some time in the future when more information has been produced. The

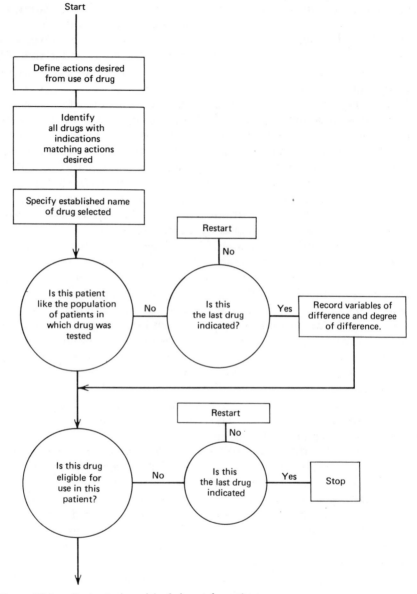

Figure 10.2.   Conceptual model of drug information use.

decision to treat newborn infants with chloramphenicol was a good decision in 1949; today such a choice would be an atrocity. Obviously, the difference lies in the change in the information base.

With the foregoing as an introduction, a model for a drug regimen

Figure 10.2   (*continued*)

plan will be presented that incorporates all the full-disclosure information in the PI. It is an elaboration of the drug information, drug
regimen planning, and drug regimen plan components of Figure 10.1.
The model (Figure 10.2) and its description are premised upon an
educational base described in part by the Input component of Figure

Figure 10.2 (*continued*)

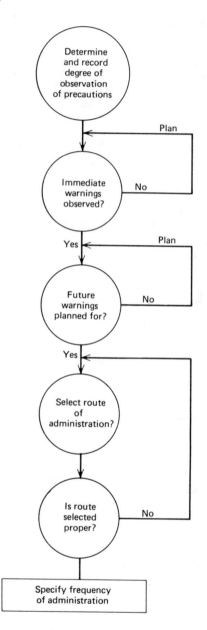

Figure 10.2 *(continued)*

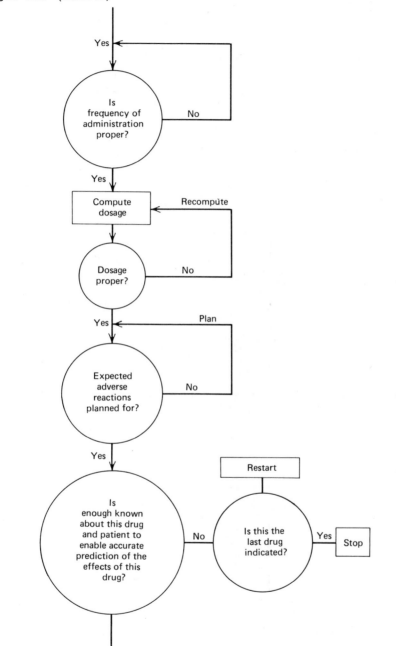

Figure 10.2 (*continued*)

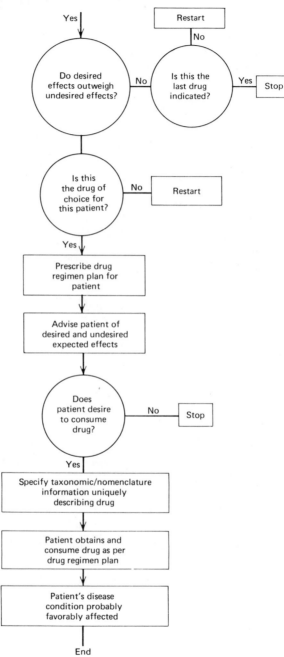

10.1 and the model depicted by Figure 10.1 as a whole. A detailed analogy to an everyday experience using an enormous information base is presented to illustrate the possibility of coping with a rapidly increasing drug information base. While the analogy is lengthy and has all the logical shortcomings inherent in the use of analogies, a careful reading should prove instructive and meaningful.

10.2   A DECISION MODEL FOR PROCESSING DRUG INFORMATION

Smith (5) has listed and described in detail the medical and social components essential to rational drug use. They are:

1. Optimum drug information.
2. Correct diagnosis.
3. Incentives for good prescribing and sanctions for poor prescribing practices.
4. Elimination of client control of the professional aspects of medical practice.
5. Acceptance (when appropriate) of the do-nothing approach to getting well.
6. Efficient division of health care labor.
7. Elimination of social selection of patients.
8. Elimination of nonessential intervention by third parties.
9. Better education in drug use for the consumer.

Here the focus is on only the first component, i.e., the use of optimum drug information in treating diseases with drugs. The position is that rational use of drug information is necessary, but not sufficient condition for rational drug use.

10.2.1   Organization of Drug Information

Careful attention to the organization of drug information will point the way toward an improved process for using drug information in disease treatment. The regulations of the US FD&C Act recommend that the information describing drugs be presented in a prescribed fashion within distinct categories. These categories, regrouped and placed within three major categories (Section 8.1) are:

A. Information describing the effects of a drug; these effects may be functional or dysfunctional.
B. Taxonomic/nomenclature information.
C. Procedural information describing how a drug is to be administered and manipulated.

Primary emphasis is on the first category because of the need to predict correctly the effects on an intended recipient. The second is also vital, however, because this type of information may be essential to locating the first type. When a drug is selected, emphasis will shift to the third category. Information in this category allows manipulation of certain variables (e.g., route of administration) which can vitally influence the effects ultimately experienced by the recipient.

10.2.2 Prescribing as Drug Regimen Planning

The prescription of a drug is best viewed as a multicomponent process. Rather than a drug being prescribed, a drug regimen plan is prescribed that must take into account the information in the preceding categories. As with any plan, the objectives toward which actions are to be directed must be identified. In a nutshell this objective is to produce a best match between a specific quantity of a drug and the patient's disease; ultimately, contact between specific cell receptors and drug molecules is desired. The information making up the host data set and its interrelationship with the information comprising the disease data set define patient signs and symptoms. These signs and symptoms determine the actions sought from use of a drug. Actions desired defines the information with which one enters the conceptual model of drug information use shown in Figure 10.2.

The indications and contraindications information for a drug entity are necessary to select a drug that will yield a functional match between the patient's disease and the drug selected. The prescriber's role consists primarily of planning the drug therapy regimen. This includes selecting a drug with the desired indications and not being contraindicated. Appropriate precautions and warnings must be taken into account in the drug regimen planning and in the actions and operations executed based on the plan. Likewise, the planning must include specification of the correct drug name, its route, frequency of administration, and dosage.

When the drug therapy regimen plan has been precisely specified, it must be directed and controlled. Ordinarily the physician is involved in the execution of these functions only to the extent required by relevant precautions and warnings. He will, for example, be responsible for periodic blood monitoring and, will usually direct the termination of the planned drug regimen. Nurses and laboratory technicians frequently perform the tasks necessary for observation of warnings and precautions.

In contrast, the pharmacist's dominant role at present in the management of the drug therapy regimen plan is only to a limited extent that of planning, although he frequently initiates termination of the plan. His primary involvement is with directing and controlling the drug therapy regimen. He is vitally and significantly responsible for setting forces in action so that the resources available to offset the patient's diesease condition are utilized to achieve the best match between the patient's specific disease and the uniquely described drug entity. Key activities include coordination of pharmacist and nursing staff activities and delegation of duties to others to execute the drug regimen plan strategy; this is equally true for outpatient and inpatient medication usage. Control of the drug regimen plan refers to ensuring the patient's progress toward the ultimate objective of the plan, improved health status. The pharmacist must determine if performance of involved persons, including the patient, conforms with the established attributes of the drug regimen plan. If performance is not in accord with the plan, the pharmacist must report this to the attending physician or to the patient, or take other appropriate action to insure achievement of the objectives of the drug therapy regimen plan. Figure 10.2 lists topically other relevant information components and depicts their interrelationships.

10.2.3   Applying Information to Patient Treatment

The application of this relevant information describing the effects of a drug involves its processing by the prescriber and others so that it becomes knowledge. Therefore the information must be processed in such a fashion that the medical deviance of the patient is affected in a positive manner.

10.2.4 Matching a Drug with a Disease

The prescriber appears to follow a two-path process in selecting a drug for disease treatment. One of these processes simply involves the establishment of a habit: upon encountering a particular disease entity, the prescriber automatically selects from memory and prescribes a drug which is prematched with the disease. His habit is a conditioned response acquired from the other pathway, which involves a cognitive process. The prescriber uses the cognitive process by first transposing the diagnosis to a list of actions desired. He then arrays all indications for all drugs into a vector. He must then make a match between the transposed diagnosis (actions desired) vector and the equivalent information statement in the indications section of the drug information being used. He uses the indications category of drug information for definition of the drug information domain relevant to indications. For all drugs that have an indication that matches a transposed diagnosis vector element a possible candidate for prescribing emerges.

Prescribing is always a "go" or "no-go" decision. When the prescriber has ascertained that a drug is indicated, the question arises: Are any of these indicated drugs contraindicated? If the answer is yes, then some other treatment must be sought that must consist of an alternate drug or procedure. The processing of the remaining drug information that should be considered in prescribing a drug treatment regimen is depicted by the interrelationships of the components in Figure 10.2.

10.3 GUIDANCE IN AVOIDING OVERUSE OF STRICT MEMORY LEARNING

Based on the technological revolution and its accompanying information explosion, both of which seem to have no end in sight, it seems that attempting to teach providers or consumers to know or remember much drug information would result in little information retention. Toffler's *Future Shock* suggests that not only does learning not occur to the desired extent, but that much forgetting and distortion also occurs (6). Relying on memory for drug information has at least four major weaknesses (1) the rate of forgetting is rapid, (2) being able to remember or recognize information does not necessarily represent understanding, (3) time and effort expended in committing information to memory and learning to recognize information detracts from time available for other kinds of learning, and (4) information stored and recalled or recognized is subject to distortion.

Most psychological studies, one's everyday experiences, and the very existence of libraries (information storehouses) suggest that these weaknesses of memory are pervasive. It seems clear that humans are very poor at information storage, whereas machines, books, and other media excel at information storage. However, humans do excel at higher order information processing tasks. This includes virtually all but the first kinds of learning listed in the next section. An everyday example of coping with large quantities of information by concentrating on concepts and principles rather than isolated facts will be described.

10.3.1 Kinds of Learning

Learning by consumers and health professionals may manifest itself in one or more of seven different forms. When expressed in terms of types of learning or things to be learned, these are (7):

1. *Memory*. Recollection or recognition of information.
2. *Translation*. Changing information into a different symbolic form or language.
3. *Interpretation*. Discovering relationships among facts, generalizations, definitions, values, and skills.
4. *Application*. Solving a lifelike problem that requires identification of the issue and selection and use of appropriate generalizations and skills.
5. *Analysis*. Solving a problem with conscious knowledge of the parts and forms of thinking.
6. *Synthesis*. Solving a problem that requires original, creative thinking.
7. *Evaluation*. Making a judgment of good or bad, right or wrong, according to standards designated by a judge.

10.3.2 Interrelationships of Kinds of Learning

The seven forms of learning and thinking described previously do not exist in a vacuum. The categories are not clearly differentiated: their theoretical development is incomplete. There is considerable overlap among any two or more categories. It may be possible for a patient who needs drug information to receive the written information with a minimum expenditure of time and money on the part of the patient and the providers. If this is so, then skills at a higher level than memory would be needed in order to process the information to make patient drug consumption a rational process. Ultimately the provider must judge whether it is the correct therapy for the patient's needs and, probably of major importance, whether the benefit from using the drug will outweigh the risks encountered. The patient (at least theoretically) must concur with the provider's conclusions (see "Does patient desire to consume drug?" in Figure 10.2). "Application" would be the category of thinking or learning most cogent and relevant for making this kind of judgmental decison. Such an application would require some elements of memory, translation, and interpretation. It usually is unnecessary for the drug information user to employ the higher order categories of thinking or learning for drug therapy purposes.

10.3.3   Further Elaboration on Kinds of Learning

The definitions previously discussed do not and cannot convey the full meaning of these terms. Within each classification level, information of either a simple or complex nature may be learned. For example, both remembering the generic name for a given drug trade name and remembering the biophysical processes of insulin secretion by the pancreas represent examples of the memory level of learning.

The seven kinds of learning are all essential, since each level is a prerequisite for learning at higher levels. After futher explanation of the meaning of memory,* it will be clearer that the memory level of learning can be reduced considerably from its present levels. The elements of memory learning are facts, definitions, generalizations, values, and skills. Facts represent knowledge acquired from direct observation or other knowledge that is noncontroversial, and they serve many roles in drug use. Some facts are important in themselves, e.g., penicillin is available in many forms, allowing for ingestion or injection as needed. The most important role of facts is to provide the building blocks for generalizations and principles, e.g., for most drugs there is some dose that is optimum for a given patient and disease.

---

* Memory, as used here, has the same meaning as remembering, recalling, or recognizing information.

Definitions are the designated meaning of words. For example, "onycholysis" is the word assigned to the set of stimuli describing the observation of fingernails and toenails which have been loosened or separated from their beds.

A generalization is a statement that declares the common characteristics of a group of drugs or ideas about drugs. For example, a generalization is the statement that the correct dose of a drug is just enough to yield the effects desired, but not enough to produce intolerable, undesired effects.

A value is a statement of the "goodness" or "badness" of something. A value judgment is the use of a value in determining the quality of an idea or act. A common value judgment is that the treatment of disease with drugs is good.

The most valuable kinds of memory are those represented by definitions, generalizations, and values. Such knowledge is usually most important in drug use. In addition, it has been shown that these kinds of learning, in contrast to the learning of facts per se, are retained longest and are more likely to be recalled when needed.

10.3.4   Use of the Telephone Directory: An Analogous, Practical Application of Ideas

Clearly, there is an enormous amount of information that is relevant to the use of a telephone and a telephone directory. There are over 130 million telephone subscribers grouped within several thousand directories which serve as storehouses for millions of facts. A phone user could profit from a careful study of a number of aspects of telephone technology. These could include, for example, a careful study of the physical and chemical aspects of telephone equipment, the history of phone directories, the management of phone companies, and the information processing necessary to update a phone directory. One could also teach students of telephone directory use the names of subscribers and their corresponding phone numbers, area codes and their derivation, etc. A potential user might have to enroll in a university School of Phone Directory Use (SPDU) to master this information.

An alternate approach would be to focus learning on concepts, generalizations, principles, and processes. Figure 10.3 depicts making a phone call in a stepwise fashion. Note that the emphasis is on the processing of information. Reflective thinking about telephone and telephone directory usage will produce a number of principles and

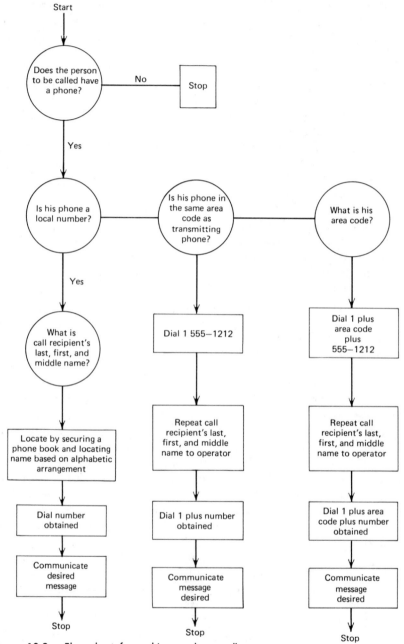

Figure 10.3.   Flow chart for making a phone call.

underlying assumptions relevant to the use of these items. Some of these concepts, principles, and generalizations are as follows:

1. A telephone is a device for talking to people when the parties are too far apart to talk in person.
2. Any telephone can be used to communicate with any other telephone, given certain knowledge.
3. Each phone is assigned a unique number.
4. A phone rings to indicate that somebody wants to talk with the person who is usually near (within hearing distance of) the phone.
5. To place a call one must (a) locate a phone (b) ascertain by the sound that is emitted if the phone is in use (c) select the number of the phone to be rung (d) communicate the number to the receiving phone through the use of the sending phone.
6. The telephone directory contains the numbers that correspond to particular phones.
7. Phone subscribers' names are listed in a logical order.
8. A subscriber's name identifies the number that will ring his phone and only his phone.
9. The method for ordering names in the phone directory is alphabetical.
10. One must memorize and be able to recall and recognize the alphabet in order to locate a desired name.
11. Names are arranged as follows: last, first and middle.
12. The last name is the primary name for arranging alphabetically.
13. The alphabetizing of the last name is sequential with first letter first, second letter second, third letter third, etc., to the last letter of the name. In the event of subscribers with identical last names, the first name is alphabetized, then the second name is alphabetized. "Ties" can be "broken" based on street address if known.
14. Phone directories contain the names and numbers of subscribers within a defined geographic area, usually a city or suburban area.
15. An area code is assigned to each city or other geographic area.
16. One can either locate a number himself or ask for assistance from a person who will select the number desired.
17. An operator is available at all times for assistance in locating numbers.
18. A special number, usually 411, must be dialed to get an operator's assistance.
19. One must know the name (first, last, and maybe middle) of a

subscriber to get operator assistance, because she uses the same process as described above for locating a number.

20. By dialing the number 1, the proper area code and 555-1212 one may ask the subscriber's number of an operator.
21. One must usually speak English to an operator.

10.3.5 Role of Principles in Phone and Drug Usage

In addition to the previous statements, reflective thinking also quickly yields an idea of the enormous amount of information represented by the various phone directories serving this country's 130 million phone subscribers. Yet it is necessary to remember or recognize only a trifling percentage of the total information in existence about telephone usage in order to utilize this modern day technological tool intelligently. Although most people know very little, if anything, about the physics of phone circuitry, this ignorance hardly impedes phone usage.

Analogous means can be employed to cope with our increasingly complex drug information base. Although it would be ludicrous to suggest that prescribing a drug regimen is as simple as using a phone, it is undeniable that an analogy exists. Phones and drugs differ largely in complexity. A phone is a technologically sophisticated device. A drug is a no less sophisticated device. The phone directory contains information essential to rational phone use. Relevant drug information sources (e.g., *Physicians' Desk Reference, American Hospital Formulary Service, AMA Drug Evaluations 1973, US Pharmacopeia, National Formulary*) contain information essential to rational drug use.

The theme here is that it is no more absurd to attempt to memorize the phone directory or directories than to attempt to memorize relevant drug information. Just as the time has passed when one could reasonably recall phone numbers used, the time has also passed when one could remember drug information reliably.

Just as was true for the flow chart in Figure 10.3 describing the process for making a phone call, many terms, concepts, generalizations, and principles must be learned before relevant drug information can be rationally processed according to the process described in Figure 10.2. Coping with the entire domain of relevant drug information also requires learning at the translation and interpretation levels, since the signs and symptoms of a patient's disease conditions must be transposed to match relevant drug information. Moreover, the interpretation level is necessary in order to select the appropriate generalizations and skills. Since a decision can always be made to prescribe no drug, evaluation learning must occur in order for a drug to be prescribed. Similarly, if more than one drug is indicated for treating a patient, then evaluation is necessary in order to choose the best drug. The learning of these kinds of skills has been treated in part in Section 10.3.

By concentrating on the key concepts, generalizations, and principles relevant to drug use, one can reduce the memory learning required. As already stated, this kind of information is retained more accurately and longer than discrete facts. The provider of drugs is freed from the tyranny of overwhelming facts, and the end product will be a more effective drug provider and improved health status for the patient.

10.4   LAYMAN AND PROFESSIONAL DRUG INFORMATION PROCESSING CAPABILITY AND PERFORMANCE

A thought-provoking and shocking book (8) contains the profound statement that most people do not know what they are talking about most of the time. This may have meaning in relationship to the well-known cliché, "a little knowledge is a dangerous thing," often misquoted as "knowledge is a dangerous thing." Yet knowledge does obligate one to incur risks, e.g., the atom bomb is a triumph of knowledge. "Ignorance is bliss" conveys the notion that not knowing may be more comfortable than knowing. Man's knowledge that he will die, while frightening to most people, certainly contributes to many of his important modes of behavior, e.g., religious. Although these modes may lead to dysfunctional effects, knowledge of his immortality has been meaningfully used to distinguish man from the lower animals.

Diverse kinds of activities are accompanied by risks, some more obvious than others. Risk-taking activities include sky-diving, skiing, going to school, marriage, riding in a car, exploding firecrackers, eating ice cream, consuming drugs, sleeping in a bed, warfare, cigarette smoking, kissing, ad infinitum. For reasons already considered, some of these are regulated and others are not. Only medication is explicitly and unambiguously relegated to a segment of society representing less than 1% of the population and forbidden to the other

99% without the permission of the 1%. There are many de facto examples of similar instances; e.g., one cannot drive a car, sell alcoholic beverages, build a house, stop going to school before a certain age, worship live rattlesnakes, marry, become a priest, etc., without complying with legal or bureaucratic standards. In all of these activities some kind of specialized capability must be demonstrated before one can engage in the desired activity.

The prescription, administration, and dispensing of drugs are restricted to those who purport to have specialized and unique capabilities. Since the physician as prescriber currently plays a dominant role as gatekeeper of the prescription drug storehouse, it follows that he alone possesses unique capability. His capability and the layman's will be examined in the context of the Input component of Figure 10.1(cf. Sections 10.4.1 and 10.4.2). The purpose of this examination will be to ascertain the relative capability of these two categories of people in relationship to one another and to other categories of people. Even though the basis for legend classification rests fundamentally on the assumption that legend drugs cannot be labeled for safe use by the layman, no known scientific study has verified this. While it seems obvious that the assumption is true, this would seem to make it relatively easy to generate evidence to substantiate it. It may well be that laymen use nonprescription drugs more rationally than physicians use prescription drugs.

Some reasonable, prudent layman must be the referent for ascertaining if a drug can be labeled for safe use by laymen. We can agree that the illiterate meets the test: a drug labeled for his use cannot be used safely. Yet as we progress up the educational hierarchy, where do we stop: Grade 1, Grade 5, Grade 10, college graduate, Ph.D., two Ph.D.s? The answer is none of these. The determination rests with both the quantity and the content of one's education. Therefore, the education of prescribers must be fundamentally distinctive and unique. Might not a test be constructed to measure one's expertise as a potential prescriber? Is possession in one's memory of certain unique facts, concepts, generalizations, or principles a prerequisite to prescribing? Is the ability to perform at levels higher than memory and translation, e.g., analysis, evaluation, the essential quality? Consideration of the problem yields the obvious point that changed capability in the student while in medical college (or veterinary, dental, pediatric, physician's assistant, osteopathic school) must be the unique causative agent responsible for the unique expertise vested in physicians and others in the health professions. (The reader will recall that this book assumes the inherent distinctiveness and separateness of diagnosis of medical deviance and prescription of its treatment.)

TABLE 10.1 NUMBER OF LECTURE HOURS DEVOTED TO THE DISCUSSION OF VARI-
OUS PHARMACOLOGIC TOPICS IN THE MEDICAL AND PHARMACY CURRICULUM AT THE
UNIVERSITY OF KENTUCKY

Topic	Medicine	Pharmacy[a]
General principles	12	9
General anesthetics	2	5
Myoneural blocking agents	1	5
Sedatives and hypnotics	3	7
Drugs in dyskinetics	1	4
Anti-infective drugs	7	25
Anticonvulsants	1	6
Psychoneuropharmacology	2	16
Analgesics	5	11
Autonomics	10	27
Cardiovascular drugs	5	27
Renal pharmacology	3	9
Endocrines	4	33
Antineoplastic agents	1	4
Drugs in allergy	1	6
Hematics	2	
Total	60	204
Approximate semester hour equivalent	6	20

[a] About 5% of the lectures deal with the chemistry and physical chemistry of drugs.
Source: T. Z. Csaky: Journal of Medical Education **48**:908 (Oct.) 1973.

Table 10.1 contains a comparative listing of pharmacologic topics taught to medical and pharmacy students at the University of Kentucky. Roughly 3½ times as much instruction is provided to pharmacy students in the pharmacologic topics listed. (A similar study done on a nationwide basis yielded comparable results (37).)

This figure suggests that pharmacists completing this program may be equipped with a better INPUT component (Figure 10.1) and decision-making capability about drugs than physicians completing the other, less intensive program. Senator Kennedy's bill (9), first introduced in 1974, and the *Malpractice Commission Report* (10) seemed to recognize clearly the need for further instruction in pharmacology and clinical pharmacology. Specifically, the latter report contained the statement:

The Commission RECOMMENDS that clinical pharmacology (i.e., the teaching of the actions, indications, side effects, et cetera, of drugs used therapeutically) be required as part of an integrated program for teaching the basics of therapeutics to all medical and nursing students and that similar attention be given to the same subjects in postgraduate and continuing medical education curricula.

Examination of the curricula of most medical and pharmacy schools tends to confirm what was shown for one university, but no study has shown this unequivocally or quantitatively for schools other than the one cited here. An objective analysis of nursing curricula content is unavailable, but available evidence tends to support the *Malpractice Commission Report* (10).

A small unpublished study, of value only as a tentative estimate of selective vocabulary ability, suggests that pharmacists and physicians have similar drug use vocabulary capability (11). The same study suggests that the drug use vocabulary for the top 200 prescribed drugs may be as large as 31,000 different words.

A content analysis was made of the words in the PIs for the top 200 drugs using a readability formula (12), and the average readability level was found to be slightly higher than Grade 12. This is slightly higher than the estimated readability of reading material designed for the adult literate population based on an analysis of the reading difficulty of 15 popular magazines (13).

10.4.1 Layman Capability and Performance in the Use of Drug Information

It is better to know nothing than to know what ain't so.—Josh Billings.

The rational layman, just as the rational professional, should clearly determine, understand, and define at least for himself the therapeutic objectives(s) reasonably eligible for selection, and then select courses of action which can be started and completed effectively, safely, and efficiently. Any limitation should be imposed only by the boundaries of present-day therapeutic science. If the outcome is not defined, how can its occurrence or nonoccurrence be recognized?

The behavior of patients who have learned some of the major principles of rational drug therapy should consist of adherence to certain predictable ways of behaving governed by certain general principles.

This statement is made on the assumption that other necessary components of rational drug use are present. The patient should be inclined to rely only on information appearing on drug labels and not on advertisements (except for advertisements of prescription drugs); alternatively, the patient should act only on drug labeling information or on information given to him by a competent person, which fits the algorithm previously described. In other words, he should be able to properly evaluate alternative information sources.

The patient should be expected to adhere to some of the basic assumptions underlying the reasons for labeling drugs. He should not be inclined to accept a prescription labeled "use as directed" because he would be aware of the unreliability of depending upon memory alone for proper drug consumption (assuming proper oral instruction was somehow obtained). He should not share his prescription drugs with others and should use only those drugs for which his own name appeared on the label. The patient should not expect drugs to be effective for treating too many illnesses; he should be aware that there is no effective drug for most aches, pains, sadnesses, tensions, or anxieties. He might be inclined to suffer sometimes rather than risk the undesirable effects of a drug because he would be aware that drugs are generally effective only for treating clinical manifestations of diseases, and are only occasionally helpful for alleviating the pain, suffering, and discomfort of behavioral problems. He should be aware that drugs are only rarely helpful for curing or relieving the discomforts of social problems. The patient should not expect drugs to relieve the problems occurring from the frustration, anxiety, or helplessness of one's job, children, family, or self, or some other attribute of his daily life style. He should expect drugs to do only what they can do. The patient should be equipped to avoid the following problems:

1. Receiving multiple prescriptions from different physicians.
2. Improperly and incorrectly self-medicating.
3. Receiving identical drugs dispensed from multiple dispensers.
4. Eating and drinking substances that cause adverse effects when consumed concurrently with certain drugs.
5. Consuming drugs at improper times and intervals.
6. Using drugs prescribed for other persons.
7. Irrationally deviating from a prescribed drug regimen.
8. Failing to comply with instructions for the proper consumption of a drug.
9. Improperly selecting a drug for the action needed.

In addition, the patient should enjoy the self-satisfaction that comes from being informed rather than ignorant.

Indeed, in order for a person to give an informed answer to the question, "Do you desire to consume this drug?" (Figure 10.2) patient education may be mandatory.

The foregoing points represent only a small sample of the total behavioral characteristics the rational and informed patient should exhibit. The following is a list of some basic pharmacological principles which should have been learned implicitly by the typical patient (or self-medicator) (14):

1. Realization that a disease state is dynamic and is a key to rational and effective therapeutics. A disease course represents a sequence, not a single event.
2. The ultimate test of the efficacy and risk/benefit ratio of a drug occurs in patients exhibiting the disease in question.
3. A controlled clinical trial ensures that the comparisons we make are as precise, as informative, and as convincing as possible.
4. Inflexibility or mischoice of a dosage regimen is detrimental.
5. The selection of the control is as critical as the selection of the experimental group in ascertaining drug effects.
6. Preliminary or pilot studies rarely provide a basis for reaching decisions on drug choices in disease.
7. For a study to have maximum relevance for patient care, its subjects should have had the same condition as the patient in question.
8. The statistical answer may mislead one to assume that the data were both valuable and valid.
9. Correct assessment of a drug regimen requires knowledge of the therapeutic dose and of the speed of drug elimination in that patient.
10. The state of a patient's health can drastically alter his drug dose requirements.
11. The fact that a particular formulation contains a specified amount of active chemical does not guarantee that this drug will be liberated upon administration.
12. The decision to use any particular drug is dependent not only upon its pharmacologic properties but also upon the health of the patient, the rate at which the drug is eliminated, the simultaneous use of other drugs, and the route and dosage form of the agent to be administered. Only after considering each of these

factors can a rational judgment be made regarding the "drug of choice."

13. For a first-order process, the half-life, given by the time required for the concentration to decline by one-half, is independent of concentration. As a first approximation, absorption of drugs from gastric, intestinal, intramuscular, subcutaneous, and rectal sites, drug distribution throughout the body, and the renal excretion and metabolism of many drugs obey first-order kinetics.

14. To produce a central effect, a drug must enter the bloodstream.

15. Response or toxicity to a drug may not appear simultaneously with drug administration or cease promptly when the drug is discontinued.

16. Comparisons between drug preparations containing the same active compound should take into account the rate and extent of drug absorption.

17. A drug must dissolve in the fluids of the gut before absorption can take place.

18. Enteric-coated tablets should not be given when an immediate effect is desired.

19. Any factor that shortens gastric emptying time increases the overall absorption rate of acidic and basic compounds.

20. Gastric emptying can be an important determinant of a patient's response to a drug.

21. The relevance of *in vitro* tests can be established only after the drug is used *in vivo*.

22. When the association constant (K) of a drug is high, any factor producing a small displacement of the drug may markedly enhance the pharmacologic effects of the drug.

23. The rate of injection of a drug must be commensurate with the clinical need and should be as slow as possible.

24. For practical purposes, distribution equilibrium is achieved when the rate of loss of drug from the blood corresponds to the rate of loss of drug from the body.

25. Drug elimination usually proceeds by first-order kinetics.

26. For certain drugs someone must be able to calculate the time at which maximal accrual of drug will occur on a fixed-dose schedule, and must carefully observe the patient until this time passes.

27. In the course of any disease, improvement or deterioration of the individual patient may be partially or totally independent of drug effects.

28. The age of the patient, young or old, may change either the ability of target organs to respond to drugs or the ability of normal systems to dispose of a drug or to oppose its effects.

29. Drug effects must be quantifiable and reproducible before genetically determined abnormal drug effects can be detected.

30. Drug administration can create diseases.

31. If objectives of efficacy have not been predetermined, lack of efficacy is difficult to recognize, and such reactions are difficult to identify.

32. Only when specific objectives have been established should drugs be added to an existing regimen. The benefit/risk ratio for each drug decreases when many drugs are given.

33. Drug effects must be continually assessed to lessen the possibility of producing toxicity.

34. The more potent the agent, the higher the risk of toxicity, either by exaggeration of the intended effect or as an inevitable ancillary action seen concomitantly with the intended effect.

35. Knowledge of drug interactions may not only prevent toxicity, but may also lead to therapeutic innovations.

36. The dosage form of a drug is a determinant of the clinical condition of the patient.

37. Even the most attractive theoretic considerations and data obtained from animal studies must be verified for efficacy and lack of toxicity in man prior to their acceptance.

38. Therapeutic interventions must be confirmed by controlled studies in the appropriate clinical context.

39. Agents given for identical therapeutic goals may have different toxic potential; this factor must be considered in selection of drugs.

Clearly, mastery of these principles places difficult demands on the layman. Many providers are likely to be deficient in the universe of knowledge from which this sample was drawn. Specialization has been society's answer to complexity; legal restriction of behavior relevant to medication usage is supposed to be a part of the solution. It might, however, be possible to teach selected principles to patients so that they may rationally consume selected drugs. Analgesics, antipyretics, hypotensives, and antibiotics would be appropriate therapeutic classes initially.

Medication Practices and Opinions

An FDA-sponsored study (15) designed to determine what factors influence the selection of a nonprescription (OTC) drug, produced discouraging results. The drug's label ranked fifth in a ranking of drug information sources. Other rankings included advertising as the most used source, with the recommendations of friends, relatives, pharmacists, and physicians as additional major sources. Reasons for not reading a label included 42% who stated they were already familiar with the products they buy. Clarity of labels was not seen as a problem by respondents, since about 80% said that OTC labels are clearly or fairly understandable. Those who found the labels not clear criticized the words as being too technical, medical, or chemical. On the other hand, almost half the respondents said that more information should be made available for OTC drugs, mainly in regard to side effects, ingredients, and what effects the medication was supposed to produce. A surprising eighty-six percent of respondents wanted the information available in written form, as contrasted with 20% who said they would like to have it via TV, magazines and newspapers.

Although 2 out of 3 respondents in the study thought that prescription labels were clearly understandable, about 1 out of 12 said the labels were not at all comprehensible. This smaller group said labels did not have enough information (31%), language was too technical (26%), and ingredient listing was not undesirable (19%). About the same fraction wanted more information for prescriptions as for OTC drugs (slightly less than 50%). The information sought most frequently was as follows (1) names/quantities of ingredients: 36%, (2) what the medicine is for: 29%, (3) adverse side effects, cautions, and whether it is habit forming. The written form was again the preference of 84% of respondents.

For OTCs, respondents said the most significant items on a label are the indications and the trademark. When those who do read OTC labels were asked what they looked for, the most frequent answers were (1) what it treats, relieves, cures, or prevents, (2) directions for use, dosage, when to stop using, (3) specific mention of active ingredients, side effects, and cautions (who should not take it). These answers are similar to those given by providers to a similar question.

One encouraging finding was that from among a list of 17 different types of OTC drugs commonly used in the home, not a single one was considered by *most users* to provide a cure. Unfortunately but perhaps understandably, 20% of those questioned believed that "cold remedies" provide a cure for the common cold. This finding is supported by another FDA-sponsored study (16) which found that only 3% of a sample of respondents reported they had used an OTC medicine to cure their ailment; diseases or conditions on which respondents were questioned were asthma (1%), allergies (3%), heart trouble (1%), high blood pressure (2%), diabetes (less than 1%), and hemorrhoids (3%).

For arthritis and/or rheumatism medicines and medicines in general respondents seemed to be unable or incapable of distinguishing a curative medicine from one which merely provides relief of symptoms. Many people believe that any drug helps them feel better; their concept of cure blends in with relief of symptoms or "getting better." Others see a prescribed drug as a curative. This view of all treatments and potential cures seems to be widespread (17).

Of those in the FDA-sponsored study who reported having used a curative medicine, the following distribution of the medicine used was reported (17):

Type of Medicine	Percentage
Unknown/unspecified prescription	35%
Cortisone	26%
Other analgesics	13%
Aspirin, Bufferin, Anacin, Excedrin	11%
Ointment/salve	8%
House remedy	4%
Uncodable responses	28%

Obviously belief in "cures" is in part the concern of patients, since about 75% of those studied said the medicine was recommended or prescribed by a health service provider, usually a physician. Demographic differences were so small that they could be attributed to methodology.

A proper and meaningful review of this report requires a brief consideration of its purpose and method. Its purpose was "to investigate fallacious or questionable health beliefs and practices and susceptibility to them" (18). Beliefs and/or practices in the following areas were singled out for investigation (19):

1. Use of vitamin pills and other nutritional supplements.
2. Use of "health foods."
3. Weight reduction practices.
4. Use of laxatives or other aids to bowel movement.
5. Self-diagnosis of ailments.

6. Self-medication for common ailments.
7. Self-medication for serious ailments.
8. Practices in the diagnosis and treatment of arthritis/rheumatism.
9. Practices in the diagnosis and treatment of cancer.
10. Health practitioners used.
11. Use of hearing aids and medication.
12. Aids to quitting smoking.
13. General health-related attitudes and opinions.

Attention in this overview will be devoted to health practices and opinions specific to the use of medicine.

The data collection process involved two basic methodological approaches. The first consisted of "a large national survey, using area probability techniques to produce a representative sample of U.S. adults, who were interviewed with an extensive questionnaire." Within the sampling error obtained in the study, this portion of the study is generalizable to the entire US population. The second type of methodology consisted of "individual and group depth interviews with people known or suspected to hold questionable beliefs or to have engaged in questionable practices."

Approximately 16 million adults (12% of the sample) indicated they would self-medicate without the assistance of a physician for longer than two weeks for one or more of the following ailments: sore throat, cough, sinus trouble, head colds, hay fever, skin problems, "helping you sleep," and upset or acid stomach. The people most inclined to medicate themselves do not differ in any important variable from those less inclined to self-medicate except that they tend to be slightly younger than the general population. Self-medicators cannot be distinguished in such variables as attitude toward the medical profession or by demographic differences.

Of the sample studied, 25% claimed to have an arthriticlike disease. However, about 1 in 5 of these respondents stated such a condition had not been diagnosed by a physician. About 1 in 5 of the reported sufferers said they had used something that was supposed to cure arthritis and/or rheumatism and not just alleviate the symptoms. As previously discussed, arthritis and/or rheumatism medicines included those prescribed by physicians and also those purchased for self-medication. For example, 13% of the reported sufferers (about 4 million people) reported having tried a medication to "lubricate their joints."

The survey included a necessarily small number of persons with cancer due to its incidence and other factors. Some of the results obtained are most inconsistent with the IND/NDA philosophy of discovering the true effects of drugs. A hypothetical "cancer cure" controversy was described in the interview, and all respondents were asked to take sides between "most scientists and doctors," who say the "cure" is worthless, and the patients of "a few doctors" who say it saved their lives. Almost half of the sample (42%), representing 50 million adults, would not be convinced by what was presented as nearly unanimous expert opinion. Not quite half (45%) of the total respondents thought the hypothetical cure should be banned by law.

In general, those interviewed appeared to be very receptive or susceptible to certain questionable practices of "doctors" and advertisers. In spite of the authoritarian portrayal of the physician in the mass media, a surprising and marked tendency was noted in those interviewed to rely on their own judgment over that of physicians. Opinions voicing distrust of physicians in the medical profession as a whole were striking; this distrust will be examined later in some detail.

Some general conclusions pertaining to health-related attitudes and opinions follow. These include:

1. "Susceptibility to health fallacies" is not an entity; tendencies to follow questionable practices in different areas are only slightly related to one another.
2. There is no consistent relationship between questionable health practices and questionable beliefs, i.e., the "generalization that fallacious practices always result from specific faulty beliefs is not supported."
3. A majority of those who have reported engaging in questionable practices are satisfied with the result they thought they obtained.
4. Many people engage in questionable health practices because they think that it is "worth a try," rather than from any false conviction that the practice is effective.
5. No single set of demographic characteristics is related to questionable health behavior in general.
6. The followers of several questionable practices seem to have a greater-than-average acceptance of advertising claims ("tonic" use, weight reduction practices, prolonged self-medication for common ailments).
7. People reporting that they engaged in questionable health practices tended to be either more critical than most people of physicians, or more inclined to trust their own judgment of a medicine when it conflicted with that of a physician.

8. People who follow questionable health practices tend to worry more about their helath than do people in general.
9. The "personality traits" of people engaging in questionable health practices tended to be indistinguishable from those less inclined to do so.
10. Older people are less likely than young people to rely on their own judgment when it conflicts with that of a physician.
11. Young people are more likely to self-medicate than older people (this is probably associated with the weight given to their own judgment).
12. Susceptibility to medical advertising and to labeling claims is unrelated to age.
13. Older people seem to be more impatient for results from medication use than younger people.
14. Older people are more prone to overreliance upon bowel movement aids, e.g., laxatives and cathartics.

Conclusions from the in-depth interviewing:

1. In general, people do not have an organized set of health beliefs and do not engage in systematic thinking about health. This means that fallacious behavior cannot be explained on the basis of questionable beliefs and systems of thinking.
2. The phrasing frequently encountered in medical literature to the effect that there is no average patient is overextended by most people so that individual response to treatment is viewed as entirely unpredictable because of the inherent uniqueness of each person. Such a view results in the notion that "anything is worth a try" and that the only way to find out if a preparation is useful is to "try it." The basis for trial and error of this type is that no matter how outlandish a claim may be, it may work for a given person even though it does not work for anyone else because that person is not exactly like anyone else. This reasoning might be correctly characterized as a kind of "rampant empiricism."
3. Rampant empiricism is most attractive to those inclined to stress their own uniqueness and judgment.
4. The "placebo effect" tends to be within the public's domain of experiences; it tends to strengthen rampant empiricism. ". . . if faith in a treatment can result in improvement, then people believe that any treatment at all can work" for them.
5. The placebo effect is successful in preventing the trial and error process from eliminating ineffective treatment. Because of the

sizable number of people willing to try a given placebo, a pool of people willing to testify to its effectiveness will always exist.

6. "Simple unaided recovery, when it *happens* [emphasis added] to coincide with a trial period, will make many people believe they hit upon something that will help them."

7. Many people are unable to distinguish between a curative remedy and a symptomatic remedy.

8. About 3 out of 4 people reported that poor health is often due to "not eating right."

9. Vitamins serve as a mass placebo because a majority of the population believes that vitamins and minerals provide more pep and energy.

10. People tend to believe that advertising claims of drugs and related items are true because of rigorous policing and regulating by advertisers that effectively prohibits serious distortions and fabrications of claims.

11. People tend to see drug quackery as that epitomized on TV as a "medicine show," where quacks sell their wares out of a Conestoga wagon or its equivalent. They believe that quackery is ". . . always so blatantly weird, preposterous, or hucksterish that [it] is easily recognizable."

12. Many victims of health fallacies are reaping the harvest of a distorted notion of health as something other than the absence of bad health; i.e., they do not see health merely as the absence of a medically deviant condition. Many people see good health as ". . . encompassing feelings of unlimited energy, freedom from anxiety and depression, and the presence of contentment and happiness." Such ends lie outside the realm of possibility because of the limitations of present-day drug technology and our understanding of human behavior.

13. To enjoy the kind of super-health desired by many laymen, one cannot merely lead an orderly existence, but must actively intervene to produce good health.

The report being reviewed also contained a number of "action implications." In other words, a number of fallacious opinions and improper practices were identified. The question is what can or should be done about them. A few of these implications are:

1. Education, often offered up as the solution for most of our problems in our country, may not have as much promise as we would like. "To the extent that fallacious practices do not result from

misinformation, supplying correct information does not solve the problem."

2. Some general orientations to health and medicine use may be subject to change by educational programs. However, ". . . the education must be fundamental and intensive, beginning in the schools; it is not likely that pamphlets and posters could have a great effect upon deeply rooted orientations under consideration."

3. While individual action based on informed opinion is essential in a democratic society, rampant empiricism or the overruling of professional judgment by lay judgment does not appear to be in the best interest of the public. "Education on such things as the nature of the scientific medicine, the importance of thorough examinations and diagnoses, and the limitations of lay knowledge, might make people less willing to disregard authoritative advice."

4. Confidence in the medical profession could be improved because a large number of people have serious doubts as to whether physicians consider the patient's welfare and best interests first.

5. A more realistic view of health as the absence of a medically deviant condition needs to be learned by the public.

The following is a presentation in greater depth of some of the points in the foregoing overview. Table 10.2 shows the results from three hypothetical situations included on the questionnaire, in which respondents were asked to weigh the judgments of physicians against direct experience by themselves or other laymen. It would be intriguing to have a candid, comparable set of responses for such professionals as nurses, physicians, and pharmacists.

Many medicines are labeled with various cautionary advice such as "if fever persists for three days, see your physician." Table 10.3 presents the results when respondents were asked to assume that they had certain ailments and had found a medicine that controlled them with continued use, and were also asked how long they would wait before consulting a physician. As previously reported, older people are less inclined to wait than younger people.

The somewhat distorted notion of the meaning of good health is augmented by a study of Table 10.4. In a sense the respondents were correct in that overweight alone is responsible for a considerable fraction of debilitating and fatal diseases, e.g., heart, circulatory, and kidney diseases. This view of illness or health adds a different perspective to the meaning of hypochondriasis. These people are not exaggerating their complaints, but are attempting to rid themselves of what would ordinarily be perceived as normal problems such as

TABLE 10.2 PERCENT RESPONDING AS SHOWN TO HYPOTHETICAL SITUATIONS BY SEX AND AGE

		Sex		Age			
	Total Sample[a]	Men	Women	Under 30	30 to 39	40 to 44	50 to 64
Use medicine recommended by a friend if physician said it was worthless?							
Yes	12	15	9	15	13	9	11
No	81	78	84	77	78	85	82
Maybe	7	8	7	8	9	7	6
Go on using medicine that seemed to help if physician said it was worthless?							
Go on	36	41	31	44	40	36	28
Stop	57	51	61	49	52	57	63
Don't know	8	8	7	7	7	7	10
Who is right in a "cancer cure" controversy? Those who say:							
it is worthless	58	57	58	61	56	55	58
it cured them	24	26	22	26	24	27	24
don't know	18	17	19	14	20	18	18

[a] Percentages may not total 100% due to rounding off of numbers.
Source: National Analysts, Inc.: A Study of Health Practices and Opinions, National Technical Information Service, U.S. Department of Commerce, Springfield, Va., PB 210978, June, 1972, p. 258.

fatigue, occasional depression or anxiety, or some other more or less natural feeling occurring in a competitive society.

Table 10.5 contains a listing of the percent of the total sample of respondents who reported degrees of agreement with 15 different statements of opinion. This listing tends to reinforce the preceding overview of the opinions and practices of a vast segment of the public. It is also interesting to observe in this table that people seem very committed to one or another position on most of these items. This is shown by the very low percentage of people who reported that they "don't know." Although one could argue with some of the opinion statements on the basis of one's own ethical position (e.g., whether

TABLE 10.3   PERCENT OF THE TOTAL SAMPLE SAYING THEY WOULD CONTINUE "EFFECTIVE" SELF-MEDICATION FOR VARYING PERIODS BEFORE SEEING A PHYSICIAN

Would See Physician:	Sore Throat	Cough	Acid Stomach	Headaches	Skin Rash
First	9[a]	9	10	9	11
1 to 3 days	36	32	40	46	41
4 days to 1 week	34	36	29	27	29
8 days to 2 weeks	10	12	7	6	7
15 days to 1 month	4	5	5	3	4
32 days to 6 months	1	1	2	2	1
More than 6 months	+[b]	+[b]	1	1	+[b]
Would not see physician	3	3	4	3	3
Don't know	2	2	4	3	4

[a] Percentages may not total 100% due to rounding off of figures.
Source: National Analysts, Inc.: A Study of Health Practices and Opinions, National Technical Information Service, U.S. Department of Commerce, Springfield, Va., PB 210978, June, 1972, p. 264.
[b] Less than 1%.

TABLE 10.4   PERCENT SAYING EACH STATEMENT IN PAIRS SEEMS MORE TRUE

	Total Sample[a]
Good health is a natural thing	40
A person has to work at it constantly to have good health	58
Don't know	2
Good or bad health results primarily from the body we are born with	14
How we take care of ourselves is more important than the body we are born with	83
Don't know	2

[a] Percentages represent respondents who choose item listed.
Source: National Analysts, Inc.: A Study of Health Practices and Opinions, National Technical Information Service, U.S. Department of Commerce, Springfield,
Va., PB 210978, June, 1972, p. 268.

children must be vaccinated against certain contagious diseases), most of the questions reflect mainstream components of medicine or health knowledge.

TABLE 10.5   PERCENT OF TOTAL SAMPLE REPORTING DEGREES OF AGREEMENT WITH OPINION STATEMENTS

	Agree Very Much	Agree a Little	Disagree a Little	Disagree Very Much	Don't Know
1. For most people who have bad health, a major reason is that they don't eat right	36	39	19	7	+[a]
2. Most of the things that advertisements say about medicines and health aids must be true, or they wouldn't be allowed to say them	8	30	34	28	1
3. Most doctors put helping their patients above everything else	43	36	16	5	+[a]
4. A lot of doctors are only interested in making money	23	39	25	14	1
5. If a medicine doesn't help you right away, it probably isn't going to do any good at all	11	19	49	21	1
6. There are a lot of old-fashioned remedies around that doctors don't pay enough attention to	24	38	23	14	1
7. Most of the things that people buy in drugstores to treat themselves are practically worthless	18	29	40	12	1
8. The medical profession concentrates too much on science and not enough on people	15	30	35	19	2
9. Despite all the scientific advances, doctors used to help their patients more than they do now	16	22	30	31	1
10. Medical doctors stick too much to the "tried and true"; they are too much against new or different ways	5	17	42	34	2

TABLE 10.5 (Continued)

	Agree Very Much	Agree a Little	Disagree a Little	Disagree Very Much	Don't Know
11. The government doesn't have any business deciding what kinds of medicines are legal	10	7	23	59	1
12. Community water supplies should be fluoridated	46	32	11	8	3
13. The law should require that children must be vaccinated or inoculated against contagious diseases	80	15	3	2	+^a
14. It is nearly impossible to know in advance whether or not a medicine will help you because what works for one person won't work for another	60	30	7	3	+^a
15. I don't care so much about a doctor's manner with his patients as long as he is a skilful doctor	38	28	21	12	+^a

^a Less than 1%.
Source: National Analysts, Inc.: *A Study of Health Practices and Opinions,* National Technical Information Service, U.S. Department of Commerce, Springfield, Va., PB 210987, June, 1972, p. 270–271.

Sources of Health and Medication-Related Information

If information is to be learned other than through personal experiences, it should prove instructive to examine sources of medication information. Although no comprehensive review will be attempted here, a review of television as a source was selected because of the large amount of time spent viewing TV. Many children watch TV more than 40 hours a week and thus spend many more hours in front of the TV set than in the classroom. While it is stylish to blame TV for everything from crime in the streets to increased sexual permissiveness (or in some "weekend widow" cases, decreased), that is not the intent here. For example, black ghetto children spend an enormous fraction of their lives watching TV with its predominant middle-class, white language and yet the dialect of these children is altered little if any.

Data on television-advertised medication and health information content are rare. However, one fruitful study (20) was done of the health information content telecast over one channel in Detroit over a typical 130-hour broadcast week.

Approximately 7.2% of the total time was devoted to health items with entertainment, profit commercials, and news being the most frequently telecast items, respectively. Nonprofit commercials (representing 36.4% of total time) contained the highest health information content of any category. The health information items did not usually contain much health information because of the intent behind the message, i.e., selling a product. The content of the health items is presented by category in Table 10.6. One interesting finding was that health information tended to be either useful and accurate or detrimental and inaccurate. The writers developed a rating scale of potential harm (worst = −27) and potential, favorable accurate items (best = +18). Figure 10.4 depicts this relationship by showing the health items score and the time devoted to items with that score. One can see that the opportunity to "know what ain't so" seems to be increased as a result of watching TV. Clearly, something needs to be done, and it would appear that starting with the fundamentals of drug information has the greatest potential.

The following tongue-in-cheek editorial, written by the editor of the *New England Journal of Medicine* to himself (in response to the article reviewed above) provides an excellent summary of what has been discussed in this chapter (21):

From time to time, the editor of this *Journal*, driven perhaps by zealous commitment to the First Amendment, publishes a polemic summons from the far right to left—Sade, for example, denying Americans their right to health care, or Harper suggesting that our hero should be Che Guevara. Most readers forgive such deviations. But with the publication of the article "Health Information During a Week of Television" (page 516 of this issue), the editor has gone too far. Not only do the authors of this derogatory tract insinuate that the nation's great television industry slights health, but they even make bold to claim that the quality of health-related material shown on TV is mediocre or even worse. There must be limits to editorial license if the traditions of our Pilgrim Forefathers are to survive.

Everyone knows, the authors' myopic and biased conclusions notwithstanding, that TV's contribution to our health is immeasurable. And

TABLE 10.6 FREQUENCY CLASSIFICATION OF HEALTH ITEMS ACCORDING TO CONTENT

	Time (seconds and %)[a]
Antidrug	7680 (23.1)
Headache and pain remedies	1860 (5.6)
Gastrointestinal remedies	1425 (4.3)
Dental remedies	1050 (3.2)
Respiratory drugs	1956 (5.9)
Vitamins	330 (1.0)
Skin remedies	180 (0.5)
Disease prevention	825 (2.5)
Physicians	9970 (30.0)
All others	7980 (24)

[a] Approximately 7.2% of total time devoted to health.
Source: Adapted from F. A. Smith, et al.: Health Information During a Week of Television, *New England Journal of Medicine* **286**:516–520 (March 9) 1972.

not only to our health, but to our marital bliss, our morale and our joie de vivre. Because of the educational efforts of TV, we know that our wives' happiness, love, endurance and resiliency will perpetually soar on high, provided they faithfully consume that elixir so rich in pep-infusing iron. Our own sagging spirits, too, will respond to this tonic, and each of us, aglow with ferriferous radiance, can proudly display "My wife!"

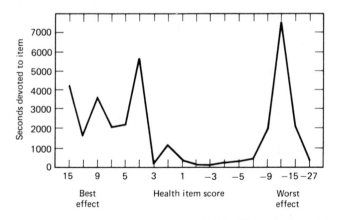

Figure 10.4. Rating scale of potential harm or good of health items televised. *Source:* F. A. Smith, et al.: Health Information During a Week of Television, *New England Journal of Medicine* 286 (10):519 (March 9) 1972.

In many other brief but pregnant interludes, TV sustains the nation's health. All of us, if we only heeded the counsel so unmistakably offered, could attain tranquil, dormant ecstasy; and while we sleep-sleep-sleep, we need not worry about that drip-drip-drip of stomach acid, for we know that the right little tablet will consume many times its weight of monster gastric acid. Nor can there be any excuse for the spouse who harasses his/her mate with the noisy and noisome effect of nasal congestion. For him who profits from the health hints on TV, night should be naught but beatitude.

Sometimes, the *Journal* publishes articles on arthritis—as if it were a problem. Obviously, its "minor aches" could be obviated and banished once and for all if people would only listen to the sanitary messages that TV brings. The documentation on the screen is certainly conclusive: a lady may be crippled at one moment by agonizing arthritis, and in the next she will be helping to produce a rousingly successful theatrical performance, but she has to be smart enough to take the right medicine.

Now, what does a housewife who feels exhausted in the morning after sending the kids to school and pushing a cart around a supermarket have in common with a grandfather who doesn't want to play with his grandchildren? Ordinarily, none of us would know, but TV helps us suspect the right answer. Is it—irregularity? YES, IT IS. And what a change it makes when the advice of a kindly friend helps these people. Regular Grandpa romps and regular housewife zooms among the stacks of produce (imagine the animalistic exuberance should these two regulars ever meet up!).

But it is for our children and their health that TV has done the most. Some might assume that TV has done enough for our children, has done its share, when it fans their desire for achievement by showing Champ Chillbone (Mr. CC) knock out eight of the enemy before gunning down 20 more, but TV knows that man cannot live by spirit alone. So Mr. CC is allowed to interrupt the adventurous mayhem and remind his young audience of their prosaic duties. 'If you want to be strong and tough like me,' Mr. CC confides in his bluff, straight-from-the-shoulder manner, 'just be sure to take your daily Vita-Cee-Cees.' And lest parents prove so recalcitrant as to ignore their children's nutritional health needs, Mr. CC earnestly adds, 'You know, fellers, Mom wants to see you strong and healthy, too. Make sure she knows about Vita-Cee-Cees.'

So if we have stuffed noses, bad breath, tension headaches, insomnia, chronic cough, bursting sinuses and creaky joints—if we feel tired instead of peppy—whose fault is it? TV wants to help us, wants to turn the effete into the robust, the deficient into the sufficient. And you, Mr. Editor, publish an article that would have us think otherwise!

After consideration of the foregoing it is perhaps comforting to have it documented that people read for almost two hours during the typical day

(22). Most of this reading is devoid of drug information except for drug advertisements. It would be interesting to prepare a similar tabulation for reading content to that presented for TV, but unfortunately this does not seem to exist. One only wishes that nearly half a billion dollars in OTC advertising would buy more.

10.4.2. Sources of Medication Information for Providers

Even if providers program themselves to proven drug information in accordance with the broad-based model depicted in Figure 10.1, using the process specific to drug information depicted in Figure 10.2, drug information is still a vital input. If the wrong information or less than optimal information is used, the means of processing will not be sufficient—no matter how valuable—to overcome this deficiency. The sources actually relied upon by providers for drug information are examined here. (Whether actual use conforms to the use advocated by sources used is discussed in Section 12.7.) These will be described in terms of (1) principal sources used; (2) frequency of use of principal sources; (3) time spent on source; and (4) content of source relative to PI content.

A number of studies have been done to determine what drug information sources are used by physicians (23–28). The more recent mailed questionnaire-based study (25) shows that the average physician spends 19 minutes each work day acquiring drug information. Another recent study (28) using a sample of 29 physicians carrying random alarm devices (activities are recorded whenever these devices go off) for a total of 5400 observations yielded an average figure of about 40 minutes for all information-seeking activities, i.e., drug and nondrug information, so the 19-minute figure seems accurate. Comparable information for nurses, pharmacists, and other health providers is unavailable.

Table 10.7 lists the frequency of use of the listed source of drug information by physicians. The *Physicians' Desk Reference* is clearly the most frequently used source of drug information; it is used about 7.5 times a week or little more than once a day. The physician spends enough time seeking drug information each day to completely read the information in PDR for two different "average" drugs. A typical physician would thus need only about 3% of the total time he spends seeking drug information to read the PI for the roughly 15 significant new drugs marketed each year. Only about a fifth of the physician's

TABLE 10.7   FREQUENCY OF USE OF SELECTED DRUG INFORMATION SOURCES BY
PHYSICIANS

Source Used	Uses Per Unit of Time	
	Mean	Standard Deviation
PDR	7.5/week	8.2
Package inserts	2.2/week	2.2
Personal peer contacts	2.2/week	3.7
Pharmacology texts	1.6/week	3.2
AMA drug evaluations	.8/week	2.2
Detailman	1.6/week	2.8
Journal ads	1.4/week	2.2
Direct mail ads	0.9/week	1.8
Pharmacists	1.1/week	2.31
Hospital staff meetings	20/year	23
Medical society meetings	4.0/year	6.7
Continuing education courses	4/year	10.5

Source: Applied Management Sciences: *Survey of Drug Information Needs and Problems Associated with Communication Directed to Practicing Physicians,* Part I, Physician Information Survey, National Technical Information Service, Springfield, Va., PB #232 679, May 8, 1974, various pages.

total information seeking time would be required to read the 30 to 50 issues of the *Medical Letter* and three or four issues of the FDA's *Drug Bulletin* annually.

A complete review of the relative use of drug information sources will not be presented; instead generalizations from the several studies available will be discussed. The PDR is ranked highest as an information source by both physicians and nurses (Table 10.8). Other studies have shown figures of 98.5% (23) and 97% (25). Several striking differences in the relative use of information sources are listed in Table 10.8. Although considerable variation can be attributed to methodology, an interesting finding is that pharmacists are listed as a principal source by 50% of the nurses studied, but by only 6% of the physicians. This difference may be due to the ready accessibility of pharmacists in hospitals, since the study included only hospital-based nurses.

Table 10.9 lists the percentage of nurses expressing full confidence in the listed drug information source. Unlike physicians, nurses generally have much greater confidence in commercial sources. In the study, however, the detailman as a source was rated a mere 12%. The infrequent solicitation of the nurse by the detailmen probably accounts for this.

TABLE 10.8 PRINCIPAL SOURCES FOR DRUG INFORMATION

	Total Nurses[a]	Total Physicians[a]
Physicians' Desk Reference (PDR)	92	61%[b]
Experience/personal knowledge		37
Journals and medical periodicals	45	27
Detailmen	6	19
Colleagues, consultants, medical society	17	13
Medical literature (nonspecific)		11
Textbooks	47	11
Compendia/drug reference books (other than PDR)	54	10
Package inserts	83	8
Direct mail		6
Pharmacists	50	6

[a] Numbers represent percentage responding to listed item as a principal source.

[b] In the same study, 82% cited PDR as "the one I use most often."

Source: Adapted from Opinion Research Corporation: *Physician's Attitudes Toward Drug Compendia*, Opinion Research Corporation, Princeton, N.J., July, 1968, p. 3; and The Nurse and Drugs Administered in Hospitals, *Medical Marketing and Media* 9(6):13–22 (June) 1974. (These figures are only roughly comparable.)

TABLE 10.9 RELATIVE CONFIDENCE OF NURSES IN SPECIFICE DRUG INFORMATION SOURCE

	Percent Expressing Full Confidence
Physicians' Desk Reference	85
Package inserts	82
Pharmacology texts	80
Hospital formulary	72
Pharmacists	61
Nursing journals	60
Bottle labels	58
Medical journals	50
Inservice programs	37
Physicians	31
Hospital displays or drug fairs	16
Pharmaceutical company salesmen	12
Other nurses	5

Source: The Nurse and Drugs Administered in Hospitals, *Medical Marketing and Media* 9(6):13–23 (June) 1974.

TABLE 10.10   SOURCES OF DRUG INFORMATION AS INFLUENCES FOR PRESCRIBING

Source	Most Believable (%)[a]	Most Current[a]	Provide Best Clinical Guidance (%)
National journals	23	25	18
Periodical newsletters	12	24	09
Compendia and other books	13	06	12
Drug company materials	04	16	05
Personal contacts	10	08	16
Textbooks	23	01	15
Meetings and courses	16	23	25

[a] Columns total more than 100% due to rounding off of numbers.

Source: Applied Management Sciences: *Survey of Drug Information Needs and Problems Associated with Communication Directed to Practicing Physicians,* Part I: Physician Information Survey, National Technical Information Service, Springfield, Va., PB #232679, May 8, 1974, unnumbered pages section.

Physicians find journal articles, meetings, and courses more reliable (25). Phsycians report that they would like to use all the information sources listed in Tables 10.8 and 10.9 more often, excluding journal advertisements, direct mail, and detailmen. Surprisingly, the PDR is not perceived as "drug company materials"; this probably accounts for the PI being cited as the "drug company materials considered most useful" by 65% of the respondents.

Of all kinds of drug information, the one that is most believable, most current, and provides the best clinical guidance, according to physician respondents, is summarized in Table 10.10. Note that non-package insert-based sources are tied for position as the most believable source. Meetings and courses were probably listed as providing the best clinical guidance partly because of their being application-oriented. The finding that only 9% of physicians responded that periodical newsletters provide the best clinical guidance seems inconsistent with the finding that one periodical newsletter, the FDA's *Drug Bulletin* influenced 42% of the responding physicians to change their prescribing patterns (31).

An important point is the source used for information of various types. Although while this was described earlier in connection with Tables 9.1, 9.2, 9.3 of Section 9.1, the reliance upon PI-based sources and non-Pi sources is important. Time is a critical factor, too. Seeking information from journal articles, meetings, and personal contacts not described in PIs is probably rational. However, seeking information from sources used to derive the PI when one is trying to gain a better understanding of a point made or omitted from a PI is to reinvent the wheel. Although no tabulations have been done, it seems clear from examination of the elements in the tables just referred to and from considering the other contents of this section that, the officially approved PI generally serves as the prime source of drug information. Its use as a source becomes clearer when one recalls that the content of the PI, journal ads, direct mail, the PDR, and what the detailman can legally say about a drug must all be essentially the same in meaning. Other sources may merely represent a second, third, or fourth retelling of basic information in the PI. Lest the reader believe that the PI is "truth" handed down from Mt. Olympus, the earlier criticism of the PI should be reviewed.

Nevertheless, the fact that the virtues of the PI may go unrecognized by large groups of drug providers is attested to by the American Pharmaceutical Association's *Evaluations of Drug Interactions* (32). A review of the contents of this publication reveals that virtually all its information about a given drug can be found in the precautions or warnings sections of the PI for the given drug. Presto, the wheel is reinvented. Since (as was previously shown) the detailman is limited to PI contact, he also seems to be inefficiently used because the provider need only read the PI to get the identical message to that available from the detailman.

10.5 RESPONSIBILITY FOR BEING INFORMED: WHOSE IS IT?

An important question for society is: Whose responsibility is it to inform the consumer as to the proper manner to take a drug?* Although some have suggested that it may be better not to inform consumers at all, the mainstream of public and probably professional opinion is that informed consumers are desirable although many providers and consumers have serious doubts about the likelihood of such an event occurring.

The answer to the question at hand depends to a significant extent on the perspective of the answerer. From the viewpoint of a consumer and citizen participant in a democratic, republican form of government, it is ultimately the responsibility of the consumer to inform

* The duty owed by the various persons occupying roles within the drug distribution system will be considered from a strictly legal viewpoint later. The argument presented here is based primarily on ethical principles.

himself. Through his choice of government form, the consumer has designated certain reperesentatives in the various branches of government to represent his interests. These representatives in turn have prescribed certain requirements which various providers must meet if they are to perform tasks reserved only to them by consumers through group action. One large group of consumer representatives appointed by consumers through their duly elected representatives is pharmacists. Pharmacy is and historically has been designated as the one occupation whose primary concern is drugs and the people who consume them. The basic purpose of most pharmacy practice acts, at least conceptually, is to insure that only pharmacists will be allowed to carry out certain drug-related activities so that the maintenance and protection of public health, safety, and welfare can be achieved. Since society has so designated pharmacists, it seems reasonable to conclude that the consumer has intended that pharmacists serve as the group responsible for seeing that the consumer is properly informed about drugs, their use, and their effects.

There are many reasons why consumers should be informed and knowledgeable about drugs and their effects. Perhaps, as previously suggested, the most basic reason of all is that by knowing about drugs and their use, the consumer's health status will likely be favorably affected. Recent research done by pharmacists and others (33, 34) has shown that when people understand why they are taking drugs they tend to consume them properly, thus reaping the greatest possible benefits while minimizing the undesired effects. Informed consumers can further the rational use of drugs. The use of modern-day equivalents of crocodile dung, leeches, and similar remedies that have been debunked by established scientific and professional groups will probably be discontinued sooner if consumers are informed. The entire history of drug quackery thrived on taking advantage of uninformed or misinformed consumers.

The need for being informed about the desired and undesired effects of drugs is one of the many problems confronting members of our technological society. Nevertheless, we have no choice as to whether we want to be informed if our health status is to be best served. Some chemical substances relieve pain, prevent seizures, relieve anxiety, induce anesthesia, assist conception, etc. Other drugs cause pain, induce seizures, produce anxiety feelings, prevent induction of anesthesia, prevent conception, etc. In order to produce the greatest chances of reaping the desired effects while at the same time minimizing the undesired effects occurring from the use of a drug, it is essential that one be informed and correctly informed. Failure, for example, to take drugs for preventing conception can result in an effect opposite to that desired. Knowledge of certain essential information cannot be delegated, it must be mastered by the consumer.

Society has seen fit to conclude that correct use of prescribed drugs is such a complex process that the information describing the effects of these drugs can only be interpreted by those licensed to prescribe and dispense drugs. The basis for the prescription drug category rests on the assumption that people cannot correctly understand the proper ways to use these drugs without intervention by a prescriber, dispenser, or administerer. For this reason the consumer is forced to rely on other persons for information as to how a particular drug is to be taken. When drugs are labelled by a pharmacist or other person according to the requirements of the law, this act is based on several assumptions which have been mentioned previously: (a) the drug user can read, (b) the drug user will read the directions on the label, and (c) the drug user will heed what he reads on the label.

A drug user must be careful to use drugs in accordance with these assumptions. For this reason drug containers are labelled by the pharmacist so that the patient does not have to rely on his memory when taking a particular drug. One must know enough to understand what is read; some initial knowledge must be present. There are many other principles which pharmacists and others can share with consumers that will enhance the drug usage process. Most of these principles have the value of principles in general; that is, by learning a principle one can then apply it to a number of particular, but different instances of drug usage. Such usage makes it unnecessary to be knowledgeable about the particulars of the information describing the effects of the large number of drugs that exist in the drug marketplace of contemporary America; one need only know enough to use what is needed. In *Future Shock* Toffler has shown us the problems and, some would say, the futility of trying to store and recall vast quantities of information. Pharmacists and others can provide some general principles for taking drugs that will obviate the need for the patient to store large quantities of information, but ultimately it is the patient himself who must be responsible for keeping himself informed.

The pharmacist is also the preferred person for providing information about the proper ways to use over-the-counter and prescription drugs (as defined by the physician) because pharmacists are the most accessible of the health care professionals who claim to be knowledgeable about drugs. The physician is an overworked, and expensive professional. Likewise, the nurse is not very accessible and can generally be communicated with only in physicians' offices or institutions.

The pharmacist, however, is readily accessible, in good supply, and is distributed fairly evenly. Also, during any relatively short period a large fraction of the population will visit a pharmacy. Moreover, pharmacists by training and society's expectations are in a position to provide the necessary information. Today, schools of pharmacy throughout the United States are giving added emphasis to the role of the pharmacist in providing needed information to drug consumers.

The pharmacist also frequently does not charge the consumer directly for information. Recent research has also shown that oral information provided by physicians to their patients is forgotten in a matter of minutes (35). The pharmacist is, and has traditionally been, the only health professional who labels drugs and thus provides written directions for the administration of these drugs.

In summary the answer to the question posed is that, although ultimately it is the consumer's responsibility to educate himself, the consumer has appointed various health professionals as providers of drug information services. The pharmacist, as the principal person assigned to the drug provision role, is in the best position to provide responsible information to the consumer.

The performance of various providers in using drug information to further the patient's own interests and the degree of knowledge of patients and providers will be examined in the following chapter.

REFERENCES AND GUIDE TO FURTHER STUDY

1. Postman, N. and Weingartner, C.: *Teaching as a Subersive Activity*, Dell Publishing Company, New York, 1969, p. 19.

2. Somers, A.: *Health Care in Transition: Directions for the Future*, Hospital Research and Educational Trust, Chicago, Ill., 1971, p. 9.

3. De Nazzo, R. V.: 18th Annual Prescription Survey of the Albany College of Pharmacy, *Medical Marketing and Media*, 9:14 (April) 1974.

4. Gagné, R. H.: Educational Objectives and Human Performance. In Krumboltz, J. D. (Ed.): *Learning and the Educational Process*, Rand McNally & Company, Chicago, 1965, p. 1–24.

5. Smith, M. C.: Social Barriers to Rational Drug Therapy, *American Journal of Hospital Pharmacy* 29(2):120–127 (February) 1972.

6. Toffler, A.: *Future Shock*, Bantam Books, New York, 1970, p. 350–364.

7. Sanders, N. M.: *Classroom Questions, What Kinds?* Harper & Row, New York, 1966, p. 3.

8. Postman, N. and Weingartner, C.: *Teaching as a Subversive Activity*, Dell Publishing Company, New York, 1969, p. 1–15.

9. Drug Utilization Improvement Act, Senate Bill 3441, 93rd Congress, 2nd Session, May 6, 1974.

10. Report of the Secretary's Commission on Medical Malpractice, Jan. 16,1973, DHEW Publication No. (OS) 73-88, U.S. Government Printing Office, Washington, D.C., 1973, p. 60.

11. Gibson, J. T.: *Drug Use Vocabulary Capability of Pharmacists and Physicians.* Unpublished manuscript, 1971.

12. Gibson, J. T. and Newton, D. S.: *Readability Levels of Package Inserts.* Unpublished data, 1974.

13. Dulin, K. L.: Readability Level of Adult Magazine Material, paper presented at National Reading Conference, Los Angeles, Calif., December 5–7, 1968.

14. Melmon, K. L. and Morelli, H. F. (Eds.): *Clinical Pharmacology Basic Principles in Therapeutics,* Collier-Macmillan, New York, 1972, various pages.

15. Nicholls, C. A. and Morrison, M.: Consumers Talk About Labeling, *FDA Consumer* **7**:4 (February) 1974.

16. National Analysts, Inc.: A Study of Health Practices and Opinions, National Technical Information Service, Springfield, Va., June, 1972, PB-210 978, p. 149.

17. National Analysts, Inc.: *ibid.,* p. 166–167.

18. National Analysts, Inc.: *ibid.,* p. ib.

19. Abstracted or excerpted from National Analysts, Inc., *ibid.,* p. ib-xviii, 82–88, 257–281.

20. Smith, F. A. *et al.:* Health Information during a Week of Television, *New England Journal of Medicine* **286**(10):516–520.

21. Inglefinger, F. J.: Hygeia on the TV Screen (editorial), *New England Journal of Medicine* **286**(10):541 (March 9) 1972.

22. Sharon, A. T.: What Do Adults Read? *Reading Research Quarterly,* **9**(2):148 (Winter) 1973–74.

23. *How Physicians Use Physicians' Desk Reference.* Alfred Politz Media Studies, New York, 1966.

24. Opinion Research Corporation, *Physicians' Attitudes toward Drug Compendia,* Opinion Research Corporation, Princeton, N. J., July, 1968 (about 60 pages).

25. Applied Management Sciences: *Survey of Drug Information Needs and Problems Associated with Communication Directed to Practicing Physicians,* Part I: Physician Information Survey, National Technical Information Service, Springfield, Va., PB #232 679, May 8, 1974.

26. Applied Management Sciences: *ibid.,* Part II: *Drug Bulletin Survey,* PB #232 680, Feb. 22, 1974.

27. Applied Management Sciences: *ibid.,* Part II: *Remedial Ad Survey,* PB #232 681, Feb. 22, 1974.

28. Hess, S. W.: Communicating with Physicians, *Journal of Advertising Research* **14**(1):13–20 (February) 1974.

29. American Journal of Nursing Company: The Nurse and Drugs Administered in Hospitals, *Medical Marketing and Media,* **9**(6): 13–23 (June) 1974.

30. Applied Management Sciences: Part I, *ibid.,* p. 3.70.

31. Applied Management Sciences; Part III, *ibid.,* p. 3.21.

32. American Pharmaceutical Association: *Evaluations of Drugs Interactions,* 1st ed., American Pharmaceutical Association, Washington, D.C., 1973, and supplements.

33. Morrow, R. and Rabin, D. L.: Reliability in Self-Medication with Isoniazid, *Clinical Research* **14**:362 (April) 1966.

34. Sharpe, T. R.: An Experimental Investigation of the Relationships between Written Drug Therapy Information and Patient Compliance with Antibiotic Therapy Regimens. Unpublished M.S. thesis, University of Mississippi, Oxford, Miss. 1973.

35. Cooper, J. D. (Ed.): The Efficacy of Self-Medication, *Philosophy and Technology of Drug Assessment,* Volume 4, Interdisciplinary Communication Associates, Washington, D.C., 1973 p. 106.

36. Reilly, M. J.: Drug Information: Literature Review of Needs, Resources & Services, DHEW Publication No. 72-3013, U.S. Government Printing Office, Washington, D.C., 1972, 122 p.

37. Aviado, D. M.: *Pharmacologic Principles of Medical Practice,* 8th ed., Williams and Wilkins, Baltimore, 1972, p. 1207–1214.

38. Palumbo, F. B.: An Experimental Study of Consumer Expectations and Knowledge of a Hypothetical Over-the-Counter Cold Preparation. Unpublished Ph.D. thesis, University of Mississippi, Oxford, Miss. 1974, 119 p.

CHAPTER ELEVEN

Laws Defining the Qualifications of Persons Responsible for the Movement of Drugs Through the Various Distribution Channels

Limiting and controlling authority for the movement of drugs through distribution channels is, as previously noted, a relatively new phenomenon. As recently as 1906 essentially no legislation existed at the federal level to control and regulate drug distribution, use, access, or availability. During this same period, laws restricting drug movement and use to physicians and pharmacists only were slowly developing. While the states were licensing pharmacists, physicians, and others in order to restrict the use of drugs to certain persons, the actual effect on the behavior of persons desiring access to and use of drugs was minimal. Control to even a limited degree seems to represent a significant departure from conditions that have existed in the past. The ancient Babylonians, for example, felt that one person was as qualified as another to advise sick people about the proper use of drugs. They advocated that ". . . the people bring their sick to the marketplace, where any passerby might ask them about their complaints and offer his advice on the remedies to be used" (1). As was suggested earlier in the discussion of the effects of limited access to prescription drugs, contemporary society has made a complete turn-about in the control and regulation of the availability, access, quality, and use of drugs.

The basic enabling legislation pertaining to the qualifications of persons responsible for the movement of drugs through the various distribution channels is contained in the US FD&C Act, which states that prescription drugs can be prescribed (it actually reads "administered") only by those persons authorized to prescribe drugs, and may be dispensed only by those persons authorized to dispense drugs. The same requirement pertains to persons authorized to administer this class of drugs. Thus the definition of persons authorized to perform a particular function is left to the individual states. Every state has seen fit to authorize only a limited class of persons to prescribe drugs. Physicians comprise the category of persons given unrestricted license to prescribe and administer drugs, or to dispense drugs for their own patients (45). (They must, nevertheless, comply with all applicable laws pertaining to labeling).

Specialized kinds of physicians are issued a restricted license to prescribe drugs depending on the intended use of the drug. Podiatrists, for example, are licensed to prescribe only drugs that are intended to affect the lower appendages. Likewise, veterinarians are licensed to prescribe drugs only for use in animals. Dentists, however, are generally issued an unrestricted license to prescribe drugs, even though they are involved with treating only a small portion of the anatomy.

Every state has seen fit to license pharmacists to dispense drugs for the general public, and to license nurses as the primary administrators of drugs. The patient is also implicitly allowed to administer drugs in an outpatient environment, although generally he is not allowed to administer drugs to himself while an inpatient. Although the law does not prohibit patient self-administration of prescribed drugs within hospitals or other institutions, institutional rules do.

The trend in legislation is to enlarge the categories of persons allowed to prescribe drugs. Present trends indicate authorizing physicians' assistants and pediatric nurse practitioners to prescribe limited kinds of drugs and, allowing nurse practitioners to prescribe certain kinds of drugs generally under the direct supervision of a physician. There is a movement within the American Pharmaceutical Association to create a third class of drugs between the present prescription and nonprescription drugs that can be prescribed by pharmacists and presumably by physicians. Such a change would prohibit the patient from prescribing for himself the drugs in this intermediate category.

Figure 11.1   Role expectation as defined by the drug control and regulatory system.

The states generally limit their qualifications for wholesalers and manufacturers to registration and (in the case of manufacturers) compliance with the Current Good Manufacturing Practice Regulations (see Chapter 6) promulgated under the FD&C Act. Many states, however, lack a regulatory input pertaining to wholesalers and manufacturers, except for the requirement that they register and periodically update this registration.

The concept of delegation of authority to role occupants will be fully developed in Chapter 12. Appreciation of the interrelationship of the various role occupants is enhanced by examining selected components of the legal system and thus augmenting understanding of the functions of a given entity. A role occupant is expected to execute normatively (see Section 11.2 for a detailed definition of norm) the functions peculiar to his role. A role occupant is a person occupying a particular role. A role is a "script" or set of behavior more or less prescribed by law or other norms for that role or job. Figure 11.1 depicts the script or role expectations placed on a role occupant by societal and personal forces, the norm of behavior for the particular role, and the sanctions used to encourage the role occupant to conform to the requisite norms.

Figure 11.2 depicts the structures of the legal system of medication control and regulation. The public makes demands on the courts and the legislature to create norms which are in turn communicated to role occupants and role sanctioning institutions, e.g., the State Board of Nursing. The sanctioning authority acts to encourage role occupants to conform to expected conduct appropriate for the protection of the public's health and safety. The dotted lines in the figure represent secondary lines of communication.

The interrelationships of medication control systems, law sanctioning agencies, and lawmakers are illustrated in Figure 11.3. This figure depicts an integrated system of influence to prescribe and enforce behavior of role occupants (providers and patients) and to secure desired performance from role occupants. Pharmacy is used as an example role for the sake of illustration, but others also belong in the categories depicted.

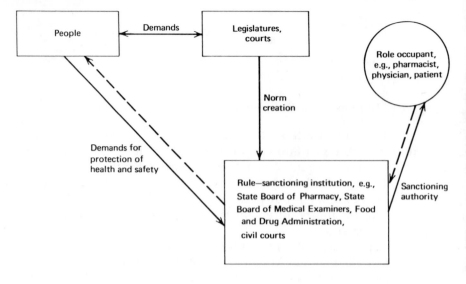

Figure 11.2.   Structure of legal system of medication control and regulation.

Since it is impossible to describe in detail the relevant characteristics of the entities and their relationships depicted in Figure 11.3, the discussion that follows will concentrate on pharmacy—an occupation in which health care function revolves entirely around medication. A "typical" practice act is described, based on a composite of some of the more progressive, typical practice acts. Nursing and medicine as roles are also briefly reviewed.

Criminal law (laws governing wrongful acts against the state) is generally codified by a legislature, whereas civil law (laws governing wrongful acts against private persons) tends almost exclusively to be left to judges to enact. (Civil and criminal law are further differentiated in Section 13.4.1). Therefore one can readily identify and describe a given portion of the law as prescriptive of unapproved behavior of a criminal nature. The emphasis tends to be toward a definitive listing of the punishment for committing forbidden acts. Likewise, the acts that are permissible for providers are relatively obscure. Since drug technology seems in many cases to be ahead of the courts, one is left with a less than definitive description of the duties of providers (and patients, too).

A pharmacy practice act of a state generally prescribes the duties of a pharmacy practitioner as limited to the practice of pharmacy. A pharmacy practice act is enacted for the purpose of protecting the public

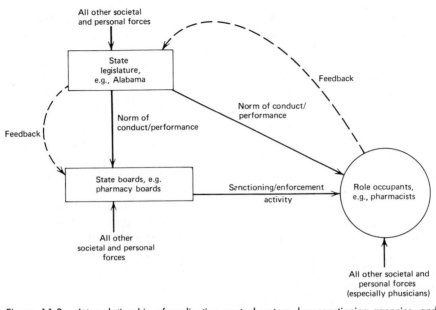

Figure 11.3.   Interrelationship of medication control system, law-sanctioning agencies, and lawmakers

health, safety, and welfare of the citizens of a particular state. The other components of an example pharmacy practice act ordinarily follow from this one basic objective and purpose. Since the purpose of a pharmacy practice act revolves around drugs, the act ordinarily reflects this in a subsection of the basic statement of purpose of the act. Typically, an act will declare that regulation of the public health, safety, and welfare includes regulating the qualifications of pharmacists and other persons allowed to compound or dispense prescriptions or other classes of drugs.

A typical act will ordinarily be introduced with a definition of the key terms used within the act, and will usually include a definition of the role to be performed by the pharmacist. It will usually include a broad, general description of the duties, responsibilities, and authority of related practitioners that will be described, briefly. A pharmacy practice act will include not only the definition of pharmacy and pharmacist, but also a definition of medical practitioner, physician, hospital, drug manufacturer, drug wholesaler, pharmacy intern, pharmacy extern, pharmacy preceptor, etc., and also a definition of various drugs based on their legal classification.

A significant component of a pharmacy practice act will provide for the establishment of a quasi-judicial and a quasi-legislative body which will see to it that pharmacists adhere to the provisions of the act. Included will be a description of the nature of the governing body typically termed "the state board of pharmacy," the qualifications for membership in the governing body, the logistics of conducting meetings and maintaining records, etc. The authority (power) of the board of pharmacy will be limited and delimited by the typical statute. The typical board of pharmacy is empowered to make certain rules to implement the pharmacy practice act of that state. In theory these rules are bounded by the pharmacy practice statute except that the board of pharmacy is ordinarily not only empowered to enforce the laws establishing the profession of pharmacy and establishing the board itself, but is also empowered to enforce its own rules and regulations pertaining to the practice of pharmacy in the affected state.

The qualifications for practicing pharmacy will be described in considerable detail. These components necessary for qualifying as a pharmacist are ordinarily described in structural terms, with some attention given to process components.

The typical act will provide for carrying out certain functions that are delegated only to pharmacy. Pharmacists in training and others usually carry the titles of pharmacy interns or, in at least two states (Alabama and Mississippi), of assistant pharmacists. Various provisions are incorporated into a pharmacy practice act for a person qualifying for a license and may very well include the amount and frequency of fee payment. Since pharmacists do not usually practice their profession outside the limits of a pharmacy, provisions are included in the typical statute to account for this.

Although the uniqueness of pharmacy is probably unparalleled by the other health professions, it is somewhat related to the profession of optometry in that a product is also supplied sometimes in conjunction with the prescription of a licensed optometrist. Likewise, a dentist ordinarily must provide his services in the context of certain kinds of equipment and assistance. Nevertheless, since a component of the pharmacist's service consists of a product, pharmacy does take on some unique aspects that are reflected in the pharmacy practice act. As previously discussed, it is essential that the various components of the drug distribution channels be identified in order for adequate drug control and regulation to occur. For this reason and others a pharmacy practice act, in the majority of states, requires registration and licensing of channel members involved in the distribution of drugs, and usually describes the conditions necessary for securing a permit or license to operate a pharmacy. Generally the act provides that a pharmacy can only be operated under the personal supervision of a duly licensed pharmacist.

In the pharmacy practice act a limitation on the retail selling of certain classes of drugs will be described. Often this will be contained in the section of the law describing the requirements and qualifications for securing a permit or license to operate a pharmacy. Restrictions on the selling of drugs will usually be described, and special restrictions may be placed on some classes of drugs, e.g., scheduled and controlled substances. These restrictions usually prohibit dealing in misbranded or adulterated drugs.

A pharmacy practice act includes considerable details about licensing requirements. These usually contain a description of an internship period. The requirements for internship training are given, and the trend is to describe qualifications or to provide for the description of qualifications in the act by the board for a teacher (usually termed preceptor) to meet in order to be allowed to train future pharmacists. Since a pharmacy has already been described as unique in that its principal concern is a product, a pharmacy practice act will also provide for the transfer of stock between drugstores in the event of change of ownership, change of location, change of name, and other relevant aspects of business.

A state statute also includes certain rules that must be observed by a state board of pharmacy in carrying out its legal obligation to enforce the act. These rules generally relate to the board's functions as a legislative and judicial arm of government, with emphasis placed on the judicial aspects. Provision is usually made for due process of law which includes notifying the accused of charges, the opportunity for a hearing before one's accuser, and appeal to a higher authority. The act contains provisions for inspection of pharmacy records, labeling requirements, and drug stocks. Typically it contains considerable detail about the nature of acts viewed as violations of the pharmacy practice act. These acts usually include such items as fraudulently obtaining a license to practice pharmacy or to operate a pharmacy, and a general prohibition pertaining to immorality and other illegal acts relating to components of other statutory or common law. The act generally provides for something less than imprisonment or fines; usually a reprimand, suspension of a pharmacy license or permit, and revocation of a pharmacy license are included as penalties. The act may also provide for the circumstances that define illegal possession of certain legal classes of drugs, and make it illegal to possess a prescription (legend) drug unless it has been dispensed in accordance with the requirements of the pharmacy practice act. Possession of a prescription drug will frequently be defined as illegal if it is not properly labeled.

Many pharmacy practice acts as well as other practice acts will contain in the statutes a code of professional conduct or provision for the formulation of a code of professional conduct by the state board of pharmacy or state pharmacy association. This kind of code will ordinarily prescribe certain high standards desired of pharmacists, although failure to meet these standards does not necessarily constitute a violation of a legal norm of conduct. The requirements of the code, if they exist at all, will ordinarily be established at a level of performance higher than the standard of conduct (norm) required of the reasonable and prudent pharmacist. However, it should be noted that as the practice is successful in securing performance according to this high calling of the code of professional conduct, common law will tend to define this level of performance as the level of the reasonable and prudent pharmacist.

A listing and topical outline of the content of a typical pharmacy practice act is presented as an aid to studying the act of a given state. The following list relates to regulation and control of most aspects of pharmacy practice:

1. Establishment and operation of a Board of Pharmacy.
2. The logistics of securing, maintaining, and continuing a pharmacist license.
3. The logistics of securing, maintaining, and continuing a pharmacy permit.
4. Qualifications for licensure as a pharmacist.
5. Board of Pharmacy membership qualifications, nomination, appointment, reimbursement policies and amounts, etc.
6. A delimiting of the powers and duties of the State Board of Pharmacy.
7. The qualifications, powers, and duties of state drug inspectors.
8. Recognition of schools and colleges of pharmacy accredited by the American Council on Pharmaceutical Education.
9. The requirement of a license to practice pharmacy.
10. Provisions for a penalty or penalties for violating various components of the Act.
11. The procedure for applying for a license to practice pharmacy.
12. The listing of the qualifications of pharmacy applicants that usually require the applicant to:
    a. be a graduate of an accredited college of pharmacy

b.   be a U.S. citizen
c.   be at least 21 years of age
d.   be of good moral character
e.   pass a pharmacy license examination
f.   serve a specified period of internship (usually one year).

13.   Provision for licensure of persons as pharmacists via reciprocity.
14.   Requirement for registration of major elements in the drug distribution channel of that state, e.g., retailers, wholesalers, manufacturers, and certain other entities distributing legend drugs or other legal classes of drugs.
15.   Requirement that each pharmacy be operated under the personal supervision of a duly licensed pharmacist.
16.   Provision for the restricting of poison sales to sales under the immediate supervision of a licensed pharmacist.
17.   A definition of filling or compounding a prescription.
18.   Provision for the sale of legend drugs only pursuant to a proper prescription issued by a practitioner authorized to prescribe legend drugs.
19.   Provision for refilling of duly authorized prescriptions.
20.   Delimiting of the physical requirements of a pharmacy prescription room and the specifications thereof.
21.   Prohibition of the offering for sale of adulterated or misbranded drugs.
22.   Prohibition of the selling of a brand of a drug different from the one prescribed by a licensed prescriber (some Acts will accept such practices provided that they pertain to the operation of a formulary and a licensed hospital).
23.   A listing and description of the grounds for revocation or suspension of licenses to practice pharmacy or operate a pharmacy under a pharmacy permit; these include:

a.   fraudulently obtaining a license or permit
b.   violation of the law as pertaining to controlled substances or legend drugs
c.   conviction of a felony
d.   violation of rules of the Board of Pharmacy
e.   gross immorality or drug addiction
f.   reprehensible conduct
g.   physical or mental incompetence
h.   illegal substitution of one brand for another
i.   colluding with another person in practicing pharmacy without a license.

24. Provision for revoking or suspending a license or permit in accordance with due process of law.
25. Provision for judicial review of any or all orders of the Board of Pharmacy.
26. Authorization to the Board to seek injunctions against violators of the Practice Act.
27. Requirements that a participating pharmacy must meet when it is serving as the preceptor pharmacy for a pharmacist intern or extern.
28. Pharmacy preceptor qualifications which usually pertain to insuring that the preceptor pharmacist is an active, full-time, licensed pharmacist who has been engaged in the practice of pharmacy for several years immediately preceding his role as a preceptor.
29. The requirement that every pharmacy, regardless of its location in an institution or elsewhere, must employ a pharmacist.
30. The requirement that any entity stocking legend drugs that are made available within that institution to its patients must either have an in-house pharmacy with a permit or secure the services of a consultant pharmacist to take direct responsibility for legend drug stock (inventory).
31. The requirement that persons dealing in mail-order dispensing of drugs obtain a permit from the Board of Pharmacy.
32. A description of the legal class or classes of drugs to which the Act will apply, e.g., legend drugs, veterinary legend drugs, non-prescription drugs, controlled substances, poisons, hazardous substances, syringes and needles, and so-called "exempt narcotics."
33. A description and procedure for promulgating rules and regulations in accordance with the provisions of the Act.
34. A description of certain technical equipment and reference books that must be kept within a pharmacy which has been issued a permit.
35. Provision for a poison and exempt narcotic register and the record-keeping requirements pertaining to these items.
36. Provisions for posting certain signs containing prescribed information spelling out when an absent pharmacist will again be available within the confines of the pharmacy.
37. A requirement for registration as a consultant pharmacist with the Board of Pharmacy.
38. A requirement for mandatory continuing education.
39. A requirement that a duly issued pharmacy permit or pharmacist license be recorded in the county of practice.

40. A caveat that the act will not apply to a practitioner (physician, dentist, veterinarian, osteopath, podiatrist) who compounds his own prescriptions for his own patients.
41. Dispensed prescription labeling requirements.
42. Information on record-keeping requirements pursuant to the dispensing of a legitimate prescription.
43. Provision for penalties for violation of various portions of the Act.
44. Provision for control and regulation of drug use within the confines of a hospital, nursing home, or similar kind of organization.
45. Dispensed prescription labeling requirements for nursing home prescriptions.
46. Provision for the content of emergency kits in nursing homes.
47. Provision for periodic review of each nursing home patient's medication regimen.

11.1   NURSING PRACTICE ACTS

Traditionally, the nurse's role in medication usage has been the administration of a single dose of a medication under the immediate direction of a physician. The role has historically been viewed as a medication function, but clearly different from prescribing or dispensing a medication. This perspective is seen by many as unduly restrictive for the modern nurse.

Nurses themselves have had a difficult time agreeing on a definition of nursing. In part this confusion arises from the attempt to define the functions of a nurse as a subset of the duties of the physician. Although the physician is given an unrestricted license which in effect authorizes the execution of any health care function, the nurse is in the difficult position (as are other health care professionals) of having to specify the nature of the restricted set of duties assigned to the nursing role.

That more than half of all nursing practice acts have been significantly amended since 1970 is ample evidence of the throes of change in nursing (2). No comprehensive review will be undertaken here. The nurse has been given restricted authority to write prescriptions in Idaho (3); and Nevada, New Hampshire, and Arizona allow nurses to dispense drugs under certain restricted circumstances.

Nurse roles differ from those of other roles in that several kinds of nurses are recognized, e.g., licensed practical nurse, registered nurse. California allows certain medical corpsmen to secure a nurse's license without going to nursing school. Georgia and the District of Columbia have permissive licensure laws which allow individuals to practice nursing without a license provided they do not claim to be licensed or use the title R.N. Other states require mandatory licensing for all who practice nursing for compensation. Some states are actively considering licensure by proficiency exam without the usual required college education; California has in part adopted this philosophy.

Movements to ease entry into the nursing profession are based on the sound principle of allowing those who can perform a given task to do so. If testing technology were sufficiently sophisticated, proficiency exams could be constructed for qualification as lawyer, pharmacist, physician, nurse, judge, etc. Such is not the case, however, and nurses are justifiably concerned that unqualified people will enter the profession.

Apart from the exceptions enumerated above, nursing is structured in a manner similar to other medication-related organizations. The women's liberation movement should help nursing shrug the mantle of traditional male dominance (from the outside) of nursing. Also, the increasing influx of males into nursing should help the profession acquire a less dependent role. The future probably holds a greater decision-making role for nurses in the prescribing and dispensing of medication. Other important sources consider the important problem of role assignment in more detail than we have done here (4, 5).

All licensure laws are principally concerned with grouping selected tasks, assigning people who meet specified qualifications to these roles (while forbidding others to perform these roles), and requiring accountability of the role occupant. A major problem arises when task assignment to roles is not done in such a way that tasks are assigned to one type of role occupant and only to that role. Likewise, a person occupying a given role may be fully capable of performing within other roles. Duties and capabilities of role occupants tend to overlap. Licensure laws for these same roles may or may not overlap.

11.2 A CONCEPTUALIZATION OF THE MEANING OF ETHICS

Whenever a set of rules is developed, the intent is always to control the behavior of someone other than the developers (although in fairness the behavior of the developers is usually purposefully included).

Diverse, more or less systematic and comprehensive, codes are written on a given subject to achieve the kinds of behavior viewed as desirable by the code developers. Examples of diverse codes are legal, moral, religious, football, courtship, cattle registration, etc.

The question: What are the criteria for determining which actions are good and bad, right and wrong, has confronted mankind in general and providers and consumers of health care in particular. Ethics, law, values, morality rights, and other norms are central, recurring concepts in the search for satisfactory answers. Legal codes are abundant, and virtually all occupations claim allegiance to something usually referred to as a code of ethics. How do these various codes relate to other guidelines or requirements for thinking or doing?

Ethics has traditionally been the discipline in philosophy to which we have looked for guidance. "Ethics" as a word has several meanings. Depending on its context it normally relates to a branch of moral philosophy or to the discipline concerned with the overall goodness or badness of particular behavior. The task of ethics is best thought of as the quest for discovering what it is that causes people to approve or disapprove of conduct. One may argue that for an action to be good, it must satisfy some desire. Is pleasure good? is a basic ethical question. Ethics may have an additional meaning, when used in the sense of a code of ethics, as a systematic listing of desired kinds of behavior for a person of a particular category (i.e., role occupant) engaged or potentially engaged in categorical acts.

The following sections represent an attempt at meaningful differentiation of several moral concepts. After a general treatment of the concepts of value, ethics, and law, attention is devoted to codes of ethics with special implications for medication use. Ideas of moral rightness or wrongness become ethical notions when reflective evaluation of the actions and their effects is relied upon. Providers must, for example, daily decide such questions as: Will the consequences of violating rules be better overall than the consequences of obeying them? Should we strive to maximize the welfare of patients as a group, or should we strive to maximize the welfare of individual patients, i.e., should we pursue hedonism or utilitarianism?

Values represent a concern with what ought to be the outcome of our actions. That is, values give rise to selecting and exhibiting one action in favor of another. Should we buy aspirin or should we contribute to the destitute children's fund? A good or service can satisfy us in two ways: (1) through its effect in producing some other and additional good or service; and (2) through its ability to involve itself to furnish in and of itself a desired end. However,

. . . when it becomes necessary to choose between two ends which offer themselves, three things are involved. First, those ends must be carefully elaborated until the complete picture is before us. Secondly, some further end must be agreed upon. Finally, those competing ends must themselves be treated as means, and evaluated as they serve to affect the other end. Reflections can thus clarify ends and evaluate means; but the acceptance of a standard for that evaluation remains something into which reflections cannot enter. That is a fundamental preference to be made upon a basis of experience and acquaintance (6).

In a practical sense certain types of acts are best not treated as good or bad in and of themselves until they have been examined and scrutinized in terms of predicting what the outcome will be if they are completed. The ethics of the drug use process implicitly prescribe as the preferred end that which produces the greater good for the individual. While certain ends in secular codes or laws may require this treatment, this may not always be the case

Yet so often have the aims which men thus dogmatically imposed upon themselves and others resulted in evil and suffering, it appears that to regard any values as quite removed from the possibility of further criticism is exceedingly apt to mean that they are incapable of any rational justification whatsoever (7).

Control of morbidity and mortality in some developing countries is having the effect of too many mouths to feed and, consequently, of marginal existence. The Bomb, too, may yet do us in.

Such careful choosing is a high calling, but may nevertheless yield results commensurate with such a calling. A goal of this approach is to achieve concentration on ends and thus avoid the confusion and needless intermingling of means and ends.

Let us forget for the moment that you said this must be done. Let us try to find out if we cannot agree on something of which we should both approve, and which we could both try to get. If we can agree on this good thing, then perhaps we should not find it so hard to argue intelligently about the best way of getting it (7).

This statement assumes that the advocates of varying positions will, once they have arrived at a particular common end, tell why each thought the end he desired was good. The various advocates would each point out the implications of their positions. Although the goal of most criminal and civil proceedings pertaining to the control and regulation of drugs is aimed toward prediction, it is nevertheless worth considering.

. . . that, when all has been said, there enter so many incalculable elements into the actions of human beings that it is still quite impossible for us to tell, in any individual case, just what will be the outcome of any particular act which they perform (8).

Does aspirin merely relieve pain or does it also alter genetic structure? This approach to the understanding of human behavior has led many to argue that study as one may human action is unpredictable. Nevertheless, it remains true that "When all has been said in favor of skepticism, it remains clear that men must act, that some acts are better than others, and that some basis of discrimination must be used" (9). To decide between consuming and not consuming aspirin requires a decision. It is important to remember that

. . . the whole purpose and essence of law is to enable us to deal with particular issues as particular examples of a general type or class. Intelligent control would be out of the question, were it not possible to discover general types and to deal with them as such. But such general types can be formulated only with limits (10).

In practice, however, this is difficult because "even with the utmost care in defining the scope of a law, ambiguities creep in almost immediately and usually grow worse as time passes" (10).

Such circumstances call for simplification. Complexity, however, will most likely be the answer. "If every situation had one law, and that obviously *its* law, the legal profession would be more like a card index and less like a science" (11). Similarly, if in the treatment of disease a particular symptom pointed to only a single cure, we might have automatic, mechanical physicians, pharmacists, nurses, and others providing cures. In real life, however, the practitioner is confronted with a number of equally appealing alternatives from which he must choose. He uses what is usually referred to as judgment to select one or more of these alternatives. It is the essence of law to determine how to apply a particular law to an uncertain case.

11.3 VALUES, ETHICS, AND LAW

Where the field of values represents concern with what ultimately ought to be, ethics represents a selection and description of what ought to be viewed from the perspective of an individual, group, society, culture or other conceptual unit of mankind. Law, however,

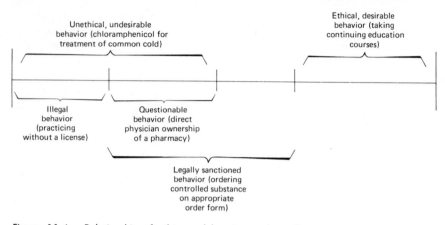

Figure 11.4.   Relationship of ethics and law in a value milieu.

represents what must be. Law incorporates a formal, publicly proclaimed and publicly enforced set of penalties which are mandatory for
persons failing to do what has been proclaimed as "must" behavior.
"Ought to" behavior may result in punishment for those deviating
from this standard, but the differentiating element is the lack of a
formalized, bureaucratized censoring or punishing of one's deviant
actions through legitimate and normal state-sanctioned channels.

Norms are established as guidelines or rules which specify the
standard of behavior for role occupants. There are several kinds of
norms, and they differ for various role occupants. Generally a norm is
premised on the claim that if the standard of behavior called for by the
norm is adhered to, then the value being sought will be attained.
These relationships are illustrated in Figure 11.4. Examples of acts that
fall along various points of the ethical to illegal continuum appear in brackets. In addition to ethical and legal norms, there are
technical norms, such as the rules for dividing fractions, computing
prothrombin time, or programming a computer; conventional norms,
e.g., nurses work 5 days a week; aesthetic norms, e.g., fat babies are
pretty; moral norms, e.g., be tolerant of racial differences, intervention
in disease is desirable, etc. For each kind of norm, adhering to that
norm will yield the "thing" sought. Adhering to the rules of "long
division" will yield the correct answer.

A crucial aspect of the concept of norm is that the normative standard is determined on an ethical, what-ought-to-be basis rather than
on a statistical basis such as the average or modal way of executing a

certain act. For legal behavior the norm is determined by the conduct of the "reasonable" man, described in detail in Section 12.6.1. In the ethical domain the norm is determined primarily by the elite of the major group to which the role occupant belongs or which represents him, e.g., the American Pharmaceutical Association has been responsible for the formulation and promulgation of ethical norms for pharmacists.

Ethics and norms can properly be viewed as more complex than we have suggested here. Ethics and ethical norms can be perceived as ends and means, respectively. Ethics is concerned with proper goal selection and selection of the proper means for striving toward the goal. A prescriber may administer an approved drug to a patient for an unapproved purpose and it may prove to be effective, but to act in accord with ethical standards he should inform the patient of his intended action and secure the patient's informed consent.

Drugs represent the vanguard of technological achievement. Their use by providers may entail choosing from several specialized kinds of norms, e.g., choosing from among religious, economic, psychological, familial, political, recreational, or other norms. For example, a physician occupies simultaneously the roles of physician, father, citizen, religious worshipper, and economic provider to his family. To act in accordance with one norm may preclude acting in accordance with another; e.g., prescribing oral contraceptives when one's religion prohibits chemical contraception. Although a pharmacist may agree to dispense a prescription after hours for an emergency situation, which represents adherence to a professional norm, this may cause him to violate the familial norm of spending some time with the children.

For the health professional the most demanding ethical decision is choosing between the norm prescribing selection of the end that best serves the patient and the norm directing that he act in the patient's best interest, even if his own best interest is compromised. The very essence of "profession" is professing to put the client's interest first. Taking the time to explain how a medication should be taken will help enhance the chances of a successful treatment outcome and thus serve the patient's interest, whereas a dimension of the provider's interest will be compromised if his income is reduced because of the time devoted to counseling. (It is easy to forget that the word "doctor" originally meant "to teach.")

The remaining portion of this chapter will be devoted to a refinement of the relationship of ethics and law, and to a description of selected ethical codes relevant to medication use.

11.3.1   The Dependence of Law on Ethics.

Law is most easily distinguished from ethics on the basis of presence or absence of power to compel performance or punish deviant performance. However, law probably would not exist without adherence to ethical norms. Most behavior depends upon mutual trust. The bank robber trusts his accomplice in the getaway car to be at the agreed location as he exits from the bank. The provider trusts the patient to keep the agreed upon appointment. The "ignorant" student trusts the professor to educate him in the subject matter of the course; and the "ignorant" patient trusts the prescriber to properly select an antibiotic to cure his infection.

Trust exerts a pervasive influence on the behavior of persons living in any situation involving direct or indirect contact with other people. Although frequent attempts are made to compel adherence to standards outside the law, careful examination will rarely show that such attempts are successful. For example, although the law can prescribe how a father's inheritance is to be divided among his children in the absence of a will, the law is unable to compel those children to love their father, or to love one another, or even to act as if they loved one another. If the legislature or court could compel love, friendship, compassion, trust, empathy, and charity, then most of the evils of present-day living would disappear. There is no way to legislate successfully against many diseases. Although it is possible to legislate against some diseases by compelling vaccinations, etc., it is difficult to prohibit or compel certain habits, e.g., cigarette smoking, wearing of seat belts, obesity, and other behaviors which, if modified, would probably increase longevity. Thus, the law may not be the proper means for persuading pharmacists to instruct patients about proper medication consumption.

Trust and cooperation are essential in virtually all societies and unquestionably in a technologically advanced society dependent upon specialization of tasks. A specialized society depends on the exchange of surplus production among the various producers: the farmer depends on the physician to deliver his baby, and the physician depends on the farmer to produce his steaks. The farmer depends on the professor of sociology to teach his sons, and the sociologist depends upon the electrician to insure that adequate lighting is available in his classrooms. Society prescribes a number of rules which are to be executed largely outside the domain of law. For example, in the United States an American father is supposed to love his children, obtain their respect, be a good economic provider, mow his law, provide certain services to the children's mother, and so on. While the law is active in compelling fathers to provide for the economic needs of children (although with less than complete success in the case of alimony), it has generally been unsuccessful in such areas as providing the proper role model or sex model behavior for children to emulate. There are a large number of roles that any one person will occupy at any given moment of life. As already suggested, people may occupy roles which require behavior that is functional for one role and dysfunctional for another. For health professionals, the primary criterion for selection is supposed to be the needs of the client rather than the needs of the provider.

The dependence of law and the very fabric of society on ethics has been well stated by Earl Warren:

> In the Law beyond the Law, which calls upon us to be fair in business, where the Law cannot demand fairness; which bids us temper justice with mercy, where the Law can only enforce justice; which demands our compassion for the unfortunate, although the Law can only give him his legal due, each of us is necessarily his own Chief Justice. In fact, he is the whole Supreme Court, from which there lies no appeal. The individual citizen may engage in practices which, on the advice of counsel, he believes strictly within the letter of the law, but which he also knows from his own conscience are outside the bounds of propriety and the right. Thus, when he engages in such practices, he does so not at his peril—as when he violates the Law—but at peril to the structure of civilization, involving greater stakes than any possible peril to himself (12).

Thus, ethics is properly viewed as the creation of civilization and is essential for its survival. A large part of the body of ethical norms is transmitted from one generation to another via the socialization process of the various societal institutions, such as the family, the school, and the church. This high calling places demanding responsibilities on individuals in general and health professionals in particular. It is the individual who must apply these ethical precepts in difficult and perplexing situations.

> This necessity requires [the role occupant] to be trained in the discernment of right from wrong and the will to accept the right, without the slightest duress. His problem is the more complicated because the issues presented by life are rarely simple. The individual usually has no difficulty in discerning absolute right, just as the Supreme Court would never be divided in its opinion if in a particular case only one constitutional principle were involved. [The Supreme Court] divides very frequently because in actual cases several constitutional principles are in-

volved and their implications, so far as these cases are concerned, are by no means the same. Similarly, the individual, confronted with life's problems, has to evaluate the relevance of one value or precept against another insofar as both concern the immediate situation. No wonder that he is frequently perplexed; and wishes he could free himself from obligations to follow the Law beyond the Law (12).

Clearly, the action required by the health care provider requires difficult decision-making. While it is true that health professionals are frequently caught up in demanding situations, it is also true that "A person may be learned or ignorant; he may be old or young, rich or poor, well or sick; whatever his condition, he has to act, and his actions have their effect on himself and generally also on his fellow man. The man of character, sensitive to the meaning of what he is doing, [must] . . . know how to discover the ethical path in the maze of possible behavior" (12). As drug technology becomes increasingly complex, the decisions which must be made by providers and patients alike become increasingly complex and difficult. Just as the decisions of the Supreme Court are divided along narrow lines reflected in close 5-to-4 decisions, health care providers will also find themselves increasingly divided as to what the best answer is under the circumstances.

The concluding sections of this chapter describe specific ethical doctrines governing provider behavior.

11.4 PATIENT'S BILL OF RIGHTS

The Patient's Bill of Rights (PBR), adopted by the American Hospital Association in 1972, will be analyzed from the perspective of its possible influence on patient and provider medication-related behavior. It is reproduced verbatim as Table 11.1. Analysis of this 254-word document is preferred over the more traditional physicians' Hippocratic Oath because it will probably have a more pronounced influence on provider and patient drug-related behavior. Moreover, there is a greater general awareness of the oath than of this more recently formulated document. The PBR will be analyzed from the perspective of ethics rather than from a strictly legal viewpoint.*

The very title of the PBR is stimulating in that it implies that these precepts are inherently owed to the patient by somebody. But the

* This section relies heavily on Horty (13).

TABLE 11.1   PATIENT'S BILL OF RIGHTS[a]

(1)   The patient has the right to considerate and respectful care.

(2)   The patient has the right to obtain from his physician complete current information concerning his diagnosis, treatment and prognosis in terms the patient can reasonably be expected to understand.

(3)   The patient has the right to receive from his physician information necessary to give informed consent prior to the start of any procedure and/or treatment.

(4)   The patient has the right to refuse treatment to the extent permitted by law, and to be informed of the medical consequences of his action.

(5)   The patient has the right to every consideration of his privacy concerning his own medical care program.

(6)   The patient has the right to expect that all communications and records pertaining to his care should be treated as confidential.

(7)   The patient has the right to expect that within its capacity a hospital must make reasonable response to the request of a patient for services.

(8)   The patient has the right to obtain information as to any relationship of his hospital to other health care and educational institutions insofar as his care is concerned.

(9)   The patient has the right to be advised if the hospital proposes to engage in or perform human experimentation affecting his care or treatment.

(10) The patient has the right to expect reasonable continuity of care.

(11) The patient has the right to examine and receive an explanation of his bill regardless of source of payment.

(12) The patient has the right to know what hospital rules and regulations apply to his conduct as a patient.

[a] Adopted by the American Hospital Association, 1972.
Source: American Hospital Association, Chicago, Ill., 1972.

definition of a right when strictly construed is something which is enforceable in a court of law. In other words when person A acquires a right, then some other person B loses a right because the person owing the right no longer has a choice as to whether that duty is to be delivered. Because of this relationship, there is always a scarcity of rights. This analysis will take the approach that rights are not necessarily owed to a patient unless prescribed by law. At present this list of patient rights is not construed by the courts as a strictly legal document. However, as more and more hospitals adopt the PBR as a set of guidelines for thought and action, the law will have an increasing tendency to incorporate the PBR within its coverage.

The Preamble to the PBR (omitted from Table 11.1) suggests an overall encompassing value which is to be achieved by adhering to the precepts listed in the PBR. If this is a correct interpretation, then each of the items in the PBR can be properly construed as a set of norms to be followed in order to yield the right appearing in the preamble, which states that " . . . these rights will contribute to more effective patient care and greater satisfaction to the patient, his physician, and the hospital organization." It is only fair to note that the patient is not the sole focus of the values implicitly contained in the PBR. On the contrary, although the patient is listed first in the Preamble, the physician and the hospital are also discussed. Perhaps the crucial aspect of the PBR has been stated pejoratively by Horty:

> . . . the hospital has a duty to protect its patients from actions of its own staff physicians should that need arise and the hospital staff must by law be aware of what is happening. And that is the crux . . . to force the hospital publicly to pledge that it will extensively monitor its own staff physicians (13).

In essence this means that the physician's conduct is the focus of most of the 12 items within the PBR. Clearly, an underlying assumption in the PBR is that it is necessary to protect patients from hospital employees, including physicians. It puts the well-being of patients ahead of all other things and people. This is almost certain to evoke considerable response on the part of affected persons; basically all providers within the hospital will be influenced, since drugs are widely used in a hospital.

The analysis here will be on an item-by-item basis following the analysis of Horty (13), except that the drug use process perspective will be the main focus of attention. The discussion which follows refers to the 12 items in Table 11.1.

Item 1 in the PBR is, of course, something that all persons can agree with as a basic right of patients. What constitutes "considerate and respectful care" may be less obvious. It is likely to affect the drug use process by triggering equivocating persons to file a law suit when they might otherwise not do so. Such an increase in suits could exert a positive control mechanism on drug use by causing drug use providers to "shape up." Similarly, it could produce an adverse effect by causing undue caution and restraint on the part of the provider in prescribing needed drugs or prescribing unnecessary drugs in order to minimize the chances of a lawsuit. Chapter 13 devotes considerable attention to this point, and the reader will be urged to conclude that at present actual lawsuits are few relative to the number of possible suits.

Items 2 and 3 have the potential to revolutionize the drug use process. Note the word "complete" in item 2. The term could be interpreted to mean everything relevant to the use of a given drug in a given patient. If no other effect occurs than to increase the amount of physician time devoted to patient education, this would have a most profound effect; a doubling or quadrupling of current time might easily occur. Such a potential time increase is no small concern because the phrase "from his physician" in this item is important. The physician is apparently designated as either the sole direct provider of information to the patient or the gatekeeper in determining what information can pass from providers to patients. This interpretation requires that the term "procedure" or "treatment" be construed to include drug therapy; such a construction does not seem to be too demanding upon the meaning of this term, since education and surgery seem to be the only other major alternative kinds of treatment. As was noted in the previous chapter, in many instances of drug use the relative risk to the patient is roughly equal to the risk associated with frequently performed operations. If it was ruled that a patient must give his "informed consent" in order to consume drugs with hazards of roughly equivalent magnitudes, this could easily revolutionize drug use within institutions.

Item 2 also requires that one interpret the meaning of the word "current." What does current information in the context of drug therapy mean? Does it mean every hour of every day, or every time a new development in the person's medically deviant condition occurs? Who is to determine when it is not medically advisable to give drug use information to the patient? Who determines when the desired standard of conduct has been adhered to by a physician or other health care practitioner? Is it necessary for nurses, pharmacists, or others to report instances in which communication between the patient or some other provider has not occurred as "prescribed?"

Item 3 contains immense potential for changing drug use. Although the direction of change suggested is not clear, it would seem to be toward improvement. In an elaboration to this item, two instructive phrases appear: (1) ". . . the medically significant risk involved, the probable duration of incapacitation," and (2) "Where medically significant alternatives for cure or treatment exists, or when the patient requests information concerning medical alternatives, the patient has the right to such information." For example, the first phrase would clearly require divulging the risk from a number of properly administered drugs since the risk parallels that from surgery; surgery, of course, already requires informed consent. Also, it seems that when a drug other than the drug of choice is being administered, the patient should be fully informed about the drug alternatives available for treatment of his particular medically deviant condition. Indeed, it may even be necessary that alternative drug therapy be described to patients when the drug of choice is being prescribed, dispensed, and administered. The meaning of the phrase "medically significant" is also unclear. Is the likelihood of experiencing mild diarrhea, for example, medically significant? It may be from the perspective of the patient but not from the perspective of the provider. Is the provider to decide?

Item 4 is self-evident. It is easy to forget that the patient is in control (at least in theory) of what is done to his body; under most circumstances he is free to leave the hospital or to terminate therapy. It is generally considered false imprisonment to detain a patient as a patient beyond his wishes.

Item 5 appears to have little if any unique meaning for drug use. However, it may affect drug use in the future if the patient maintains that his privacy is interfered with through the use of drugs without his permission for teaching purposes. This may tend to retard legitimate drug experimentation in teaching centers and elsewhere.

Although item 6 does not seem to be unique, it should be commented upon briefly. With the use of "emotional" drugs such as methadone and drugs used to treat venereal infections, it is essential that providers involved in this kind of drug use keep patient information confidential. Such an apparently innocuous question as: "What is this drug being used for?" may offend a patient who is receiving penicillin for treatment of gonorrhea. It nevertheless appears to be the intent of this item to insure confidentiality of patient information. It is wise to remember that the patient is supposed to be the one who controls access to and confidentiality of information about him. It seems to be a frequent mistake on the part of providers to construe "confidential" as meaning confidential to providers, i.e., under the control of providers, when this is the very opposite of the facts. At least one court has ruled that the information in the patient's records belongs to him, whereas the physical record itself belongs to the provider; there is an amazing paucity of cases on this point.

Item 7 may at first appear to have basically the same effects on drug use services as on other hospital-based services. The meaning of "capacity," whether intended to mean ability or "if it is a policy of the hospital to offer that catgory of services" is largely irrelevant to drug usage. This confusion over the meaning of the word capacity is likely to affect nondrug use services significantly. The key word here appears to be *services*. If *services* is interpreted to mean only hospital/hotel type services, then drug therapy would be exluded; but if the word is intended to include medical services, medication would clearly be a vital part of those services. A number of possibilities arise when drug services are included within this item. For example, if a patient requests a drug order for a pain reliever or for some other drug, is the hospital supposed to act "within its capacity" and make a "reasonable response" to provide this "service" to a patient? Would such a request include, in the instance of a voluntary medical staff, contacting the prescribing physician at home in order to ascertain if a desired drug can be administered? This interpretation might have a positive effect regarding such drugs as RhoGAM®, which requires administration within the first 72 hours after birth. The patient might consider this item a legitimate basis for exerting his claim for this desired service, since it would ordinarily fall within the capacity of a hospital and would generally be construed as not outside the scope of a "reasonable response."

Item 8 appears to have most relevance in two broad areas of concern. In the instance of a prescriber who has a proprietary interest in a nursing home or in the pharmacy within a nursing home, the patient would have the right to be made aware of this relationship and might possibly choose not to act on the advice of his physician. It is doubtful that this item was intended to require prescribing physicians who own stock in relabeler drug companies to divulge this interest to patients. In a proprietary hospital owned by a physician or group of physicians, it would be a marked departure from existing practices to inform the patient that physician ownership of the pharmacy resulted in direct payments to the owner-physician. It seems a rather unreasonable expectation for hospitals to serve as the enforcing or policing agent for insuring adherence to this particular item.

Item 9 has already been addressed in part under items 2 and 3. Basically it relates to the straightforward research undertaken in teaching hospitals and, to a lesser extent, in other hospitals. It appears to cover the gamut of drug experimentation; it pertains to drug experimentation both for treatment purposes and solely for the production of new information. Significantly, in addition to looking to the researchers (usually physicians) for accountability, this item also places accountability upon the hospital itself. This approach seems valid since the hospital is providing the physical site, facilities, personnel, and other resources essential for executing research. It does not seem unreasonable for the hospital to control physicians' and other researchers' conduct and to formulate policies and procedures to monitor drug experimentation. Such control is one more step toward

TABLE 11.2 DECLARATION OF HELSINKI*a*

I. BASIC PRINCIPLES

1. Clinical research must conform to the moral and scientific principles that justify medical research and should be based on scientifically established facts.

2. Clinical research should be conducted only by scientifically qualified persons and under the supervision of a qualified medical man.

3. Clinical research cannot legitimately be carried out unless the importance of the objective is in proportion to the inherent risk to the subject.

4. Every clinical research project should be preceded by careful assessment of inherent risks in comparison to foreseeable benefits to the subject or to others.

5. Special caution should be exercised by the doctor in performing clinical research in which the personality of the subject is liable to be altered by drugs or experimental procedure.

II. CLINICAL RESEARCH COMBINED WITH PROFESSIONAL CARE

1. In the treatment of the sick person, the doctor must be free to use a new therapeutic measure, if in his judgment it offers hope of saving life, reestablishing health, or alleviating suffering.
(If at all possible, consistent with patient psychology, the doctor should obtain the patient's freely given consent after the patient has been given a full explanation.) In case of legal incapacity, consent should also be procured from the legal guardian; in case of physical incapacity the permission of the legal guardian replaces that of the patient.

2. The doctor can combine clinical research with professional care, the objective being the acquisition of new medical knowledge, only to the extent that clinical research is justified by its therapeutic value for the patient.

III. NONTHERAPEUTIC CLINICAL RESEARCH

1. In the purely scientific application of clinical research carried out on a human being, it is the duty of the doctor to remain the protector of the life and health of that person on whom clinical research is being carried out.

2. The nature, the purpose and the risk of clinical research must be explained to the subject by the doctor.

3a. Clinical research on a human being cannot be undertaken without his free consent after he has been informed; if he is legally incompetent, the consent of the legal guardian should be procured.

3b. The subject of clinical research should be in such a mental, physical and legal state as to be able to exercise fully his power of choice.

TABLE 11.2   (continued)

3c.	Consent should, as a rule, be obtained in writing. However, the responsibility for clinical research always remains with the research worker; it never falls on the subject even after consent is obtained.
4.	The investigator must respect the right of each individual to safeguard his personal integrity, especially if the subject is in a dependent relationship to the investigator.

[a] Introduction omitted.

Source: Declaration of Helsinki, World Medical Journal **11**:281 (Sept.) 1964.

securing adherence to legal requirements for experimentation on humans, called for by various ethical doctrines such as the Declaration of Helsinki and the Nuremberg Code (Section 11.4; Tables 11.2 and 11.3). Additional problems created by item 9 revolve around the definition of what constitutes experimentation with drugs. If experimentation is construed to include the use of approved drugs for unapproved purposes, this would represent a significant change in existing philosophies of hospital employees and medical staffs. Such an interpretation would be a marked extending of the control on physician researchers vested in the US FD&C Act. As previously described, the only mechanism for controlling provider behavior under the FD&C Act is an after-the-fact civil action based on malpractice. Chapter 13 shows that this is a largely unused or ineffective procedure. Item 9 puts teeth into the idea that drugs should be used principally only for a clearly defined purpose, and when the patient is fully informed and has given his consent for departure from the proven standard of safety and efficacy. Although this item pertains primarily to teaching hospitals, it is also essential that community hospitals using ordinary drugs or treatment in an experimental way establish protocols and monitoring procedures for the practices within their own area of responsibility.

Item 10 is a frequently overlooked component of health care. The American Public Health Association in its publication on this subject has listed continuity of care as one of the essential elements of health care (42). This item also has more significance than might be expected in regard to the use of drugs. Frequently a patient is sent home with inadequate drugs or prescriptions for drugs; even more frequently, a patient is sent home without adequate information for consuming the drugs given to him by a provider. This item suggests a significant departure in the hospital's perception of its role in that the hospital implicitly must get involved in monitoring the patient's needs for

. . . (b)   Informed consent means that the consent of such humans (or the consent of their representatives) to whom investigational drugs are administered primarily for the accumulation of scientific knowledge, for such purposes as studying drug behavior, body processes, or the course of a disease, must be obtained in all cases and, in all but exceptional cases, the consent of patients under treatment with investigational drugs or the consent of their representatives must be obtained.

(c)   "*Under treatment*" applies when the administration of the investigational drug for diagnostic, therapeutic, or other purpose involves medical judgment, taking into account the individual circumstances pertaining to the patient to whom the investigational drug is to be administered.

(d)   "*Exceptional cases*" . . . are those relatively rare cases in which it is not feasible to obtain the patient's consent or the consent of his representative, or in which as a matter of professional judgment exercised in the best interest of a particular patient under the investigator's care, it would be contrary to that patient's welfare to obtain his consent.

(e)   "Patient" means the person under treatment.

(f)   "*Not feasible*" is limited to cases wherein the investigator is not capable of obtaining consent because of inability to communicate with the patient or his representative; for example, the patient is in a coma or is otherwise incapable of giving consent, his representative cannot be reached, and it is imperative to administer the drug without delay.

(g)   "*Contrary to the best interests of such human beings*" applies when the communication of information to obtain consent would seriously affect the patient's well-being and the physician has exercised a professional judgment that under the particular circumstances of this patient's case, the patient's best interests would suffer if consent were sought.

(h)   "*Consent*" means that the person involved has legal capacity to give consent, is so situated as to be able to exercise free power of choice, and is provided with a fair explanation of pertinent information concerning the investigational drug, and/or his possible use as a control, as to enable him to make a decision on his willingness to receive said investigational drug. This latter element means that before the acceptance of an affirmative decision by such person the investigator should carefully consider and make known to him (taking into consideration such person's well-being and his ability to understand) the nature, expected duration, and purpose of the administration of said investigational drug; the method and means by which it is to be administered; the hazards involved; the existence of alternative forms of therapy, if any; and the beneficial effects upon his health or person that may possibly come from the administration of the investigational drug.

When consent is necessary . . . the consent of persons receiving an investiga-

TABLE 11.3 (continued)

tional new drug in Phase 1 and Phase 2 investigations (or their representatives) shall be in writing. When consent is necessary under such rules in Phase 3 investigations, it is the responsibility of investigators, taking into consideration the physical and mental state of the patient, to decide when it is necessary or preferable to obtain consent in other than written form. When such written consent is not obtained, the investigator must obtain oral consent and record that fact in the medical record of the person receiving the drug.

Source: 21 Code of Federal Regulations 310.102.

drugs when he is sent home. For example, since only about 3 million of some 23 million hypertensive patients are under adequate control, implementation of item 10 would encourage current efforts to stimulate health care practitioners to carry out certain acts necessary to insure patient compliance with the prescribed drug regimen.

Item 11 could affect the way drugs are used in hospitals because of its potential economic effects. Since it is the practice of most hospitals to use the pharmacy department as a revenue-generating department to make up for revenue deficiencies in other departments (e.g, room service charge), making the cost of drugs better known to patients might have a long-term tendency to depress prices of drugs to patients. It might also have the negative effect of singling out unit doses of drugs as inordinately expensive on a per dose basis, since it is difficult for a patient to perceive all the resources necessary for provision of medication on the basis of a unit dose system. In these days of accountability, knowledge of drug prices might provide some small amount of pressure to retard or impede the much-needed provision of pharmacy services via unit dose. (Unit dose is defined in Section 12.4.1.)

Item 12 is very important because it relates to how much information the patient is given about the basic rights contained in the PBR. Delivery would be facilitated if the patient was made aware of the precise nature of his rights. If the hospital has a duty to print and make available the particular items comprising its own modified patient bill of rights, it will be conducive to the patient's greater demand for the various items contained in his own PBR. This item could be criticized as being so broad and general as to lack meaning. Although it is subject to various interpretations, the word "conduct" seems to pertain primarily to the various methods by which the patient is handled or processed throughout his stay in terms of hospital routine, places and methods of treatment, and so on. If the patient were fully aware of the policies and procedures pertaining to "stat" (immediately) or "PRN" (as needed) drug orders, he might be more inclined to request these types of medications. Since these types of medications are mostly analgesics and psychotropics, this change in medication use practices might relate more to the patient's attitudinal perception of his hospital stay than to his "medical" perception of his stay. Such a change might well be against the patient's interests.

It is important to recognize and maintain a central focus on the dominant concern of the PBR with the patient as a human being who ought to and must have his dignity preserved. Offering no set of laws or listing of rights can guarantee for the patient the kind of treatment he has a "right" to expect under existing ethical and technological capabilities; only health care providers themselves can achieve this. Apparently the provisions in the items generally may tend to add to the overall cost of health care, since more time will be necessary on the part of health care practitioners to educate in order to secure the necessary informed consent of the patient through each critical step of his sojourn as a patient. Increased cost may attentuate patient efforts to seek needed care and thus serve the antithesis of the PBR's purpose. Although health professionals will probably react negatively, at least in part, to the accountability aspects of this very important document, it is also likely that health professionals will find many positive points. In a sense the PBR is merely a means of enforcing the already existing professional claim that the patient's interests are given priority.

Although other ethical codes will not be reviewed, it is perhaps instructive to consider the *Code of Ethics* adopted by the American Pharmaceutical Association in 1967 (14). The most important part of this code is its section 1 which says: "The pharmacist should hold the health and safety of patients to be of first consideration; he should render to each patient a full measure of his ability as an essential health practitioner." Clearly, the various codes encourage norm-setting at levels consistent with protecting the public's health and safety pertaining to medication-related behavior on the part of providers. Perhaps a code of ethics for consumers is needed to encourage similar responsible behavior. The patient must act consistent with his own role. The norm for patient behavior seems to be lower than is appropriate for maximum benefit from medication use. A patient who cannot perceive the added care provided by unit dose over the traditional "floor stock" system will have a tendency to act against his own best interest if he is to decide which system to use.

11.5   THE "ETHICS" OF DRUG USE/EXPERIMENTATION

Quotations are placed around the word ethics in the heading of this section because of the special nature of drug use and experimentation. Regulations (15) have been promulgated, based on section 505(i) of the Act (16) to regulate experimentation with people consuming drugs that are regarded as new drugs. These regulations are very similar to two ethical codes: the *Nuremberg Code* and the *Declaration of Helsinki*. Thus, both ethics and law are clearly concerned with this issue. Why? Do not researchers always act in the best interest of their patients or clients? Unfortunately the answer is an unqualified no. The reasons for ethical failings are many and are outside the scope of this section (17).

Some noted studies which fail to conform to the minimum ethical norms include the following:

1. Injection of live cancer cells into chronically ill patients who were not even aware that they were subjects in an experiment (18).
2. Administration of placebo oral contraceptives in a double-blind experiment designed to find out whether some of the reported side effects of the "pill" were physiological or psychological. The women were not told they were receiving a placebo, although they were told to use vaginal cream because the "pill" they were given might not be completely effective (19).
3. In one experiment 41,119 patients were given a test for pain tolerance as part of their regular checkup. They were told it was a test for "pressure tolerance." Each person placed his (or her) heel in a viselike machine and was instructed to stand the pressure as long as he could. Comparisons were made on the basis of age, sex, and racial differences in pain tolerance (20).
4. Nine normal, women patients were injected with epinephrine at the rate of 4 grams per minute, to seek a method for evaluating antiarrhythmic drugs. Arrhythmias were produced at least twice in each person. The informed consent of subjects was not obtained. The researchers stated that they "accepted the role of guarantor of the patient's rights and safety" while they were artificially inducing abnormal heart rhythms (21).
5. To test the effectiveness of cromolyn sodium in blocking asthmatic attacks, 9 children, ages 11½ to 16, who suffered from asthma were intentionally subjected to "challenge doses" of antigens to produce an asthmatic attack. Each child experienced at least one severe attack. Regular bronchodilator medication was withheld for 18 hours prior to the study (22).

6. Succinylcholine, which causes temporary muscle paralysis including inability to breathe, was used to determine the drug's effectiveness as an agent in behavior modification. Institutionalized subjects exhibiting certain kinds of deviant behavior were selected as subjects (22).

7. To determine the value of hyposensitization therapy for treating bronchial asthma, 130 children were studied prospectively for 14 years. Of these, 91 received ineffective "buffered saline injections" according to an elaborate injection schedule. "No mother or child in the study knew that any sort of study was under way" (23).

8. In order to test the effectiveness of vaginal contraceptive foam, 2932 women from five clinics agreed to participate in a study by using only foam as a means of contraception. The testing included a newly developed dispenser. The results included 94 pregnancies (24).

9. To test the effectivenesss of penicillin in preventing rheumatic fever, 109 military men were randomly assigned (without their knowledge) to placebo and injectible penicillin groups. In the controls 2 men developed rheumatic fever and 1 developed nephritis (24).

10. To test the effectiveness of sulfonamides in preventing rheumatic fever and glomerulonephritis, a control group of 500 men received a placebo, and another group of about the same size received sulfadiazine. Rheumatic fever developed in 5.4% of those treated with sulfadiazine and in 4.2% of the control group (24).

11. To determine conclusively whether chloramphenicol causes aplastic anemia, 41 randomly chosen patients were given either 2 or 6 grams of the drug per day. Bone-marrow depression developed in 2 of 20 patients given 2.0 grams and in 18 of 21 given 6 grams of chloramphenicol daily; 12 control patients did not develop these problems (25).

12. "Melanoma was transplanted from a daughter to her volunteering mother, 'in the hope of gaining a little better understanding of cancer immunity and in the hope that the production of tumor antibodies might be helpful in the treatment of the cancer patient.' Since the daughter died on the day after the transplantation of the tumor into her mother, the hope expressed seems to have been more theoretical than practical, and the daughter's condition was described as 'terminal' at the time the mother volunteered to be a recipient. The primary implant was widely excised on the twenty-fourth day after it had been placed in the

mother. She died from metastatic melanoma on the four hundred and fifty-first day after transplantation. The evidence that this patient died of diffuse melanoma that metastasized from a small piece of transplanted tumor was considered conclusive" (26).

13. "There is a question whether ureteral reflux can occur in the normal bladder. With this in mind, vesicourethrography was carried out on 26 normal babies less than forty-eight hours old. The infants were exposed to X-rays while the bladder was filling and during voiding. Multiple spot films were made to record the presence or absence of ureteral reflux. None was found in this group, and fortunately no infection followed the catheterization. What the results of the extensive X-ray exposure may be, no one can yet say" (26).

14. Newborn premature babies were randomly assigned to four treatment groups, where one group served as the control group and each of the three remaining groups received different drug combinations. The babies' parents were unaware that an experiment was being conducted. An equally good answer could have been obtained through the use of the epidemiologic method including the pooling of relevant information from many hospitals. (The details and reference to this experiment have been presented in Chapter 8 and in Table 8.6).

While the foregoing studies primarily involved ethical deviance by physicians, one should not conclude that physicians are any worse (or better) than any other group of providers. Physicians received the most attention mainly because they shouldered the most responsibility. The reader should review the study described in Chapter 8 and the study design suggested by Table 8.6; it should be noted that informed consent was totally lacking and that physicians, nurses, and perhaps even pharmacists were also involved. An important point to remember is that in order to do what is right one must first know what is right.

This section will be limited to a consideration of the three documents mentioned earlier. Since the FDA regulations are largely derived from ethical codes, the latter will be reviewed first.

The *Nuremberg Code* was generated by the Nuremberg military tribunals, which conducted the War Crimes Trials after World War II. It will not be presented verbatim because it has largely been superseded by the *Declaration of Helsinki*. It is instructive, however, for the student to review the "medical experiments" which were conducted under the Nazi regime (27). The reader should note carefully the gradual erosion of ethical standards that culminated in the infamous experiments. Could these experiments be repeated today?

The *Declaration of Helsinki*, as adopted by the World Medical Association, is reproduced as Table 11.2. This is an important, but very general document. Although many argue that it is so general that it is of little value, a reading of it will show otherwise. It consists of three major sections: the first enumerates some basic principles of human experimentation, the second pertains to experimentation concomitant with treatment, and the third deals with experimentation for purposes of extending knowledge.

Note that treatment-associated experimentation does not call for unqualified informed patient consent. Nontherapeutic research, however, must be done only with the permission of the subject; permission must be given freely and must be based on an informed decision including the purpose, nature, and risk of the experiment. The Declaration allows for instances in which informed consent need not be obtained in writing.

The search for deficiencies in such a terse statement as the *Declaration of Helsinki* will require reading between the lines. For example, the subject's right to continuing review of his decision is not considered. "Informing" a subject might be misconstrued as "telling" the subject the required or relevant information. The word "understand" is absent from the statement.

The FD&C Act (28) requires that sponsors of an investigational study obtain a certification from the clinical investigators that they will inform human beings of the use of drugs (and the necessary controls) for experimental purposes. The Act also requires that informed consent be obtained except in unusual circumstances. Table 11.3 lists the interpretive regulations promulgated by the FDA to enhance compliance with statutory requirements. In general these regulations are well regarded and are thought to represent high standards of conduct which are, nevertheless, flexible enough not to impede experimentation. Note that discretion on the part of the experimenter is severely curtailed; the average patient is put in the driver's seat. The word "understand" also appears in this statement. Written consent is required for Phases 1 and 2 of drug investigational studies.

The scientific method rather than armchair speculation is usually the most effective means of ascertaining if hypotheses are verifiable. In drug experimentation an important question is: "Does actual performance adhere to the required standards of conduct for experimenters?" A study was made of the conduct of human experimentation at a large medical school and teaching hospital (29). The methodology consisted of personal interviews with the research subjects and review of the records of an institutional peer review committee entrusted with overseeing clinical investigations. Most of the 51 women interviewed were subjects in a double-blind drug study for inducing labor in pregnant women. Results showed that the review committee was vigorous and active in the pursuit of its function. Specific findings were as follows:

1. Twenty (39%) of the labor-induction subjects were unaware that they were subjects in an experiment.
2. Most subjects showed little evidence of having given serious consideration to their decision to take part in the research and of developing accurate risk and benefit estimates of participation.
3. A detailed examination was made of the weaknesses in the informed consent process. Role confusion between the role of patient and the role of research subject was also examined in terms of the amount of information and restriction on the information available in decision-making.
4. Clinic patients were less likely to serve as research subjects than as "raw material" for research, and did not generally have the research used for their own benefit.
5. Five types of subjects were identified: (a) unknowing, (b) unwilling, (c) indifferent, (d) benefiting, and (e) committed subjects. Subjects tended to vary along a continuum of relative coercion to relative freedom in the decision to participate.
6. Recommendations were made that included the need for a continuing monitoring procedure to supplement traditional peer review procedures governing the conduct of clinical investigators.

The principal investigators in the two projects studied were sensitive to ethical issues, and generally indicated their willingness and desire to follow proper procedures in getting the informed consent of subjects.

This study illustrates the difficulties encountered by well-intentioned investigators in adhering to ethical standards. The study doesn't represent isolated conditions. In a large-scale survey (10) of 350 physician researchers in 424 different human studies, respondents stated that 18% of the studies involved more risk than benefit to subjects (30). The means for rectifying unethical behavior are not clear. The teaching of ethics in health care institutions, especially medical schools, appears to be a fruitful place to start. Apart from the claim of allegiance to the Hippocratic oath, medical students currently receive very little ethical training; one study (31) showed that only 13% had as much as one lecture or seminar on the ethical problems of human experimentation. Data for other health care providers are anecdotal, but it seems that more ethical instruction is needed by all types of providers.

For further study on the increasingly important concept of the ethics of human experimentation, several excellent sources may be consulted (32–39).

REFERENCES AND GUIDE TO FURTHER STUDY

1. Stevenson, L. G.: Official Control of Administration of Drugs, *Experimental Medicine and Surgery* **22**:147 (January) 1964.
2. Kelly, L. Y.: Nursing Practice Act, *American Journal of Nursing* **74**(7):1310–1319 (July) 1974.
3. Idaho State Board of Medicine and State Board of Nursing. Minimum Standards, Rules and Regulations for the Expanding Role of Registered Professional Nurse, Boise, Idaho State Board of Medicine and State Board of Nursing, June, 1972.
4. U.S. Department of Health, Education and Welfare: Report on Licensure and Related Health Personnel Credentialing (DHEW Publication 110. (HSM) 72-11) U.S. Government Printing Office, Washington, D.C., 1971.
5. U.S. Department of Health, Education and Welfare: Secretary's Committee to Study Extended Roles for Nurses. Extending the Scope of Nursing Practice, U.S. Government Printing Office, Washington, D.C., 1973.
6. Columbia Associates in Philosophy: *An Introduction to Reflective Thinking*, Houghton Mifflin Company, New York, 1923, p. 220.
7. Columbia Associates, *ibid.*, p. 221–222.
8. Columbia Associates, *ibid.*, p. 233.
9. Columbia Associates, *ibid.*, p. 240.
10. Columbia Associates, *ibid.*, p. 268.
11. Columbia Associates, *ibid.*, p. 269.
12. Warren, E.: Speech at Louis Marshall Award Dinner, Jewish Theological Seminary of America, New York, November 11, 1962.
13. Horty, J. E. (Ed.): Patient's Bill of Rights, *Action Kit for Hospital Law*, March, April, 1973, Parts I and II respectively. (P.O. Box 4663, Pittsburgh, Pa. 15206).
14. American Pharmaceutical Association: Code of Ethics, American Pharmaceutical Association, Washington, D.C., 1969.
15. Title 21, *Code of Federal Regulations*, 310.102.
16. 21 *U.S. Code*, 355(i).
17. For a disjointed but comprehensive review of this subject, see The Kennedy Hearings, Hearings before the Subcommittee on Health, 93rd Congress, 1st Session, 1973, Part 1 (336 p.), Part 2 (791 p.), part 3 (1185 p.), U.S. Government Printing Office, Washington, D.C., 1973.
18. Katz, J.; Jr.: *Experimentation with Human Beings*, Russell Sage Foundation, New York, 1972, 1159 p. (This is an excellent source. It contains numerous in-depth case descriptions including transcripts of actual testimony of participants in controversies.)

19. Goldzieher, J. W., Moses, L. E., Averken, E. *et al.*: Nervousness and Depression Attributed to Oral Contraceptives: A Double-Blind, Placebo-Controlled Study, *American Journal of Obstetrics and Gynecology,* **111**:1013–1020 (December 15) 1971.

20. Kennedy Hearings, Part 1, p. 272.

21. Kennedy Hearings, Part 1, p. 244.

22. Kennedy Hearings, Part 1, p. 267.

23. Kennedy Hearings, Part 1, p. 268.

24. Kennedy Hearings, Part 3, p. 1164.

25. Kennedy Hearings, Part 3, p. 1165.

26. Kennedy Hearings, Part 3, p. 1167.

27. Alexander, L.: Medical Science Under Dictatorship, *New England Journal of Medicine* **241**:39–47 (July 14) 1949.

28. 21 *U.S. Code,* 355(i).

29. Gray, B. H.: *Human Experimentation in Medical Research: A Sociological Study.* Unpublished Ph.D. thesis, Yale University, 1973, 298 p.

30. Kennedy Hearings, Part 3, p. 1044.

31. Kennedy Hearings, Part 3, p. 1048.

32. Yacasua, L. T.: Morality, *Phi Delta Kappan,* **55**(9):608–610 (May) 1974.

33. Freund, P. A. (Ed.): *Experimentation With Human Subjects,* George Braziller, New York, 470 pp. (This reference contains insightful and searching essays (with comments on most essays by another writer) on many problems of drug experimentation on humans.)

34. Bloom, M. J.: Non-therapeutic Research Involving Human Subjects, *Syracuse Law Review* **24**(3):1067–1094 (Summer) 1973.

35. Anonymous: Informed Consent—A Proposed Standard for Medical Disclosure, *New York University Law Review* **48**:548–563, (June) 1973.

36. Epstein, R. L. and Benson, D. J.: The Patient's Right to Know, *Hospitals* **47**(15):47–52 (August 1) 1973.

37. Anonymous: Universal Declaration of Human Rights, *United Nations Bulletin* **J6**:6–8 (January 1) 1949.

38. Anderson, R. D.: The Patient's Bill of Rights, *Voices* 12/60, **1**(12), (December) 1971. American Society of Hospital Pharmacists. (This is an audio cassette of a very "homey" presentation on the duties owed by a pharmacist to a patient, with a pharmacist speaking for both patient and pharmacist.)

39. Barber, B.: *Research on Human Subjects: Problems of Social Control on Medical Experimentation,* Russell Sage Foundation, New York, 1973.

40. Sollitto, S. and Veatch, R. M.: *Bibliography of Society, Ethics and the Life Sciences,* Institute of Society, Ethics, and the Life Sciences, Hastings-on-Hudson, New York, 1973.

41. National Council on Crime and Delinquency: Prisons, Inmates and Drug Testing Summary Report of the Conference on Drug Research in Prisons, August 6–8, 1973, Research Center, National Council on Crime and Delinquency, Davis, Calif.

42. Meyers, B. A.: *A Guide to Medical Care Administration: Concepts and Principles,* Volume 1, American Public Health Association, New York, 1969, p. 32–35.

43. Hershey, N. H. and Bushoff, S. H.: *Informed Consent Study,* Aspen Systems Corporation, Pittsburgh, Pa., 1969, 49 p.

44. Curran, W. J.: Public Warnings of the Risk in Oral Polio Vaccine, *American Journal of Public Health* **65**(5):501–502 (May) 1975.

45. Fink, J. L., III: The Realities of Law and Medicine: The Physician Extender and Therapy By Prescription. Paper presented at the Third Annual Conference on New Health Practitioners, Association of Physician Assistant Programs, St. Louis, Mo., April 7, 1975, 12 p. (This brief paper describes the basis for statutory authority for prescribing drugs. The point is emphasized that federal statutes are, conceptually, drug-(object) oriented whereas state statutes are practitioner-oriented; 67 references are cited.)

CHAPTER TWELVE

The Scope of the Legal Duty Owed by Providers to Recipients

The basic skeletal model for delegating power and authority to selected people in our society at the national, local, and generally even the small committee level is (1) Assignment of duties (responsibilities) to certain role occupants (people), (2) Assignment of sufficient authority (power) needed to perform the duties assigned, and (3) Accountability of role occupants for proper performance. This model assumes that society itself has ultimate authority and therefore is ultimately accountable for all acts whether committed by members acting as individuals or as groups. It also incorporates the assumption that society is informed and is capable of acting rationally and intelligently in its own best interest.

Although this conceptual model has existed as a fundamental Anglo-Saxon heritage premised on the principles laid down by Blackstone (1,2), the relative emphasis seems to have shifted considerably. While today cries of too much control and regulation are heard from many assigned the exclusive privilege to perform certain duties, things are much better from the perspective of the provider than in the distant past. Arabian pharmacists had to cope with people who had a tendency to be untrusting (3). They were ". . . watched and supervised by the *muhtasib,* who was required to, 'Make them fearful, try them, and warn them against imprisonment. He must caution them with punishment. Their syrups and drugs may be inspected at any time without warning after their shops are closed for the night.' "

Arabian physicians did not seem to have it any better. They ". . . were required to make copies [of prescriptions] for the close relatives of the sick of all those prescriptions employed in treatment, so that in the event of the patient's death the family would be able to submit these to the community's chief physician for his opinion of the knowledge and care displayed therein" (4).

Lest the reader jump to the too hasty conclusion that the degree of accountability was simply an early forerunner of peer review, he is reminded that if the chief physician detected negligence or deficiency the deceased patient's family could demand blood money.

12.1   DUTY AND SOURCE OF DUTY

The scope of the legal duty owed the patient by the various practitioners involved in the provision of drugs and drug-related services generally is contained in the various State Practice Acts and in the common law of the particular state. Generally a State Medical Practice Act defines the practitioners licensed to prescribe drugs; and the State Pharmacy Practice Act generally defines and describes the persons allowed to dispense drugs. The same situation applies to State Nursing Practice Acts and legislation for other health care categories, e.g., veterinarians, podiatrists, and dentists.

The common law of a particular state generally defines the scope of the duty owed by a particular practitioner more definitively than the State Practice Act for a given type of practitioner. Usually the duty owed by the particular practitioner is defined as that which would be exercised by the reasonably prudent practitioner of that genre. For example, physician specialists are legally held to a higher standard of care than are physician generalists. The same applies for pharmacy specialists and pharmacy generalists and other health care practitioners.

As will be shown, behavior might be required, preferred, permitted, tolerated, disapproved, or prohibited; the matter is complicated by the variability inherent in the drug use process. Basically, behavior can be perceived as prohibited, required, or optional. Prohibited behavior seems to be easy to describe; i.e., behavior of a certain kind may be prohibited for all role occupants or only one or two categories of role occupants. Required behavior usually has meaning only when a patient-provider relationship is established; certain behavior unique to that relationship may then be required. Optionable behavior presents the bulk of the problems. Basically, however, it relates to the notion that behavior neither required nor prohibited for a role occupant can be performed or not performed at that person's discretion. To a greater extent than for other role occupants, many acts that need to be performed to serve the patient are at present optional for pharmacists. Obviously, other normative systems besides law are important as behavioral determinants for pharmacists, nurses, physicians, and others. To be consistent with the conceptual model, one can look upon optional duties, if taken on by an individual permitted to do so, as self-assigned. Generally when these duties are undertaken, the other components of the model automatically become operative and applicable.

12.2   CONCEPTUAL MODEL OF DELEGATION—ELABORATION

The basic model for delegating power and authority to selected people has already been sketched. Close examination of this model and its assumptions yields considerable understanding of the duties owed, authority delegated, and accountability exacted from the various practitioners involved in the delivery of drugs to patients.

The assignment of duties or responsibilities to certain people is an all-inclusive statement. The law attempts to prescribe in general terms the duties of unique categories of providers. For example, a state pharmacy act will prescribe exclusive or near-exclusive duties for pharmacists in regard to the procurement, distribution, delivery, labeling, storage, record keeping, etc., of drugs to patients. By the very act of designating only specific people (a segment of society) for assignment to these prescribed roles, other people are usually prohibited from carrying out the duties prescribed for the particular health care profession involved. As has been shown, statutory law serves as only one of the two major sources of law which prescribe the duty owed by various role occupants. Case (common) law is probably the most important body of law which prescribes the duties of role occupants. It makes no difference in establishing the duty owed as to the source of the law. Statutory or case law serve equally well in defining the duty owed.

A number of observations and conclusions can be made pertaining to the assignment of duties to only a segment of society. When the conceptual model is accepted as the real (existential) model, the only mechanism immediately obvious for a particular profession to limit its responsibilities is limitation of the responsibilities prescribed in the relevant legislation. For example, for pharmacists to minimize their responsibilities to the population in the state in which they receive their exclusive right to serve as pharmacists, they would opt for no duties. The corollary of this is also ture. Maximum responsibility goes hand in hand with acquiring maximum duties to be performed in a particular occupation. Physicians serve as the prototype profession that has been delegated or assigned a very significant set of responsibilities to perform for society.

The assignment of duties must be accompanied by sufficient authority for a role occupant to perform the duties assigned. The various practice acts of a state generally accomplish assignment by designing a set of duties to be performed and limiting the performance of these duties to a designated class of role occupants. The theory of delegating authority has taught us that a role occupant should receive only sufficient authority necessary to perform the duties assigned to him. Otherwise, authority that exceeds the desired or necessary authority level may be used to further the role occupant's own interests at the expense of the person who is supposed to be served. It is also clear from examination of this component of the basic model of delegation of power that the greatest amount of authority that can be obtained functionally by a role occupant will be that which accompanies a maximum of duties. Conversely, authority is minimized or is zero when a role occupant has few or no duties. Generally the law, either statutory or common, will prohibit the delegation of authority to persons not so authorized by the various licensure boards. For example, a physician cannot usually delegate to a nonphysician the authority to prescribe drugs that are restricted to prescription by a licensed practitioner.

The third component of the model, accountability, will now be described. A role occupant who has been assigned duties and has received delegated authority is held accountable for his acts by the people who delegated to him his authority and responsibilities. The law generally prescribes certain criteria or conditions that a role occupant must meet when he is providing some good or service, as defined in the assignment of duties component of a state practice act. A norm is established that defines how a particular role occupant or collectivity ought to act. As in all instances of delegation of authority, the responsibility ultimately returns to the person who delegated it originally. In the United States this is, in all cases, the people. Since the people delegated authority for lawmaking to the legislature, and since the legislature in turn delegated certain authority to the various role occupants, accountability for performing the duties of a given role resides with that occupant.

Each of the three components of the model presents certain problems pertaining to their underlying assumptions. A vast amount of knowledge is assumed to be present on the part of the people delegating authority to the role occupants. It assumes that the patients of the various role occupants (pharmacists, physicians, dentists, veterinarians, podiatrists, etc.) are aware of the scope and nature of the duties assigned to the role occupants. Since a patient may be unaware of the delegation of a duty to a particular person, it is difficult for him to follow through on the other two components of the model. If the patient is not informed as to the limits and scope of the authority delegated to the role occupant, the patient does not know within what bounds the role occupant must act. Thus, the patient cannot readily know when the role occupant has exceeded his authority. Since knowledge of the duties and authority assigned to the various role occupants is an essential ingredient of accountability, it is difficult for accountability to be exacted from these role occupants.

Most laws assigning duties to role occupants prescribe that the duties performed be executed according to certain norms established either in statutory or case law. Since some of the products and services that are rendered by the role occupants are extremely complex and rarely encountered by a patient, it is difficult for him to know what the norm of performance is for a given service or product he receives. For example, few patients are knowledgeable enough to know that the norm for administration of potassium penicillin is a 10-day drug regimen. In order for a physician or pharmacist to be held accountable for providing drugs for this minimum time period, the patient must be aware that the 10-day period exists.

These and a number of other problems have created the necessity for frequent intervention in the patient's behalf in regard to the duties assigned, authority delegated, and accountability exacted from the various role occupants. As our society becomes increasingly complex and dependent on technological methods, processes, and products, often only the particular role occupant or his peers are fully informed about the norm for a particular duty. Such role specialization has given rise to the modern concept of self-regulation by the various role occupants (although "consumerism" is clearly on the increase in the health care sphere). For example, physicians are frequently held to be the only people capable of understanding the norm of conduct to which a physician must adhere when a particular duty is performed.

This turn of events makes it necessary for a patient who feels he has been wronged by a provider to secure the cooperation of another provider in order to rationally establish deviance from the norm. This creates a number of problems: notable among them is the "conspiracy of silence" among physicians. This point will be developed later.

Since the average citizen is usually incapable of making a determination himself about the appropriateness of a duty or service rendered by a role occupant (according to the law), he has allowed various professional groups to act in his behalf. For example, since only a physician is fully informed as to the norms, standards, criteria, and other qualities of a particular physician-rendered service, it follows that no other person will be involved in determining the accountability that may be exacted from a physician. It also becomes apparent that since the nature of the duties are perceived as complex, only a given role occupant is competent to decide the needed authority level for adequate performance of the duty by a like role occupant. The result is that a duty whose nature and other related circumstances are rather uncertain is assigned by society; the quantity and nature of the authority necessary for adequate performance of this duty determined by the role occupant is also determined by his peers. A number of problems created by this arrangement are outside the scope of this discussion. However, the prevailing problem is one of economics. The patient, although generally not knowledgeable regarding the nature of the duties, quantity, and quality of authority necessary for their performance and the performance level of the role occupant, is nevertheless required to pay for the service or product rendered. Unfortunately, such problems of economics have resulted in many instances in which the patient's best interests are not served. Modern examples of abuses are found in the high noncompliance with drug regimen rate, adverse drug reaction rate, and drug interaction rate which frequently occur to the unsuspecting, uninformed, but nevertheless paying patient.

The principal formal mechanism established by society for accountability of practitioners who deviate from the required norm rests with the criminal and civil statutes that prescribe public and private remedies for harm that befalls a citizen because of a role occupant's deviance from the established norm, as determined by the role occupant's peers. Criminal law provides a time and/or money penalty for persons convicted of deviating from the requried norm. Civil law, principally the tort and contractual components of civil law, provide for remedies to a person who has suffered at the hands of a role occupant who deviated from the required normative standards.

The criminal sanction imposed on a given role occupant is generally described and included in the legislation prescribing the duties, authority, and other requisites of a given practitioner. These components, using a state pharmacy practice act as an example, have already been discussed. The nature of civil and criminal sanctions imposed on one who is suspected of not conforming with prescribed laws is described in the next chapter.

12.3 THE ACCESSING OF ONE ANOTHER BY PROVIDERS AND CITIZENS

Although the model previously described for assigning duties to certain persons, delegating the necessary authority for performance of those duties, and requiring accountability for performance by various role occupants reflects actual use by society, its effects and effectiveness derive from contacts among individuals. Society, of course, consists of diverse individuals, primarily citizens. The decision to become a patient must usually be initiated by the citizen himself, who seeks out a practitioner who has been assigned the duties necessary for provision of a desired service. Upon locating an appropriate, authorized role occupant, a citizen contracts with that provider for a service and/or product. Under this arrangement the patient is the principal and the provider is the agent. While in practice it seems to be a fact of life that providers direct patients, the law is set up or so prescribed that the rules for contracting regulate the individual and private encounter between a citizen/patient and a citizen/provider. The laws of agency and contract and the laws regulating and controlling the interactions of people in the area of torts adequately define the prescriptive norms for provider and patient behavior.

12.4 UTILITY AND IMPORTANCE OF KNOWING DUTY OWED

The use of a drug in disease treatment is an increasingly complex undertaking. With the increasing prevalence of drugs that must be used only when periodic laboratory tests are run (e.g., blood prothrombin time), when dosage adjustment must occur frequently, when discontinuing one drug and continuing another can profoundly affect a drug recipient even to the extent of inducing death or serious illness, it is of paramount importance to patients and providers alike that an understanding of the duty owed be clear, unambiguous, and communicated to the affected parties.

Understanding of the duty owed is desirable for a number of reasons. If a provider owes a legal duty to a patient, then both can look to the law as a sanctioning institution that stands ready to punish a provider failing to perform that duty. On the other hand, if no legal duty is owed and it appears desirable from the patient's perspective that it be furnished, then either provider or patient can appeal to nonlegal motivational factors for producing the action desired. A misunderstood duty will explain this point. The DHEW *Medical Malpractice Report* (5) presented the finding ". . . that there is no factual basis for the commonly-asserted belief that malpractice suits are likely to stem from rendering emergency care at the scene of accidents." The fear of playing the good Samaritan is simply unfounded in fact. An example of a hypothetical need will clarify this point. If a person suffers a snakebite while deer hunting with a group including a physician, it is clearly better from the victim's viewpoint for the physician to render aid. However, a legal duty is almost certainly not owed the victim by the physician. The law does not compel the physician to come to the aid of the victim, i.e., the law will inflict no punishment (either fine or imprisonment) on the physician for failure to act even if his actions would prevent the victim's death. The victim may appeal to the physician on a nonlegal basis. If the victim were the physician's father, the motivational appeal might be love. If the physician and victim were opposing members of feuding (as in blood feuding) groups, the victim might appeal to the physician's religious belief in the golden rule, or the victim might make an economic appeal by offering money, or the victim might appeal to the physician's fear of dying by threatening to kill the physician with his deer rifle if aid is not forthcoming. If the physician does come to the aid of the victim, however, he must act as a reasonably prudent physician of the same learning and skill would act under the same circumstances.* Thus a legal duty would be created after the physician went to the aid of the victim, although under the circumstances it would be minimal. As previously stated, liability is least likely to be incurred by inaction. Yet a provider cannot practice his trade without incurring liability. It is

---

* However, it is possible that a specific statute may exist granting qualified immunity to a physician acting in an emergency such as this. The HEW Malpractice Report recommended enactment of such a statute (see reference 5, p. 16–17).

not inconceivable that the law of a given state might contain a special provision creating a duty on the part of a physician to treat a snakebite victim who is a member of a mutual deer hunting party. Under this condition, failure to act by the physician would expose him to liability for nonfeasance, i.e., failure to perform an act required by law, resulting in an injury.

Although the snake bite example may seem farfetched and unreal, it probably is not an extreme example. Even if the physician has his black bag available and equipped with a variety of anti-snake bite venom ampules,* he will have at least two serious problems in deciding to administer the drug.† If the identity of the snake is unknown, proper selection of anti-snake bite serum will be difficult. Even if proper selection of serum is accomplished, there is still the possibility of an adverse reaction, including death, due to anaphylactic shock from serum allergy. The labeling for the drug clearly states that tests are to be conducted to determine if the intended recipient is allergic to horse serum, and that epinephrine should be available for treating shock. The physician may not have the materials or other resources needed to test the victim for sensitivity to horse serum, and he may not have the necessary antidote for serum reaction. If he goes ahead, disregarding the approved labeling statement for the anti-snake bite serum, he may risk a malpractice suit.‡

An alternative method of examing the complexity and importance of the concept of duty is to look at a paradigm (model) of possible acts that could occur due to medication use in people. By examining potential behavior it will be possible to consider major or most behavioral acts that might lie within the domain of law. Figure 10.2, previously described as a model for drug information use, can be used as a referent for grossly describing the universe of possible drug-related behavior. To begin with, the law (other than in exceptional conditions such as venereal disease) does not prescribe that patients must seek drugs when they perceive themselves as ill or diseased.* The decision

* This is unlikely because snake bite is so rare that many times the serum must be specially flown in by plane.
† This modification of the example assumes complete knowledge on the part of the physician and the victim of malpractice, and also assumes recovery of the victim.
‡ Examples such as this served as the basis for the *Malpractice Report* recommendation that qualified immunity be granted for life-threatening emergencies.
* As described in the literature on illness behavior, people are expected to act in accordance with what is described as the "sick role," but the determinants of this expectation lie with the social, psychological, and organizational makeup of society and individuals.

is left to the patient just as it is the individual's responsibility to decide whether he wants to smoke cigarettes. The actions desired for relief from a disease must be correctly matched with some drug, and the best drug to produce the desired effects while keeping the undesired effects at a minimum is the drug of choice. The law allows the patient to select his own medication in some instances, and requires that the patient seek the services of a prescriber in others. Whether the law requires that the prescriber use the skill and learning of a reasonable and prudent practitioner under similar conditions is of considerable importance to all concerned. Each of the decision points (Figure 10.2) is meant to be grappled with and answered by *somebody*.

In the instance of prescription drugs where only unique, legally licensed persons (mainly pharmacists, physicians, and nurses) can legally prescribe, dispense, or administer drugs, this somebody must assist the patient in his desired drug consumption. For example, consider an instance in which a patient receives a drug, e.g., potassium penicillin G for the treatment of a sore throat caused by an identified beta-hemolytic streptococcal bacterium, takes the drug for 4 days, feels better and then discontinues the drug. A few days or weeks later the patient discovers he has rheumatic fever. For the sake of illustration and simplicity, we will assume that failure to take the drug for at least 10 days caused the rheumatic fever. Was a duty owed on the part of one or more providers to participate in certain acts that would have resulted in a nondisease outcome, or was it the patient's duty to commit these acts? In a typical case a patient would have visited a physician's office and would have encountered the physician and a number of nurses. After receiving a prescription, the patient would have visited a pharmacy and would have encountered a pharmacist and a number of salespeople. The patient, after receiving the desired drug (defined by people other than himself), would have paid the pharmacist just as he did the physician. The physician prescribed the drug, and included the directions for taking the drug and the quantity to be provided in the written prescription supplied to the pharmacist by the patient.* If all the major parties involved had each known their respective duties and those of the other parties, the patient's drug consumption might have been proper and a preventable, but tragic disease might have been avoided. Although no duty might have been owed, a duty would be owed conceptually, in the spirit of the law.

---

* The issue of which of these persons would have been liable, if any, will be considered later.

One additional variant will be used to describe further the concept of duty owed. An analogy can gainfully be made to law as a regulator of human behavior during the game of football. Increased understanding can be obtained by contrasting the complex with the simple, the uncertain with the certain, the subjective with the objective. Football rules exist to enhance the achievement of the aims of those playing (real and vicariously) football. In a sense the duty to abide by the rules of football is like the duty owed to patients by providers. Players on side A and side B contrast with the provider and recipient of a drug or drug-related service, respectively. In both instances the common good of the opposing groups is served by cooperation and playing in accordance with the rules of the game. Each team is aware that the other team is striving toward a similar goal: scoring points. At this point the analogy to the use of drugs is not quite parallel. Whereas in football the teams work against one another in order to make points, in drug use money (and intangible rewards) is being sought by one team member, and a drug effect is being sought by the other team member. In drug use both can "win," whereas in football only one team can win. Cooperation rather than competition is desirable, since cooperation by both parties will tend to increase both their chances of winning the game.

State practice statutes are one source of law for defining the duty of a role occupant, e.g., a nurse. By design and because of the relative permanence of these statutes they are written in fairly broad terms which tend to define the duty owed in a general way, if at all. Moreover many acts, such as the use of a recently approved new drug, e.g., an oral contraceptive pill for males, cannot be specifically taken into account because the drug was unknown at the time of enactment of the statute. The function of the courts includes ruling on the duty owed for acts committed that are not explicitly or specifically described in statutes. Fundamentally, the courts make a rule on a retrospective basis to fit some particular case.

Drug technology is a rapidly evolving field, and most changes tend to add to the complexity of the drug use process. Some, e.g., the Commissioner of the FDA, have suggested that physicians should be allowed to prescribe only selected drugs. Indeed, only certain approved physicians and pharmacists can prescribe and dispense methadone for maintenance therapy. (The FDA lost an important court case on this point; the court ruled that restrictions on which pharmacists could dispense were improper) (6).

12.4.1 Importance of Changes Occurring in Definition of Duty Owed

The pharmacy profession is changing to meet the challenge of increasing complexity in the drug use process. Pharmacists are becoming more involved in drug-history taking, maintaining patient medication profiles, reviewing drug use (restrospective, concurrent, and prospective), administering drugs, prescribing drugs, and patient consultation on the effects of drugs and methods of drug consumption. Many of these represent functions in areas of activity that have simply not been performed in times past. These functions were not being performed by patients, pharmacists, physicians, nurses, or others. The law did not require that these acts be executed. Moreover, ignorance of the necessity for these acts probably accounts to a large extent for the lack of a law requiring desired performance.

Although case law has been slow to develop in the areas of pharmacist involvement described (due to factors that will be explained later), some changes in these directions have occurred in state and federal law. Three specific statutes will be described, primarily because they represent the first and, because of their pacesetting effects, the most significant laws. These are: the requirements of a New Jersey law (actually an administrative ruling by the New Jersey Board of Pharmacy, upheld by the courts) requiring that pharmacists maintain a patient profile, the Washington State law (actually an administrative ruling) requiring that pharmacists properly instruct patients on how to take their medicine, and the federal *Conditions of Participation* for Skilled Nursing Facilities (SNFs) requiring that pharmacists review each patient's drug regimen monthly.

The New Jersey law requires a patient system "devised so as to enable immediate retrieval of information necessary to enable the dispensing pharmacist to identify previously dispensed medication at the time a Rx is presented for dispensing" (7). The law contains a key feature requiring that pharmacists "must examine the patient's profile record before dispensing the medication to determine the possibility of a harmful drug interaction or reaction." If the potential exists, he must "take appropriate action to avoid or minimize the problem," which includes consulting with the patient's physician. The profile law also requires that the patient's allergies, idiosyncrasies, and chronic conditions be recorded. Apparently the court felt that existing and needed information (previously described in the conceptual model for drug use in Figure 10.2) was not being obtained and used as it should be, because it stated: "The evidence submitted to the Board in this case clearly pointed out the dangers inherent in the compounding and dispensing of Rx drugs due to harmful interaction or reaction because of allergies or idiosyncracies of the patient."

Additional evidence contributing to the ruling showed that pharmacists had successfully used patient profiles for years, and persuasive evidence of "about 24,000 deaths each year in the U.S." from adverse drug reactions was presented.

Specific duties (responsibilities) of a pharmacist in charge of a prescription department have also been listed by the New Jersey Board of Pharmacy. These duties include:

1. Employing and supervising personnel in the prescription department.
2. Maintaining accurate records of all prescription medication received and dispensed.
3. Ensuring that medication dispensed is in conformance with the prescription received.
4. Maintaining the security of the prescription department and its contents.
5. Ensuring that only pharmacists provide professional consultation with patients and physicians.
6. Ensuring that only pharmacists or interns accept telephoned prescriptions and renewal authorizations.
7. Ensuring that all dispensed medication is properly labeled.
8. Ensuring the use of prescription labels naming the pharmacist-in-charge.
9. Ensuring the posting of the name of the pharmacist-in-charge so it is visible from the outside.
10. Prohibiting the presence of misbranded drugs in the pharmacy.
11. Operating the prescription department in an orderly manner.
12. Ensuring the delivery of complete service to the community.
13. Ensuring that the prescription department is operated in conformance with good pharmaceutical practices.
14. Ensuring that the pharmacy does not engage in improper advertising.
15. Notifying the board when he terminates his duties as pharmacist-in-charge.

The requirements are much more specific than is usually the case with state practice acts or regulations.

An example of the potential use of a patient profile occurred in early 1974, shortly after the last appeal based on the above ruling was adjudicated. The FDA urged pharmacists to keep records of the lot numbers and brands of digoxin dispensed because certain lots were being recalled due to new testing standards that resulted in evidence of improper potency. Without proper records, proper recall down to the patient level would be impossible. Even in the absence of a requirement by the FDA of recall to the consumer level, it is obvious that the patient's interest would be served in this case by a recall to the patient level. Thus an adequate patient profile is a means to this end.

The *Conditions of Participation* (8) comprise a part of the standards by which providers (technically vendors) of services under the Medicare or Medicaid program must abide in order to be approved to participate in these programs. Approval is necessary for payment to be made to a provider.

The Condition for pharmaceutical services in nursing homes (SNFs) describes the required structural and process components of quality for drugs and drug services provided to eligible recipients. The requirement has been added that "the pharmacist reviews the drug regimen of each patient at least monthly, and reports any irregularities to the attending physician. The pharmacist submits a written report on the status of the facility's pharmaceutical service . . . at least quarterly." This new requirement is noteworthy for defining the duty owed in a number of ways. It is part of the law (via a regulation) for those providing services to Medicare and Medicaid eligibles. Moreover when a court is deliberating the standard required for other patients, the standard required for these patients may be used to determine if the same standard is owed to other patients. The standard is important because it is fairly objective and has the support of the US Social Security Administration and also of a number of organized pharmacy groups such as the American Society of Hospital Pharmacists, the American Pharmaceutical Association, and the American Society of Consultant Pharmacists.

The ruling of the Washington State Board of Pharmacy, similar to the one described above, requires that

> With each new prescription dispensed after January 1, 1974, the pharmacist, in addition to labeling the prescription in accordance with preexisting requirements must orally explain to the patient or the patient's agent the directions for use and any additional information, in writing if necessary, to assure the proper utilization of the medication or device prescribed. For those prescriptions delivered outside the confines of the pharmacy, the explanation shall be by telephone or in writing. PROVIDED, that this shall not apply to those prescriptions for patients in hospitals or institutions where the medication is to be administered by a nurse or other individual licensed to administer medications, or to those

prescriptions for patients who are to be discharged from a hospital or institution (9).

This regulation, apparently adopted in lieu of a mandatory patient profile record, clearly states that a pharmacist now owes his patient a legal duty to take certain measures to enhance the chances that a patient will take his medicine properly. Although this law is limited to the state where it was enacted, it may be looked to by other jurisdictions searching for a definition and standard of the duty owed a patient by a pharmacist.

Findings of independent study groups as to preferred, more effective, or safer ways of rendering defined services may serve as a referent for courts to determine the duty owed to a complaining person. For example, the General Accounting Office (GAO) did an extensive study (10) resulting in an 888-page report which included recommending and endorsing the unit-dose system* of drug distribution because it was determined to be not only the most economical but also the safest patient care system for institutional drug distribution.

Based on this study, a complaining patient could argue that a sustained drug injury due to a distribution error would not have occurred if the safest (as defined by the prestigious GAO) distribution system had been used. Indeed, it is not inconceivable that the doctrine of *res ipsa loquitur* could be invoked.†

12.5 EXAMINATION OF PROVIDER/PATIENT RELATIONSHIP

Providers and patients may engage one another without entering into any formal or explicit agreement per se. Most transactions between providers and patients do, however, result from agreement between the involved parties. Although the agreement may be unspoken and implicit, it is nonetheless as real and binding as an explicit, written contract. It is not necessary and perhaps not even usual for either the provider or the patient to fully understand the legal nature of the mutual relationship established, since the obligation of provider to patient is created independently of whether the parties understand

---

* Unit dose system: a system of drug distribution for providing a patient a single unit of use dosage entity whose integrity is maintained from point of original packaging by means of recording essential drug use information on the drug labeling. For further understanding, see reference (11).
† Literally, "the thing speaks for itself." This doctrine is discussed later.

their legal relationship. A contract need not be in writing to be enforceable, but a verbal contract is obviously more likely to be distorted because of the problem of remembering the terms of the agreement.

12.5.1   Means of Terminating a Provider/Patient Relationship

A contract between a provider and a patient differs to some degree from most other types of contracts in that the mutual relationship can be terminated almost at will. A patient can terminate the services of a pharmacist, nurse, or physician at any time. A provider can usually do the same, if sufficient notice is given the patient so that services may be sought elsewhere.

12.5.2   What Provider Agrees To

The law prescribes the duties a provider must execute if a provider/ patient relationship is established. The principal requirement for a provider is that the acts he commits in the service of a patient will be carried out with the reasonable care of an average provider of his particular type, e.g., pharmacist, podiatrist, etc. The reasonable care concept is specific to the type of practitioner the provider considers himself to be. For example, a physician specialist, when operating within his area of expertise, is supposed to provide "reasonable care" defined in terms of the care which would be provided under similar circumstances by a specialist rather than a generalist. In other words, the level of care to which a specialist must adhere is usually higher than that required of a generalist.

12.5.3   What Patient Agrees To

The patient also has certain duties, some delegated to him by society, others which he owes himself. They can be summarized by saying that the patient must act as a reasonable patient would act, i.e., the patient must exhibit the reasonable care of an average patient of his particular type. Such behavioral expectations include, for example, the presumption that an honest drug history will be given, and that even if a drug produces pain as an adverse reaction the patient will cooperate with and follow the drug dosage regimen schedule and other suggestions of the physician or other provider. It is assumed that the patient will inform the provider of the effects he has experienced in the course of his treatment, or appears to be experiencing, so that the provider can know and use as appropriate other relevant information possessed by the patient. The patient must act as a prudent patient would act under the same circumstances. He cannot pretend to know little or nothing of his own drug-related problem when he actually possesses such knowledge.

12.5.4   What Provider Does Not Necessarily Agree To

As already suggested, both patient and provider are interested in a favorable outcome from the use of a drug. Nevertheless, the state of drug technology is such that the outcome of drug usage cannot be predicted with complete accuracy. Unless a provider explicitly agrees to produce a desired outcome for a patient from the use of a drug, no desired outcome is guaranteed. If a patient secures an agreement or guarantee from a provider that a desired treatment outcome will be forthcoming, then the provider can be held to his promise. The usual rules of contract apply when such a guarantee is provided. A patient may interpret the physician's or other provider's remarks to have a different meaning from that intended by the provider. Nevertheless, if an express contract can be shown to have been in effect between the concerned parties, the contracting parties can be held to their promises. It is important to note that when a guarantee is provided, a patient will be able to prove his own case if he takes it to court, even without a physician or other provider to give expert testimony as to the failure of the treatment. The burden of proof, although technically not shifted to the provider, seems to rest with the provider since he must show that the guaranteed result was actually produced. It is wise for both provider and patient to set down in writing the conditions of an explicit contract guaranteeing certain desired outcomes or encompassing certain unusual conditions. It is also prudent to secure the services of a lawyer in producing such a contract.

12.6   OVERVIEW OF BROAD DUTY OWED

The idea of a duty owed seems to be directed mainly toward insuring that some minimum standard of action is adhered to when a provider or patient renders a service to another. This supposition rests on the idea that some uniform standard of behavior should be exhibited by a

reasonable man of a given type (12). The variability of human behavior is of such magnitude that it is impossible to fix a definite rule
in advance for all conceivable human conduct that has previously been
noted and described. Nevertheless, what is sought in the ideal situation is a rule which will serve as a written plan to describe the course
of action required. It is important to recognize that when a rule is
selected for a given situation, all other alternatives for action have
been eliminated. Likewise, law as a system for directing human action
needs a plan that will yield a guide to action rather than to thinking,
and will detail the exact manner in which a certain activity must be
accomplished. Such a plan would serve to establish a usual or customary method of handling future activities.

On the more general level there is a need for a plan that can serve as
a generalized statement or understanding, which guides or channels
thinking in decision-making for providers and recipients of drugs and
related services. Rather than trying to describe rules or procedures for
all possible acts, the intent here is to lay down some general
guidelines for thinking, i.e., to provide a formula, so that when a given
generalizable activity is encountered the guideline or formula can be
used in order to ascertain the rule that should prevail for the duty
owed. Law is derived by constructing a generalization based upon
observation of some, but never all particulars.

12.6.1 Reasonable Man Concept

The concept of duty owed and standard of care necessary is structur-
ally simple. Suppose, for the sake of explanation, that all men are as of
this moment required to say "greetings to you" within 3 seconds
when a female comes within a 5-foot imaginary circle, with the center
of the circle extending through the center of the head of the male and
perpendicular to the floor or ground. Saying "greetings to you" would
become the duty owed. The standard of care would be the standard
way the reasonable man would utter the phrase (unless the statute
covering this act required some other standard). The conduct according to the prescribed principle would be evaluated on an individual
basis. If a man is arrested and ultimately tried (or is sued in a civil
court) for failure to properly express the greeting, it must first be
established that a duty was owed and then the standard of care
observed where the phrase (if uttered) "greetings to you" ascertained.
Clearly, in this farfetched and simple hypothetical example, establishing such facts as nearest distance the woman came to the man,
whether the required phrase was uttered, the tone of voice, emotions

expressed in the voice, etc., is rather difficult. As events become more complex and important, so does the determination of the duty owed and the standard of care necessary under the circumstances of some act.

The courts have dealt with this problem by prescribing a uniform standard of behavior in terms of the actor's physical attributes, mental capacity, knowledge, and skill. The key to this approach is that when the duty is ascertained, the degree of care actually provided can be compared with that owed and a determination as to equity can then be made.

The duty owed is that of the reasonable man of ordinary prudence (13). The reasonable man is a fictitious person who walks the earth only in the minds of courts, lawyers, and (theoretically) citizens. His role is somewhat analogous to that of the market model of economics. Although the model itself and its requirements may be difficult to meet in reality, it serves as a useful referent for selecting alternatives for action. A quote from a court case in the 1930s gives the flavor of the reasonable man concept:

> He is an ideal, a standard, the embodiment of all those qualities which we demand of the good citizen. . . . He is one who invariably looks where he is going, and is careful to examine the immediate foreground before he executes a leap or a bound; who neither star-gazes nor is lost in medita- tion when approaching trapdoors or the margin of a dock; . . . who never mounts a moving omnibus and does not alight from any car while the train is in motion . . . and will inform himself of the history and habits of a dog before administering a caress; . . . who never drives his ball until those in front of him have definitely vacated the putting-green which is his own objective; who never from one year's end to another makes an excessive demand upon his wife, his neighbors, his servants, his ox, or his ass; . . . who never swears, gambles or loses his temper; who uses nothing except in moderation, and even while he flogs his child is meditating only on the golden mean. . . . In all that mass of authorities which bears upon this branch of the law there is no single mention of a reasonable woman (14).

The cry of the incompetent: "It is I, not the reasonably prudent man, who is defendant here," (15) will fall on deaf ears as far as our courts are concerned. The reasonable and prudent patient, pharmacist, physician, or other person is not to be identified with the ordinary person of that type because the ordinary person might occasionally do unreasonable things. One must not yield to the notion of concluding that the reasonable man is synonymous or equal in meaning to the average man. The reasonable man is required to act as the average reasonable or prudent person of that type would act under similar circumstances, i.e., he is required to act with average carefulness. For professions in general and the medical profession in particular the reader is reminded that the profession itself, via the expert witness, defines the care expected. Poignant and tragic examples of a whole profession being in error can be found in the drug use field. An especially touching example was the large number of needless deaths in the 1800s that were caused by physicians and nurses who, despite a clear and articulate warning by the noted (then chiefly for literary achievements) Oliver Wendell Holmes, insisted on following practices resulting in puerperal (childbirth) fever and deaths of mothers shortly after the fourth day postpartum. The obstetrics department of a hospital and its two leading professors not only insisted on rejecting and attacking Holmes's explanation, but also attacked Holmes himself. Although Holmes ultimately prevailed, his Viennese counterpart, Semmelweiss, had gone insane some 20 years earlier mainly because of the failure of the establishment to accept his theory which later served as a basis for Holmes's empirical observations. In these instances virtually all the members of an entire profession were wrong. The reasonable man then is a prudent and careful man who always acts within the limits expressed in the standard (16).

12.6.2   Physical Attributes of the Reasonable Man

The conduct of the reasonable man is expected to vary depending on the situation that confronts the actor. A person fails to act reasonable only when he fails to do what the reasonable man would have done under the same or similar circumstances (16).

The reasonable man standard is specific in that the physical attributes must be those of the actor in order to ascertain the reasonable man of that description. For example, a patient who is blind would be judged in accordance with the behavior of the reasonable, prudent blind person. Nevertheless, the blind person will still be expected to conduct himself in accordance with his knowledge of his blind condition.

12.6.3   Mental Capacity of the Reasonable Man

The reasonable man is assumed to have some mental capability. He is assumed to be capable of inputting or perceiving information and making a decision based upon this perception. It seems to be an assumption of the reasonable man's mental capacity that he will act rationally and will not be ruled by his emotions, as might sometimes occur with an average person. The average person may be congenitally retarded, may be a fool, may be stupid, may be easily excitable due to his temperament, may be inclined to make decisions without the requisite minimum level of factual knowledge, or may otherwise act irrationally. The reasonable man standard, however, does not take this into account.

Practitioners involved in medication control and regulation are assumed to have a mental capacity at least equal to that of the reasonable, prudent practitioner of that unique type.

12.6.4   The Reasonable Man's Level of Knowledge

The reasonable, prudent man is expected to possess some knowledge. As used here, knowledge is defined as ". . . a belief in the existence of a fact, which coincides with the truth. It rests upon perception of the actor's surroundings, memory of what has gone before, and a power to correlate the two with previous experience (17)."

The knowledge level assumed includes an understanding of the everyday phenomena of nature as well as an understanding of some basic principles such as the law of gravity, the fact that the sun rises daily, that water is necessary for the maintenance of life, that some substances induce death when ingested, etc. Any individual who has led a normal existence should have learned considerably more than is suggested by the foregoing minimum, e.g., there are drugs which can prevent disease, sexual intercourse can be entertaining, going to church is generally regarded as a favorable activity, stealing is undesirable from the viewpoint of society, a government exists, cars without brakes will not stop, telephones can be used to talk with people who are far away, etc.

This discussion makes the point that some degree of knowledge is assumed to exist on the part of any actor. What level of knowledge is required for a given person is best left to be determined on a case-by-case basis. The level of knowledge required is minimum. The knowledge, skill, and intelligence required may involve a special class of persons rather than the average man. For example, someone who specializes in decarbonizing automobile engines is more knowledgeable than the average person about the adverse effects of effluent from automobile engines. Similarly, professional persons such as pharmacists, dentists, physicians, nurses, and others involved in drug control and regulation are said to possess special knowledge and skill. The knowledge, skill, and intelligence requirements of professionals must be equal to the minimum possessed by a reasonable, prudent person of that unique type.

State statutes generally include a requirement that a licensed health professional possess a standard minimum of special knowledge, skill, and ability. For example, a physician specialist is required to possess a higher level of these attributes than a generalist. If an appendix is removed by a generalist, the level of knowledge and the skills required need not be as high as those of a surgeon who specializes in such tasks. The minimum knowledge and skill level for a unique health professional is generally determined by comparing the standard of care provided in the same community or communities of a similar size and nature or, more recently, in the nation as a whole. The important point is that the minimum knowledge and skill of a professional involved in providing drugs and related services is determined by looking to the practitioners themselves. The level can be determined (according to the rules of legal procedure) only by securing testimony from an appropriate practitioner; e.g., a physician would be needed to testify about the minimum standard of skill and knowledge necessary for a fellow physician of a particular type.

In a nutshell, "the cumulative effect of all of these rules has meant that the standard of conduct becomes one of 'good medical practice,' which is to say, what is customary and usual in the profession" (18). This means of resolving a complex problem is of tremendous importance to providers and consumers of drugs and related services. Such a requirement for testimony allows professional groups the privilege of setting their own legal standard of conduct merely by adopting their own practices. An alternative explanation (19) is that courts have been reluctant to overrule the learning of another profession especially such an esteemed profession as medicine. Metaphorically speaking, we might say that this is a way of arguing that courts are not inclined to second-guess the pilot when beginning a cross-country flight in a commercial jetliner. It takes too much knowledge and skill to know what questions to ask of the pilot and too much knowledge and skill to process and utilize the answers obtained if the questions are asked of the pilot.

12.6.5 Hypothetical Duties Owed

Figure 10.2 included a variety of decisions that must be made, and included answering the question, "Does the patient desire to consume the drug?" This is supposed to be a patient decision directly or by proxy. Clearly, the conceptual model for drug usage depicted suggests that the patient is informed and aware of the desired and undesired expected effects of a given drug before the drug is consumed. In theory it is the patient's decision whether to consume the drug in order to experience the desired effects at the expense of the undesired effects. But is it also the duty of the patient's physician, nurse, pharmacist, or other person acting in the patient's behalf to advise the patient of the desired and undesired expected drug effects? This is the acid test. For if no duty is owed by the provider of a drug or drug service, then the law does not support a patient who does not receive desired or necessary information.

For example, the use of a particularly well-known drug, chloramphenicol, results in the death of about 1 person out of every 20,000 people who receive it (see Section 13.8.1.). The incidence of poliomyelitis induced by poliomyelitis vaccine, while small, is nevertheless known (less than 1 case in 40 million people treated) (21). Many "everyday" drugs such as aspirin exert undesired effects. Antihistamines cause drowsiness and create problems in operating machinery, including driving automobiles. Thus the foregoing question has not been answered by the courts specifically for drugs.

A recent California case on this subject resulted in the ruling "that an integral part of the physician's obligation to his patient is a duty to disclose the available choices of therapy and the significant dangers involved in each alternative" (22). In this case the courts found that "the patient, as a reasonably prudent person, would have decided not to undergo surgery had his physician provided him with the information necessary to make an informed evaluation of the risk." The patient was informed by the court that he was entitled to recover damages sustained as a result of the hazard that was not made known to him. Although this case does not relate specifically to drug therapy it is nevertheless relevant, since some drug therapy is more risky than some surgical procedures (see Section 8.1.1 for statistics on relative risk).

The US FD&C Act unambiguously requires the investigator in phases 1, 2, and 3 of the investigational new drug research studies to communicate the expected effects, both desired and undesired, which have been shown to occur from use of the drug. However, even for this component of the drug use process there is a legal way for providers (almost exclusively physicians) to withhold information from patients, at least in phase 3 research studies. As previously reported, if the physician deems it in the patient's best interest not to communicate to the patient the experimental nature and intended use of the drug, he may legally choose this approach. The courts may look to the level of information disclosed by a drug prescriber, dispenser, or administrator in good standing within his respective community to define the duty owed to disclose information to patients. In the California case the court ruled that "a medical doctor has a duty to explain to the patient in lay terms the complications that may occur. Further, the doctor must reveal such additional information as a skilled practitioner of good standing would provide under similar circumstances." If a drug which produces adverse effects as serious as adverse effects from surgery is needed and recommended to the patient, then the physician has the duty to fully inform the patient about the potential undesired effects, possible or probable, from that particular drug. Similarly, this could well apply to such widely used drugs as oral contraceptives.*

The results of several court rulings have been that a physician is under no obligation (duty) to warn his patients of undesired effects that may occur during treatment, if the physician has reason to believ that the health of the patient will be adversely affected if such facts are disclosed. However, in the California case mentioned earlier, "the court found that the physician had no reason to believe harmful effects would follow had the patient been appraised of the significant danger involved in his surgery" (22). It seems, with the increased educational level of the population, the increased use of drugs for otherwise healthy people, and the accelerated use of drugs for chronic conditions, that a provider (especially a physician or pharmacist provider) would be hard pressed to defend his failure to fully disclose the desired and undesired effects of a drug consumed by a patient. The Patient's Bill of Rights, adopted by the American Hospital Association (Section 11.2), easily leads to the conclusion that at least within a hospital setting an ethical duty is owed to the patient to fully inform him of all aspects of patient treatment, including drug therapy. The PBR, however, is an ethical goal and has no legal stature.

Ambiguity in stating the legal duty of the provider to fully inform the patient does not detract from the importance of knowing whether a provider owes the duty to fully inform the patient of the desired and undesired effects of a drug. From patient and provider perspectives it remains important to identify and describe some problems created if such a duty is owed. For example, in general one-third of placebo

---

* Other grounds, such as the contents of the officially approved labeling of oral contraceptives, could be used to define in whole or in part the duty of disclosure owed by a provider to a patient. (See also reference 23.)

drugs that act on the central nervous system are fully effective in relieving pain in patients receiving these drugs (24). This is true despite overwhelming pharmacologic evidence that the relief of pain gained from placebo use is not physiologically based. If the patient is informed about the nature of the drug and the undesired and desired effects which may occur, he may be robbed of the otherwise beneficial effects he could have experienced from the drug. Added to this very real problem is another serious problem of time, expense, and the overall technical difficulty of educating patients. A certain minimum level of educational achievement is necessary on the part of the patient for him to be able to receive, act on, understand, and otherwise cope with information describing the effects of drugs. To the extent that patients are not educated to understand this information, problems will occur. A physician or pharmacist could very well spend an hour or more in an attempt to produce reasonable understanding on the part of a single average (prudent) patient. Clearly, although this might be consistent with our ideals of individual rights, it will nevertheless increase many of our problems of proper access to desired and needed health services. Providing this additional information service will probably add a tremendous burden to our already overburdened and too expensive health care services and products.

When asked about the problems and anxiety associated with fully informing the patient, a noted physician witness before the House Intergovernmental Relations Subcommittee replied: "You could say that about any drug. If every patient that I treat with penicillin—I don't tell them that you can get a rash and this and that and that you might die from it. I would only be able to see five patients a day if I did this with every drug that I prescribe all day long" (25).

12.6.6 Specific Duties Owed by Pharmacists

Few cases specifically describe the duties of a pharmacist. Moreover, such cases often involve gross departures from prudent behavior and hardly relate to negligence in exercising professional judgment. Some cases are outdated and may not stand as precedents for modern-day pharmaceutical practice. (Strict liability cases involving pharmacists are beyond the scope of this book.) Nevertheless, there are enough instances to list some specific duties owed by pharmacists. The following list can be useful as a source to show what a pharmacist's behavior should be under similar circumstances (26):

1. Pharmacists must not sell a harmful drug when a beneficial drug is called for (27).
2. The pharmacist owes "the highest degree of prudence, thoughtfulness, and vigilance" (27).
3. When the purchaser of a dangerous drug is a minor, the pharmacist must exercise special care if the sale involves a highly potent drug (28).
4. A pharmacist owes through his implied warranty a duty to compound a drug as prescribed by a duly licensed physician (29).
5. A pharmacist owes the duty to use due and proper care in filling a prescription (29).
6. The proper methods are supposed in the compounding process (29).
7. The duty is owed to provide a drug that has not been adulterated by some foreign substance (29).
8. The pharmacist must call the physician for clarification when the prescription has been illegibly written (30).
9. A pharmacist owes a duty to refrain from dispensing a lethal dose of medicine even though it was prescribed by a physician (31).
10. The pharmacist must see to it that the purchaser understands, when an unusually large but nonlethal dose is called for, that a larger than usual amount is being provided (32).
11. Violation of federal or state statutes is viewed as negligence per se (33).
12. When a pharmacist incorrectly fills a prescription and later discovers that fact, he must call or contact the purchaser (34).
13. A pharmacist must employ people who know the difference between the various drugs held or offered for sale (35).
14. The owner of a pharmacy is liable for the injuries induced by a nonpharmacist employee who illegally fills a prescription, providing that the customer thought the nonpharmacist had the authority to so fill the prescription (36).
15. A pharmacy owner is liable for the acts of his employee as long as that employee acts within the scope of his authority (37).
16. A pharmacist must discover deteriorated drugs that are present in his pharmacy (38).
17. At least one court (28) has ruled that the pharmacist has the duty to advise the purchaser of a drug which might interact with another drug to produce an injurious effect, assuming the pharmacist has cause to believe that the patient does not know this fact himself.
18. A pharmacist ordinarily does not owe the duty to protect a drug purchaser from unexpected reactions to a particular drug (39,40).

19. A pharmacy which sells a drug under its own name assumes a responsibility equal to that of the manufacturer of the drug (41,42).
20. A pharmacist must correctly advise a customer about the similarity of two compounds (43,44).
21. A pharmacist must not substitute another drug, e.g., an OTC drug, for a prescription that results in the patient being injured due to failure to receive the drug prescribed (44).

12.6.7 Duty to Provide USP Dispensing Information

The *United States Pharmacopeia* (USP) has historically served as a standard to insure the identity, purity, quality, and strength of a drug. Moreover, the very listing of a drug in the USP was evidence of a drug being of greater value than unlisted drugs. Traditionally, the USP has contained a listing of the major use or uses of a drug and has carried certain information relevant to dispensing drugs, e.g., "store in a cool place," "protect from light." Due to the assumption of the compounding function by drug manufacturers, however, the volume has been of little direct value to practicing pharmacists or physicians. State pharmacy practice acts have nevertheless continued to require that all pharmacies maintain a current copy of the USP.

The USP XIX has made a significant change regarding the quantity and nature of dispensing information appearing in the volume. The new information in the USP monographs is specifically intended to guide pharmacists when consulting with patients. Such information pertains primarily to storage conditions, side effects, contraindications, and operations that might be of benefit to the patient. The pharmacist is encouraged to use his professional judgment in selecting what, if any, information to provide to his patients. Three examples of dispensing information contained in USP XIX are (70):

1. Atropine sulfate tablets:
   Dispensing information—
   Note: Antacids such as alumina gels may interfere with absorption if taken simultaneously.
   Advice: Notify physician if skin rash, flushing of skin, or eye pain occurs. Dryness of mouth, difficult urination, blurred vision, and sensitivity to light may occur.
2. Chlordiazepoxide hydrochloride:
   Dispensing information—

Advice: Drowsiness may occur which may impair ability to drive
or perform other tasks requiring alertness. Avoid alcoholic beverages. Notify physician if sore throat, fever, or unusual bleeding or
bruising occurs.

3.   Penicillin G Potassium tablets:
Dispensing information—
Note: Inquire whether patient is allergic to penicillin.
Advice: Notify physician if skin rash occurs. Preferably taken 1
hour before or 2 hours after meals.

12.6.8   Duties Owed for Regulating Controlled Substances

While controlled substances represent only approximately one out of
every seven drug issuances, their control permeates the drug distribution channels and regulates the behavior of providers and patients.
The regulations of the CSA include approximately 150 pages (45).
Clearly, it would be wasteful, duplicative, and not very instructive to
describe these regulations in minute detail. This section is concerned
with general principles and policies governing controlled substances,
and the reader should refer to the *Code of Federal Regulations* or the
Federal Register for the specifics governing a particular event (46).
Although the pharmacist is the provider most affected by the controlled substances regulations, the physician and, to a lesser extent,
the nurse are also significantly affected by these regulations.

Labeling Requirements

Each commercial drug container must have on its label a symbol
designating the schedule to which it belongs. These were previously
described and depicted in Section 7.2.1. The pharmacist or other
person dispensing a controlled substance to a patient is not required
to place these symbols on the dispensed prescription label. The pharmacist or other dispenser must place the same information on the
prescription label as is required for any other legend drug as required
by the US FD&C Act plus one additional piece of information. This
information consists of adding to the FD&C Act labeling requirements
the statement: "Caution: Federal law prohibits the transfer of this drug
to any person other than the patient for whom it was prescribed." The
dispensed prescription labeling requirements have been described
under Section 9.2.4, and the labeling information items are listed in

Table 9.4. It is important to note that these labeling requirements pertain to anyone who acts in the dispensing role. In addition to pharmacists, this includes physicians and other practitioners who supply drugs directly to their patients and bypass the typical pharmacy. Any nonlegend controlled substance must also be labeled to meet the requirements for a nonprescription drug (Table 9.5). All practitioners owe the duty to their patients to label a dispensed drug in accordance with applicable regulatory provisions. Intrainstitutional labeling should be sufficient to uniquely identify a product. In addition to the usual labeling requirements, the product's schedule should probably be identified, e.g., through the use of color codes.

Duty to Register

Every entity within the drug distribution channel, with the exception of the patient, must register either directly or indirectly in order to perform a role in the distribution of this legal class of drugs. Pharmacies must register in all cases. Physicians and other prescribers must also register with the Drug Enforcement Administration (DEA) under most circumstances. However, physicians and other prescribers need not register when they are practicing exclusively within an institutional environment, i.e., prescribing solely for inpatients. If the hospital or other institution is registered under the CSA, then each prescriber need only add a suffix to the hospital's registration number in order to be within the requirements of the CSA.

Individual pharmacists do not have to register under the CSA, probably because they are registered with their respective state board of pharmacy. However, physicians and other prescribers are required to register when providing prescriptions for outpatients because even though they are registered with their respective boards, these boards are not primarily concerned with the control and regulation of drugs.

Duty to Use Order Forms for Schedule II Controlled Substances

A triplicate order form must be used for the transfer of controlled substances in Schedule II. A registrant desiring the proper order forms must obtain these by completing a special requisition form and submitting this to the DEA. He must use this required order form only for Schedule II controlled substances; substances in other higher numbered schedules may be ordered without relying on these DEA order forms. Each registrant must be careful to keep certain records and record certain information on the Schedule II order forms when he receives the items ordered. A space is provided on the order form for recording the necessary information. The basic purpose of the order form is to serve as a means of ensuring to a greater degree than for any other class or subclass of drugs that only authorized channel members operating under strict channel rules can secure quantities of Schedule II drugs. It is noteworthy that a gap exists in the traceability of this schedule of drugs, due in part to the failure of the regulations to require that each physician order prescription blanks from the DEA. If blanks were ordered then the quantity produced under the quota allotment for Schedule II substances could be matched with the quantity prescribed and the quantity dispensed of any given Schedule II controlled substance; complete accountability for all drugs could then be obtained. DEA-issued order blanks would provide for a precise reconciliation of the dispersal of whatever quantity of the particular controlled substance was manufactured. Such a provision will probably be required in the future; this prediction is based on some of the findings from various congressional hearings held on this general subject (71).

Duty to Keep Records

The duty to keep certain records prescribed in the CSA rests most heavily upon pharmacists, especially those practicing at the community level. Every pharmacy engaged in handling any controlled substance must keep complete and accurate records of all receiving and dispensing transactions. Such records must be maintained for a period of 2 years.

The records of all inventories and other records of controlled substances in Schedule II must be maintained separately from all other records of the pharmacy. All inventories and records of controlled substances in Schedules II through IV must be maintained separately, or must be in such form that they are readily retrievable from the ordinary business records of the pharmacy.

In order to augment proper record keeping and to maintain accountability through the traceability of these drugs from their origin to the ultimate recipient (the patient), an inventory requirement was first instituted for May 1, 1971. At that time every registrant must have taken and must, every 2 years after that date, take a complete and accurate record of all stocks of controlled substances on hand. Specific directions must be adhered to when taking the inventory record.

The pharmacist or other provider who receives, stores, or dispenses controlled substances must generally adhere to the record-keeping and inventory requirements. However, physicians and other prescribers are largely exempt form the dispensed prescription record-keeping requirements. Exemption appears to be premised upon the somewhat tenuous assumption that physician providers will maintain a record of quantities of controlled substances prescribed or administered to patients in the medical record maintained for the individual patient. Although the research is scanty as to how well such records are kept, it suggests that contemporary records are grossly inadequate to achieve proper control of these substances.

The regulations are so detailed that they describe virtually every conceivable situation that might be encountered. For example, a particular duty is owed to distribute controlled substances among pharmacies, physicians, hospitals, or nursing homes in a prescribed fashion. Basically, this provision allows for a pharmacy or other registrant to dispense a controlled substance without being registered as a distributor, provided that not more than 5% of the total number of dosage units of all controlled substances is distributed and dispensed during the 12-month period immediately preceding some predetermined date.

Various other detailed rules are prescribed in the regulations to ensure that complete control (with the shortcoming noted above) is attained. The record-keeping requirements control Schedule II drugs so stringently that virtually any unaccounted for quantity can be traced to the responsible person. The requirement for traceability and control of higher numbered scheduled substances is almost as stringent except that order forms are not required.

Duty to Store Controlled Substances Securely

Pharmacies, but apparently not prescribers, must store controlled substances to help ensure that only authorized channel movement occurs. Originally the CSA regulations required storage of controlled substances in Schedule II in a locked, substantially constructed cabinet or safe. Later, the regulations were amended to allow the dispersal of controlled substances throughout the noncontrolled stock in such a manner as to obstruct theft.

Any pharmacy wishing to dispose of excess or undesired stock of controlled substances must contact the nearest DEA office and request the necessary forms. This form must be completed in triplicate and forwarded to the DEA office along with a cover letter stating that the controlled substances are not desired and that the pharmacy wishes to dispose of them. The DEA office will authorize and instruct the pharmacy in the proper manner of disposal. This will usually include provision for transfer of the undesired controlled substance to an agent authorized to receive these drugs under the Act, or by delivery to the DEA office, or by destruction of the controlled substances in the presence of a DEA agent. Occasionally, other means determined by the DEA office may be allowed on a special case basis.

To complete the traceability of controlled substances, aberrations in authorized channel movement that occur from drug theft must be reported to the DEA office if a significant loss is discovered. The pharmacy must complete a special form and forward it together with a report to the nearest DEA office.

Duty to Issue and Fill Prescriptions Properly

A prescription for a controlled substance is a legitimate prescription only when issued for a legitimate medical purpose by a practitioner who has established a practitioner-patient relationship and is acting in the course of his usual professional practice. It is illegal for a pharmacist knowingly to fill a prescription for a nonlegitimate controlled substance. For example, a dentist who decides to prescribe morphine sulfate tablets to treat his wife's sore toe has not issued a legitimate prescription, and if the pharmacist is aware of the circumstances he cannot legally fill this prescription, i.e., the pharmacist does not have the necessary authority for filling this prescription. Although the responsibility for proper prescribing and dispensing of controlled substances rests upon the prescribing practitioner, this does not allow the pharmacist to escape liability. If, for example, a veterinarian prescribes a drug for a human but writes the prescription ostensibly for the person's pet, the pharmacist is obligated to not fill the prescription if he is aware of the circumstances.

All prescriptions for controlled substances must be dated and signed on the day they are issued and should bear the full name and address of the patient and the name, address, and registration number of the practitioner. Where written prescriptions are required, they must be written in ink or other suitable means not subject to tampering, and must be manually signed by the practitioner.

Schedule II prescriptions must be in writing and cannot be refilled. However, a special provision is made for emergency oral authorization of Schedule II prescription drugs if the prescriber furnishes a written prescription within 72 hours. The meaning of "emergency" is narrow, and the regulations should be consulted for details (45). Prescriptions for controlled substances in Schedules III, IV, or V may be issued either orally or in writing by a duly authorized prescriber and these prescriptions may be refilled if authorized. However, the prescription may not under any circumstances be refilled more than 6 months after the date issued, or be refilled more than 5 times after the date issued. A new prescription is required when these conditions can no longer be met.

Although only a duly authorized prescriber can authorize a new prescription or the renewal of an existing prescription, a nurse or other nonauthorized prescriber can transmit an authorization message from a prescriber to a dispenser. An office receptionist cannot legally authorize a prescription refill because the duty owed rests with an authorized prescriber. While a prescriber cannot delegate this duty, a receptionist can communicate a message from the prescriber to the dispenser.

The pharmacist owes a duty when refilling a prescription for any controlled substance in Schedules III or IV to enter on the back of that prescription his initials, the date the prescription was refilled, and the amount of the drug dispensed.

Special provisions appear in the Act for the partial filling of Schedule II prescriptions. In essence, partial filling is permissible; the remaining portion of the prescription may be supplied within 72 hours, but cannot be supplied after this period. Partial filling is specific to controlled substances in Schedule II. The requirements are essentially the same for Schedule III and IV controlled substances because the rule which applies in both instances is that only a duly authorized prescriber can authorize the movement of a controlled substance through legitimate distribution channels.

Retail Dispensing Restrictions for Nonprescription Controlled Substances

Schedule V is the schedule of controlled substances which generally contains nonprescription items. In theory, any substance in any schedule may be a nonprescription item and may be dispensed without a prescription at retail. However, the regulations provide that stringent conditions be met when sales of these items occur. They include the following requirements:

1. The dispensing must be made only by a pharmacist or pharmacist intern and not by a nonpharmacist employee even if under the direct supervision of a pharmacist. When the pharmacist has determined whether he will authorize the sale of a controlled substance, clerical personnel can complete the transaction including cash or credit transactions or delivery by a nonpharmacist.
2. The pharmacist must not authorize the sale of more than 8 ounces

or more than 48 solid dosage units of any substance containing opium, nor more than 4 ounces or more than 24 solid dosage units of any other controlled substance to be sold to the same purchaser within any 48-hour period.
3. The purchaser must be at least 18 years of age.
4. The pharmacist must establish suitable identification of the purchaser, including proof of age if he deems it appropriate.
5. The pharmacist must maintain a bound record book containing the name and address of the purchaser, the name and quantity of controlled substance purchased, the date of each sale, and initials of the selling pharmacist. He owes a duty to maintain this record book for a period of two years from the date of the last transaction entered in the record book, and he owes a duty to make this available for inspection by duly authorized DEA representatives.

He must not commit any act which would conflict with others. For example, if a local law forbids the selling at retail of a given controlled substance, pharmacists owe a legal duty to refrain from selling this substance.

The pharmacist and the physician have been singled out for special attention in their role as educators. The National Commission on Marihuana and Drug Abuse in its now famous second and final report, "Drug Use In America: Problem in Perspective," has clearly spelled out duties owed by providers regarding controlled substances and related drugs. The report states: "Both doctors and pharmacists should expressly warn patients of the risks of dependence, overdose, and use in conjunction with similar drugs such as alcohol, when prescribing or preparing psychoactive drug medication" (68). The Commission singled out the pharmacist: "At the retail level, all pharmacists should verify the identity of persons seeking prescription psychoactive drugs. They must also vigorously enforce the regulations which apply to over-the-counter cough preparations containing codeine" (69). Unfortunately, these recommendations have received little constructive attention from medicine and pharmacy.

12.7 USE OF DRUGS FOR UNAPPROVED-APPROVED USES AND DUTIES OWED

A detailed explication has already been made to show the sources and origin of information describing the effects of drugs, in particular the effects of drugs approved by the FDA. Although some facts surrounding the issue of which drugs are to be used to treat particular instances of medical deviance will seem surprising at first, upon further reflection and study of the complex issues involved they will become more understandable. To suggest that it is not mandatory that a prescriber (almost always a physician) adhere to the information derived from the sources described and summarized in the officially approved labeling may seem strange. However Representative L. H. Fountain, Chairman of the Intergovernmental Relations Subcommittee in testimony on new drugs used for unapproved purposes elicited the following remarks from W. W. Goodrich, then General Counsel to the FDA:

> Now, I do not think they really believe that myself, but they believe quite strongly, and Mr. Buchanan pointed out: there is not any direct control under the Federal law over the physician who orders a drug for you and, say, ordered the wrong one. He does not violate any Federal law when he does that. He may be guilty of malpractice or something of that kind, but there is just not anything in the Food, Drug, and Cosmetic Act that monitors the propriety of his choice of a drug for use (47).

Moreover, it was even possible for a person to be advised or to have it suggested to him by the FDA that the officially approved labeling need not be adhered to. This is evident from a memorandum of a telephone conversation between an FDA dermatologist and an inquiring patient on the subject of whether methotrexate should or can be used for the treatment of psoriasis. An excerpt from this memorandum states:

> We [the FDA dermatologists] were able to tell Mr. Green that the FDA has not officially established a policy on the use of this drug in psoriasis. As a personal opinion, however, I feel that the drug is a valuable agent in some recalcitrant cases, and I believe that this is dermatological consensus at this time. Methotrexate is not without its side effects and, in fact, a few deaths have been attributed to it. In summary, we told Mr. Green that he in his position would have to weigh the potential advantages against the potential disadvantages in his particular case, and that this was not a decision that we could make here at the FDA (48).

The matter was still not completely clear. Representative Fountain elicited a response at odds with the previous FDA response when he asked the following question (49):

> Now, Doctor, did you mean by your statement that the physician is free to employ a drug, whether it is approved or not under the new drug provisions of the law, for any condition which, in his medical judgment,

he feels is indicated in the treatment of the patient, regardless of the toxicity or the dangers or the unproven merit under FDA rules of the drug?

Representative Fountain's question ultimately received a "no" answer (50). The Commissioner of the FDA in response to an inquiry as to whether a particular inquiring physician would be breaking the law by using an approved drug for an unapproved use gave the following advice (51): "If the patient were injured there may be a basis for recovery for malpractice depending on the reasonableness of the experimental use."

The point was made at the beginning of this section that the demarcation marking the boundary between the duty owed and the other requirements of law is extremely difficult. The extremes may be black and white, but the vast middle ground seems to be various shades of gray. It is nevertheless instructive to examine the duty owed. Consideration of hypothetical but possible real-life examples will shed light on this issue.

Suppose that a physician obtains a drug history for a 7-year-old patient, and finds that the child is apparently sensitive to ampicillin. In spite of this, the physician decides to prescribe ampicillin to "find out for sure" if the child is allergic to ampicillin, even though both ampicillin and erythromycin are indicated for the infection present. Later, the child is treated in the local hospital emergency room for a serious allergic reaction. The physician then prescribes erythromycin succinate, and the child experiences no further adverse reactions. The package insert for ampicillin contains the warning that it is not to be given when the patient is known to be allergic to it; the PI for erythromycin indicates that there is no cross-sensitivity with ampicillin. Did the prescribing physician owe a duty to the patient not to prescribe ampicillin? The pharmacist who filled the prescription kept a patient profile record which allowed him to identify the potential problems of allergy. However, after verifying the allergic condition with the child's father, the pharmacist filled the prescription for the child. The physician was not called because he was already aware of the facts. Did the pharmacist owe a duty to refrain from filling the prescription? Would the fact that the child's parent was a college professor and was told of the potential allergic problems alter the duty owed by the pharmacist or the physician?

Suppose again that a patient presents himself to a duly licensed prescriber (physician) and is diagnosed as having pernicious anemia, but finally receives a drug other than Vitamin B_{12} (the only drug indicated for treating this particular deficiency disease), the drug of choice. Is a duty owed the patient to supply the needed drug?

Consider an instance of the opposite kind of behavior. A nonpregnant woman, after a complete physical examination by an obstetrician-gynecologist, is pronounced in good health; in the course of the examination, however, her blood type is found to be Rh negative. Later she gives birth to an Rh-positive child, with no drug administered to her to prevent development of Rh-negative disease (erythroblastosis fetalis). After her second pregnancy the same physician delivers a mentally retarded, deformed baby with the abnormal conditions conclusively shown to have been caused by RH-negative antibodies acting on the blood of the fetus. Was a duty owed to provide the drug needed?

Consider a further example: A teenager is treated for severe acne with a drug not approved by the FDA for treating acne in teenagers. The teenager's acne is cured, but a near fatal blood dyscrasia develops due to the acne-curing drug. Is the provider liable for the resulting injury?

To complete the circle, additional examples must be examined. Imagine a patient suffering from cardiac arrhythmia whose physician determines that lidocaine hydrochloride is the drug of choice for treating this condition. The officially approved labeling, however, fails to include the use of lidocaine hydrochloride for this particular purpose. What is the physician's position if the patient does not receive the lidocaine and suffers a fatal heart attack? What is the physician's position if he administers the lidocaine hydrochloride and an adverse reaction develops even though the desired effects occur from the drug. Does the answer change if the desired effects do not occur and there is an adverse reaction instead?

What is a physician's position regarding the use of diazepam for the treatment of status epilepiticus when the officially approved labeling for this drug does not contain this indication? What is a physician's position regarding the prescription of propranolol for the treatment of angina pectoris or hypertension when the labeling for this drug also does not reflect these particular indications? The list of questions can go on ad infinitum.

To complete consideration of the complexity of the issues involved, one must consider the pharmacist's position when he dispenses the drug if he is clearly aware that the drug is intended for a use other than that approved within the labeling. What is his duty? What is a nurse's position or duty owed when she administers a drug, knowing that the indication is not FDA-approved? Should the patient be informed? Is it the duty of the pharmacist, the nurse, or the prescriber to communicate this information to the patient?

The above examples constitute actual situations that must be dealt with by providers and patients involved with drug use. The labeling requirement extends not only to providers but fundamentally affects patients. The role of apprved labeling in determining the manner, conditions, and limitations of drug usage assistance provided to patients will now be described.

12.7.1   Duty to Use Drugs to Match Package Insert Indications

In 1967 an incident, termed a therapeutic mishap, in which a textbook dose two to four times that of a PI dose resulted in the death of a 8-year-old child (52), helped initiate a journalistic skirmish which peaked with publication in the *Federal Register* of a proposal about the use of approved drugs for unapproved purposes (53). The basic disagreement centered around whether prescribers owed a duty to patients to prescribe drugs only in accordance with officially approved PI indications. The controversy was complicated by the unobjective stands taken by the American Medical Association (AMA) and the Food and Drug Administration (FDA). The principal point of debate involved the amount of authority inherent in a PI, i.e., whether a prescriber must prescribe only in accordance with this officially approved source of information. Basically, the AMA's position was that the PI serves only to inform physicians of the recommendations of the drug manufacturer, but does not force them to comply with the suggestions. The FDA's position was that the recommendations of the PI are the best available drug use information source. Although these viewpoints are not necesarily opposed, the two groups succeeded in misinterpreting each other.

Such controversies sometimes shed light on the issues, but in this instance what the law is must ultimately be resolved by regulation or court decision. Several aspects of the PI have been clearly established by courtroom action. In 1954 one court held that the information in the PI was "a proper method of use" (54). A California court in 1957 allowed admission of the PI as evidence, but stated that the insert did not establish the standard of care and deviation from its recommendations did not constitute experimentation (55). Nevertheless, the general statements of the PI have been accepted as proof of the existence of drug information that responsible prescribing physicians should have known about and adhered to (56). One court ruled that when differences of opinion over doses exist among specialists, the recommendations of the PI are not binding (57). The courts have held that the physician must be aware of the warning and dosage recommendations of the manufacturer. This particular ruling stemmed from a decision regarding injury to a 9-month-old infant caused by the use of an antibiotic labeled "not for pediatric use" (58). Along these same lines, a New Jersey court determined that it was the obligation of the physician to be aware of the previous history of the patient with regard to the use of drugs; the pharmacist's duty and liability seem not to have been considered as part of these cases (59). The New Jersey case was also interesting in that the PI was accepted as applicable for defining the standard of care among dentists.

One of the more noteworthy cases involving chloramphenicol occurred in 1970 (60). In its opinion, the court stated that where a drug manufacturer recommends the conditions under which a drug should be prescribed, the disorder it is designed to relieve, or warnings and other precautionary measures to be observed, a physician's deviation from these recommendations is prima facie evidence of negligence if competent medical testimony states that the patient's injury is a result of the physician's deviance (60). In this case the court also ruled that the manufacturer had no duty to warn the lay public regarding the dangers of prescription drugs.

A pharmacist may receive prescriptions for legend drugs when the intended use differs from the indications appearing in the PI. Pharmacists violate no federal statute in filling such prescriptions because the regulation of both medicine and pharmacy is generally left to the individual states. The pharmacist is also exempted by the container labeling requirements of Section 503 of the US FD&C Act (61).

12.7.2 Duty to Publish Only in Accordance with Package Insert Information

The case already cited in which an 8-year-old child died from an unusually high drug dose clearly identifies the possibility that adverse effects can occur from indiscriminate, faulty, or otherwise erroneous information appearing in textbooks. On the other hand, serious questions arose when the remarks of authors of textbooks, medical journal articles, or other scholarly works were limited by the FDA or any other regulatory agency. After much gnashing of teeth and emotion on the part of organized medicine's representatives, the ultimate conclusion was that a physician or other author is free to express his opinion concerning a drug; the FDA has not had and does not have any jurisdiction over such published material. It seems reasonable that a resulting mishap from improper use of a drug based on textbook information ought to be documented to justify deviation by the defendant from the manufacturer's suggested use. Section 13.14 contains a brief overview of the extent to which the PI recommendations are observed in actual drug use.

The results and conclusions of a conference held in 1968, in which representatives of the FDA and the AMA's Council on Drugs responded to 22 questions, were published in a later issue of the *Journal of the American Medical Association* (62). The top legal persons in the FDA were represented at this conference, and the AMA Council on Drugs was represented by its chairman, Dr. John Adriani. Most of the conclusions reached during this conference were ultimately substantiated by the *Federal Register* release of August, 1972 (53). The question as to what extent a physician may deviate from drug use recommendations as described in the PI was raised, and the conclusion was that a physician may use a drug in any amount and for any purpose he sees fit. In the event that a physician deviates from the PI instructions, the burden of proof may rest with the physician if the PI is admitted in court as evidence of the proper use of a drug. On the other hand, the PI may be used by a physician's defense attorney as evidence to indicate that the physician was using the drug in an accepted and approved manner and also to show that the FDA approved the drug. Proper usage as described in the PI, however, does not assure immunity from legal action or from liability.

A question also arose about the extent to which an author of a scientific article may deviate from drug usage recommendations in his article on drug information. The conferees concluded that a physician or other author is free to express his own views concerning a drug; however, it is wise, although not mandatory, that a notation be made in an article that the dosage or dosage form of a particular drug differs from an officially approved dosage or dosage form. In the event of a mishap occurring because of incorrect information in a textbook, the injured party can use a PI showing the basis for proper use of the drug as evidence in court.

It was also concluded that following the recommendations of the PI does not necessarily absolve either the manufacturer or the physician of liability in the event of an adverse reaction. Although the use of a drug in conformance with PI labeling may strengthen an argument in favor of the defendant's or the manufacturer's position in court, it does not necessarily absolve either of liability. Any patient is free to institute proceedings against any party regardless of whether the PI includes a listing of the hazards experienced.

If a drug is indicated for treatment of a particular disease and the physician fails to use it, the prescriber may be liable for any injuries occurring to the patient because he failed to receive the indicated drug. If the physician or other practitioner is able to provide valid reasons and convince the court that he was justified in not using the product, this may be sufficient to absolve him of any liability. A physician is not required to prescribe a drug because it is effective in treating a specific disease mentioned in the labeling. Nevertheless, the PI may be admitted as evidence to demonstrate that such a drug is available for a specific purpose. If a physician is ignorant of the fact that a given drug is available and specific for a purpose and he fails to use it while others in his community usually use it for the purpose being considered, and if the reasonable physician would have used it had he known of its availability, then he could be accused of negligence and an action filed against him for malpractice. A physician probably owes a duty to prescribe an indicated drug when the appropriate condition is observed in the patient, unless he can justify some other course of action.

12.7.3 Duty to Adhere to Nonindications Package Insert Content

One of the more interesting aspects of the entire journalistic controversy including the FDA *Federal Register* response is the almost complete disregard of PI information other than indications (including actions and uses). Even if a drug had to be used only in accordance with officially approved indications, this would not be nearly as demanding as would be the case if adherence to the entire PI information was required. Other than in the courts, little or no consideration has been given to deviations from contradictions, precautions, warnings, dosage and administration, or other nonindications aspects of the PI. These other portions apparently can be deviated from, ignored, considered in part, or in other ways not relied upon without exciting an iota of interest in the FDA or the AMA. For example, if the duty was owed that prescribers must perform a thorough physical examination of all new recipients of oral contraceptives (a precaution), this would dramatically alter the practice of gynecology and the way in which this particular drug is prescribed.* For example, drug use review of Medicaid prescriptions in Alabama (63) revealed that approximately seven times as many units of indomethacin were being consumed by these patients as aspirin units. The PI at that time stated that in-domethacin was to be used only after a trial with salicylates had been unsuccessful (64). Clearly, a requirement that the precaution section of the PI be rigorously observed would affect the prescription of drugs in Alabama and probably in other states.

Consideration of one case which did not reach the appellate level will shed light on potential developments in this area (65). The official labeling for oxsoralen included a statement that photosensitivity and especially sensitivity to sun rays often resulted when the user's skin was exposed for more than a minute. After a physician testified that even if he had known of the sensitivity problem he would still have prescribed the drug, the jury awarded $7,750 to the plaintiff. Both the physician and the pharmacist shared in paying the award. The award was to compensate the patient for severe skin damage, including possible permanent skin depigmentation and increased susceptibility to skin cancer. The court ruled that the pharmacist and the physician should have advised the patient about the warnings contained in the PI. The patient should have received proper instruction regarding exposure to light. The manufacturer was not held liable because the warning was clearly present in the PI. The jury apparently felt that the patient was not actually warned as claimed by the defendant physi-cian.

12.7.4   Duty of Nonprescribers to Adhere to Package Insert

There is little or nothing in the literature about the pharmacist's or the nurse's duty in regard to dispensing or administering drugs outside the limits of the PI information. Although this seems reasonable based on the tasks traditionally performed by these professionals, it ap-pears to be a questionable judgment for contemporary conditions. Further court decisions may result in a definitive ruling about the duties owed by pharmacists, nurses, and other nonphysician person-nel in dispensing, administering, etc., drugs outside the scope and limits of the PI information.

Consider one of the few cases specifically related to the issue raised

---

* According to one estimate, two-thirds of oral contraceptive recipients do not receive any kind of physical examination (23).

here. In this instance the pharmacist was held liable for failure to advise the physician of the adverse effects of methysergide; the case did not reach the appellate court (66). The pharmacist was found negligent in not warning the physician of the side effects listed in the PI, since the effect experienced by the plaintiff was one of several listed in the methysergide PI. The pharmacist, the physician and the manufacturer shared in paying $350,000 to the plaintiff for damages suffered, including endocardial fibrosis. This case coupled with the oxsoralen case may point to future developments regarding the duty to act in accordance with nonindications PI information.

The section which follows will conclude examination of the duty owed pertaining to the use of approved drugs for nonapproved purposes. It will discuss the role of the PI in its proper historic, regulatory, and statutory context.

12.7.5 Statutory Basis for Determining How Approved Drugs Are to be Used*

Section 505 of the US FD&C Act prohibits the introduction or delivery for introduction into interstate commerce of any new drug without the filing of an IND plan or approval of an NDA. The new drug provisions of the FD&C Act apply only at the moment of shipment in interstate commerce and not to action which occurs after shipment in interstate commerce; this is unlike the adulteration and misbranding provisions of the Act. This statutory provision furnishes the foundation for the conclusions ultimately made in this section.

The major objective of the drug provisions of the FD&C Act is to assure that drugs will be safe and effective for use under the conditions of use prescribed, recommended, or suggested in the labeling for a given drug. The procedural mechanism for achieving this objective rests with the statutory prohibitions pertaining to movement of a drug in interstate commerce as specifically described within the statute. When a new drug is approved for marketing, the conditions of use that have been approved are required to be set forth in detail in the full disclosure labeling. This labeling exists mainly as the package insert, and the abbreviation "PI" will be used in the remainder of this section to indicate the equivalent of full disclosure. The requirements

---

* This section relies heavily upon the *Federal Register* proposed rule entitled "Legal Status of Approved Labeling for Prescription Drugs; Prescribing For Uses Unapproved by the Food & Drug Administration" (53).

which this labeling must meet have been described in detail earlier. Its origin was also described. PIs present a summary of drug use information, which the supplier of the drug is required to develop from accumulated clinical experience, and systematic drug trials consisting of preclinical investigations and adequate, well-controlled clinical investigations that demonstrate the drug's safety and effectiveness.

If an approved new drug is shipped with the approved PI in interstate commerce, and neither the shipper nor the recipient intends that it be used for an unapproved purpose, the requirements of the new drug portion of the FD&C Act are satisfied. After the drug has entered interstate commerce, the new drug provisions of the Act no longer apply. This makes it legal for a physician to prescribe a different dosage for his patient, or to vary the conditions or use from those approved by the FDA. Apparently practitioners engaged in dispensing or administering drugs for unapproved purposes or under unapproved conditions are also free to pursue whatever course of action they deem desirable.

The FDA contends that interpretation of the Act in such a way that practitioners and particular physicians are free to exercise their own discretionary judgment is consistent with the legislative history of the Act and its amendments and the congressional intent of the Act. This is based on repeated statements found in the history of the Act attesting that Congress did not intend the FDA to interfere with medical practice. Moreover, several references occur which support the claim that the bill was understood not to claim to regulate the practice of medicine, especially between the physician and his patient. Legislative history also shows that Congress considered it the patient's right to seek civil damages in court if he encountered evidence of malpractice, and declined to place any legal restrictions upon the medical profession. The problem of malpractice in the United States has traditionally been left to the discretion of the states and has been exercised via the varied civil laws pertaining to malpractice and, to a lesser extent, via various statutory laws regulating the various health care professions.

On the other hand, while congressional intent was not to interfere with the practice of medicine, it is clear that it did intend that the FDA determine and approve for marketing only those drugs for which there exists substantial evidence of safety and effectiveness. This means that the FDA is authorized to determine what information about drugs constitutes truthful, accurate, and full disclosure to permit safe and effective prescription by the physician. When a drug is determined to be safe and effective, the onus falls upon the prescriber to make a final judgment as to which, if any, of the available drugs his patient will receive in light of the information contained in their labeling and other adequate scientific data available to him.

The Act does not prescribe the duty of filing an investigational new drug plan for prescribing an approved drug for unapproved usages, or that the prescriber submit to the FDA data concerning the therapeutic results and the adverse reactions obtained for a physician. It would seem to be in the best interest of the physician and the public that this be done. Such a use is investigational, and the prescriber should take account of the scientific principles, including the moral and ethical considerations, applicable to the safe use of investigational drugs in human beings if nonlegal considerations enter into a judgment as to the duties owed. Data so reported can lead to warnings against dangerous unapproved uses or, on the other hand, to acceptance of previously unknown uses.

As has been previously described, considerable concern has been expressed by physicians and, to a lesser extent, by others that failure to follow the labeling of a drug may render the practitioner laible for malpractice. Labeling is not controlling on this issue, although it may in some jurisdictions be admissible in court as evidence of what would constitute proper use of a drug. The purpose of labeling is not to impose or preclude the imposition of liability from the use of a drug. It is to provide truthful information in summary form of the functional and dysfunctional effects of a drug.

When the FDA finds that an approved new drug is being used for unapproved purposes, the FDA is obligated to investigate these conditions thoroughly and to take whatever action is warranted in order to protect public health. Alternative courses of action include requiring a change in the labeling to warn against or to approve the unapproved use, seeking substantial evidence to verify the unapproved use, restricting the channel of distribution, and even withholding approval of the drug and removing the new drug from the market in extreme cases.

The FD&C Act regulations (67) require that the PI contain appropriate information with respect to *all intended* uses of the drug. Thus where a manufacturer or his representative, or any other person in the chain of distribution, does anything that directly or indirectly suggests to the patient or his representative that an approved drug may properly be used for unapproved uses for which it is neither labeled nor advertised, that action constitutes a direct violation of the Act and is contrary to what is permitted by law. For example, if a physician knowingly causes the shipment of furosemide (Lasix) in interstate commerce for the purpose of using this drug to treat very young children, he will be in violation of the Act unless he previously secured proper authorization from the FDA. Similarly, if a physician causes methotrexate to be shipped in interstate commerce, intending to prescribe it for the treatment of acne in teenagers, he will be in violation of the Act. It seems that pharmacists dispensing methotrexate, when they are aware of its intended uses and when they have caused it to be shipped in interstate commerce, would also be liable for violation of the Act. Refraining from dispensing or prescribing is a potentially demanding requirement. For example, if a pharmacist is aware that a particular physician routinely prescribes propoxyphene hydrochloride for the relief of mild pain in pregnant women, is he in violation of the Act when he causes the drug to be shipped in interstate commerce intending to supply it to the pregnant patient? He may be because the PI contains the statement that this drug has not been shown to be safe in pregnant women. Thus, the burden of justification would rest with the physician and with the pharmacist to show that it was safe for use in this condition.

REFERENCES AND GUIDE TO FURTHER STUDY

1. Ehrlich, J. W.: *Ehrlich's Blackstone*, Part 1, Capricorn Books, New York, 1959.

2. Ehrlich, J. W.: *Ehrlich's Blackstone*, Part 2, Capricorn Books, New York, 1959.

3. Stevenson, L. G.: Official Control of the Administration of Drugs, *Experimental Medicine and Surgery* **22**:150 (January) 1964.

4. Stevenson, *ibid.*, p. 151.

5. Report of the Secretary's Commission on Medical Malpractice, Appendix, Reports Studies and Analysis, DHEW Publication No. (OS) 73–89, U.S. Government Printing Office, Washington, D.C., 1973, p. 16.

6. United States District Court for the District of Columbia: *Journal of the American Pharmaceutical Association* **NS 14**(8):400–403 (August) 1974. (The complete opinion appears here.)

7. Chapter 14, Title 45, New Jersey Revised Statutes.

8. Conditions of Participation, 45 *Code of Federal Regulations*, 249; 20, *Code of Federal Regulations*, 405.1127.

9. *Revised Code of Washington*, West Publishing Co., Section 18.64.

10. Comptroller General: Report to the Congress, Study of Health Facilities Construction Costs, General Accounting Office, November 20, 1972, p. 540–556; 363–380.

11. Hassan, W. E.: *Hospital Pharmacy*, 3rd ed., Lea & Febiger, Philadelphia, 1974, p. 323.

12. Prosser, W. L.: *Law of Torts*, 4th ed., West Publishing Company, Minneapolis, Minn., 1971, p. 149.

13. Prosser, *ibid.,* p. 150.

14. Prosser, *ibid.,* p. 150, quoting from A. P. Herbert, *Misleading Cases in the Common Law,* 1940, p. 12–16.

15. White, A. A.: The International Exploitation of Man's Known Weakness, *Houston Law Review* **9**:894 (May) 1972.

16. Prosser, *ibid.,* p. 151.

17. Prosser, *ibid.,* p. 157.

18. Prosser, *ibid.,* p. 165.

19. Prosser, *ibid.,* p. 165.

20. Center for Disease Control: *Morbidity and Mortality,* **23**(51):435 (December 21) 1974.

21. Curran, W. J.: Public Warnings of the Risk in Oral Polio Vaccine, *American Journal of Public Health,* **65**(5):501–502 (May) 1975.

22. American Pharmaceutical Association Legal Division, *Alabama Pharmacy Journal,* **4**:15 (January) 1973.

23. Competitive Problems in The Drug Industry, Select Committee on Small Business, U.S. Senate, Part 15 (January 14, 15, 21, 22, 23, 1970), Part 16 (February 24, 25; March 3, 4, 1970), and Part 17 (Appendixes, no hearing date), U.S. Government Printing Office, Washington, D.C., 1970, p. 5921–7324.

24. Goldstein, A. et al.: *Principles of Drug Action* (xerox ed.) John Wiley and Sons, New York, 1974, p. 780–783.

25. Roenigls, H. H., Jr.: Testimony Before Intergovernmental Relations Subcommittee, New Drugs For Unapproved Purposes, July 29, 30, 1971, U.S. Government Printing Office, Washington, D.C., p. 124.

26. Crumley, M. G.: Professional Liability of Pharmacists, *Defense Law Journal* **22**(5):471–490 (April) 1973.

27. Burke v. Bean (1962) 363 S.W.2d 366.

28. Krueger v. Knutson (1961) 111 N.W.2d 526.

29. McLeod v. W. S. Merrell Company (Fla. 1965) 174 So. 2d 736.

30. Jones v. Walgreen Co. (1932) 265 Ill. App. 308.

31. People's Service Drug Stores, Inc. v. Somerville (1932) 1961 Md. 662.

32. Tombain v. Conners (1912) 85 Conn. 231.

33. Scott v. Greenville Pharmacy, Inc. (1948) 48 S.E.2d 324.

34. Burke v. Bean (1962) 363 S.W.2d 366.

35. Tucker v. Graves (1920) 17 Ala. 602.

36. Nesci v. Angelo (1924) 144 N.E. 287.

37. Moses v. Matthews (1914) 146 N.W. 920.

38. Potter v. Krown Drugs 214 So. 2d 198.

39. Singer v. Oken (1949) Misc. 1058, 87 N.Y.S.2d 686.

40. Conneliuson v. Arthur Drug Stores, Inc. (1965) 153 Conn. 134.

41. Tiedje v. Harvey (1931) 329 N.W. 611.

42. Highland Pharmacy v. White (1926) 131 S.E. 198.

43. Willson v. Faxon (1913) 101 N.E. 799.

44. Audreotalla v. Gaeta (1927) 156 N.E. 731.

45. Title 21, *Code of Federal Regulations*, Part 300 to end.

46. ASHP Guidelines for Institutional Use of Controlled Substances, *American Journal of Hospital Pharmacy* **31**:582–588 (June) 1974.

47. Hearings Before the Intergovernmental Relations Subcommittee, U.S. House of Representatives, 92nd Congress, July 29, 30, 1971, New Drugs Used for Nonapproved Purposes, U.S. Government Printing Office, Washington, D.C., 1971, p. 32.

48. *Ibid.,* p. 59.

49. *Ibid.,* p. 61.

50. *Ibid.,* p. 62.

51. *Ibid.,* p. 64.

52. Goddard, J.: FDA Papers, *Clinical Pharmacology and Therapeutics,* **8**:753 (July–August) 1967.

53. 37 *Federal Register,* August 22, 1972, p. 16877.

54. Julien v. Barker *et al.* (July 8, 1954) 272 P.2d 718.

55. Salgo v. Leland Sanford, Jr., University Board of Trustees (October 22, 1957) 317 P.2d 170.

56. Sagal, E. L.: The Drug Package Insert, *Trial* **7**(2):59–52 (March–April) 1971.

57. Brune v. Belinkoff (April 3, 1968) 235 N.E.2d 793.

58. Anderson, B.: Package Inserts as Evidence, *Journal of the American Medical Association* **208**:589–590 (April 21) 1969.

59. Sanzari v. Rosenfeld (January 23, 1961) 167 A.2d 625.

60. Mulder v. Parke Davis and Company and Mork (December 18, 1970) 181 N.W.2d 882.

61. 21 *U.S. Code Annotated*, 353(b)(2).

62. Adriani, J. (Chairman, AMA Council on Drugs): Notes on the Package Insert, *Journal of the American Medical Association,* **207**(7):1335–1338 (February 17) 1969.

63. Mesel, E.: The Patient-Care Viewpoint, in Proceedings Computer-Based Information Systems in the Practice of Pharmacy, July 19–21, 1971, University of North Carolina, Chapel Hill, N.C., p. 1–35.

64. Physician's Desk Reference, 25th ed., Medical Economics Publishing Company, Oradell, N.J., 1971, p. 947.

65. Tonnesen v. Paul B. Elder Company (California Superior Court, Santa Clara County, Docket No. 288356, March 8, 1974).

66. Mahaffey v. Sandoz, Inc. (Kansas Sedwich City District Court, Case No. C-20275, May, 1974).

67. Title 21, *Code of Federal Regulations*, 1.106.

68. U.S. National Commission on Marihuana and Drug Abuse: *Drug Use in America: Problem in Perspective,* U.S. Government Printing Office, Washington, D.C. 1973, p. 379.

69. *Ibid.,* p. 382.

70. United States Pharmacopeial Convention, Inc.: *U.S. Pharmacopeia,* 19th rev., Mack Publishing Co., Easton, Pa., 1974, p. 41, 80, 364 respectively.

71. See for an overall view of various proposals, Diet Pill (amphetamines) Traffic,

Abuse and Regulation, Subcommittee to Investigate Juvenile Delinquency, U.S. Senate, Feb. 7, 1972, U.S. Government Printing Office, Washington, D.C. 749 p.

72. Salisbury, R.: The Effect of Monitoring Patient Drug Profiles upon the Legal Liability of the Pharmacist, paper presented at the First Annual Meeting of the American Society for Pharmacy Law, San Francisco, Calif., April 23, 1975, 13 p.

73. Campbell, R. K.: Compliance by Washington Pharmacists with the Patient Information Regulation, paper presented at 122nd Annual Meeting, American Pharmaceutical Association, San Francisco, Calif., April 19–24, 1975.

74. Campbell, N. A.: The Pharmacist's Responsibility to Determine a Prescriber's Practice Limitations, paper presented at First Annual Meeting of the American Society for Pharmacy Law, San Francisco, Calif., April 23, 1975, 8 p.

75. Forst, B. E.: Decision Analysis and Medical Malpractice, *Operations Research,* **22**:1–12 (January–February) 1974.

CHAPTER THIRTEEN

Remedies: Laws Defining the Effects on Persons Failing to Act According to Prescribed Principles

If a prince is to be trusted, it must be not because he is 'good', but because it is against his interest to be 'bad.' (1)

13.1 CONCEPTUALIZATION OF EXACTING OF ACCOUNTABILITY

Exacting of accountability is one of the key components of the larger control and regulatory model. This term refers to the act of checking to determine if performance of a duty has occurred and if the level of performance is acceptable. It too is based on a conceptual model. The model for the exacting of accountability is based on three major steps:

1. Establishment of standards of performance.
2. Measuring actual performance.
3. Taking corrective action against deviation.

Although the focus of this chapter is on the last step, attention to all three is necessary. The purpose of exacting accountability is to ensure to the maximum extent possible the achievement of the objectives desired from medication use. When the exacting of accountability is examined in elemental form the following steps can be defined:

1. Establishment of desired role occupant performance standard pertaining to medication use.
2. Execution by role occupants of acts pertaining to medication use.
3. Measurement of actual performance of role occupants.
4. Comparison of actual performance to the standard established for each role occupant.
5. Description and quantification of deviations.
6. Determination of which, if any, role occupant should have performed the acts at issue.
7. Analysis of causes of deviations of actual versus established performance standard.
8. Creation of a plan for corrective action.
9. Implementation of plan for corrective action.

The best plan for exacting accountability does not correct deviations efficiently and effectively, but rather prevents the occurrence of deviations. A major plan for corrective action rests with the punitive provisions of criminal and civil law.

A large portion of this book has been devoted to describing in detail the standards established for behavior as various decisions and acts making up the medication use process occur. Specific chapters have described the *standard* of performance of role occupants in their roles as providers and patients. To a lesser extent a description of the *actual* performance of selected role occupants has been sketched; a more detailed examination of the actual performance of selected providers will be presented later in this chapter.

The major thrust of this chapter is toward a description of the means of exacting accountability from providers when deviation has occurred. The deviation must result in an injury either to the public or to an individual, or both. A major issue involves an evaluation of whether the deviation constitutes a lack of careful conduct by the role occupant.

13.2   THE INFERENTIAL MODEL FOR DRUG USE

Drugs are legitimately used in our society to treat medically deviant conditions. The goal of therapy is to produce some desired effects or changes in the body while at the same time minimizing the undesired effects from consumption of a given drug. A given drug is effective for treating only a definite and limited number of medically deviant conditions. As previously described, the goal of most drug therapy is to obtain a best match between the actions of a drug and one or more medically deviant conditions.

The patient and provider both desire a predictable and unvarying relationship between consumption of a drug and its effects. However, the only way to be certain that a given drug will produce only the expected number and quantity of undesired effects is to administer the drug to a person with the medically deviant condition and observe the results. If the desired results are readily discernible, one can be reasonably positive that the desired functional effects of the drug have been achieved. However, it is always possible that the body's natural defense mechanisms rather than the administered drug were responsible for the "cure." Even under these rather unlikely circumstances for determining the effects of a drug with certainty, there is still doubt that a subsequent, identical medically deviant condition in the same patient, with the same etiology, and treated with the same drug will give the same results. One element of change is the patient himself. Biologically, initial exposure to a drug may affect the patient's body in such a way that a later treatment regimen will produce effects unlike those of the first exposure.

As suggested, the means described above for determining the efficacy of a given drug is neither feasible nor realistic. Therefore some inferential method of matching a patient's particular medically deviant condition with an indicated drug must be used. The data gathered by this method, which may be *in vivo* or *in vitro* and pertains to the safety and efficacy of a drug, is summarized in the relevant literature. Information describing the effects of a unique drug is summarized for patients in general in the package insert and other relevant information sources describing the effects of a given drug. But both patient and provider who intend the drug to be administered for a particular medically deviant condition desire and need to obtain an estimate of the effectiveness of a given drug product through some *in vitro* method. Generally, no acceptable or satisfactory *in vitro* test exists. Therefore one must rely upon the information derived from patients in general to predict the effect that will be experienced from administration of a drug in one particular patient. To the extent that the patient differs from other patients on whom the drug was tested, the results are not likely to be the same as anticipated. Also, the predictability of drug effects in a given human being is not very reliable when animal data are used to make this prediction.

13.3   RELATIONSHIP OF THEORETICAL MODEL TO THE EXACTING OF ACCOUNTABILITY

The uncertainty described in the situation may lead to serious problems for both patient and provider. Neither can be certain about the effects of a given drug administered to a given patient. When patient and provider expectations differ, dissatisfaction on the part of either or both is likely to occur. In the case of patient dissatisfaction, the seeds for discontent, unhappiness, and ultimately a malpractice suit germinate and sometimes give rise to the patient seeking compensation from the provider for real or imagined damages. To the extent that a provider did not base his prediction of expected results on available information and data, and to the extent that he did not act on the information as a careful, reasonable, and prudent practitioner would have acted, he is exposed to the possibility of having to pay the patient for any damages (injuries) that may have occurred from the use of an administered, prescribed, or dispensed drug. When the deviating provider intentionally strays so far from the norm that extraordinary injuries occur to the patient, remedies other than civil may be sought. Such actions may ultimately result in the provider being imprisoned or required to pay a compensatory sum of money for his deviant act, or both. The nonprovider may likewise be punished if he engages in behavior prohibited by law or fails to behave as prescribed by medication law. The sections that follow will add more detail to the conceptual model for control and regulation of users and providers of drugs and related services with primary emphasis on the procedures for exacting accountability from role occupants.

Each act created by a legislature almost invariably carries with it a penalty specifying the fine or period of imprisonment which will be imposed upon a law breaker, i.e., an accountability clause. Generally, under common law this penalty must be specific enough so that a would-be wrongdoer can be informed as to what penalty would be imposed upon him for breaking a particular law. The US Food, Drug & Cosmetic Act, the U.S. Comprehensive Drug Abuse Prevention and Control Act (the Controlled Substances Act is a part of it), the State Provider Practice Acts, the State Food, Drug & Cosmetic Acts, the State Uniform Controlled Substances Acts, and other drug-related acts generally include a definitive listing of penalties that may be incurred by a wrongdoer.

Civil penalties incurred by a person not complying with various laws are generally determined on a case-by-case basis in a court proceeding. The amount of money exacted is generally based upon present value of future earnings of the offended person coupled with certain kinds of special awards, including punitive damages.

The penalty for failing to comply with any of these laws may vary from as little as a $50 fine to lifetime imprisonment, depending upon the particular crime committed and the particular jurisdiction governing the act committed by the wrongdoer. The following sections will consider civil and criminal penalties in detail.

13.4 LAW AS A CONCEPT

Law in general and medication law in particular are concerned with controlling and regulating the behavior of people. At the core of the concept of law lies a set of assumptions which purport to account for a person's behavior. One of these assumptions pertains to responsibility. A major premise of law is that one acts in a manner consistent with factors that lie within the personality of the individual. Since a person can choose how he wants to act, he should be free to reap the consequences of his behavior. Based on this proposition, the law is designed to prevent certain behavior through the enticingly simple mechanism of promising the contemplating actor that a promised punishment will be forthcoming if the contemplated act is attempted or completed in a way that deviates from requirements modified by the circumstances of the event.

Motivation—why people do the things they do—has been the subject of many articles and books by many people learned and not so learned, famous and not so famous, and the controversy rages on. The contemporary behavioristic view, articulated most clearly by B. F. Skinner, contends that there is little or no personal decision involved in behavior and hence no guilt, no responsibility. Punishment is a means of redirecting behavior and is future-directed. No retribution is rationally consistent with this theory. Psychoanalytic theory tells us that motivation lies in unconscious love and hate attachments derived from experiences primarily in the developmental years. Others advocate—both apostles of old and contemporary apostles—that instinct determines behavior; in the deterministic, instinctive interpretation of behavior the genetic code has preordained one's behavior. Clearly, the extremes are the old nature-nurture, good-bad, free will-determinist, pleasure-pain, stimulus-response theories of motivation and learning.

As was stated earlier, regardless of the etiology of behavior society exists and believes that some behavior is desirable over other behavior. How then is the desired behavior to be achieved? Can we wait until all the facts are in? No, we must act now, remembering all the while to be prepared for the serious possibility of being wrong. The positive view of risk-taking includes risking being right, too.

The problem faced by law is somewhat like that of an engine powering a car. If it is not controlled and regulated, it may go—indeed, will go—in an undesired direction. Once it has been set in motion, its speed and destination will probably be undesirable if the car is not controlled and regulated (one may quarrel that the analogy is already shaky because the car for most people is a means to an end that is well defined). The end desired is transportation from one place to another with provisions that include arriving alive and well, etc. With health behavior, ends and means are not as clearly demarcated as the ends sought through the use of a car. To return to the control and regulation of the behavior of the car: the goal can be achieved through several means, some of which are more consistent with the car owner's long and short-range uses of the car than others. For example, the speed of a car can be controlled by appropriate manipulation of the accelerator or by applying the brakes. It would also be possible to control the car's speed by removing the water or oil and allowing the car to overheat. Since we understand what motivates a car much better than we understand what motivates a patient, we can select control mechanisms consistent with the intended short- and long-term uses of the car. If we did not possess this knowledge, we might not know that some source of energy must be made available to supply the car power. Therefore, once the desired cruising speed was reached, we would be quite surprised to learn that a continuous energy source was required to continue movement at the desired speed.

The point is that medication law is to a large extent a control mechanism. The value judgment has been made that some control is preferred over no control. Whether the control range is achieved by depressing or raising the "accelerator" of the car of society is frequently—perhaps usually—unclear. But the accelerator has been installed, and when the decision has been made that under certain circumstances the accelerator is to be depressed, the provision is also made that raising the accelerator or failing to depress it when an appropriate objective is defined will result in punishment.

The sciences—physical, biological, and social—are all relied upon to serve as sources of knowledge to help define means to ends. Values, religion, and philosophy are relied upon to produce an answer to what ends are desirable. To the extent that error or ignorance is present within these bodies of knowledge, error and ignorance will be present in the law. If we think, based on our understanding of the effects of drugs, that administering a contraceptive to a group of people will stimulate the birthrate, then we will experience a birthrate markedly unlike that desired. If a law is enacted based on this information, it too will fail in producing the outcome desired.

"The first sign of wisdom . . . is to understand that there can be observed regularities in social behavior which are subject to study and analysis" (2). While man can and frequently does act rational, man can and frequently does act irrational. Only by taking into account the fact that man influences his environment and is in turn influenced by his environment and that there are a number of diverse forces interacting with law and other forces to control, and direct, and regulate behavior, can we come to control behavior. Some claim that laws are enacted by those in power to further the interest of the people in power (3). The theory of bureaucracy tells us that members of bureaucracies act in concert to maximize rewards and minimize strains both for the organization as an entity and for the members of the organization.

> Just as an engineer must fail who tries to design an aircraft without taking into account the laws of physics, so the [producer and user of medication law] must fail who tries to design a legal structure without taking into account the laws of social science. Freedom is a recognition of this entity; we are not free if we ignore the forces operative in the real world (4).

It is quite possible that one can escape an understanding of the importance of law in a complex, industrialized society. Nevertheless, it is quite probable that law and its institutions form the most important single social force shaping the structure of any complex, democratic society. Ultimately, law is not concerned with rules or procedures or policy, but rather with behavior. Rules, procedures, policies, and generalizations are merely means used to arrive at the behavior that is to be exhibited by the members of that society.

With these qualifiers of the law in mind, the structure of law will be examined and also the process which must be relied on when the law is to be used to attempt the correction of some private or public wrong.

13.5 STRUCTURE OF PUNITIVE COMPONENT OF LAW

The conceptual model for control and regulation of users and providers of drugs and drug-related services can be applied to explain the punishment* for deviating from role requirements. The model prescribes that society (1) delegate (assign) duties to roles, (2) delegate authority for performance of duties to role occupants, and (3) exact accountability from those assigned duties to perform. Recall the following salient points:

1. The various state practice acts serve as vehicles for assigning duties to roles.
2. The USFD&C Act, the various state practice acts, the state and federal controlled substances acts (or their equivalents), and certain other acts serve as vehicles for delegating authority to providers and patients to perform acts assigned to the various roles and to restrict others from performing assigned duties.
3. The common and statutory laws in general and certain component parts of the acts named above serve as means of exacting accountability from patients and providers.
4. For receipt of a drug or drug-related service by some particular person, the laws regulating contracts and agency serve as a means to the desired end.
5. Exacting accountability falls mostly upon the patient (recipient) or the patient's representative receiving the drug or drug-related service. If the patient recognizes or suspects something improper or lacking in the product or service received, the laws of malpractice or tort serve as tools for exacting accountability.
6. If someone other than the patient or provider suspects that either the patient or provider has acted in a manner inconsistent with his role and if the deviation from the norm is perceived as an act against the public, then the rules of criminal law serve as the basis for exacting accountability.

These briefly but correctly depict the legal structure for controlling and regulating the behavior of medication users and providers. The major principles underlying the points enumerated above will be listed within the broad categories or statutes which follow and each will then be described in general terms.

Examination of the elements of a tort will serve as a foundation for further elaboration on the main thrust of this section: methods for exacting accountability, taking into account the circumstances surrounding the claimed tort. A tort is an injury or wrong to another person that occurs because a duty owed was breached (not fulfilled or

---

* Punishment as used here includes being required (forced) to pay compensatory and related awards to those injured by legitimized role occupants.

not properly fulfilled). It has four elements: legal duty owed, legal duty violated, injury occurred, and violation of legal duty owed caused injury. A key point to a tort action is the requirement that an allegedly injured person prove his claim according to the rules and principles of law within a court. The behavior of people is clearly more rational if one can anticipate the legal ramifications from the pursuit of each of the alternatives available for action.

The duty owed by a role occupant has been described conceptually and as a part of particular statutes including the USFD&C Act, and the USCSA and State Controlled Substances Acts. The common law principles pertinent to an understanding of the duty owed have been articulated in Chapter 12. Moreover, the foregoing is also true when it pertains to a coherent explanation of the authority vested in a role occupant necessary for execution of his duty.

Attention will now be directed to an account of sanctions available when a person claims one or more elements of a tort are present. After a discussion of the fundamental principles of torts, attention will be devoted to other sanctioning components of the law, especially criminal sanctions.

13.5.1   Civil (Private) Law and Criminal Law Contrasted

Figure 13.1 depicts the gross components of law as they exist in the United States. Civil and criminal law represent the two major divisions. It is also clear that drug-related malpractice comprises only a small portion of the law. Although the acts in Figure 13.1 are depicted as independent, those falling within the domain of civil and criminal law may be governed by one or both components of the law. As sketched in Figure 13.2, some acts may be both criminal and civil. An individual may be prosecuted for a criminal act and yet may be required to pay damages in a civil trial for the identical act. The civil and criminal trials resulting from students being shot by national guardsmen at Kent State University were possible due to this philosophy of law. This is due to the nature of the two kinds of law. Civil law is mainly concerned with individuals and their interrelationship with other private persons. An act viewed as undesired and deleterious to the individual may not be perceived similarly by society; the converse is also true. Selling unauthorized legend drugs may constitute a crime, and thus persons innocently injured from the effects of the involved drug may be successful in getting a court to require the seller to compensate the injured party.

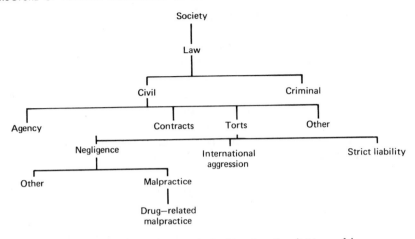

Figure 13.1. Macro structure and interrelationship of major divisions of law.

13.5.2 Divisions of Civil Law

Figure 13.1 also depicts the major subdivisions of civil law. The primary components of most relevance to civil law are agency, contracts, and torts. The law of torts is the major subdivision of law that involves medication-related claims. Within torts the major areas of concern are termed "strict liability," "intentional aggressions," and "negligence" (5). The law of malpractice is included in negligence. Major and primary emphasis has been and will be devoted to malpractice because about 90% of cases are negligence cases, and another 5% are contract cases (6). Most developed malpractice law pertains to physicians. The trend seems to be toward greater involvement of others who "practice" their profession, e.g., pharmacists and nurses. Anyone can be negligent, regardless of his occupation. Thus, the discussion in Chapter 12 on duty owed pertains not only to health professionals but to others as well. All people owe a general duty to act carefully in their interpersonal relationships.

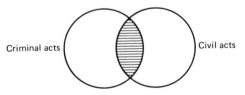

Figure 13.2. Relationship of two major divisions of law.

13.5.3 Remedies Provided by the Law of Torts

People do not go to court regarding a malpractice question unless some individual or representative of the public is seeking a change in behavior of the person named in the complaint, or unless he believes that an injury has occurred or may occur at the hands of the accused. Although for a number of reasons the objectives sought by litigants appear to be diverse, on close examination they can be shown to fit chiefly into a relatively small number of categories. These can be correctly subsumed under the following major categories (7):

1. The court may be asked to merely declare that the plaintiff possesses certain rights, or
2. The litigant may request that the court order certain actions to prevent a threatened wrong against the complaining person, or
3. That the court act to undo a wrong already done, or
4. That the court [in lieu of taking steps 1–3] award the complaining person the monetary compensation necessary to offset or equal the loss sustained by the complaining person at the hands of the defendant.

Remarks made here relate only to the fourth category.

Tort actions are directed toward the goal of compensating an injured plaintiff for injuries sustained. Punishment per se is not the goal. The law of torts is fundamentally concerned with restoring the person to his previous state, i.e., that existed before the injury. Obviously in cases of serious injury, e.g., death, caused by tortious injuries, no actual restoration can be accomplished. Nevertheless, the basis of tort law rests on the achievement of equality between the injury received and payment of money by the defendant, i.e., restitution for that injury.

13.6 CHANGING PUBLIC SENTIMENT TOWARD MALPRACTICE

A consumer newsletter, *Moneysworth*, devoted a substantial portion of an early issue to the subject of malpractice in an article headlined "When to Hire a Negligence Lawyer" (8). The author went on to urge the reader: ". . . if the tragic time ever comes when you are seriously hurt because of someone else's negligence, don't flub it. It could be the worst financial mistake you ever made." This article also introduced itself with the statement: "For many people, the only time in their lives when they have a chance to lay their hands on as much as $100,000 is when they're injured because of someone else's carelessness." Clearly, readers were being encouraged and exhorted to seek justice in accordance with the purest and most demanding conceptual models of delegation of authority to providers by society. Increased per capita malpractice claims (primarily for physicians) tend to underscore the apparent eagerness of the public to accept this newsletter's philosophy at least if not its specific advice. (See Section 13.9.5 for a description of the relationship between the rate of malpractice cases and selected variables, e.g., education.)

What the complaining person can get from the person accused of injuring the patient is money. But what must such a complaining person do to get the money he feels is coming to him? How can he force the allegedly offending person to pay the compensatory sum of money? On the other hand, the defendant is equally concerned with avoiding payment. How can an innocent defendant show that the plaintiff's claim is false or invalid?

The issues confronting both the plaintiff and the defendant are depicted and described in Figure 13.3. The interrelationship of the issues and elements to be dealt with is also depicted. The figure goes beyond the formal, conceptual depiction of the issues to show actual situations that sometimes occur.

Figure 13.3 depicts the interrelationship of the duty owed, negligent performance of duty, the injuries from acts of providers, the liability of providers, claims and suits filed by patients, and compensation paid by providers and received by patients.

Injuries are depicted as the area lying inside rectangle 1, 2, 17, 21 of Figure 13.3. These injuries represent the dysfunctional effects of received drugs upon a patient. These dysfunctional effects may or may not be caused by negligence. The drug is known to have caused the injuries.

Negligence of providers is shown as rectangle 3, 5, 14, 18. Negligent behavior may or may not result in an injury to a patient, a suit or claim need not necessarily be filed, and compensation will not necessarily have to be paid.

Rectangle 6, 9, 24, 25 represents and describes the nature of instances revolving around acts which result in a suit or claim. A suit or claim may be filed in the presence or absence of injury, and when the injury is or is not the result of negligence.

Compensation is depicted by rectangle 10, 11, 22, 23 in Figure 13.3. Note that not all legitimate patient claims result in compensation. On

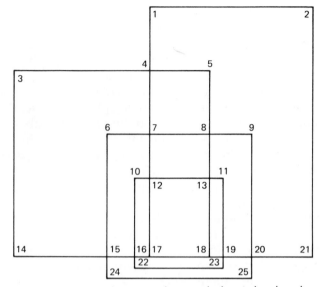

Figure 13.3.   Drug injuries, negligent conduct, and drug-induced malpractice claims.
Rectangle 1, 2, 17, 21: all drug injuries, whether or not caused by negligence.

Rectangle 3, 5, 14, 18: all instances of negligent conduct by providers of drugs and drug-related services, whether or not such conduct caused injuries.

Rectangle 4, 5, 17, 18: all injuries caused by negligence. These are the actionable injuries under the current tort system of liability and, theoretically, should result in the payment of compensation.

Rectangle 6, 9, 24, 25: all malpractice claims and suits filed.

Rectangle 6, 7, 15, 16: all claims in which there is negligence but no injury. Claims in this zone are usually made by disgruntled patients who are dissatisfied with the results of treatment or with the manner in which it was provided.

Rectangle 8, 9, 18, 20: all claims and suits where there is injury unrelated to negligence.

Rectangle 15, 20, 24, 25: logically, there might be some claims and suits even in the absence of injury or negligent conduct.

Rectangle 10, 11, 22, 23: all claims and suits where compensation has been paid.

Rectangle 10, 12, 16, 17: all claims and suits where there is negligence but no injury. On rare occasions, the conduct of a drug provider may be so reprehensible that settlement is made in the absence of any injury to avoid adverse publicity and embarrassment.

Rectangle 13, 11, 18, 19: all claims and suits in which compensation is paid for injuries not caused by negligence. Occasionally the injury may be so devastating to the patient that a suit is compromised and payment is made even in the absence of negligence, to avoid the possibility of a larger award by a sympathetic jury.

Rectangles 13, 11, 18, 19; 10, 12, 16, 17; and 16, 19, 22, 23: all claims and suits paid that, under the present tort system of liability, are theoretically not justifiable for actual compensation. *Source:* Adapted from Report of the Secretary's Commission on Medical Malpractice, January 16, 1973, DHEW Publication No. (OS) 73-88, U.S. Government Printing Office, Washington, D.C., 1973, p. 23.

the other hand, compensation may be provided in the absence of legitimate claims, e.g., when no injury or negligence is present, when negligence occurs without an injury, or when an injury occurs without negligence.

13.7 APPLICATION OF TORT PRINCIPLES BY ACTUAL OR POTENTIAL LITIGANTS

The discussion to this point has been almost exclusively concerned with the application of the law in real-life situations. The goal has not been to equip the reader to be a lawyer, but merely to be able to anticipate and understand the lawyer's use of relevant general principles in his legal reasoning. However, since patients and providers and others involved in the control and regulation of drugs must act, knowledge of legal principles should result in selection of an action alternative consistent with the intent of the law. Knowledge of the procedures for proving the prima facie tort case (described in the forthcoming section) is instructive in helping a person understand his responsibility and obligation under the law.

Surprisingly, the approach of many providers to understanding and explaining the law of torts frequently omits the most essential element in a tort action, namely, the occurrence of an injury. The occurrence of injury is left to be discovered and brought forth by the injured person himself. (Of course, this need for injury identification also applies to a legal representative of the injured person.) Given that an injury is suspected to have happened or may possibly happen, it is essential to identify the tort and to differentiate it from other possible legal wrongs. The identity of the tort will probably markedly affect the liability owed.

The nature of the plaintiff's interest which has been or may be injured is the key factor to be determined by the contemplating actor, since the injury largely determines the amount of damages that will ultimately be paid by the offending actor. The second major factor to be determined is the nature of the defendant's or potential defendant's conduct. A pharmacist, for example, may fail to advise a patient of the need to reduce his sodium warfarin dose when the patient's phenobarbital is discontinued. He or she may owe one standard of performance if the failure was intentional, another if the advising was required by statute, and yet another if the failure to advise occurred because the pharmacist was up all of the previous night at a poker game. He or she may also have owed no duty to advise the patient. If he voluntarily undertook actions defined as optional for his role, his standard of conduct was also affected.

13.7.1   Prima Facie Malpractice Case

Predicting the whole gambit of a potential or actual tort case should commence with an examination of the prima facie case itself. Prima facie means the set of essential items that must be present and proven in order for damages to be collected by the complaining person (plaintiff). Such a case consists of (1) an act or omission to act by the actual or potential defendant, (2) duty of due care owed, (3) a breach of duty (by failure to adhere to applicable norms, i.e., to act carefully), (4) an injury to complainant, and (5) violation of a legal duty caused the injury.

The key issue of law (as opposed to issues of fact) revolves principally around a determination of whether a duty of due care (duty to act carefully) was owed, or whether some special duty was owed that was imposed by statute or case law as, for example, that imposed by the typical pharmacy, medical, or nurse practice act. Liability may arise because a duty was owed to act and a person either failed to act and an injury resulted, or a person did not act as a reasonable man would have under the circumstances and therefore an injury resulted. The standard of care is always that owed by the standard of care which the reasonable man would have performed had he acted under the same circumstances.

The amount of care owed, i.e., the standard of performance required, depends on the circumstances surrounding the particular act or contemplated act; but the standard of performance of a duty owed for a given circumstance is always constant. A duty owed may vary in accordance with the circumstances, but once the duty owed is established the standard does not vary. For example, a pharmacist confronted by a person exhibiting signs of acute pain from an angina pectoris attack may provide a dose of nitroglycerin on an emergency basis without proper prescriber authorization. The pharmacist is held to the standard of care of a reasonable, prudent pharmacist under the circumstances. As the need for immediate action occurs or the risk of harm varies, the amount of care required also varies, but the standard always remains the same. The standard is always the amount of care which the reasonable and prudent (careful) pharmacist or other person of the actor's training and experience would have exercised under the circumstances surrounding the actor at the time of his act.

Many other facts and factors other than those cited above enter into a determination of the standard and amount of care owed. For example, the coverage of a particular act by a statute is relevant to ascertaining the standard and duty of due care owed. The relationship of the plaintiff and the defendant, the ages of the involved parties, the mental abilities of the involved parties, and many other relevant factors are involved in establishing the duty of due care owed under particular circumstances.

Proving or speculating about the possibility of being able to prove breach of duty depends on whether the plaintiff or potential plaintiff can establish that the defendant's behavior fell short of the duty owed to the complainant. If this can be shown, then a breach of duty has occurred. A breach of duty may be caused by:

1. Malfeasance: performing an unlawful act that results in injury to another person.
2. Misfeasance: performing a lawful act in a negligent or careless manner that results in injury to another person.
3. Nonfeasance: failing to perform an act which one is legally bound to do, or which is required of a person occupying a particular role.

When a determination can be made that an act occurred, that a duty was owed, and that a breach of duty occurred, then a negligent act is established. However, the injury that is supposed to have occurred must be documented, and must also be shown to have been the direct result of the negligent act.

The legal doctrine of *res ipsa loquitur*, which means literally "the act speaks for itself," may be invoked to show that a breach of duty occurred merely by virtue of showing that the act itself took place. For example, if a patient who has previously experienced no adverse effects from taking a hypotensive drug develops a sudden loss of consciousness shortly after ingestion of the drug, this may serve as sufficient proof that a negligent act occurred. In order to establish the applicability of *res ipsa loquitur*, three essential factors must be established:

1. It must be shown that the accident was of a type that does not normally occur in the absence of someone's negligence.
2. The indicated source of negligence must be shown to be within the scope of a duty owed the plaintiff by the defendant.
3. It must appear that neither the plaintiff nor any third party in any way contributed to or caused the plaintiff's injury.

Where the duty involved is one imposed by a statute, the doctrine of *res ipsa loquitur* will not be applied; instead the doctrine of *negligence per se* will probably be applied. In an incident involving a statutory duty, actual breach of duty must be proved in all cases where the defendant is held liable for his deviance from the required statutory norm. Also, if it can be shown that the act that appears to be a breach of duty is in fact justified, then there is no breach of duty. The effects of invoking the doctrine of *res ipsa loquitur* are complex. The most important point to be made from the perspective of both plaintiff and defendant is that in malpractice cases the burden of obtaining expert witnesses tends to be shifted to the defendant's position rather than residing with the complaining patient.

As stated above, if a defendant can show that his actions were justified considering the circumstances, then no breach of duty has occurred. For example: if a physician deviates from the approved labeling for some drug and can justify his deviant act, then no breach of duty will have occurred. He might relate experience of his own which reasonably suggests that the drug is effective, or seek testimony from colleagues to show that the drug is effective for the intended purpose, or he might recall some scholarly article to that effect (if this is permitted by the jurisdiction and court involved). A number of other elements are necessary to determine whether the injury was actually caused by the behavior of the defendant or the contemplating defendant. These include the contributory negligence rule which, if applicable, says in effect that the injury sustained would not have occurred had the plaintiff not acted the way he did; thus the defendant would not be responsible for the injury. (Other relevant issues which will only be mentioned here include the rule of concurrent liability, the material factor rule, and whether or not other actors were involved in inflicting the injury on the complainant). Moreover, cause is not sufficient proof. Proximate cause, which means essentially direct causation, must be proved. For example, if a pharmacist dispenses an antibiotic to a terminally ill cancer patient when morphine is called for, and the patient dies, in order for damages to be exacted from the pharmacist it must be shown that failure to dispense the morphine actually caused the patient to die.

Causation is an extremely complex issue and will not be covered in detail here. Imagine the difficulty of trying to prove that diethylstilbestrol injections into pregnant women resulted in uterine cancer in the offspring of these women some 20 years later. The numerous cases in Europe involving the thalidomide issue of the late 1950s and early 1960s, furnish adequate evidence of the difficulty of proving that consumption of thalidomide directly caused phocomelia and other malformations observed in infants.

Numerous other points must be considered by a contemplating actor. For example, a rule of law is that a tortfeasor (wrongdoer) takes his victim as he finds him. Thus, if a pharmacist of his own volition and authority decides to dispense a single phenobarbital tablet to a person who unknown to the pharmacist is also taking sodium warfarin, the pharmacist is held to the same duty and standard of care as if he had known the patient had the disease for which the sodium warfarin was being administered.

It is essential that there be proof of actual damages to the complainant. If the damage or injury is absent, even though all the other elements of the *prima facie* case are present, then no liability exists. For example, a physician may fail to administer RhoGAM, a drug used to prevent Rh-negative disease (erythroblastosis fetalis) in the offspring of Rh-negative women who give birth to a child with Rh-positive blood, and it may be proven that the physician owed a duty to administer this drug to his patient, and it may also be proven that the duty owed was breached. In addition, however, it must also be shown that an injury occurred. In this example, if a baby was born with Rh-negative blood, then no injury could exist because of the nature of the blood type. Therefore no liability would be owed, and no payment for damages could be extracted from the defendant.*

At first it is difficult to grasp the intent of awarding of damages under the law of torts. In the instance of malpractice, the intent is to compensate the victim rather than to punish the offending person. The idea is to replace the legal right that was injured with a sum of money. For example: if a child's leg is amputated due to negligent action on the part of physicians or nurses and the child is awarded damages of $40,000, then according to the conceptual intent of the law the child and the offending persons have achieved a restoration of the original condition of the child. In other words, the leg has been exchanged for $40,000 and, at least in theory, everybody is satisfied.

The amount of damages awarded or recovered is computed on the basis of the injuries sustained, including the pain, suffering, and resulting disabilities and other limitations on a person's behavior imposed by the damage sustained. Frequently, special damages such as the cost of hospitalization, medical expenses, drugs, or the inability to carry on one's former job are also compensable. Special damages

---

* Due to the fear and emotional trauma generated by the knowledge of the omission for the time period between children, a tort action might be possible or derivable from the facts of the case.

create special problems when mentally retarded or aged people are injured, because these people are often unable to hold jobs. Since the present value of their future wages thus approximates zero, these people have in economic terms no worth, or even a negative value. Similarly, instances in which unwanted pregnancies occur due to a dispensing error by a pharmacist may result in a claim by the pharmacist that the error resulted not in damages, but rather in a gain. This conclusion may be reached because children are viewed as an asset with positive value in our society. Questions of the value of life and limb must nevertheless have a dollar value assigned to them and, although a person or his family may consider him to be unique, irreplaceable, and consequently of infinite value, the law does not take this view.

13.7.2 Negligence per se

When a duty is imposed by a statute, it may or may not create the possibility of establishing both the owing of a duty and a breach of that duty. However, most statutes relevant to drug control and regulation tend to be criminal in nature, and thus tend to omit specifying a civil remedy. Two key requirements for establishing negligence per se are proof that a statutory duty was clearly owed and that legislative intent was present. The core of this concept is the idea that acting contrary to what is commanded by a statute is in and of itself evidence of failure to act carefully, i.e., of being negligent in executing a legal duty owed.

13.8 GENERAL DESCRIPTION OF TYPES OF INJURIES FOR WHICH COMPENSATION IS SOUGHT

Currently, the issue of malpractice, especially malpractice pertaining to physicians and hospitals, is receiving an increasing amount of attention. What is the magnitude of this problem? What, if any, is the injury that is claimed to have been suffered? Are people who file malpractice claims only slightly injured or are they very severely hurt? The following list represents an overview of selected facts which should place in perspective the magnitude of the malpractice problem in general. These findings are not specific to medication-related malpractice (9):

1. A medical malpractice incident is a relatively rare event; claims are rarer, and jury trials rarer still.
2. Out of every 158,000 patient visits to physicians only 1 malpractice incident is alleged or reported.
3. Only about 1 claim out of every 250,000 patient visits results in an assertion for damages, for a maximum annual total of 18,000 assertions (not cases or claims) of malpractice.
4. Only 1 court trial is held for every 10 claims closed.
5. Most physicians have never had a malpractice suit filed against them, and most physicians who are sued are sued only once.
6. Only about 6.5 claim files are opened annually for every 100 active practitioners.
7. Only about 16% of physicians (based on figures from one state) are sued in a typical year.
8. Only 21% of hospitals experience 2 or more malpractice claims per year.
9. About two-thirds of the hospitals in this country have no malpractice claims in a typical year.
10. Most patients have never suffered a reported medical injury due to malpractice, and very few have made a claim alleging malpractice.
11. The average person who lives 70 years will experience about 400 patient-doctor contacts.
12. The chances that any person living to age 70 will assert a medical malpractice claim in his lifetime is 1 in 39,500.
13. The number of pharmacists sued is negligible compared to the number of physicians sued.
14. Most pharmacists are sued for negligence in distribution and labeling practices rather than because of adverse effects of drugs.
15. Few nurses are sued for negligent acts pertaining to the use of medication.
16. There is less than 1 chance in 100,000 that any one physician-patient contact will give rise to a malpractice claim.
17. There is only about 1 chance in 10,000,000 that the dispensing of any one prescription will give rise to a malpractice claim.

The degree of injury claimed by a person filing a malpractice claim may of course range from the extreme of death to the opposite extreme of only slight emotional or mental suffering. Figure 13.4 depicts the percentage of alleged injuries according to the severity of the injury claimed. This figure shows that about 18% of alleged claims resulted in death, and an equal fraction resulted in permanent injury. Exclud-

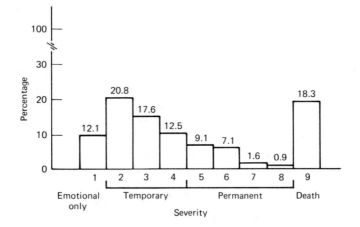

Figure 13.4. Severity of injuries alleged in medical malpractice claim files closed. *Source:* Report of the Secretary's Commission on Medical Malpractice, DHEW Publication No. (OS) 73-88, U.S. Government Printing Office, Washington, D.C., 1973, p. 11.

ing the patients who died, however, about two-thirds of the alleged injuries were temporary. To what extent drugs caused or were involved in these injuries is unknown.

13.9   MAGNITUDE AND NATURE OF INJURIES SPECIFIC TO MEDICATION

Since recognition of drug-induced injury by those who are injured by drugs has been slow to develop, very few court cases have been reported. Table 13.1 lists the distribution of cases by type of alleged physician negligence. The listed figure of 3.3% (132 cases for a 2-year period, or 66 cases for 1 year) suggests that the problem of drug-induced injuries is miniscule. Based on the figures listed in the preceding section, the maximum possible number of alleged claims would be about 300.

The fact that such estimates pertaining to drug-induced adverse effects exist is understandable when the findings of a General Accounting Office (GAO) study are examined. The GAO study found that about 80% of a randomly selected sample of FDA adverse reaction reports "were incomplete in one or more categories of information." Some FDA medical officers did not even know of the existence of the

TABLE 13.1   DISTRIBUTION OF CASES BY TYPE OF ALLEGED NEGLIGENCE

Alleged negligence	All Cases[a]	
	Number	Percent
Failure to diagnose (total)	417	10.4
Improper treatment (total)	3600	89.6
Drug-related	132	3.3
Surgical	1005	25.0
Medical equipment	336	8.4
Infection	60	1.5
During examination, etc.	303	7.5
Fracture or dislocation	273	6.8
Use of restraints, etc.	444	11.1
Anesthesia-related	117	2.9
Transfusion-related	75	1.9
Injection site	75	1.9
Abandonment	69	1.7
Casting-related	78	1.9
Legal theory	153	3.8
Gross misunderstanding	6	.1
Facilities	57	1.4
Unknown	417	10.4
Total	4017	100.0

[a] Data are for a two-year period.
Note: A claim is an instance of alleged malpractice brought either formally or informally for a lawyer's consideration. A claim becomes a case when a lawyer agrees to take the case and his client agrees to the fee arrangement.
Source: Report of the Secretary's Commission on Medical Malpractice, Appendix, Reports Studies & Analysis, DHEW Publication No. (OS) 73-89, U.S. Government Printing Office, Washington, D.C., 1973, p. 150.

adverse reaction reporting system (10). However, other information derived from research reports of actual versus preferred use of drugs and of adverse reactions can lend perspective to the number and nature of cases that might have developed had the individuals involved been more knowledgeable and inclined to seek legal redress.

For example: some 4,000,000 people were estimated to have received Chloromycetin (chloramphenicol) in a single year, although no more than about 400 of these people should have received this drug (11). At a mortality rate of 1 in 20,000, approximately 200 deaths and 200 court suits* should have occurred as a result of the provider-directed drug

* These figures are approximations. For a more precise set, see reference 12.

consumption for a 1-year period (12). This section is understandable only in the context of the relative benefit and risk regarding the functional and dysfunctional drug effects under consideration. The intent is to show that drug injuries do occur at a rate much higher than that suggested by malpractice data. Each instance of injury must be evaluated on its own merits. However, the evaluation is relatively easy if it can be established that the drug was not indicated. Dysfunctional effects, whatever their magnitude, will always exceed functional effects when the latter are zero. It may frequently be the case that dysfunctional effects are so inconsequential that the injury sustained will amount to a trivial complaint.

The point also includes isolating some of the grosser manifestations of drug-induced injuries, arguing all the while that lack of sufficient documentation on a national basis prevents precise and reliable estimates of such injuries even for the most popular drugs. It seems that fairly gross, obvious, and significant injuries must be identified before sufficient professional attention is devoted to a drug to produce information akin to that in this section. The first product to be described will be chloramphenicol.

13.9.1   Chloramphenicol-induced Avoidable Injury

Figure 13.5 lists specific conditions for which chloramphenicol was given; the cases depicted were taken from the AMA's *Registry of Blood Dyscrasias,* i.e., reported cases of chloramphenicol use resulting in a blood dyscrasia. Of 408 reported cases, the reason chloramphenicol was given was cited in 71%. Chloramphenicol would probably not have been the drug of choice for more than 7% of the cases. In the Senate drug hearings (11), the general estimate of the percentage of chloramphenicol-use issuances in which the drug was clearly not indicated ranged from 90% upward, with about 95% being the most frequently cited estimate. The conclusion the reader is encouraged to reach is that chloramphenicol has had the potential for generating more legitimate malpractice suits than have actually been brought to the attention of lawyers.

The feelings of ambiguity and bewilderment experienced by people adversely affected by drug use is best expressed by those who have suffered or been sacrificed (depending upon one's perspective) at the altar of undesired drug effects. A touching letter to a manufacturer of chloramphenicol expresses this (13):

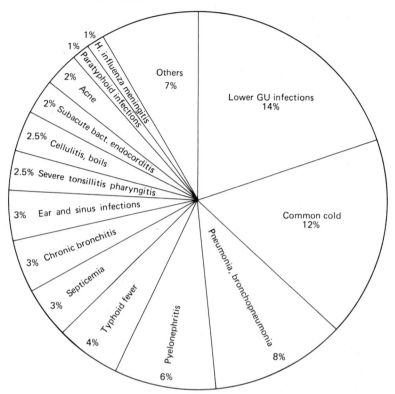

Figure 13.5. Specific reasons for prescribing chloramphenicol (based on 288 cases in which the reason for prescribing chloramphenicol was cited). *Source:* W. R. Best: Chloramphenicol-Associated Blood Dyscrasias—A Review of Cases Submitted to the American Medical Association Registry, *Journal of the American Medical Association* 201(3): (July 17) 1967.

"Parke Davis & Company,
Detroit, Michigan

GENTLEMEN:

My sister, ..., died May 3, 1967 after taking, by prescription, the antibiotic chloromycetin produced by Parke Davis and Company. Marion was 44 years old. To the best of my knowledge, after discussion with the attending doctors, the medication was responsible for the complete destruction of blood platelettes at the beginning. General infection at the end because of the absence of white corpuscles in her blood was the immediate cause of her death.

A post-mortem has been authorized, the results of which are not completed. .... took the antibiotic while on a trip to Europe. The prescription was filled in Spain, after a doctor's examination. She refilled the prescription once, twelve capsules. The total intake was 22 capsules. Two capsules were not taken.

The first administration of the drug occurred in October, 1966. The first indication of the nature of her illness was discovered state-side in February, 1967. We hope your interest in the case will prompt you to discuss the illness in detail with the doctors involved whose names I will gladly furnish on request.

I am sure you will understand that I have made attempts to become familiar with this drug since my sister's tragic illness and death. I understand that serious and fatal blood dyscrasias have been known to occur in the past. I understand that the serious consequences of the administration of the drug are published for the benefit of the medical profession. I understand precautions are urged stating blood studies are essential during treatment with the drug. Perhaps it is not practical to advise the patient in the same manner, but I assure you Marion would have weighed the advice carefully before accepting the treatment prescribed had she been given the opportunity to do so.

The illness for which chloromycetin was prescribed was not of a serious nature. Furthermore, the writing on the bottle containing the two remaining capsules is in Spanish, a language not understood by Marion.

We know that the drug is beneficial to countless more people than it is fatal to others. It is difficult to find comfort in this fact. . . . . was a vital, well regarded, loved person who held a responsible well paying job and supported her mother. I cannot be bitter or vindictive, because this fine woman has suffered a greater loss than I, and she is neither bitter nor vindictive. I can, however, write to tell you of the tragic consequence of the drug taken by my sister. I can write to complain that her death seems needless to those left behind and that this drug manufactured to cure has taken a life.

. . . . Mother . . . none of us . . . seek liability from your Company. It is our sincere hope that something can be done to prevent the recurrence of the tragedy to another. We feel strongly the utter lack of professional responsibility on the part of the doctor. Is it possible the man did not understand the potential effects or had insufficient advice concerning the drug from the company? Is it impractical to suggest that those to whom chloromycetin is available for administration should indicate, in writing, that they understand all of the undesirable effects the drug may produce in the human body during therapy, and after? If blood studies which are recommended during treatment could prevent a fatality, shouldn't they be mandated instead of merely recommended? Should the drug be withdrawn from a foreign market where the people entrusted with its administration may not be as professionally responsible as American doctors?

It is difficult to be objective and not allow emotions to be a part of this letter, since experiencing the tragedy of . . . .'s death. Her Mother, her sister and I, however, feel a compelling responsibility to write to you, the drug manufacturer to express our concern that other deaths may occur needlessly if a more responsible attitude is not taken by the maker of the drug, and the medical profession entrusted with its administration.

I will be pleased to receive a reply.
Very truly yours,

NAME WITHHELD"

Unfortunately, in at least some countries the facts described regarding Name Withheld's sister, Marion, are being repeated even now for at least some drugs.

13.9.2 Oral Contraceptives

An argument will be made that a prima facie case can reasonably be made against a significant number of prescribers of oral contraceptives. (The figures presented here are only rough estimates.) The entire subject of oral contraceptives (OC) is complex and controversial. Over 1400 pages of Senate hearings testimony were devoted to this subject at the time the patient brochure for OC use was issued (14).

The argument that potential malpractice cases exceed actual cases will be presented as it pertains to oral contraceptive consumption. This will be based on the finding that about two-thirds of the women who received prescriptions for "the pill" received no information about its dysfunctional effects. They also did not have a physical exam and a Pap smear before the pill was prescribed (14).

The estimated number of current OC users is approximately 6 million, based on the *National Prescription Audit* (15) and the second *Oral Contraceptive Task Force Report* (16). The estimated mortality rate for the age 20–34 group of OC users is 1.5/100,000, and 0.2/100,000 for non-OC users, for an incremental death rate of 1.3/100,000 users due to OCs. Therefore, with 1.3/100,000 incremental deaths for an estimated 6 million users, approximately 78 people die annually from OC use. Of these 78, 52 people die with virtually no information from either the prescriber or the dispenser about the risk of dying. In addition, the incremental hospitalization rate of OC users over non-OC users is 42/100,000 users. This yields 2520 incremental hospitalizations due to OCs, and two-thirds of this amount is 1680. Thus 1732 people (1680 + 52) or their families could reasonably pursue a malpractice case against the prescriber and perhaps also against the dispenser of OCs. The legal question at issue here is whether a duty was owed to secure the informed consent of OC users prior to the prescription and dispensing of OCs.

For a significant subset of these persons a much better case could be made using grounds other than informed consent. For about 1732 (two-thirds) of these women who did not receive the desired physical exam and Pap smear, the likelihood of exacerbation of already existing conditions was present. This includes all the women with thromboembolic and related disorders, impaired liver function, known or suspected cancer of the breast, estrogen-dependent neoplasia, and undiagnosed abnormal genital bleeding. Also, it is obviously unlikely for a woman to associate certain problems she may develop from OC use if she has not been advised about what effects may occur. Prevention of preventable problems is thus thwarted.

13.9.3 Pharmacist-induced Patient Injury

Since pharmacists have only recently begun to assume a decision-making role in drug therapy, they are involved in very few malpractice cases. Two of the major malpractice insurance underwriters for pharmacists claims to have no data describing the incidence of malpractice among pharmacists (17, 38). A sampling of the kinds of injuries experienced by patients has been provided by Smith (18). Critical incidents were gathered by a mail survey of pharmacists who had been identified as practicing a "high level" of community pharmacy. Written reports were provided by the pharmacists; and it is unlikely that these reported incidents would be an exaggeration of the facts, at least for negative incidents. Table 13.2 lists the category of incident, its definition, and a description of negative results for a sample of 237 incidents. It is obvious that an important number of adverse effects are caused by acts of pharmacists. To communicate the nature of these negative incidents, a slightly edited list is presented here.

1. A geriatric patient entered the pharmacy with a prescription for sodium salicylate. I did not fill the prescription as such but gave her a bottle over the counter. The physician called a few days later and was very upset over my action. It seemed the patient complained of pain and the physician wanted this as a placebo prescription to prevent giving her a stronger analgesic which he felt she did not need. Consequently, good relations were lost between physician and patient.

2. I received a new prescription for Thorazine concentrate for a boarding home patient from one of our state mental hospitals. I dispensed it as usual but failed to instruct the nursing personnel as to the need for diluting the medication in another vehicle. About a week later one of the workers at the home told me that they had nearly fought with the patient for two days trying to get him to take the prescribed dose directly into his mouth from the dropper. They had finally read the manufacturer's label (which I had covered with my pharmacy label) and put the medication in juice. The patient was now doing fine.

3. A man came in and asked for a laxative. I asked him whether he wanted something that would work immediately or after a night's rest, and he said he wanted something to work immediately. I asked no more questions. He went over to the soda fountain, took the medication (citrate of magnesia) and left. In about 10 minutes he was back and wanted to use our bathroom. I let him. After about 30 minutes I had to go downstairs for something else, and I could hear someone moaning in the bathroom. I checked and it was he. I called an ambulance, got him comfortable in the truss room, and also called a doctor. The doctor got there first but suspected that maybe the man was faking. They took him in an ambulance to the hospital, did some testing, and finally put him into surgery about one hour after admission. A ruptured appendix

TABLE 13.2 FREQUENCY DISTRIBUTIONS OF OUTCOMES BASED ON NUMBER OF END RESULTS

Category	Definition	Negative Results ($N = 237$)	
		Description	%
Patient end results[a]			
1. Longevity	Expected duration of life at time of incident		
a. Life saved/death caused		a. Death caused by actions of omission or commission	< 1
b. Length of life		b. Decreased	
2. Physical abnormalities	Diseases, state, conditions, and their complications 2. Anatomical ⎱ 3. Physiological ⎰ abnormalities (signs) 4. Biochemical	Unimproved, unchanged, duration prolonged unnecessarily. Caused, made worse, or unnecessarily deteriorated while under care.	5.9
3. Psychological abnormalities	Psychiatric syndromes, e.g., schizophrenia, or psychological entities, e.g., cardiac neurosis	Unimproved, unchanged: duration prolonged unnecessarily. Caused, made worse, or unnecessarily deterioriated while under care.	0
4. Physical symptoms	Subjective complaints of patient caused by biological abnormalities, e.g., pain, dizziness, weakness, anxiety, depression	Unrelieved, unchanged, duration prolonged unnecessarily. Caused, made worse, or unnecessarily deteriorated while under care.	2.1

5. Psychological symptoms	Subjective complaints of patients caused by emotional problems	Unrelieved, unchanged, duration prolonged unnecessarily. Caused, made worse or unnecessarily deteriorated while under care.	2.9
6. Function	Functioning of patient as an individual (self care, work, school) as a member of a family (role as parent or mate) as a member of society (community, church)	Individual function, Family function, Social function } worsened	< 1
		Subtotal	12.2

Process outcomes[a]

7. Compliance	Patient's diligence in following physician's instructions about medication, diet, activity, habits, follow-up and continuity of care with same MD	Decreased	2.1
8. Risks and unnecessary procedures	Potentially harmful or unnecessary procedures, tests, surgery	Incurred or increased	9.2
9. Hospitalization	Duration, frequency, appropriateness	Unnecessary or unnecessarily prolonged	0
10. Cost	Direct expenditures or loss of income.	Increased unnecessarily	3.4
11. Proper drug use		Patient does note use drug in accordance with accepted procedure	< 1

[a] Sanazaro and Williamson distinguish between patient end results and process outcomes. In the former, the end results refer specifically to changes in the patient as a person or in the attributes of the disease or condition. None of these categories is uniquely dependent upon medical intervention. In contrast, process outcomes occur only when the patient receives medical care. . . . These do not occur during the natural history of disease in the absence of medical intervention. *Source:* Adapted from M. C. Smith: Patient End Results of Community Pharmacy Service, *Journal of American Pharmaceutical Association,* **NS14**:(3) (March) 1974.

was the problem. There were also peritoneal ulcers, and one ulcer was almost paper-thin. He lived, and all came out fine but the one dose of that purgative could have almost been the cause of death.

4. A woman hypochondriac patron was taking Seconal placebos. We were making the placebos by emptying the active ingredient and replacing it with lactose. This woman was paranoid, and one day she suspected what we were doing. She opened a capsule, tasted the powder, and then called the pharmacist and confronted him with her suspicions. He admitted that we were doing just what she suspected. She blamed us for all her problems, even though the physician had prescribed the placebo. This incident could have been prevented by common-sense judgment on the part of the pharmacist. He should have known the instability of the woman, and could have tactfully reassured her that she was getting just what the doctor ordered.

5. This incident involves a patient who had frequent dizzy spells accompanied by severe headaches. She often watched television promotions of headache medications and felt that there was no need to see a doctor. Therefore she came in for something for her headache. Having several prescriptions to dispense with no time to secure previous conditions and activities that led up to her complaint, she was sold Empirin Compound tablets. After a few days we were informed that she had had a slight stroke, which probably could have been prevented with proper advice and treatment in the early days of her symptoms.

6. A woman with an earache went to an ear-nose-throat doctor and received two prescriptions. One was for an antibiotic capsule and the other for Nilstat suspension with the directions, 1 cc three times a day. On the next afternoon after the prescriptions were dispensed, the woman called the pharmacy wondering if the Nilstat was to be placed in the ear as she was currently doing. Because of the way Nilstat looks she wasn't sure if it was an ear drop or not. It was explained to her over the phone that it was to be taken orally and not to be used in the ear. In a couple of hours the daughter of the lady came into the pharmacy and said they had called the physician and he told them that we should have placed on the label "for the throat." The prescription was shown to the daughter along with an explanation that it was labeled as the doctor had specified on the prescription. The daughter was very upset and left the pharmacy.

7. This incident concerns a prescription I misread as 25 mg, which was actually 2.5 mg. It could have had serious results, but fortu-

nately things worked out satisfactorily. It was a prescription for Coumadin, and the doctor indicated the strength as /0025. At the time I dispensed the prescription, I commented to the daughter of the patient that it was somewhat unusual to be using a dose that high. The patient and daughter went to see the doctor a couple of days later, and the daughter happened to mention to a nurse that it apparently was a high dose. The nurse checked the situation, reported to the doctor, and it was necessary to restabilize the patient. The patient reported the mistake to me and I discussed the problem with the doctor. I did not lose the patient as a patron, but it certainly affected our relationship.

8. This incident concerns a new patient of the pharmacy who expected her first child. Her obstetrician had given her a prescription for prenatal vitamins. The directions to the patient were poorly written, and the pharmacist hastily interpreted them as saying one capsule twice a day instead of one capsule once a day. After the first supply was used, the patient returned with another new prescription for the same vitamin. This time the prescription was dispensed correctly. Upon examining the second prescription label the patient called the pharmacy and asked why the directions were different. She became alarmed when it was explained to her that an error had been made. Fearful of any damage to her unborn baby, the pharmacist informed the physician of his error. The physician assured him that there was nothing to fear in this case. The pharmacist called the patient and explained that he had conferred with the physician and that no harm had been done. Perhaps this was not enough, because the patient never returned to the pharmacy.

9. I make it a habit to explain directions for new prescriptions and to caution my clientele about any obvious side effects. A new patron came into my pharmacy one day with a prescription for Declomycin. I cautioned her about prolonged exposure to the sun with this drug. Unknown to me, this patient was very much an alarmist about drugs and interpreted the caution to mean that this drug was very dangerous and potent. She immediately called the doctor and asked him why he gave her such a potent drug, and said that she wasn't going to take it under any circumstances. Naturally he called me and expressed his feelings about the situation, which were highly negative. I still feel it is necessary for the pharmacist to give this information to patients, and I still do. However, I also feel it is necessary to know your customer first and use the correct approach in explaining these things.

13.9.4   Adverse Drug Reactions

In hospitalized patients, a significant number of adverse drug reactions occur. Estimates vary widely, a reasonable estimate being that at least 5% of exposures result in an adverse drug reaction (19). The frequency of more than 15 life-threatening events occurring in 411 patients is presented in Table 13.3. Although these events could be keyed to particular drugs, this has not been done because the point is that even if the lowest figure of 0.05% is taken as an estimate of life-threatening events in the population, this would mean (since about one-half the population consumes prescription drugs in a year (20)) that 50,000 people annually would experience a life-threatening event. If the high figure of 0.85% is taken as the best estimate, then the figure of life-threatening events would be 850,000 people. These values are within the range of the 160,000 yearly hospitalizations

TABLE 13.3   FREQUENCY OF LIFE-THREATENING EVENTS

Life-threatening Event[a]	Number of Patients	Percent of All Patients
Arrhythmia	98	0.85
Bone marrow depression	45	0.39
CNS depression	37	0.32
Fluid overload	33	0.29
Hemorrhage	31	0.27
Renal failure	28	0.24
Hyperkalemia	26	0.23
Hypotension	22	0.19
Fluid or electrolyte disturbances	21	0.18
Hypoglycemia with complications	14	0.12
Superinfection	12	0.10
Liver failure	8	0.07
Anaphylaxis	6	0.05
Corticosteroid complications	6	0.05
Other	24	0.21

[a] Drug-attributed events were classified as life-threatening by the investigators after careful clinical evaluation. For the purposes of this table, each life-threatening episode was counted only once in terms of the event judged to be the primary one. For example, if the administration of potassium chloride led to hyperkalemia, arrhythmia, and death, the primary adverse event was classified as hyperkalemia and not included under arrhythmia.

Source: R. R. Miller: Drug Surveillance Utilizing Epidemiologic Methods—A Report from the Boston Collaborative Drug Surveillance Program, *American Journal of Hospital Pharmacy* **30**(7):590 (July) 1973.

estimated from data reported by the Commission on Professional and Hospital Activities (39). Although little data is available quantifying the incidence of adverse drug reactions in ambulatory settings, the conclusion is inescapable that a large number of life-threatening and less serious dysfunctional effects occur from drug consumption. To the extent that care was not exercised in prescribing, dispensing, and administering these drugs, a claim for liability against one or more providers seems reasonable.

Adverse Effects from Selected Drugs and Drug Classes

The indications section of the indomethacin package insert clearly states that it is to be used only after aspirin or other salicylate therapy has been attempted unsuccessfully. Data from the Alabama Medicaid drug use review program show that the required prerequisite salicylate therapy was the exception rather than the rule. In 1970 2.4 million units of indomethacin were dispensed and only 0.55 million units of aspirin were dispensed under the Alabama Medicaid Program (21). This is more than a fourfold greater use for indomethacin than for aspirin, even though aspirin is indicated for many more conditions than indomethacin. Thus it seems reasonable that needless injuries were experienced by many indomethacin users. Although this information is somewhat dated, there is little to suggest that much improvement has occurred or that prescribing habits in Alabama are unique.

Numerous hearings before the various subcommittees of the US Senate and House of Representatives have dealt at length with the general subject of antibiotic misuse. In a recent article discussing the real danger of antibiotics, the authors warn "Unfortunately, antimicrobial agents are prescribed for mumps, measles, chickenpox, infectious mononucleosis, viral gastroenteritis, and upper respiratory infections but are worthless in these illnesses" (22). Published studies and data bear out the correctness of this statement. Table 13.4 shows that a patient will probably receive an antibiotic prescription from a physician for treatment of the common cold.* Presumably, these prescriptions will be filled by a pharmacist. Since antibiotics aren't indicated for the common cold, the patient is in a position to receive no benefit and some risk. The risk occasionally extends to permanent brain dam-

---

* A "Request for Proposal" issued six years later by the US Food and Drug Administration to seek research which can answer the question, "Why do physicians use antibiotics the way they do," suggests that the same sort of problem lingered on for at least six more years.

TABLE 13.4   TREATMENT OF THE COMMON COLD IN PHYSICIANS' OFFICES[a]

Type of drug	Percentage of Patients[b] Visiting a Physician Receiving a Prescription and/or Drug (%)
Broad- or medium-spectrum antibiotic	31
Oral cold preparation (antihistamine and decongestant)	29
Pencillin	22
Cough preparations	12
Cold and cough preparations	11
Nonnarcotic analgesics	10
Topical nasal and ophthalmic preparations	8
Sulfonamides	6
Antihistamines	5
Narcotic analgesics	2
All others	13

[a] Data from National Disease and Therapeutic Index based on analysis of 1128 patient visits.
[b] Percentage exceeds 100% because patients may be issued more than one prescription.
Source: Competitive Problems in the Drug Industry, Hearings Before the Select Committee on Small Business, Advertising of Proprietary Medicine, Part 3, U.S. Senate, December 8, 1972, p. 1184.

age, as happened in an instance involving a 30-year-old father. He consumed penicillin, which was contraindicated because he was severely allergic to it. This information was written in several places in the patient's chart, but the physician did not read the chart. The physician wrote the prescription and the pharmacist filled it; the patient took the antibiotic and suffered brain damage from the allergic reaction which resulted (23). (The plaintiff received $650,000 which places him in the "elite" of the less than 3 in 100 who receives more than $100,000; see Table 13.6 for a listing of award distribution.)

A study given considerable attention by the professional press and by Congress strongly suggests that antibiotics are incorrectly used (24). This study showed that antibiotics are used rationally for about 20% of antibiotic exposures and are used irrationally in about two-thirds of the instances, with the remaining therapy being questionable.

Another study yielded similar results (25). Here the reasons for selection of the actual drug prescribed were compared with the indications appearing in the officially approved PIs and the *Medical Letter*

(26) for selected drugs. In this study, rational therapy measured approximately 32% and irrational therapy approximately 19%, with almost half of the remaining therapy categorized as questionable. The most interesting finding was that only about 10% of the total cases studied were definitely and conclusively shown to be in agreement with the drug of choice as defined by the *Medical Letter* (26). Only about 14% of the 167 cases reported in this study were shown conclusively to agree with the PI indications (26).

Neither of the preceding studies described provided a meaningful estimate of the degree or severity of adverse reactions occurring from the use of antibiotics. However, the report of another study (27) is interesting not only because it relates directly to the question of incidence of adverse effects due to drugs, but also because it was solely concerned with the use of antibiotics intravenously (a particularly hazardous route of administration). This study also compared the actual use of drugs with FDA-approved use, and found that only about 29% of the drug use issuances studied agreed with the officially approved PI. The most surprising aspect of the study, however, was the finding that approximately 15% of the patients involved had died. Although four different tables were presented to depict the relationship between mortality and the receipt of a nonindicated drug, no statistically significant cause-and-effect relationships were found. Moreover this portion of the study was conducted on an *ex post facto* basis, and the authors cautioned the reader to avoid a cause-and-effect relationship conclusion. However, the report does raise interesting and provocative questions as to the liability owed to deceased patients by the physicians, nurses, pharmacists, other role occupants, and the hospital involved in providing medications to these patients (27).

The foregoing reviews of various studies and statements pertaining to the adverse effects of different therapeutic classes are intended to show that there is ample opportunity for a patient to reap more dysfunctional than functional effects from the use of drugs. Due to the underdevelopment of information in the specialty area of drug use, it is currently impossible to give a reliable estimate of the precise incidence of adverse effects due to these drugs. One must also be cautious to note that even if the incidence of adverse effects was determined to the last decimal place, it remains to be shown that these adverse effects occurred due to the negligence of pharmacists, physicians, nurses, or patients. It seems likely, nevertheless, that patients do suffer because of the negligence of practitioners and also because of their own negligence and ignorance. The malpractice system appears to be ineffective as a control mechanism.

13.9.5 Factors Correlated with Malpractice Claims

A study was made of medical malpractice in the United States utilizing available data and a multiple correlation and regression analysis methodology (28). The cases in the study were from each of the 50 states and the District of Columbia. Professional liability claim rates, the dependent variable, were obtained for all the states from the Professional Survey conducted by the Law Department of the American Medical Association.

Two groups of independent variables were analyzed. The first group consisted of legal variables reportedly influencing rates of professional liability claims. These were the doctrines of *res ipsa loquitur,* informed consent, charitable immunity, the "locality" rule, and the statute of limitations. Second, a group of structural variables thought to be relevant were studied. These included certain demographic variables and such factors as the number of internship programs per state, measures of physician and lawyer supply, availability of hospital beds, and hospital expenses.

Predictive variables were patient median school years completed, which explained one-third of the variation in malpractice claims rates among the states, and general hospital expenses per patient-day. The doctrines of *res ipsa loquitur* and the statute of limitations were significant predictors. These four predictor variables explained 55% of the variation in claims from state to state.

The researcher who executed this study questions the professional license and mandate procedures of the states. The proposition was advanced that an educated population, as its educational level improves, will increasingly restrict the domain of professional decision-making. In essence this study is consistent with the societal demand for greater accountability from several segments of contemporary society.

Although the data on which this study was based were necessarily dated, the findings are provocative. There is at least a suggestion that as patient educational level improves and the consumer movement builds up steam, the malpractice control system will be more effective as a control mechanism. The doctrine of *res ipsa loquitur* is being applied by an increasing number of jurisdictions and at an increasingly frequent rate. The cost of health care is increasing at a rate challenged only by that of food and petroleum products; this rate suggests that as hospital expenses increase, malpractice cases will increase. One must also note that this study was based on malpractice in general and not drug-related malpractice.

The data on actual court cases involving nurses suggest only a small number of nurse-induced injuries. The nurse is a key provider and is thus a prime actor in administering more than 25% of all prescription drugs. Therefore it seems unlikely that her performance is markedly different from that of the other providers reviewed.

13.9.6 Other Examples of Drug Injury

The particular examples of drug therapy cited were related for a number of reasons, including availability of data and magnitude of usage. From a search of the legal literature, one will find that a relatively small number of drugs are disproportionately represented. These include diethylstilbestrol, chloroquine hydrochloride, indomethacin, oral contraceptives, chloramphenicol, betahistine hydrochloride, antibiotics as a class, halothane, prednisone, thalidomide, and polio vaccine. While the list contains drugs no longer marketed, e.g., thalidomide, others are valuable. A drug's value probably should not be judged on the basis of the number of malpractice cases it generates.

13.10 PRINCIPLES AND PROCEDURES: ASSERTING A CLAIM FOR COMPENSATORY DAMAGES ALLEGEDLY OWED

A court trial, although a relatively infrequent event as a percent of total patient claims, is a complex affair.* It is instructive to begin a discussion on this subject by first examining the components of a trial. Major components consist of the court (judge or judges), the plaintiff (the person seeking compensation), the defendant (the person trying to avoid paying compensation), the jury (when a jury trial is elected), the lawyer for the plaintiff and lawyers for the defendant, and lots and lots of words.†

* Less than 10% of patient claims result in a court trial (29).
† Lawyers relate to words as dentists do to drills. The nature of the dental carie to be corrected, the location of the tooth, the presence of gum disease, age of the patient, other diseases present, etc., influence the selection of the proper drill for a dentist. Likewise, a lawyer selects with the utmost care the word necessary to express the idea he wishes to convey. The lawyer is not unlike a walking thesaurus or synonym dictionary. In his use of the language he will carefully select from among idea, concept, conception, thought, notion, and impression before selecting the word idea which appeared in the foregoing sentence. Law books don't contain "pictures."

A key concept is that regardless of what is stated, shown, acted out or otherwise communicated within a courtroom, most conduct must adhere to prescribed rules. These rules relate mainly to who can communicate what and when and what issues of fact can be the referents for this information. A court case is not completely unlike a football game. There are opposing coaches (the respective opponents' lawyers), opposing teams or players (the plaintiff vs. the defendant), and the rules of playing football, which correspond to the rules of evidence in law. Just as in football one can score a touchdown only by acting in accordance with the rules if he desires to have it counted as part of his score. One must likewise abide by the rules in a court proceeding to present the information and the meaning intended.

It is not the intent of this section to instruct the reader in all or even most aspects of a trial. The purpose is rather to carve out a structure for a trial, and to describe the components of the structure so that they can be visualized clearly.

A trial is concerned with (1) issues of law: the rule of law for the particulars of the case at hand, and (2) issues of fact: the facts for the particulars of the case at hand. The accused in a criminal trial and the defendant in a civil trial are leading participants in a fairly prescriptive process. Two major characteristics of this process are (1) the presumption of innocence on the part of the accused, and (2) the adversary system of justice. The former is self-explanatory. The latter characteristic assumed its modern aspects in the early 1800s (30). The adversary system provides for proof of facts alleged by one side and a similar right for the opposing side. The proof must be presented only according to procedural rules of law. Another major aspect of the system is the right to cross examine witnesses of the opposing sides.

A legal action in a trial can be looked upon in terms of an analogy to a syllogism. The rule of law becomes the major premise, the facts of the case at issue form the minor premise, and the verdict or judgment is the conclusion. For example, suppose a statute provides: if a pharmacist responsible for operating a pharmacy within this state allows prescriptions to be filled during his temporary absence, he shall be guilty of improperly practicing pharmacy and fined not less than $1,000. The statute would become the major premise of the syllogism, whose minor premise might be: the accused, on the 21st day of January 1976, in Professional Apothecary Pharmacy, on 210 S. Gay Street, Auburn, within this State, between the hours of 10 A.M. to 3 P.M. allowed prescriptions to be filled in this pharmacy for which he was responsible. The conclusion would be that the accused is guilty of the act charged, and is liable to a fine of at least $1,000. The accused can dispute (1) that the rule of law as laid out is the rule for this instance, or contend (2) that the facts alleged are not true, or both. The court (judge or judges) rules on the issues of law and, assuming the major premise, the prosecuting attorney would have to prove the issues of fact alleged in the minor premise. The prosecution must, according to the procedural rules of law, persuade the jury that the facts as originally described are true.

A number of salient generalizations are listed below pertaining to the conduct of a trial:

1. There can be no crime without a law and no punishment without a law.
2. Counsel (in a criminal action) must generally be supplied if the accused cannot afford to employ his own.
3. In the case of an appeal (in a criminal action) the state must generally supply a copy of the record to the indigent appellant.
4. Facts are never true or false but rather more or less probable.
5. The rules of evidence require that proofs be addressed to show whether or not the illegal or wrongful acts alleged occurred, and not whether or not some other such acts occurred, and not whether the accused is in general good or bad.
6. Information relevant to the inquiry can be acquired only through the testimony of witnesses who claim to have direct knowledge about the facts to be proven, or through real evidence such as medical records, needles for injections, apothecary balance, etc., or via the expert witness.
7. Hearsay or "second-hand" testimony is prohibited (but expert witnesses are allowed; also allowed in at least one state are package inserts and textbooks) (31).
8. Conviction in a criminal case must be on the basis of "proof beyond a reasonable doubt." In a civil case the decision rests with the side which has "presented a preponderance of evidence," i.e., more than 50% of the evidence.

13.11 SALIENT POINTS REGARDING A TRIAL

Each time a witness testifies before a court the probability that what is recorded by the witness depends on his credibility, which is a function of five principal factors (32) (1) the opportunity to see the event he reports on, (2) his capacity to observe, (3) his capacity to remember, (4) his capacity to report observations to the court, and (5) his truthfulness in reporting what he has observed.

After the evidence is obtained, the jury may or may not have the opportunity to rule upon the issues of fact and apply the law to the fact. In a civil case either the plaintiff or the defendant may move for a "directed verdict." This is a request granted by the judge when "reasonable men" could not possibly disagree about the likely outcome if the evidence went to the jury, that is, when all the evidence points conclusively in one direction. In a civil case then, a jury considers a case only when reasonable men could differ as to the conclusion to be drawn from the evidence presented. The liability is not clear-cut if a case is heard by a jury; both sides think they have a reasonable chance of winning.

The major criterion for differentiating between criminal and civil cases is the nature of the proof that must be offered. The requirement for proof is more demanding in a criminal case than a civil case. A civil case can be won by the party that is successful in showing that the weight of the evidence (more than 50%) rests with its side.

A criminal case requires proof beyond a reasonable doubt. Loosely, the requirements for a criminal conviction are that no reasonable men could disagree about the appropriateness of the conclusion reached. However, there is evidence to suggest that this might not be the case. One reason for the difference in the nature of proof required is that the civil case is directed primarily toward settling disputes. A criminal conviction lowers the status of the convicted person. Many civil liberties are forfeited when a criminal conviction is handed down in all felony cases. In a civil case the only item at issue is a sum of money, which will either remain with its original possessor or be transmitted to the other party at the conclusion of the trial. A civil case is a controversy between two private persons, whereas a criminal case is looked upon as a controversy between a private person and the State (even though the charge may evolve from one private person killing another through an erroneous act such as dispensing 10 times the proper dose of a drug).

The foregoing differentiation between the nature of the civil trial and the criminal trial is perhaps comforting because it may be argued that reasonable men would agree according to the criterion prescribed for both civil and criminal cases. However, there is considerable evidence of both a bureaucratic and value nature that suggests such a differentiation may be true in form or appearance only. (For further study of this aspect of a trial, see reference 33.) It seems fair to say that for both opponents and proponents the trial, while lacking in some respects, seems to be the best available means for reconciling differences among private persons or between the State and private persons. A number of facts, however, make the trying of a case particularly difficult, especially in the medication use area. Some of the difficulties encountered are

1. The facts of a typical case are difficult to remember, particularly in a long trial.
2. The judge's explanation to the jury of the law or laws governing the controversy are frequently almost incomprehensible to the typical juror.
3. Juries, regardless of the manner in which they are chosen, reflect the values of the particular segment of society from which they are taken and probably represent their own unique values.

Confounding the differentiation between the functions of the judge and the functions of the jury are the methods by which judges can control juries. For example, a judge can direct a verdict of acquittal in a criminal case or may direct a verdict for either side in a civil case. The judge can influence the jury by the manner in which he explains the law governing the facts to be decided in the case. Judges can declare specific issues to be issues of law rather than of facts. The matter of whether or not the doctrine of *res ipsa loquitur* is to be applied in a particular case is thus of utmost importance to both parties involved. In this instance the judge determines whether this rule of law applies to the facts being cited in the case.

   Table 13.5 is a summary of the major components of the malpractice resolution system. Major components are listed on the left of the table. In order to properly consider the time element, the table should be studied beginning at the left and top of the table, going across and then down the page, and ending with the right-hand entry in the bottom row.

13.12   SOME PRINCIPLES OF CRIMINAL LAW

Law has been defined as a system of rules for directing human behavior. The human behavior that is directed pertains to the relationship between man and his fellow man, between man and the State, and between man and inanimate objects. For some countries the relationship of man and his ideas—what one can think or at least

TABLE 13.5 SUMMARY OF MALPRACTICE DISPUTE RESOLUTION SYSTEM

Structural elements	Jurisdiction of the parties and the subject matter	Patient initiates by filing a complaint or declaration by the patient	Decision maker: Court 1. Judge 2. Jury (most frequently included)	Purpose: to ascertain liability and damages owed to be sustained	Determine with finality responsibility
Initiation	The facts to sustain a legal theory must always be alleged	Parties involved: generally unlimited, if service of process can be achieved; minimum of plaintiff and defendants	What is sought? Money. Amount: generally unlimited. A few jurisdictions still prohibit joinder of claims in tort and contract.	Extensively used; imaginatively used for their stated purpose, and tactically for delay.	
Case preparation	Highly formal, expensive, complex, adversarial, time-consuming, painstakingly thorough, and burdensome to answering party.	Availability of medical records and evidence: testimony/subpoena	Who provides expert medical advice? Claimants.	Procedure: rules exist in almost all jurisdictions. Effectiveness varies greatly with local custom and active participation of judges.	

Time ⟶

Case Hearing	Rules: Carefully designed to ensure that only the most reliable evidence is heard by the jury. Complex, and fraught with grounds for error and appeal.	Relationship of plaintiff/defendant—public; confrontation. Witnesses generally excluded unless terrifying. Scandalous or shocking testimony may be heard with public excluded.	Record of proceedings: generally required and made.	Conditions for hearing testimony: always under oath as a matter of right, to ensure that testimony is carefully considered and solemnly given.	Cross-examination always permitted. Generally limited to any material matter raised in direct examination. Wide latitude generally given to derive truth.
					Power to subpoena witnesses: broad power.
Disposition	Finality: verdicts and judgments are final and *res judicata,* subject only to appeal.		Enforcement: execution and levy.		Appeal: Review is by appellate tribunal. New Trial may be granted if appellant is successful. Frequently obtain finality on appeal.

Time ⟶

Source: Report of the Secretary's Commission on Medical Malpractice, Appendix, Reports Studies and Analysis, DHEW Publication No. (OS) 73-89, U.S. Government Printing Office, Washington, D.C., 1973, p. 219–222.

discuss—is also within the legal domain. The law establishes a norm of conduct (action) to which all persons affected by the law, as prescribed in legislation or cases, must adhere.

The raison d'être for law is mainly a function of industrialization and its accompanying reduction of space between persons. When people are not exposed to one another, no conflicts arise because of the lack of opportunity for conflict. As men repeatedly come into contact with one another, however, a greater number of opportunities arise for conflict. Law is the social instrument selected to optimize the relationship between two persons.* As suggested, this relationship may include a relationship between one person and the possessions of another or a relationship between a person and the State, which represents a collective of men.

Law as a system of rules for directing human behavior exists somewhat independently of other systems but is nevertheless dependent in part on these systems. Often, although conflict arises between the potential actor and the rightness or wrongness of the contemplated act, what is morally wrong may or may not be legally prohibited. For example, a child who is swimming too far from shore may be struggling to keep from drowning. A man on the beach who observes the child may or may not take action to save her, even though a rescue attempt would involve no danger to his own safety because of the ready availability of a life preserver which is within easy throw of the child. If the man elects to photograph the drowning girl (rather than enter the water or act to save her) with the intent of publishing the pictures acquired, he has acted immorally (according to most people). However, since the law does not compel him to take any action, he would be legally innocent of any wrongdoing (35).** Theoretically the law exists separately from the ethical/moral system; actually, however, it is founded upon the cultural and religious values, and mores of the legislators who enact the law and the judges who interpret it, thus creating common law.

The method of classifying crimes, namely, felonious acts, misdemeanors, and treasonous acts reflect the foregoing account of the moral interrelationship with the legal system.† Some crimes are classified as both morally and legally wrong and are considered bad in and

---

* This suggests a social system, e.g., a democracy, in which exists relative freedom to act within only broadly constricted limits, as contrasted with tribal or patriarchal societies in which freedom of action is relatively nonexistent (34).

** An actual case similar to this in which no effort was made to rescue a child drowning in a swimming pool is reported in a court case (35).

† This discussion will not include treason as a crime.

of themselves. Murder is such an example. The other major area for categorizing crimes consists of simply delineating certain acts as crimes because the legislature has prohibited them. Felonies and misdemeanors are differentiated on the basis of prison time imposed on a wrongdoer, the kind of facility in which he is incarcerated, and in other ways. These crimes may be perceived as lying at opposite ends of a continuum. Intermediate points along this continuum comprise crimes between misdemeanors and felonies. The classification of crimes discussed above should not be confused with the demarcation between crimes and torts. Crimes are defined as actions of such seriousness that they are regarded as infringements on the rights of the public at large, whereas torts have been defined as wrongs in which the injury is primarily of concern to a particular individual or set of individuals.

13.12.1.   General Principles Pertaining to Criminal Law

As defined in Chapter 1, a principle is a description of the interrelationship among two or more concepts. This statement is true for principles describing criminal law and for principles describing anything that exists. Recall also that a concept is a symbol or group of symbols representing a class of stimuli with common characteristics which relate to objects, events, and persons. Concepts are described in terms of attributes that can vary in nature, value, or ways in which they can be combined. In order to communicate efficiently it is necessary to classify stimuli according to common characteristics, disregarding the uncommon, or different, or unequal characteristics that describe the object, event, or person under discussion. This manner of learning and study, however, also tends to create a desire for more information and bewilderment about the appropriateness of the generalization.

The other alternative is to attempt to describe each particular stimulus relevant to criminal law. To engage in such an undertaking is clearly beyond the scope of this book and the ability of this author. However, it may be meaningful to offer some principles to serve as a guide for those wishing to pursue this subject. Accordingly, the list that follows represents some of the key generalizations of criminal law and in many instances of civil law as well (36).

1. The federal government receives its power from the people as defined within the US Constitution.

2. The federal government has only the power granted to it in the Constitution; all other power is either granted to the states or remains with the people.

3. The power of a particular state is limited to the power granted through that state via its state Constitution.

4. No state law may be enacted at any state level that is not in agreement with the state Constitution.

5. Courts must make every effort to hold statutes constitutional. Holding a statute as unconstitutional is viewed by the courts as a solution of last choice.

6. The federal government and the state government may have concurrent jurisdiction on a given subject.

7. Statutes must be written in precise enough terms for a particular wrongdoer of ordinary ability to be fully informed about the punishment which he will incur if he violates a statute.

8. The defendant in a criminal case receives every benefit of the doubt.

9. In a federal case, criminal statutes are to be construed strictly when they work against the accused and liberally when they benefit the accused.

10. The US Constitution prohibits the passage of law on an after-the-fact basis which makes acts already committed illegal.

11. The US Constitution prohibits double jeopardy by the same sovereign. However, both the state and the federal government may prosecute a person for a given infringement of the law. This means, that a person may be exposed to double jeopardy for the same crime within this limited context.

12. The combination of the elements that must be present in order for a crime to have occurred are described as *corpus delicti*.

13. The federal courts, the state courts, and their subdivisions may have jurisdiction over a particular issue of fact or law.

14. A system of rules has been established whereby jurisdiction is defined in terms of territory, person, and subject.

15. Every crime requires an act which takes a variety of forms and which may lead to a variety of complex, diverse legal problems.

16. The law does not prescribe punishment of a person for what he thinks.

17. Generally, the law does not punish a person who commits an otherwise criminal act unless an evil state of mind is shown to exist.

18. Possession in and of itself is ordinarily not considered a crime; it must be shown to coexist with an evil state of mind in order to be

categorized as a crime. Possession of controlled substances is a notable exception.

19. Status is construed as a condition or state of being; in and of itself status cannot constitute a crime.

20. Several means exist for committing an offense:
    (1) the act may be done by the wrongdoer's own hand,
    (2) the act may be committed through an inanimate agency, e.g., an ax, hypodermic syringe,
    (3) an innocent human being (one who is unaware of his criminal role or is an unwilling actor) may be used as the instrument for committing a crime,
    (4) a nonhuman agency may be used to commit a criminal act, or
    (5) a noninnocent human may conspire to commit an offense.

21. A crime occurs due to the execution of a prohibited act or the failure to perform an act required by law.

22. A cause-and-effect relationship must be established between the act of the accuser and the harm alleged to have been done by the wrongdoer.

23. A man is presumed to intend the natural and probable consequences of his acts.

24. A wrongdoer takes his victim as he finds him; e.g., a person may be deemed to have caused the death of a hemophiliac when a hemophiliac is killed by a wrongdoer who intended only a body blow.

25. The defendant's act must be shown to have been the proximate cause of the injury or harm done to the victim.

26. Proximate cause may be established by showing a direct cause-and-effect relationship between the action and the harm done.

27. Proximate cause may be established by showing that the defendant's actions set off a chain of events which culminated in harm; e.g., erroneous administration of a nephrotoxic drug to a patient already suffering from kidney disease causing poor excretion can result in a buildup of the drug to a toxic level and cause death.

28. The prosecutor may prove that proximate cause was discovered by showing that the action of the accused placed the victim in a position that substantially increased the risk to the victim of being harmed by some other cause.

29. At least three significant elements must be shown for a crime of attempt to have occurred:
    (1) the doing of an act,
    (2) which tended toward the commission of a crime,

      (3)   but which fell short of completion, so that the crime was not consummated.

30. Generally, most crimes require a combination of act and intent.

31. A person is presumed innocent of an alleged crime until such time as his guilt is proven beyond a reasonable doubt.

32. Repenting in and of itself does not relieve a wrongdoer of the penalty prescribed by law for the commission of a given act.

33. Motive and intent have different meanings: motive is construed as those desires or wants which compel, drive, or forcefully direct a person to intend to do something.

34. A man may be responsible for unintended consequences of his conduct.

35. General criminal intent is all that is usually required in most crimes.

36. When specific intent is to be proven, it must be shown that the wrongdoer desires the prohibited result that occurred.

37. Lack of specific intent sometimes constitutes complete justification for committing an otherwise criminal act.

38. Recklessness is construed as a less wrongful state of mind than intent. A reckless state of mind is said to exist when an actor acts, not intending harm, but with complete disregard for the rights and safety of others, causing harm to result.

39. Negligence acts are usually voluntary, but do not rise to the level of intended conduct.

40. Every individual owes a duty, varying with circumstances, to other people to not infringe upon their welfare or safety.

41. Negligence may constitute a civil or criminal wrong.

42. Negligence may occur even when the accused is unaware of the consequences of his conduct, even though a reasonable man would be aware of the consequences of his conduct.

43. Strict liability for an act committed may constitute a crime merely by showing proof that the act was done; no proof of intent or state of mind is necessary.

44. Our system of justice is predicated on the theory that man acts of his own free will.

45. The US Constitution provides every citizen the right to believe anything he wants to believe.

46. Any of the following may constitute a defense or justification for the commission of an otherwise criminal act: insanity, intoxication, infancy, immunity, statute of limitations, mistake of fact, mistake of law, entrapment, consent, duress, custom, or religious belief.

The reader is reminded that the items listed above are generalizations. Particularization of individual acts to evaluate alternative behavior strategies is not an easy undertaking.

13.13 "PUNISHMENT" FOR VIOLATION OF MAJOR LAWS AND LEGAL PRINCIPLES

The scope of this section is largely descriptive. The reader may think that the nature of punishment is such that if act A is committed, then punishment B will be imposed on the offender. This is probably not the case, but the point will not be pursued here. What will be pursued is mainly the answer to the question, "If a person is convicted of committing illegal act A, what is the prescribed penalty B"? Penalty is used here to include the damages awarded plaintiffs in civil proceedings.

Table 13.6 lists the distribution of amounts paid on medical malpractice claims settled in a recent year. Note that more than one-half the claimants received less than $3,000. Less than one claim in 1,000 resulted in a claim for $1,000,000 or more. In these instances of civil cases, where the law provides for a determination of the penalty on a case-by-case basis, the remedy prescribed by law and the remedy awarded by law are perfectly congruent.

More than 75% of claims result in dropping, not pursuing the claim, or in accepting payment of the amount of the providers' charges.

Table 13.7 lists the penalty for specified acts prescribed by the Comprehensive Drug Abuse Prevention and Control Act of 1970. The penalty increases in severity as one progresses from the higher to the lower numbered schedules. These terms are fully defined in the statute itself and relate primarily to acts classified or associated with drug abuse as that term is popularly construed. Since drug abuse is not the subject of this book, the reader is directed to the statute.

Conviction of providers under this statute is so rare that a review will not be presented. Usually conviction is associated with acts classified within the popular meaning of drug abuse. The selling of prescriptions without benefit of a proper examination or provider-patient relationship is generally involved when physicians are prosecuted under this act. Pharmacists are usually prosecuted for trafficking in illicit drugs in a gross manner; nurses are treated similarly.

The penalty contained in most state statutes for practicing a provider profession without a license or for violation of the respective state

TABLE 13.6 DISTRIBUTION OF AMOUNTS PAID ON MEDICAL MALPRACTICE CLAIMS
CLOSED FOR A ONE-YEAR PERIOD[a]

Total Settlement Costs of Incidents, in Dollars	Percent of Incidents	Cumulative Percent of Incidents
1–499	21.1	21.1
500–999	16.0	37.1
1,000–1,999	12.3	49.4
2,000–2,999	10.1	59.5
3,000–3,999	3.0	62.5
4,000–4,999	2.7	65.2
5,000–9,999	13.4	78.6
10,000–19,999	10.0	88.6
20,000–39,999	5.3	93.9
40,000–59,999	1.3	95.2
60,000–79,999	1.0	96.2
80,000–99,999	0.8	97.0
100,000 and up	3.0	100.0
	100.0	

[a] 70% of claims in 3 years or less.
Source: Commission Study of Claim Files Closed in a Year, Report of the
Secretary's Commission on Medical Malpractice, Department of Health, Edu-
cation, and Welfare, DHEW Publication No. (OS) 73-88, Washington, D.C.,
January 16, 1973, p. 11.

practice act is generally low. The average penalty is approximately 1
year in prison and/or a $1,000 fine for pharmacists, physicians, and
nurses; however, it varies considerably. In Alabama, for example, the
penalty for practicing medicine without a license is 1 to 3 months in
jail and/or a $50 to $500 fine; in other states the maximum penalty is as
much as 5 years.

State acts regulating controlled substances usually duplicate the
penalty provided in the federal statute. Most states have enacted their
version of the Uniform Controlled Substances Act. Penalties are generally much more severe than those in the federal act. State penalties also
involve mainly acts falling within the common meaning of drug abuse.

The criminal penalties listed in the US FD&C Act are 1 year in
prison and/or $1,000 fine for the first violation and up to 3 years and/or
$10,000 for the second conviction. The Act also provides for seizure of
goods existing in violation of the Act. It also contains a provision for
seeking an injunction. Under this statute FDA officers are not given
the power to arrest an offender. The most important control features

TABLE 13.7 PENALTIES PRESCRIBED BY THE COMPREHENSIVE DRUG ABUSE PREVEN-
TION AND CONTROL ACT OF 1970 FOR THE LISTED ACT

1. "Unintended" illicit manufacturing beyond quotas up to $25,000 (this carries a civil penalty only).
2. Simple possession ≤ 1 yr. and/or ≤ $5000 (can be expunged from record if person is age 21 or less).
3. Distributed by person > 18 to person < 21: 2 to 3 times that not meeting age requirements.
4. General manufacturing, distributing, dispensing of narcotics: ≤ 15 years and/or ≤ $25,000.
5. General manufacturing, distributing, and dispensing of nonnarcotic controlled substance in C-I, C-II, or C-III.
   A. C-I, C-II, or C-III: ≤ 5 years and/or $15,000.
   B. C-IV: ≤ 3 years and/or $10,000.
   C. C-V: ≤ 1 year and/or $5,000.
6. Continuing Criminal Enterprise:
   A. ≥ 10 years up to life, ≤ $100,000 and forfeiture of profits.
   B. Double the amount for second conviction.
7. Dangerous special drug offender: ≤ 25 years.

Note: A second conviction generally carries a penalty twice that of the first.
Source: Public Law 91-513, Section 400.

are the control procedures inherent in the IND and NDA procedures (see Chapter 8) and culminating in the FDA's power to approve or not approve an NDA.

13.14 NEED FOR AN ALTERNATE CONTROL MECHANISM

It has been shown that both the malpractice system and the criminal law system are ineffective in enhancing the safe and effective use of drugs in this country. Such control systems are at best after-the-fact control mechanisms. Although many providers (especially physicians) believe that peer review is an effective and desirable control mechanism, the facts do not support this assertion. Generally, peer review has been a failure, at least from the perspective of the client. There is no alternative control mechanism to the malpractice system at the present time, and prospects too are few (51). However, the recently enacted Professional Standards Review Organization Act (PSRO) appears to be a candidate for insuring more effective use of all health care services. This act does not specifically pertain to the use and review of drugs, although one can easily infer that drugs are included within the category of "services rendered."

The only really bright light on the horizon shines from the recently modified regulations for skilled nursing facilities and intermediate care facilities (described in Chapter 12) which require the review of each patient's drug regimen monthly by a pharmacist (for skilled nursing facilities) and by a pharmacist or nurse (for intermediate care facilities). To a lesser extent, the provisions of the acts enabling the creation of health maintenance organizations which encourage drug use review (before, during, or after, initiation of therapy) are encouraging. Ultimately, one may argue persuasively that an informed public is essential for rational use of drugs, although it need not necessarily be a public equipped to act as its own health care provider. It need only master the necessary key control principles relevant to the use of medication in a complex society. The public must require providers to be accountable to their clients directly or indirectly. While this is no easy task, it does seem desirable and perhaps essential as drug technology becomes more pervasive, insidious, and important in its effects on human behavior in our society.

The teaching of the principles of medication law in colleges of medicine, pharmacy, and nursing has the potential for enhancing the rational use of medication. The teaching of medical ethics in which providers are taught what is right and why certain behavior is evaluated as good would probably increase the rational use of drugs. Perhaps the greatest need is for increased instruction in the area of clinical pharmacology in colleges of medicine and nursing. The *Malpractice Commission Report* recommended "that clinical pharmacology . . . the teaching of actions, indications, side effects, etc., of drugs used therapeutically be required as part of an integrated program in teaching the basics of therapeutics to all medical and nursing students and that similar attention be given to the same subjects in post-graduate and continuing medical education curricula" (37). It is probably surprising to most people that such a recommendation is necessary; one would think clinical pharmacology was already a major component of such curricula.

The recent emergence of clinical pharmacy as a concept and the apparent readiness of the professional pharmacist to become more involved in the therapeutics of drug use offer a long-term solution to the problem of medication use and misuse. Ultimately, the conceptual model for delegation of authority, duties, and requiring accountability must prevail. A new health care practitioner will probably emerge as the "expert" for the prescription of drugs. Whether this emerging practitioner will be a pharmacist, nurse, or merely an additional medical specialist, has yet to be resolved. Previous experience suggests that medical specialization will not yield the desired outcome and will probably be prohibitively expensive. The clinical pharmacist will only be successful in fulfilling this role if the pharmacist casts aside his traditional preoccupation with the physical sciences and takes on increased knowledge and activity in the biological and behavioral science areas of patient care.

REFERENCES AND GUIDE TO FURTHER STUDY

1. Russell, B.: *Power*, Unwin Books, London, 1938, p. 198.
2. Chambliss, W. J. and Seidman, R. B.: *Law, Order, and Power*, Addison-Wesley Publishing Company, Reading, Mass., 1971, p. 505.
3. Yacasua, L. T.: Morality, *Phi Delta Kappan* **55**(9):608–610 (May) 1974.
4. Chambliss and Seidman, *ibid.*, p. 506.
5. Prosser, W. L.: *Law of Torts*, 4th ed., West Publishing Company, Minneapolis, Minn., 1971, p. 26–27.
6. Report of the Secretary's Commission on Medical Malpractice, Appendix, Reports Studies and Analysis, DHEW Publication No. (OS) 73-89, U.S. Government Printing Office, Washington, D.C., 1973, p. 219–222.
7. Meyers, L.: *American Legal System*, rev. ed., Harper & Row, New York, 1964, p. 152.
8. Belli, M. W.: When to Hire a Negligence Lawyer, *Moneysworth* **2**(6):1 (December 27) 1971.
9. U.S. Department of Health, Education, and Welfare, DHEW Publication No. (OS) 73-88, Washington, D.C., January 16, 1973, p. 11–12.
10. Werble, W. (Ed.): *FDC Reports*, 36: T & G 7 (March 11) 1974.
11. Competitive Problems in the Drug Industry, Hearings before the Senate Subcommittee on Competitive Problems in the Drug Industry, Part 6, Nov. 29, 1967, February 6, 8, 27, 29, 1968, U.S. Government Printing Office, Washington, D.C., 1968, p. 2487.
12. Best, W. F.: Chloramphenicol—Associated Blood Dyscrasias, *Journal of the American Medical Association* **201**(3):99 (July 17) 1967.
13. Competitive Problems in the Drug Industry, Part 6, *ibid.*, p. 2354–2535.
14. Competitive Problems in the Drug Industry, Hearings before the Senate Subcommittee on Competitive Problems in the Drug Industry, Parts 15, 16, 17, U.S. Government Printing Office, Washington, D.C., 1970.
15. IMS America Ltd: *National Prescription Audit*, 12th ed., 1973, IMS America Ltd., Ambler, Pa., p. 9.
16. Competitive Problems in the Drug Industry, Hearings before the Senate Subcommittee on Competitive Problems in the Drug Industry, Part 17, U.S. Government Printing Office, Washington, D.C., 1970, p. 6851.

17. Ahlers, D. B.: American Druggists' Insurance Company. Personal communication, June 26, 1974.

18. Smith, M. C.: Patient End Results of Community Pharmacy Service, *Journal of the American Pharmaceutical Association* **NS14**(3):131–139 (March) 1974.

19. Miller, R. R.: Drug Surveillance Utilizing Epidemiological Methods—a Report from the Boston Collaborative Drug Surveillance Program, *American Journal of Hospital Pharmacy* **30**(7):589 (July) 1973.

20. Rabin, D. L.: Use of Medicines: A Review of Prescription and Nonprescription Medicine Use, *Medical Care Review* **29**(6):673 (June) 1972.

21. Mesel, E.: The Patient-Care Viewpoint. *In Proceedings Computer-Based Information Systems in the Practice of Pharmacy*, July 19–21, 1971, University of North Carolina, Chapel Hill, N.C., 1971, p. I–35.

22. Caldwell, J. R. and Cluff, L. E.: The Real and Present Danger of Antibiotics, *Rational Drug Therapy* **7**:1–2 (January) 1973.

23. Arzata v. Southern California Permanente Medical Group, California Superior Court, Los Angeles County, Docket #SOC26677, Sept. 13, 1973, citation 28:95 (January 1) 1974, cited in *Clin-Alert*, #52, March 26, 1974.

24. Roberts, A. W. and Visconti, J. A.: The Rational and Irrational Use of Systemic Antimicrobial Drugs, *American Journal of Hospital Pharmacy* **29**:832 (October) 1972.

25. Gibbs, C. W. Jr. et al.: Drug Utilization Review of Actual versus Preferred Pediatric Antibiotic Therapy, *American Journal of Hospital Pharmacy* **30**(10):892–897 (October) 1973.

26. Anonymous: Handbook of Antimicrobial Therapy, *Medical Letter* **14**(2) (January 21) 1972.

27. Gibson, J. T., et al.: Intravenous Antibiotic Usage in High Risk Patients Compared to FDA-approved Usage, *American Journal of Hospital Pharmacy* **30**(2):116–123 (February) 1973.

28. Berman, E. Z.: Medical Malpractice: A Question of Professional License and Mandate. Unpublished Ph.D. thesis, Rutgers University, N.J., 1973, 152 p.

29. Commission on Medical Malpractice, Appendix, p. 21.

30. Chambliss, W. J. and Seidman, R. B.: *Law, Order and Power*, Addison-Wesley Publishing Company, Reading, Mass., 1971, p. 422.

31. Watkins, v. Potts, 122 So. 416 (1929).

32. Chambliss and Seidman, *ibid.*, p. 423.

33. Chambliss and Seidman, *ibid.*, p. 431–433.

34. Unger, R.: *The Place of Law in 'Modern' Society: Sketch for an Interpretation*. Unpublished manuscript, Yale University Law Library, about 1971, 183 pages.

35. Handiboe v. McCarthy, 1966, 114 Ga. App. 541, 151 S.E.2d 905.

36. Chamelin, N. C. and Evans, K. R.: *Criminal Law for Policemen*, Prentice-Hall, Englewood Cliffs, N.J., 1971, various pages.

37. Malpractice Commission Report, *ibid.*, p. 60.

38. Maulin, A. M.: Administrator, American Pharmaceutical Association Professional Liability Program, St. Louis, Mo., personal communication, May 29, 1975.

39. The Leading Causes of Admissions PAS Hospitals, 1969, *Commission on Professional and Hospital Activities* **9**(7):1 (May 17) 1971.

Uncited References

40. Bedan, H. A.: The Death Penalty as a Deterrent: Argument and Evidence, *Ethics,* **80**(3):205–217 (April) 1970.

41. See also *Scientific American* **229**(3):23–175 (September) 1973. (This entire issue is devoted to the role of medicine in human life.)

42. Brody, H.: The Systems View of Man: Implications for Medicine, Science, and Ethics, *Perspectives in Biology and Medicine* **17**(1):71–92 (Autumn) 1973. (This relatively brief article coherently integrates concepts from the three major subject areas described.)

43. Pfizer Laboratories: *An Introduction to Physician's Liability for Battery, Negligence, and Acts of Others: A Programmed Review for Physicians,* Educational Design, Inc., and Pfizer Laboratories, New York, 1966, 47 pp.

44. Williams, A. J.: Law and Medicine, *Medicine, Science and the Law* **12**:154–170 (July) 1972. (This article defines legal medicine for an emerging nation, Nigeria.)

45. Carroll, J. B.: Words, Meanings, and Concepts, *Harvard Educational Review* **34**: 178–202 (Spring) 1964.

46. Wade, O. L. and Beeley, L.: Monitoring Adverse Reactions to Drugs: Toward a Therapeutic Audit, *International Journal of Health Services* **4**(1): 109–123 (Winter) 1974.

47. U.S. Government Printing Office: *Medical Malpractice: The Patient Versus the Physician,* Washington, D.C., 1969, ca. 1400 pages. (This document contains a verbatim transcription of selected court cases.)

48. Blumberg, A. S.: The Politics of Deviance: The Case of Drugs, *Journal of Drug Issues* **33**(2):105–114 (Spring) 1973.

49. McDonald, W. F.: Administratively Choosing the Drug Criminal: Police Discretion in the Enforcement of Drug Laws, *Journal of Drug Issues* **33**(22):123–134 (Spring) 1973.

50. Stephan, J. and Kellogg, E. H.: The World's Laws on Contraceptives, *American Journal of Comparative Law* **22**(4):615–651 (Fall) 1974.

51. Senate Bill number S2697, introduced on Nov. 21, 1975 by Senator Kennedy, contains several provisions for restricting usage of a drug to FDA-approved indications.

CHAPTER FOURTEEN

How to Keep Current on Legal Norms of Behavior

A professor teaching a course on the subject of this book is supposed to have replied to the question of how to keep current on medication law that he was always careful to check his mail before coming to class. Otherwise, he might be out of date. A pharmacist, serving as a state surveyor certifying nursing homes for meeting the Condition of Participation for Pharmacy Services (1), claimed in jest that he had requested a big computer with printout capacity. Each morning he would have the computer print the rules nursing homes were to abide by for that day. Both these remarks underscore the rapid changes associated with medication and regulatory law. This book has dealt with the important principles of medication law and behavior. Often, the provider (and, increasingly, the patient) is interested in knowing the specific aspects of an act or in determining the current status of a principle. This chapter is devoted to that goal. Since most law involving provider and patient medication-related behavior is regulatory rather than statutory, regulatory law will be the major focus of this chapter.

We often hear statements to the effect that an educated man is one who knows where to find the answer to his question. While it may be nearer the truth that the educated man is one who knows what questions to ask, in either case information access is important and is also a problem. A primary aim of this book is to assist the reader in framing his questions. Although this chapter discusses information retrieval and especially the use of indexes and other references, knowing only where to find it can be taken too far. Hal Draper (2), a science fiction writer, provides us with an example of the ultimate of *Future Shock* (3). In his study he extrapolates the rate of information growth to the ultimate extreme. He adds the element of the ultimate condensation of information through the use of (then) modern technology. The result is indexes to indexes to indexes solely as a means of access to information on classification and indexing. Due to the advancement of information condensation technology, all human knowledge (except, of course, the entry key) has been stored electronically within a single drawer. Due to an error of identification and classification, the information on the location of the drawer itself was lost beyond recall. The result was the collapse of a complex civilization. The patient and provider are advised to keep tabs on the location of their "key"—and to keep their key up to date or all may be lost.

One learns through informed channels that a particular medication has been removed from the market, e.g., oral hypoglycemics; that a new drug has been approved, and yet another drug has been reclassified as a controlled substance. Dispensers hear rumors that they no longer must keep Schedule II controlled substances separately from other drugs, and prescribers hear rumors that the quantity of a controlled substance prescription is now limited. A physician learns that a certain ingestible contraceptive must be provided only after the patient's informed consent is obtained. Consumers and providers frequently learn of changes through their respective news sources. Often, both are left with the impression that changes are made according to the whim of some government bureaucrat. Although there may be an element of truth in this view, changes in behavior prescribed at the federal level must be brought about in accordance with prescribed statutory and regulatory procedures. An example will serve to depict this orderly progression.

On March 7, 1972, the FDA Commissioner proposed that nitroglycerin sublingual tablets (NST) be dispensed only in lots of 100 or less and only in the original, unopened container. He also suggested that certain warning statements be placed on the labeling for this drug to warn the pharmacist and the patient of the need for the new kind of packaging. This proposal was published in the *Federal Register* of March 7, 1972 beginning on page 4918 (4). The following warning statements were to be added to prescriptions for NST: (1) Warning: This drug should be stored in a cool place and dispensed only in the original, unopened container. (2) Warning: To prevent loss of potency, keep these tablets in the original container. Close tightly immediately after use. The proposal included an explanation of the need for the suggested changes: new packaging materials allowed leakage of the nitroglycerin from the tablets and resulted in subpotent tablets. Also, transference to certain kinds of packages by the patient and the dispenser resulted in subpotent tablets, therefore warning statements were necessary. Studies were referred to substantiating the FDA's information. Interested persons were invited to mail their comments on the proposed rule changes to the DHEW within 60 days of the proposal. The address for comment was listed: Hearing Clerk, Dept. of Health, Education and Welfare, Room 6–68, 5600 Fishers Lane, Rockville, Md. 20852. Anyone interested can write to this address and explain his reasons for disagreement or express his opinion about changes needed.

On August 5, 1972, the Commissioner of the FDA announced the final order pertaining to NST, which appeared on page 15858 of the *Federal Register* of that date (5). It stated that the order would take effect on September 1, 1972 (usually more time is allowed, but this date was selected to correspond with a relevant USP date). The first part of this final order consisted of a summary of the comments and responses to the earlier proposal. (The rule-making procedure was expedited because of a lack of opposition to the principle of assuring that nitroglycerin preparations possess their purported potency. Often there is enormous opposition to a proposed rule.) Comments were received from six manufacturers, two state organizations (one of which represented the Law Enforcement Committee of the National Association of Boards of Pharmacy), the USP, three individuals, a general hospital, a pharmacist, and a plastics container manufacturer.

The first comment was taken into account and an amendment to the rule providing for the possible use of nonglass containers was added. To the objection that a container size up to 100 was unduly restrictive on prescriber and patient, data were referred to which showed that multiple openings of containers result in increasing loss of potency. Comments on the USP's definition of "cool place" resulted in amending the first warning so that the pharmacist was directed to store the NST at controlled room temperature and to dispense the tablets only in their original, unopened container.

One objection to the short period for implementation was explained by referring to the USP change effective September 1, 1972, pertaining to new packaging requirements for nitroglycerin. To the objection that NST containers were too small for adding the new warning, the Commissioner ruled "that the pharmacist will be able to label them in a satisfactory manner" with available technology. Manufacturers of sustained-release nitroglycerin products objected to inclusion of their products. The provision for exemption was added pending receipt of adequate data substantiating these claims. A plastics manufacturer submitted limited data to substantiate the stability of NST in his containers. The FDA promised to review the data and amend the new rule, but until such a change is made, no plastic containers will be allowed. After considering each of the comments a final order was published in the *Federal Register* to take effect on September 1, 1972. This order has been added to the *Code of Federal Regulations* (CFR) as (21 C.F.R. 3.90).

The FDA or any other administrative agency must make rule changes according to appropriate statutory provisions (6). In the example cited above, the order was promulgated because certain sections of the US Food, Drug and Cosmetic Act provide that drugs must be stable and other sections provide authority for specifying labeling. The FD&C Act specifies that the Secretary of Health, Education and Welfare (HEW) is the official responsible for execution of the provisions of the Act. A citation providing for the delegation of authority by the HEW Secretary to the FDA Commissioner is also listed in the order.

The process of rule-making occurs briefly as follows: (1) Congress enacts a law (an Act), (2) provision for administrative rule-making appears in the Act, and (3) the designated agency makes the rule. The procedures which must be followed by the FDA will be described, but other agencies, e.g., the DEA, must abide by a similar procedure. "Administrative law" is the term used to describe rules, orders, and regulations promulgated by a federal agency. These rules ae aired at an administrative hearing. Such a hearing must be conducted as provided for in the Administrative Procedures Act, and certain sections of the US FD&C Act or other relevant Acts. Technically, hearings are either of the adjudicatory type or rule-making type. These two types of hearings can be contrasted as follows:

Adjudication	Rule-Making
1. Directed to a few people	1. Directed to a large number of people
2. Accusatory	2. Educational
3. Retrospective	3. Prospective
4. Based upon somebody's past conduct	4. Based upon policy or likely future conduct
5. Process relies heavily on Section 505 of FD&C Act	5. Process relies heavily on Section 701 of FD&C Act

The first step in rule-making must be the publication of a *Proposal* describing the rule intended. It must be published in the *Federal Register*, so that all interested persons may have an opportunity to present their views regarding the proposal either orally or in writing. After sufficient time has elapsed for receipt and consideration of comments filed on the proposal, the next document published is a *Proposed Order*, which must also appear in the *Federal Register*. Any person adversely affected may file objections to any portions of the proposed order and explain why they are objectionable. Such a person may request a public hearing. The law provides that the very filing of objections stays (postpones until resolution) those provisions of the order to which objections are made. The next step might be termed *stays filed or not*. The FDA must publish in the *Federal Register* a notice specifying those parts of the order which have been stayed by the filing of objections. If no objections have been filed, a statement to this effect must be published. If requested, a public hearing must be held and the time and location of the hearing must also be published in the *Federal Register*. The hearing is conducted in a manner similar to that of a trial. Witnesses may be called and cross-examined. The proceedings will be transcribed by a court stenographer. The Hearing Examiner will listen to the FDA Commissioner. The next step consists of publication of a *Tentative Order* in the *Federal Register*. Any party to the hearing may object to any provision of the tentative order by submitting written arguments and a request for oral argument to the FDA Commissioner. After all exceptions and arguments have been acted upon, a *Final Order* will be published in the *Federal Register;* the date of effectiveness of the order is also specified. This ends the agency proceeding. The final order may be appealed to the appropriate Circuit Court of Appeals of the United States by any person who claims to be adversely affected by it. As with all cases, the Supreme Court at its discretion may review the decision of the lower court.

In summary, providers or patients or any other person may participate in the formulation of rules and regulations in the following ways (6):

1. File comments to published proposals.
2. File objections to proposals and request hearings.
3. Participate in hearings and present evidence to support their arguments.
4. Present oral arguments about exceptions to a tentative order.
5. Ask a court to review the agency's action.

An agency order results from an adjudicatory procedure. Basically, this type of procedure is equivalent to the administrative rule-making procedure described. Adjudicatory procedure occurs most frequently in regard to the approval or disapproval of a new drug application (NDA). At the discretion of the FDA, the applicant is given an opportunity for a hearing on the question of whether the application is approvable (7). Similarly, if a previously approved NDA is being withdrawn, the FDA may allow the applicant a hearing to argue his case. The grounds for approval or withdrawal of approval are described in the Act (8) and in the regulations (9). Generally, the applicant is entitled to a hearing. Recent Supreme Court decisions have given the FDA greater discretion in this matter. Now, an entire class of drugs may be removed from the market without each individual NDA applicant being given the opportunity for a hearing.

If a hearing is held, the process is very similar to the administrative procedure described. Publication in the *Federal Register,* however, begins with the publication of a tentative order.

Obviously the *Federal Register* (FR) is an important document; a former FDA Commissioner considers it the single most important document published in the United States daily. The FR is published daily (with certain exceptions, such as the day after federal holidays), and is actually a daily supplement to the *Code of Federal Regulations* (CFR). The CFR contains all regulations current at the time of its printing, and the regulations to the US Statutes, which in turn are contained in the United States Code (USC).

If an individual wishes to determine whether a prescription for a Schedule II controlled substance expires after a certain period, he can begin his search by consulting the alphabetical list of Acts by popular name in the *US Code Congressional and Administrative News* (USCCAN). He will find that the Controlled Substances Act (CSA) is contained in 21 U. S. Code 801, et seq. He will learn from reading section 202 of the CSA that the answer to his question will be found in title 21 of the CFR. By consulting the table of contents in the six volumes comprising title 21, he will then be directed to 21 CFR 306, i.e., section 306 of title 21 of the CFR. By searching the table of contents for part 306, he will learn that 306.11 will probably contain the answer to his question. After reading 21 CFR 306.11 it will be necessary to check the FR to determine if any changes in this section of the CFR have been promulgated as a final order. Depending on the date of the CFR, he should begin with the latest cumulative index and check the list of CFR sections affected. To be current, the latest daily issue of the FR will also have to be checked. If the check of pertinent CFR sections reveals a change in a regulation, this supersedes the CFR. In checking for rule changes, care must be taken to avoid confusion of final orders with rulings that are not yet final; the effective date must also be noted to determine the exact time of applicability of a new rule. It is possible to secure a copy of a final order or of any rule change proposed by writing to the Hearing Clerk (see address listed earlier) and requesting the appropriate document; specifying the correct CFR section or, better still, the FR citation increases the likelihood of timely receipt of a document. While the FR serves as a supplement to the CFR the material preceding the order itself is often informative. Thus, by consulting the explanatory material and reading each FR notice pertaining to a given rule, one augments his understanding of the final rule.

14.1   HOW TO FIND OUT ABOUT NEW LAWS

A law is enacted by Congress, and even though it may not take effect immediately it is often desirable to know its content. Opportunity for influencing the regulations promulgated from the law depends on knowledge of the statute itself. Usually medication-related law must await the writing of administrative regulations before it becomes effective, e.g., the Comprehensive Drug Abuse Prevention and Crontrol Act (DAP&C) of 1970, enacted on October 27, 1970, did not go into effect until May 1, 1971, for most of title 2 (the controlled substances act portion) because of the necessity for promulgating enabling regulations provided for in the DAP&C Act.

The *slip law* is the first published form of a new act to be available. A copy of a slip law can usually be obtained on request from one's Congressman or Senator, or by writing to the House or Senate Clerk. The *session laws,* termed *U.S. Statutes at Large,* are the next official form in which a statute can be located. For medication law, the *U.S. Statutes at Large* are reenacted to form part of the USC. Most medication law can be found in Title 21 of the USC, abbreviated 21 USC. The *US Code Annotated* contains the same text as the USC plus (10) (1) annotations of court decisions, interpreting, construing, and applying each section, (2) editorial notes and analytic discussions on particular statutes or provisions, (3) references to opinions of the attorney general and to legislative history, and (4) supplementation by annual pocket parts, quarterly pamphlets, and revised volumes as necessary.

For most students of medication law and behavior the USCCAN is an excellent source. It contains (1) the text of enacted laws, and (2) selected congressional committee reports as part of the Act's legislative history.

The *Congressional Information Service* (CIS Index) contains an up-to-date index to all congressional hearings arranged by subject, bill number, committee, and title.

The first reference that should be consulted by the student of medication law and behavior is the *Commerce Clearing House, Food, Drug and Cosmetic Reporter* (CCHFDCR). This publication is almost as current as the FR. It contains a current listing section which lists by CFR number the changes in the CFR via the FR, and also contains a full listing of the citations for a rule either in process or final. By noting the date in the CCHFDCR, it is possible to search forward to the present in the FR and thus save considerable time.

The research aids described above are relevant to law other than the example acts cited. The regulations governing medication law and behavior within nursing homes are, for example, also found in the federal regulations (1, 11).

State law is relatively more difficult to describe because there are 50 different states to contend with. Usually a copy of a given state statute can be found by getting a copy of the *Sate Code* from a general library. Then a search of the reference aids in the code, e.g., list of acts by popular name, will lead to the desired law. The various practice acts can be located in this way and also State Uniform Controlled Substances Act (or its equivalent). If a state has enacted a State Food Drug & Cosmetic Act (or its equivalent) it will also appear in that state's legal code. The simplest way of obtaining copies of practice acts is to get the address of the Board of interest from a library and request a copy of the desired practice act from that board. Copies of state laws regulating hospitals, nursing homes, and related institutions can usually be obtained from the appropriate State Health Department or its equivalent. State Senators and Representatives can also frequently secure copies of desired acts and regulations for their constituents.

An efficient and effective means of ascertaining if your state has enacted a State FD&C Act and its contents is to search the CCHFDCR. In this publication an "All States" volume describes for each state the content of the State FD&C Act or its equivalent.

It is a serious deficiency of most state governments that a state equivalent of the *Federal Register* is not published. Many states rely upon promulgation of rule changes via publishing in designated newspapers. A check with a given state Attorney General's office will inform one as to how that state and its various boards announce rules and regulations.

The provider of services will probably find that the most efficient means of keeping up to date is to maintain membership in his profession association. Usually, these organizations supply newsletters or news journals that keep their membership posted on current developments. Patients will have to rely on newspapers or their local libraries. National newspapers such as *The New York Times*, the *Wall Street Journal*, and the *Washington Post* frequently summarize changes in the law and occasionally carry the full text of a new law or regulation. There is at least one consumer newsletter, the *Health Law Newsletter* (12), that is designed for use by laymen.

14.2 FORCING ADMINISTRATIVE AGENCIES TO ADHERE TO RELEVANT PROCEDURES

In January 1974, the National Organization for the Reform of Marijuana Laws (NORML) filed a suit against the US Drug Enforcement Administration (DEA) (13). NORML claimed that the DEA improperly rejected their position to consider the reclassification of marijuana from Schedule I to Schedule V of the CSA or to remove marijuana from control under the CSA. The US Court of Appeals ruled in favor of NORML to the extent that the DEA was told to consider the petition on its merits. The Court ruled that the DEA's contention that marijuana must be classified within Schedule I because of the treaty requirements of the Single Convention On Narcotic Drugs was invalid. The Court pointed out that the Single Convention coverage pertains to cannabis and cannabis resin, which are defined to exclude marijuana leaves.

Reconsideration of the CSA is necessary to explain the NORML petition (see Section 7.2.1). The CSA was an attempt to rationalize the federal government's control program for dangerous drugs. Congress contemplated that the statutory classification would be subject to continuing review by the DEA in accordance with the statutory criteria for classification of a controlled substance within one of the five legally defined schedules. Reclassification was to be based on data, studies and information not available at the time of passage of the CSA. The Act provides that marijuana shall initially be classified as a Schedule I

Controlled Substance (CS). Authority is provided in the CSA for removal or rescheduling of a CS. The CSA provides that proceedings for removal or transfer of a substance may be initiated on the petition of any interested party. The CSA also provides that the DEA "must request from the [HEW] Secretary a scientific and medical evaluation and recommendation before starting proceedings to remove a substance. The Secretary must consider the statutory criteria in making his recommendation." The DEA must abide by the Secretary's finding. A part of the CDAP&C Act of 1970 provided for a Presidential Commission to make recommendations for the appropriate control of marijuana, so that the information so generated "will be of aid in determining the appropriate disposition [of the classification] of marijuana in the future."

The title given to the Presidential Commission Report, generally referred to as the *Shafer Report,* was *"Marijuana: A Signal of Misunderstanding."* This report contended that marijuana does not meet the criteria for classification in Schedule I or II because (in part) it has neither an actual nor a relative "high potential for abuse." In effect the Court's ruling was that the DEA (then the Bureau of Narcotics and Dangerous Drugs) acted on its own and without any statutory reason for its argument. Thus, the DEA was ordered to follow its own rules.

Patients, consumers, and others can force an agency to abide by what they see as statutory and regulatory requirements. While a little grumbling may be good for the soul, writing one's thoughts and channeling them properly will better serve to produce desired changes. Doing one's duty may be difficult, but the long-range effects may make the future more pleasant. An excellent example of this can be seen by examining the comments submitted regarding a proposal to limit the quantity of controlled substances called for in a prescription, and to limit the period during which a prescription for a controlled substance can legally be filled (14, 15). The comments are detailed, but clearly reveal nuances of medication use unlikely to be known by the DEA or the FDA.

This brief overview has only scratched the surface of the vast library holdings relevant and useful to the understanding of medication law and its influence on behavior. Additional references are provided to aid the student who needs more on the use of finding aids than is presented here (16–18). The use of legal references requires a different set of library skills from those needed for the general library. Most law libraries will provide needed assistance, and the general library usually has a specialist who will assist the interested reader in his search.

REFERENCES AND GUIDE TO FURTHER STUDY

1. Title 20 *Code of Federal Regulations,* 405.1127.

2. Draper, Hal: Ms Fnd In a Lbry. In Groff, C. (Ed.) *Seventeen Times Infinity,* Dell Publishing Company, New York, 1969.

3. Toffler, A.: *Future Shock,* Bantam Books, New York, 1971, p. 2–6.

4. 37 *Federal Register,* March 7, 1972, p. 4918.

5. 37 *Federal Register,* August 5, 1972, p. 15858.

6. Brennan, W. E.: Administrative Hearings in FDA, *FDA Papers* **2**(6): 14 (July–August) 1968.

7. 21 *U.S. Code,* 355 (C).

8. 21 *U.S. Code,* 355.

9. Title 21 *Code of Federal Regulations,* 130, et seq.

10. Cohen, M. L.: *Legal Research in a Nutshell,* West Publishing Company, Minneapolis, Minn., 1971, p. 87.

11. 39 *Federal Register,* Jan. 17, 1974, p. 2231 and Title 20 *Code of Federal Regulations,* 405.1127.

12. Health Law Newsletter, *National Health Law Program,* Los Angeles, Calif., published monthly.

13. Commerce Clearing House: *Food, Drug, Cosmetic Law Reporter,* 1974 (paragraph 41076, for a summary of this case).

14. 37 *Federal Register,* 15933, August 8, 1972.

15. 37 *Federal Register,* 10372, May 20, 1972.

References not Cited

16. *Price, M. O. and Bitne, H.: Effective Legal Research,* Little, Brown & Company, Boston, 1969.

17. West's Law Finder, *A Research Manual for Lawyers,* West Publishing Company, Minneapolis, Minn., 1967, 65 p.

18. *How to Use Shepard's Citations,* Shepard's Citations, Inc., Colorado Springs, Colo., undated, about 35 p.

Index